Western Balkans

Slovenia
p304

Croatia
p115

Bosnia & Hercegovina
p78

Serbia
p265

Montenegro
p195

Kosovo
p176

North Macedonia
p232

Albania
p47

Mark Baker, Joel Balsam, Virginia DiGaetano, Peter Dragicevic, Lucie Grace, Vesna Maric, Anja Mutić, Isabel Putinja, Iva Roze Skochova, Brana Vladisavljevic

CONTENTS

Plan Your Trip

The Guide

Zlatni Rat (p158), Croatia

Predjama Castle (p331), Slovenia

Zadar (p138), Croatia

Toolkit

Storybook

Neretva Canyon, Bosnia & Hercegovina

WESTERN BALKANS

THE JOURNEY BEGINS HERE

I was born and raised in Mostar, Bosnia and Hercegovina, and even though I emigrated to the UK at the age of 16 during the 1990s war, my life has always been intricately tied to the Western Balkans. Perhaps because I left so young, I made sure I travelled the entire region many times over, (re)discovering its many mountains, rivers, lakes and islands, and doing a lot of swimming in my beloved Adriatic sea. I am always happy to see travellers witness the gifts of these beautiful lands, as well as their many paradoxes – the locals will never leave you short on hospitality, humour and spectacular anecdotes, or food! I love the colourful character array of the local people, the natural beauty of the Western Balkans and the fact that, across the region, an authentic, inimitable way of life persists despite the many political shifts of the past.

Vesna Maric

@vesnamarx

Vesna is a travel writer and literary author – her memoir, Bluebird, *charts her experience of emigrating to the UK as a teenager.*

My favourite experience is taking the train – or a drive – through the **Neretva Canyon** (pictured above), between Mostar (p100) and Sarajevo (p84). The views of the Neretva and the dramatic canyon are perennially breathtaking.

WHO GOES WHERE

Our writers and experts choose the places which, for them, define the Western Balkans.

FLORIAN MUHARREMI/SHUTTERSTOCK ©

As I kicked my feet up after hiking from Valbona to Theth in Albania's **Accursed Mountains** (p188), a strange feeling swept over me: what if I didn't leave? This tranquil retreat from stressful city life has everything I need: awesome nature, fascinating culture and tasty traditional food. Then I remembered how extroverted I am, and my deadlines...but the Accursed Mountains had me questioning everything – and I reckon it will do the same for you.

Joel Balsam

@joelbalsam / joelbalsam.com

Joel is a freelance journalist who writes about travel, culture and the environment.

NENSY/SHUTTERSTOCK ©

The **Logar Valley** (p327) in Slovenia is one of the most magical places I've ever been. The narrow roads from Ljubljana leading into the thickest mountain forests suggest travelling into the very depths of the world, but then you arrive at this almost supernatural clearing and a majestic, impossible valley opens itself up to welcome you. One cannot but be transformed there, which is after all the whole point, isn't it?

Virginia DiGaetano

virginiadigaetano.com

Virginia DiGaetano is a Rome-based writer desperately trying to learn how to whistle.

BEAUTIFUL MONTENEGRO/SHUTTERSTOCK ©

My favourite experience is cruising on **Lake Skadar** (p220). Every boat trip I've taken has been completely different, whether birdwatching amongst the water-lily meadows or calling in at remote island monasteries.

Peter Dragicevich

@peterdragnz

Born in New Zealand but with family roots in the former Yugoslavia, Peter has written dozens of guidebooks for Lonely Planet – including the first-ever edition of this book, not long after Montenegro regained its independence.

ECSTK22/SHUTTERSTOCK ©

Back in **Belgrade** (p270) after many years abroad, I enjoy its theatres, bookstores, rural bounty at its green markets, and the fact that people always have time to meet for a coffee. Kalemegdan (pictured) remains my favourite place in the world for contemplation. Nothing beats the living-is-easy ethos of summer nights on Dorćol's leafy streets, though quiet walks through a blanket of snow – when White City lives up to its name – come close. Layers of history lend beauty to every crumbling facade.

Brana Vladisavljevic

Brana is a freelance editor and translator based in Belgrade, Serbia.

DENNIS VAN DE WATER/SHUTTERSTOCK ©

An old man selling ice cream in Zagreb once told me 'this is the country of joy and dreams' and that sums up how I feel about Croatia. It's a wonder – from the natural sights like the travertine waterfalls in **Krka National Park** (p144; pictured) to architectural marvels that range from the Gothic in **Šibenik** (p146) to modernism on **Krk** (p133). It's a country that repeatedly makes my jaw drop.

Lucie Grace

@80bathes / @LucieGraces

Lucie Grace is a travel and culture writer, based between Croatia and Thailand, who has a lifelong passion for wild swimming.

CONTRIBUTING WRITERS

Mark Baker

markbakerprague.com

Mark is a writer about travel and history – and the author of a nonfiction book on Cold War history.

Anja Mutić

@everthenomad

Born and raised in Zagreb, Anja returned to Croatia after 20 years spent abroad. From her Zagreb base she now runs Storyline Studio, a creative content agency for tourism, travel and hospitality.

Isabel Putinja

@isabelswindow

Isabel is a travel writer, solo walker and slow traveller living in Istria, Croatia.

Iva Roze Skochova

ivaroze.com

Iva is a travel writer and journalist, who is on an endless journey to find that one destination she isn't going to enjoy. Suggestions welcome.

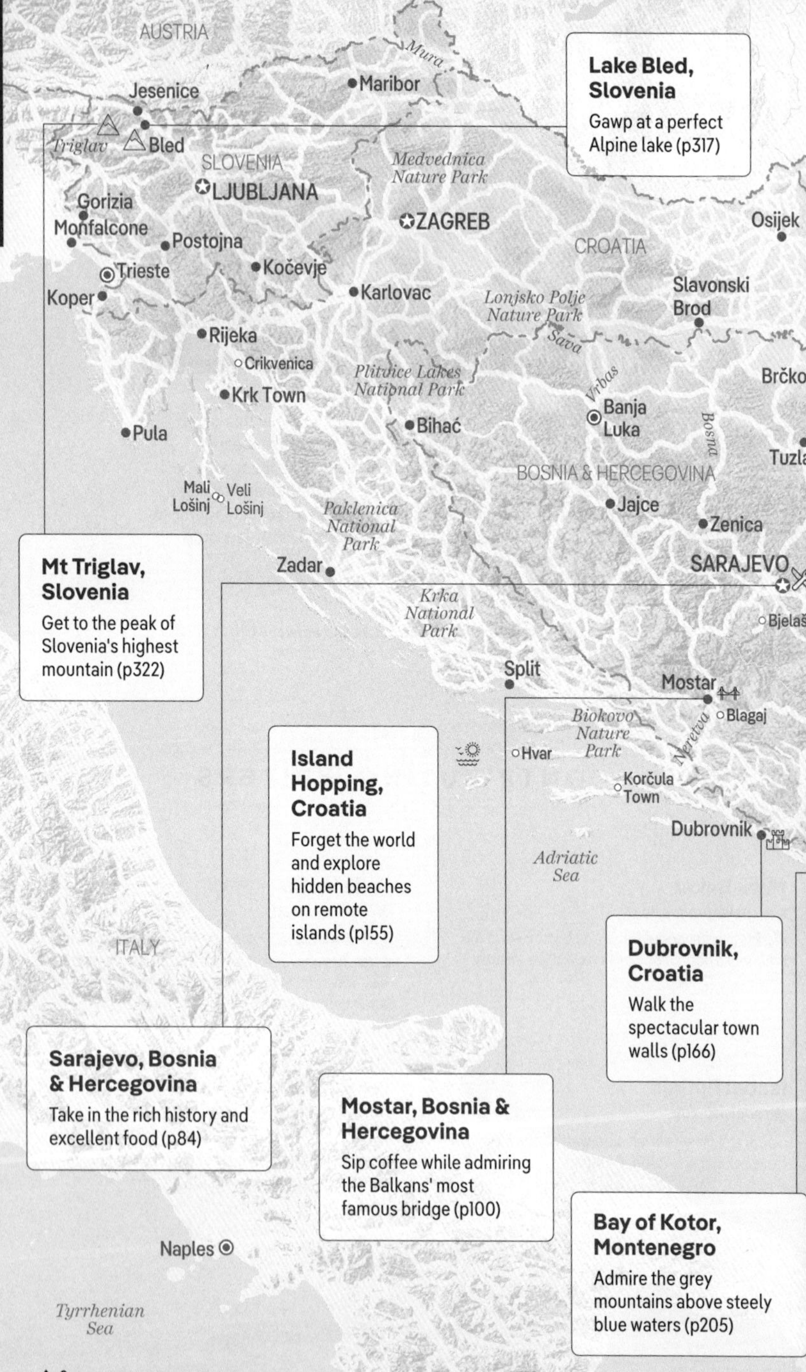

Lake Bled, Slovenia
Gawp at a perfect Alpine lake (p317)

Mt Triglav, Slovenia
Get to the peak of Slovenia's highest mountain (p322)

Island Hopping, Croatia
Forget the world and explore hidden beaches on remote islands (p155)

Dubrovnik, Croatia
Walk the spectacular town walls (p166)

Sarajevo, Bosnia & Hercegovina
Take in the rich history and excellent food (p84)

Mostar, Bosnia & Hercegovina
Sip coffee while admiring the Balkans' most famous bridge (p100)

Bay of Kotor, Montenegro
Admire the grey mountains above steely blue waters (p205)

Vojvodina, Serbia
Admire the Secession-style architecture of genteel Subotica (p282)

Belgrade, Serbia
Dive into the exciting cultural, dining and nightlife scenes (p270)

Durmitor National Park, Montenegro
Take in the dramatic beauty of the rugged peaks and plunging canyon (p223)

Peja, Kosovo
Climb the Peaks of the Balkans Trail through Montenegro and Albania (p188)

Shkodra, Albania
Take the Lake Koman Ferry and hike the Accursed Mountains (p63)

Pelister National Park, North Macedonia
Witness wildlife and hike up to glacial lakes (p258)

Lake Ohrid, North Macedonia
Swim in the spectacular lake and admire Byzantine churches (p246)

Berat, Albania
Gaze at the gorgeous ensemble of Ottoman houses (p69)

OUTDOOR ADVENTURES

Craggy mountain ranges stretch along the Western Balkans, offering endless opportunities for hiking, biking, rock climbing and paragliding. In their shadows are rowable lakes, raftable rivers and scramble-able canyons. Rocky mountains and terracotta-roofed towns plunge spectacularly into crystal-clear waters all along the Adriatic coast. Albania's riviera still has donkeys wandering through olive groves abutting secluded bays, while Croatian islands are quiet off-season. Winter offers access to Europe's cheapest ski resorts.

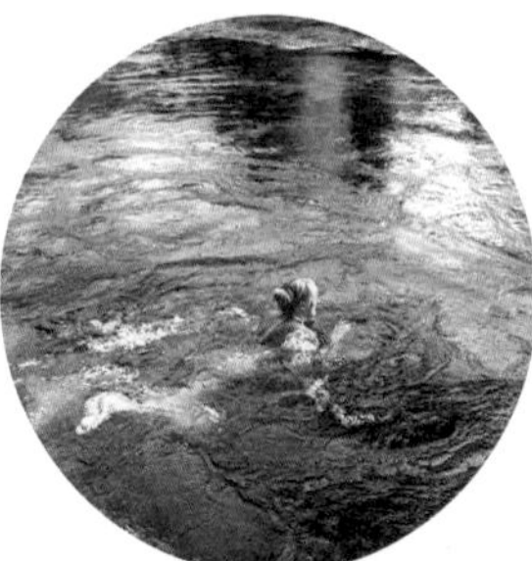

FROM LEFT: IWCIAGR/SHUTTERSTOCK ©, JANA JANINA/SHUTTERSTOCK ©, ANDREW MAYOVSKYY/SHUTTERSTOCK ©

Hiking

Bring proper hiking boots, as the limestone on the mountain tracks can be hard going. Be prepared for sudden downpours.

Swimming

In summer, pack your swimming gear whether or not you're heading to the coast; there are plenty of rivers and lakes to cool off in.

When to Hike

The best months for hiking are from May to September, especially late August and early September, when the summer crowds will have largely disappeared.

Canyon Matka (p242), North Macedonia

BEST OUTDOORS EXPERIENCES

Get to grips with extreme sports in ❶ **Bovec** (p324), Slovenia, offering everything from canyoning to hydrospeeding.

Raft the rapids of Montenegro's ❷ **Tara River** (p225) hidden within Europe's deepest canyon.

Windsurf at Croatia's famous ❸ **Zlatni Rat** (p158), amid crowds of swimmers and windsurfers in summer.

Hike the snow-capped peaks and traditional mountain villages of Albania's ❹ **Accursed Mountains** (p65), one of Europe's most remote corners.

Paddle your way through the gorgeous ❺ **Canyon Matka** (p242), only 15km from the North Macedonian capital.

OLD TOWNS

The Western Balkans has more stunning old towns than you can point your phone camera at, reflecting the political and religious shifts across the many centuries of local history. Choose from the gorgeous marble streets of Dubrovnik and the walled town of Kotor, the Ottoman market quarter in Sarajevo and Byzantine-churches-on-every-corner in Ohrid. Witness the Classical period in Split's old centre, the Venetian-Gothic in Piran and Jajce's Bosnian Church remnants.

Cyrillic

It's well worth getting to grips with Cyrillic (it's not as difficult as it looks) – it's useful for road signs and postings in remote areas.

Holy Site Attire

Churches and mosques throughout the region require visitors to be dressed respectfully, which means no shorts or bare shoulders for men or women.

Cultural Flavour

The movement of invaders, settlers and traders across the region over the centuries has given the Western Balkans an intricate cultural patchwork and unique flavour.

FROM LEFT: TOOYKRUB/SHUTTERSTOCK ©, DIA TV/SHUTTERSTOCK ©, SUMMIT ART CREATIONS/SHUTTERSTOCK ©

Dubrovnik (p166), Croatia

BEST OLD TOWN EXPERIENCES

Admire the marble-paved streets and glorious sea views from the resplendent city walls of ❶ **Dubrovnik** (p166).

Witness the dramatic location of ❷ **Kotor** (p200) between the sea and the steeply rising grey mountainside.

Enjoy a Bosnian coffee in Baščaršija, ❸ **Sarajevo** (p84), the bustling old Ottoman quarter.

Wander between Byzantine churches and ancient ruins in ❹ **Ohrid Town** (p250), located on the shores of one of Europe's deepest and oldest lakes.

Get your fix of the Venetian-Gothic architecture in the historic core of ❺ **Piran** (p332), set on a narrow peninsula jutting into the Adriatic.

Postojna Cave (p328), Slovenia

SPECTACULAR SCENERY

The incredible vistas and breathtaking scenery across the Western Balkans are unforgettable. Running from the north to the very south of the region, you'll witness scenery that is dramatic, serene, looming or soothing – sometimes simultaneously. The sight of crashing waterfalls, turquoise waters, crumpled mountain ridges, still lakes and lush, dark forests is unfailingly life-affirming.

Pristine Alps

The area around the borders of Albania, Montenegro and Kosovo is one of the least-touched alpine regions on the continent.

Tree Planting

In North Macedonia, millions of trees have been planted each year since the inaugural national tree-planting day that was set up in 2008.

BEST SCENERY EXPERIENCES

Enjoy light walking in Croatia's ❶ **Plitvice National Park** (p142) and turquoise waters, lush forest and cascading waterfalls.

See a unique pocket of the world from the ferry across ❷ **Lake Koman** (p65), in Albania's remote mountainous north.

Admire the spectacular zigzags of the ❸ **Uvac River** (p294) in southwestern Serbia – best seen from above.

In Slovenia, witness ❹ **Postojna Cave** (p328), one of the world's largest karst cave systems with unrivalled rock formations.

Swim in the emerald waters of Bosnia & Hercegovina's ❺ **Kravica Waterfall** (p105), at the base of this broad, beautiful arc.

Griffon vulture, Uvac Canyon (p294), Serbia

WILDLIFE

The Balkans is a refuge for many of the larger mammals that were almost eliminated from Western Europe 150 years ago. The rugged forests of the Dinaric Range from Slovenia to Albania shelter wolves, red deer, roe deer, lynx, chamois, wild boar and brown bears, as well as griffon vultures, golden eagles, kestrels and peregrine falcons.

Forests

Highland forests include silver fir, spruce and black pine, broad-leafed beech forests grow at medium elevations, and lower down is a huge variety of oak species.

Lakes & Birds

The great lakes of Skadar, Ohrid and Prespa in the south of the region are havens for Dalmatian pelicans, herons and spoonbills.

BEST WILDLIFE EXPERIENCES

Visit the dolphin reserve at ❶ **Lošinj** (p136), which protects the Adriatic's only known resident pod of dolphins.

See bears in the wild near ❷ **Novo Mesto** (p339).

Spot wetland birds at ❸ **Lake Skadar National Park** (p220), an important bird reserve, including the Dalmatian pelican, pygmy cormorant and whiskered tern.

Keep an eye out for griffon vultures swooping about, along with 130 other bird species at ❹ **Uvac Canyon** (p294).

Witness bears rescued from confined cages, given room to roam in semi-wooded enclosures at Kosovo's ❺ **Bear Sanctuary** (p181).

ANCIENT SIGHTS

It's been said that the Balkans have produced more history than they can consume. Indeed, the many invaders, settlers and traders back and forth across the region over the centuries have created an intricate mixture of cultures, societies, religions and ethnic identifications. All this has left the relatively small region with a wonderfully diverse and rich set of remains that visitors can witness and appreciate both in major cities and in more remote locations.

FROM LEFT: PHILIP WILLS/SHUTTERSTOCK ©, BEARFOTOS/SHUTTERSTOCK ©, ALEKSANDAR TODOROVIC/SHUTTERSTOCK ©

What's in a Name?

The Balkan Peninsula is the name erroneously given to the landmass stretching into the Mediterranean east of Italy, terminating in the outspread fingers of Greece.

Linguistic Mysteries

It's thought that the modern Albanian language, a linguistic oddity unrelated to any other language, is derived from ancient Illyrian.

Religious Front Line

The fault line dividing the Roman Empire from the Byzantium ran right through the centre of the Western Balkans.

Arena, Pula (p130), Croatia

BEST ANCIENT SIGHT EXPERIENCES

Stand in awe of Split's imposing and remarkably intact ❶ **Diocletian's Palace** (p150), Roman architecture in the city's beating heart.

Wander around the enchanting 2500-year-old ruins of ❷ **Butrint** (p59) scattered throughout a forest on Albania's Ionian coast.

Admire Belgrade's ❸ **Kalemegdan Fortress** (p270), a promontory on the Danube that has been destroyed over 40 times and fortified since the Celtic period.

Take in the atmosphere of ❹ **Kokino Observatory** (p243), an archaeo-astronomical site, where the ancients performed complex lunar calculations.

Get Classical in ❺ **Pula** (p130), with its magnificent 1st-century amphitheatre, a complete Roman temple and triumphal arch.

Krka National Park (p144), Croatia

SWIMMING

There are good swimming spots along the entire coast, from Slovenia to Albania, and throughout the Croatian islands. Beaches come in a variety of textures: sandy, shingly, rocky or pebbly. Aside from the beaches, there are amazing swimming spots – lakes, rivers and waterfalls included – throughout the region. Keep your swimwear handy!

Water Temperatures

In summer the Adriatic water temperature can reach over 25°C, and it's usually over 20°C from June right through to October.

Swimming in Landlocked Serbia

Landlocked Serbia offers some good swimming, from city beaches on the Danube and Sava Rivers – Novi Sad's Štrand and Belgrade's Ada Ciganlija.

BEST SWIMMING EXPERIENCES

Dip into lakes at ❶ **Krka National Park** (p144).

Enjoy sublime views over the walled resort village of ❷ **Sveti Stefan** (p212) while lazing on the beach adjoining the island's causeway.

Dive into ❸ **Lake Ohrid** (p246), one of Europe's deepest and oldest, and a true beauty.

Cool off at ❹ **Perućac** (p290) on Tara mountain in Serbia's west.

Discover Albania's best beaches, around the town of ❺ **Dhermi** (p61).

Odprta Kuhna (Open Kitchen; p312), Ljubljana, Slovenia

NIGHTLIFE

The Western Balkans are nothing if not party loving – there are ample opportunities to join the locals, whether they're dancing, drinking, or (always) smoking. You'll find some party beaches too, and fancy island clubs, as well as turbo-folk-blasting bars and nightclubs. Live music is available most weekends across the region. Take your pick.

BEST NIGHTLIFE EXPERIENCES

Party the night away at one of the many clubs in ❶ **Belgrade** (p274), and go bar-hopping in the Dorćol quarter (p275).

Visit ❷ **Rijeka** (p126) during its brilliant annual Ri Rock Festival – the city's music scene is the best in Croatia.

Check out the particularly lively scene in and around the famous Blloku neighbourhood in ❸ **Tirana** (p50).

Hop between pubs, cafes, cocktail bars and a set of scruffy clubs in an old army barracks in ❹ **Ljubljana** (p310).

Go to a post-beach sundowner and then on to cocktails, followed by crowded little dance bars, in ❺ **Hvar** (p157).

Montenegrin Miami

Scores of flashy beachside bars and clubs have earned Budva, the walled town on Montenegro's coast, the nickname 'the Montenegrin Miami'.

Dress Smart

It pays to have a smart set of clothes for visiting the better restaurants and clubs; people in the Balkans dress to impress.

WINING & DINING

Foreign invaders have plundered the Balkans for millennia and the region's cooks have plundered right back, incorporating Venetian, Austrian, Hungarian and Ottoman flavours. Locally produced olive oil, truffles and wine hold their own against the best in the world, as does the seafood, herb-grazed lamb and abundant bounty of fresh fruit and vegetables. Expect to find offers from the sleekest gourmet experiences, to barbecued meats and traditional grandma-home-cooked dishes.

FROM LEFT: XSEON/SHUTTERSTOCK ©, T.SABLEAUX/SHUTTERSTOCK ©, JUSTIN FOULKES/LONELY PLANET ©

Wine Tastings

Call ahead to reserve wine tastings. Many wineries are happy to welcome visitors but may not be equipped to handle walk-ins.

Taming the Tipple

Don't say no to the *rakija*...but do go easy. It may come in many forms, from plum to apricot and quince – but it's always strong!

Booking Ahead

When eating out, it pays to book ahead at the very top places, especially during the peak season and on weekends.

Vipava Valley (p337), Slovenia

BEST FOOD AND WINE EXPERIENCES

Get served up truffles, wild asparagus and fresh seafood in ❶ **Istria** (p130), and taste top drops in the wineries.

Taste the homespun cooking of ❷ **North Macedonia** (p232), from paprika-tinged sausages to stuffed peppers and foraged mushrooms.

Don't miss the *burek* (meat pie) or *ćevapi* (small grilled kebabs) in ❸ **Sarajevo** (p84).

Enjoy gourmet treats and tour the wine cellars of Slovenia's ❹ **Vipava Valley** (p337) by car or bike.

Find amazing wine and olive oil on the Dalmatian coast near ❺ **Korčula** (p160) together with fresh seafood.

COUNTRIES & CITIES

Find the places that tick all your boxes.

Slovenia
p304

Croatia
p115

Bosnia & Hercegovi
p78

Slovenia

A GEM, HIDING IN PLAIN SIGHT

All visitors are mesmerised by the sheer beauty of tiny Slovenia – from the soaring peaks of the Julian Alps to the subterranean magic of Postojna Cave. The list of activities on offer is endless. An assault on Mt Triglav is a consummate Slovenian experience. Slovenia's wines and food are superb.

Croatia

LIVING UP TO THE HYPE

Croatia's islands cater for almost anyone's idea of idyllic. The country's best assets are its fantastical walled towns, ranging from tiny hilltop Hum to the coastal drama of Dubrovnik. The core of the city of Split sits behind ancient Roman palace walls. The influence of Venice differentiates Croatia's coastal cuisine from the rest of the region.

Bosnia & Hercegovina

RICH HISTORY, WILD NATURE, WARM WELCOME

Bosnia's mixed Muslim, Christian and Jewish heritage is reflected in its food, culture and architecture. Rebuilt historical centres showcase its history: the scars of recent horrors are still visible, socialist monuments sprout from rural landscapes and Ottoman and Austro-Hungarian buildings loom in urban centres. Bosnia is great for kayaking, rafting, skiing, hiking and mountain biking.

Montenegro

MOUNTAINS, COAST AND ANCIENT TOWNS

Tiny Montenegro crams an awful lot into a small space, including sandy beaches, jagged mountain peaks and dramatic gorges. Seaside Kotor is one of the country's most extraordinary sights. Nearby Perast is a vision from distant Venice, while Cetinje – high up in the mountains – is the heart of Old Montenegro.

Serbia

DIVERSITY OFF THE BEATEN PATH

With art nouveau architecture up north, fine examples of socialist modernism in Belgrade, Ottoman Novi Pazar and Orthodox churches throughout, Serbia is more diverse than you might think. The all-out edgy Exit Festival has Serbia firmly on the international music map. Back-to-nature experiences are orientated around rivers.

Serbia p265
Montenegro p195
Kosovo p176
North Macedonia p232
Albania p47

Kosovo

A YOUNG AND BEAUTIFUL NATION

Kosovo's medieval monasteries have outstanding frescoes, an age-old atmosphere and forbidding walls that have withstood the turbulence of times past and present. Cosmopolitan Pristina has a mix of modern shops and Turkish-style bazaars. Prizren's old town is a showcase of Ottoman-era architecture. The hills around Peja (Peć) are ideal for scenic hiking.

North Macedonia

NATURE AND HISTORY

North Macedonia's churches house important medieval art, while its monasteries are all about dramatic settings. Lake Ohrid is ringed by swimming spots, while at Lake Prespa you can hike and visit an island populated by tortoises and pelicans. Hikers can enjoy untouched mountain landscapes. Traditional, homemade-style food abounds.

Albania

STILL UNDERRATED, SOMEHOW

The more isolated parts of Albania's gorgeous Ionian coast are a delight, while the country's mountains are some of Europe's most spectacular. Village life is still governed by traditions that have long been forgotten elsewhere. In Tirana, cafe culture rules the day before club culture takes hold of the night.

IHOR PASTERNAK/SHUTTERSTOCK ©

Bay of Kotor (p205), Montenegro

ITINERARIES

Best of the Balkans

Allow: 2 weeks **Distance:**1540 km

Consider this a 'greatest hits' of the Western Balkans, taking in a slice of each of the eight countries featured. It can easily be tackled on public transport, although a car will give you more flexibility for exploring the extraordinary countryside along the way.

1

CAPITAL CITIES ⏱2 DAYS

Start by city-hopping through four of the capitals: **Ljubljana** (p310) in Slovenia, **Zagreb** (p120) in Croatia, **Belgrade** (p270) in Serbia and **Sarajevo** (p84; pictured) in Bosnia. While the first two are cute, mid-sized, Central European cities, Sarajevo's fascinating cultural fusion lets you know that you're on the east side, while Belgrade is a hub of history, culture and nightlife entertainment.

2

MOSTAR & DUBROVNIK ⏱3 DAYS

Stop to take a look at the famous bridge in **Mostar** (p100; pictured), spend the day wandering around the Old Town and see the famous bridge divers hurl themselves into the Neretva River. Head to the ancient walled city of **Dubrovnik** (p166), and take a couple of days to explore its walls, churches, galleries and restaurants; if the season is right, swim off the rocks outside the walls.

3

MONTENEGRO ⏱4 DAYS

From Dubrovnik, hop across the Croatia–Montenegro border to its 'mini me' **Kotor** (p200). A couple of days exploring Kotor and the **Bay of Kotor** (p205) are well spent – the landscape of steely mountains and seas is bound to leave you in awe. From here you can take an extraordinary drive via **Budva** (p208), **Podgorica** (p221), the breathtaking **Morača Canyon** (p228; pictured) and through the mountains to Kosovo.

FROM LEFT: SERGII FIGURNYI/SHUTTERSTOCK ©, MEHMETO/SHUTTERSTOCK ©, BERND ZILLICH/SHUTTERSTOCK ©

LJUBLJANA
SLOVENIA
START
ZAGREB
HUNGARY
ROMANIA
Osijek
CROATIA
Danube
Novi Sad
Slavonski Brod
13 hrs
Karlovac
Rijeka
Sava
BELGRADE
Smederevo
Šabac
Bijeljina
Bihać
Banja Luka
BOSNIA & HERCEGOVINA
Tuzla
SERBIA
Kragujevac
Jajce
Zenica
Drina
Čačak
Kraljevo
Kruševac
Zadar
SARAJEVO
Višegrad
Bjelašnica
Drina
Split
Mostar
Blagaj
Novi Pazar
MONTENEGRO
Mitrovica
PRISTINA
KOSOVO
2.5 hrs
Nikšić
Peja (Peć)
Dubrovnik
4 hrs
PODGORICA
Prizren
Kotor
Budva
Lake Skadar
Shkodra
5 hrs
Adriatic Sea
Ulcinj
NORTH MACEDONIA
TIRANA
Durrës
2.5 hrs
Ohrid
ITALY
END
Elbasan
Lake Ohrid
0 100 km
0 50 miles
Bari
Berat
ALBANIA

4 KOSOVO & NORTH MACEDONIA 3 DAYS

Spend a day in historic **Prizren** (p185; pictured) and a night in **Pristina** (p180), checking out its cacophonous architecture, before continuing on to North Macedonia. Cross the border and spend a day or two amid the old-world architecture of **Ohrid Town** (p250) on the shores of the lake, swimming and admiring the wealth of Byzantine churches. Cross into Albania and drive to its capital.

5 ALBANIA 3 DAYS

Two days in **Tirana** (p50) will give you a chance to explore its lively daily life, museums, galleries and excellent restaurants, and make sure you don't miss the city's vibrant nightlife.

Detour: *If you have time, drive out to* ***Durres*** *(p55) and explore a slice of the Albanian Adriatic, swimming and sunbathing before returning to Tirana to take your flight back home.*

SERGIY VOVK/SHUTTERSTOCK ©

Zlatni Rat (p158), Brač, Croatia

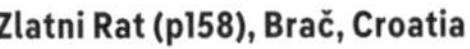

ITINERARIES

Cruising the Coast

Allow: 3 weeks **Distance:** 1697km

This itinerary traces a leisurely path along arguably the Mediterranean's most spectacular coastline, from the Adriatic Sea in Slovenia and Croatia, and all the way to Albania's Ionian coast. Driving is the best way to trace the whole route.

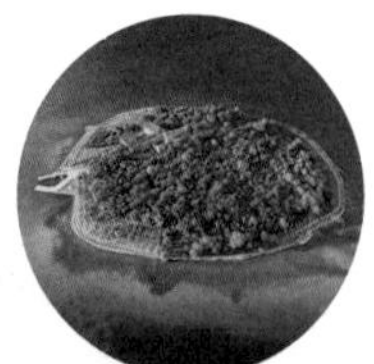

1 PULA 2 DAYS

Start by exploring the Istrian peninsula, starting in beautiful **Pula** (p130). Admire its perfectly preserved 1st-century Roman amphitheatre and catch a concert here. Stroll along its *lungomare,* tracing the rocky coastline along a path rich with the scent of pines, and swim in the Adriatic. Learn about olive oil production. Take a day trip into the interior to visit Istria's historic hill towns and experience its exemplary cuisine. Head towards Rijeka.

2 RIJEKA, KRK & LOŠINJ ISLANDS 5 DAYS

Head to the regional rock capital of **Rijeka** (p126), a buzzing, cosmopolitan city with great food. Next, drive to **Krk** (p133; pictured), Croatia's largest island, famous for its long beaches, seaside towns and a wealth of cultural heritage. Don't miss its wine and olive oil. Take another ferry to **Lošinj island** (p136), and explore the gorgeous towns of Mali Lošinj and Veli Lošinj.

3 DALMATIA 4 DAYS

Set aside your second week for exploring Dalmatia. Drive back to mainland Crikvenica, below Rijeka, and first detour to **Plitvice National Park** (p142) to witness its famed waterfalls. Plunge down to **Zadar** (p138) and wander through the slippery marble streets of the old town. Keep cruising the coast to the sun-kissed city of **Split** (p148), home to Diocletian's Palace (pictured) and gateway to the Dalmatian islands.

FROM LEFT: ECSTK22/SHUTTERSTOCK ©, XBRCHX/SHUTTERSTOCK ©, XBRCHX/SHUTTERSTOCK ©

4 THE ISLANDS 4 DAYS

After a night on party- and beach-loving **Hvar** (p153), explore the historic Hvar Town. Spend another day exploring Pakleni Islands (pictured). Take a catamaran to **Brač** (p158), where you can swim at Bol beach and eat at one of the island's restaurants. Another ferry ride will take you over to **Korčula** (p160), where the Old Town is a picturesque fortified gem and Lumbarda is peaceful and idyllic. Head to Dubrovnik.

5 DUBROVNIK & MONTENEGRO 3 DAYS

Start your last week in the famous walled city of **Dubrovnik** (p166). Heading further south, cross into Montenegro and drive around the extraordinarily beautiful **Bay of Kotor** (p205), taking in the palazzo-packed **Perast** (p205) and the lovely beaches around the Bay. Swim in the Adriatic and then press on to the fortified old town of **Kotor** (p200; pictured).

6 MONTENEGRO & ALBANIA 3 DAYS

Continue down the coast, stopping in **Budva** (p208) for the obligatory photo of **Sveti Stefan** (p212; pictured). Spend the night in buzzy **Ulcinj** (p213) before crossing into Albania, following the coast as the sea switches from Adriatic to Ionian. The last two nights are on the Albanian Riviera, stopping in **Durres** (p55) and heading on down to **Gjipe Beach** (p62) and the ancient ruins of **Butrint** (p59).

SLAVENKO/SHUTTERSTOCK ©

Bosnia & Hercegovina section of the Via Dinarica (p109)

ITINERARIES

Remote Ramblings

Allow: 4 weeks **Distance:** 1633 km

If you've got a few months to spare, excellent fitness and a local crew handling the logistics, you could tackle the extraordinary 1261km cross-border Via Dinarica (p109) hiking trail. If not, this driving itinerary roughly traces the route, allowing for a series of day walks in national parks.

1

SLOVENIA 5 DAYS

Start in the Slovenian capital, **Ljubljana** (p310), where you can enjoy some good bar and restaurant life over three days before heading into the wild. Stop for a look around **Postojna Cave** (p328; pictured) and discover a vast karst cave system created by a river, housing the olm, an endemic aquatic salamander. Continue across the Croatian border to Plitvice National Park.

2

CROATIA 5 DAYS

Continue on to busy but beautiful **Plitvice National Park** (p142; pictured), rich in waterfalls, pitch your tent and do some hiking in the national park. Next, discover the green paths of **Lika** (p142) – you can even spend a few nights in a tepee or a tree house near the town of **Gospić** (p143). Move onto exploring the waterfalls and lakes of **Krka National Park** (p144), excellent for a couple of days' hiking.

3

BOSNIA & HERCEGOVINA 6 DAYS

Cross the border of Bosnia and Hercegovina and drive to the ski resort of **Bjelašnica** (p93). From here, you can hike to the lost-in-time villages nearby and sample traditional Bosnian cuisine. Continue on to **Sarajevo** (p84) for a taste of the Bosnian capital before driving to **Višegrad** (p96; pictured) to view the famous bridge. Push on to **Sutjeska National Park** (p97), where mountain hiking awaits.

FROM LEFT: WENILIOU/SHUTTERSTOCK ©, BEST-BACKGROUNDS/SHUTTERSTOCK ©, IGOR POPOVIC 911/SHUTTERSTOCK ©

4

MONTENEGRO, KOSOVO & ALBANIA ⏱ 6 DAYS

Enter Montenegro and spend two days in **Durmitor National Park** (p223; pictured) and then another day in lakeside **Biogradska Gora National Park** (p227). Cross into Kosovo and base yourself in **Peja** (Peć; p188). Visit its famous monastery and tackle the walking tracks in the **Rugova Valley** (p189). Continue down into Albania and head to **Valbona** (p66) in the Accursed Mountains.

5

NORTH MACEDONIA ⏱ 5 DAYS

Valbona is the official end of the Via Dinarica. From here you can take day hikes into the mountains or organise a cross-border trek, venturing into Montenegro's **Prokletije National Park** (p227; pictured). Finally, press on to North Macedonia and spend a couple of days in the villages of **Mavrovo National Park** (p256) before finishing up in the capital, **Skopje** (p238).

HIVAKA/SHUTTERSTOCK ©

Tara River, Durmitor National Park (p223)

ITINERARIES

Capitals, National Parks & Historic Towns

Allow: 3 weeks **Distance:** 1127 km

A trio of capital cities – Belgrade, Sarajevo and Podgorica, five national parks and a medley of historic towns punctuate this route through the heart of the Balkans, traversing Serbia, Bosnia and Hercegovina, and Montenegro.

1 SERBIA 5 DAYS

Start your journey with three days in Serbia's rambunctious metropolis, **Belgrade** (p270). Once you've explored its museums, fortress, smoky cafes and lively bars, take a detour northwest to **Novi Sad** (p276), the principal city of the nation's Vojvodina region. From here it's only a half-hour drive to **Fruška Gora** (p279); set aside a day for hiking, wine tasting and expeditions to historic Serbian Orthodox monasteries (pictured).

2 BOSNIA 5 DAYS

Head south to **Tara National Park** (p290) and explore the forested mountains and dramatic Drina River canyon. Cross the border into Bosnia and visit **Višegrad** (p96), the town immortalised in Ivo Andrić's acclaimed novel *The Bridge on the Drina*. From here, **Sarajevo** (p84) is due west and worthy of a multiday stay. Soak up the sights, sounds and tastes of its Baščaršija quarter (pictured).

3 HERCEGOVINA 4 DAYS

After feasting on *burek*, baklava and Bosnian coffee in the shadow of historic mosques, churches and synagogues in Sarajevo, continue on to sun-scorched Hercegovina, along the emerald-hued Neretva River. Gaze at the exquisite Ottoman centre in **Mostar** (p100; pictured). Pause in **Blagaj** (p103) to visit the peaceful *tekke* (dervish house). Go east to **Sutjeska National Park** (p97), distinguished by its mountain scenery.

FROM LEFT: MIRKO KUZMANOVIC/SHUTTERSTOCK ©, BERND ZILLICH/SHUTTERSTOCK ©, MO WU/SHUTTERSTOCK ©

Danube
Novi Sad
CROATIA
Slavonski Brod
Fruška Gora National Park
2
2hrs
Pančevo
1
START
Sava
Brčko
Bijeljina
Šabac
BELGRADE
Smederevo
Banja Luka
Tuzla
Drina
BOSNIA & HERCEGOVINA
SERBIA
Kragujevac
Jajce
7hrs
Drina
Zenica
Čačak
Tara National Park
SARAJEVO
3
Višegrad
Kraljevo
Kruševac
Bjelašnica
Sutjeska National Park
Durmitor National Park
Novi Pazar
Split
Mostar
Blagaj
4.5hrs
Mitrovica
MONTENEGRO
6hrs
Peja (Peć)
PRISTINA
KOSOVO
Lovćen National Park
Dubrovnik
PODGORICA
Prizren
Kotor
4
Cetinje
Lake Skadar
ALBANIA
Adriatic Sea
Budva
2hrs
Shkodra
Tetovo
Ulcinj
5
END
NORTH MACEDONIA
0 100 km
0 50 miles

4

MONTENEGRIN MOUNTAINS ⏱ 5 DAYS

Hop across the border and spend days hiking and rafting in **Durmitor National Park** (p223). One night is enough to get the gist of the modern capital, **Podgorica** (p221; pictured), and allow another to explore the museums and galleries of **Cetinje** (p215). From here take the spectacular route through **Lovćen National Park** (p219) and down the precipitous, serpentine road to **Kotor** (p200).

5

MONTENEGRIN COAST ⏱ 3 DAYS

Kotor is a walled gem positioned within the innermost fold of the fjord-like **Bay of Kotor** (p205; pictured). With this town as a base, head over for a look at the still-charming walled town of otherwise-overdeveloped **Budva** (p208) and pause along the highway for the obligatory photo of the fortified island village of **Sveti Stefan** (p212). Stop for the night in buzzy **Ulcinj** (p213), and enjoy its sandy beaches.

WHEN TO GO

The Western Balkans can be visited any time, but the region is at its best in late spring, summer and early autumn.

While the cities can be visited any time of the year, winter generally offers fewer facilities, and the weather cools down. But there's plenty of culture on offer to keep you busy in the cities even mid-winter, and there is skiing around Sarajevo.

Outdoor activities – such as hiking and climbing – are best kept for late spring and early autumn. Beach time and river swimming and rafting are perfect in the scorching summer months – keep in mind that beaches get quite crowded in the high season (July and August) and that facilities are practically nonexistent in winter. Hikes can be done in midsummer too, depending on the temperatures.

Check out the festival season in Croatia, Serbia and Bosnia and Hercegovina, where you can catch music – techno, folk, rock, you name it – and film festivals.

I LIVE HERE

MOUNTAIN ADVENTURES

Metodi Chilimanov is owner of SharOutdoors. @chilimanoff

I fall in love with North Macedonia over and over again. I can go rock climbing or kayaking in Canyon Matka, biking on Mt Vodno, hiking in Mavrovo National Park or free-ride skiing and ski touring on the Shar Mountain. The majestic Shar Mountains, my home, have taught me everything I know about mountains. I feel privileged to be able to guide many fellow adventurers around this incredible landscape.

Canyon Matka (p242), North Macedonia

BEST TIMES TO VISIT ACROSS THE REGION

Ideally visit Ljubljana between April and October, Belgrade between May and November, Sarajevo between May and September, Dubrovnik between May and October, Tirana between June and September and Skopje between May and October.

Weather Through the Year (Zagreb)

January	February	March	April	May	June
Ave. daytime max: **4°C**	Ave. daytime max: **5°C**	Ave. daytime max: **11°C**	Ave. daytime max: **17°C**	Ave. daytime max: **21°C**	Ave. daytime max: **26°C**
Days of rainfall: 6	Days of rainfall: 7	Days of rainfall: 7	Days of rainfall: 9	Days of rainfall: 9	Days of rainfall: 9

SCORCHING SUMMERS

In summer, pack your swimming gear whether or not you're heading to the coast; the interior can get scorching hot and there are plenty of rivers and lakes to cool off in.

Music & Film Festivals

Thousands of revellers enter the state of **Exit** within the walls of the Petrovaradin Fortress in Novi Sad (p276). International headlining acts draw music lovers from all over the continent. **July**

Held over three days at Poljud Stadium, Split's electronic-music fest then heads to the islands for the rest of **Destination Ultra Croatia Music Week**. **July**

Since it grew out of the ruins of the 1990s war, the **Sarajevo Film Festival** (p91) has become one of the largest film festivals in Europe. Commercial and art-house flicks are showcased, mostly with English subtitles. **August**

Croatia's most fun and glamorous, **Motovun Film Festival** presents a roster of independent and avant-garde films. Nonstop outdoor and indoor screenings, concerts and parties take over the medieval streets of this Istrian hilltop town. **July**

I LIVE HERE

COASTAL BEAUTIES

Sanja and Jon Kawaguchi run Kawa. @kawa.dubrovnik

Pelješac is our favourite escape during busy summer months in Dubrovnik. We take a quick roadside stop for oysters in Mali Ston, lunch straight out of the sea at Kobaš, swim in cerulean waters at wild Pržina beach, then take the old coastal road past steep vineyards and old villages towards Viganj. In the morning, across the bay, the sound of church bells of Korčula is enchanting. The air smells of sea, salt and pine trees.

Oysters, Mali Ston, Croatia

Carnivals & Traditional Music Festivals

Serbia's **Guča Festival** (p289) is one of the most exciting and bizarre events in all of the Balkans. Hundreds of thousands of revellers gather to damage their eardrums, livers and sanity over four cacophonous days of trumpet-fuelled revelry. **August**

The **Vevčani Carnival**, in North Macedonia, is a traditional pagan carnival thought to have existed for 1400 years, and is still celebrated with elaborate costumes, music and general revelry. **January**

The **Rijeka Carnival** (p128) is the most salubrious carnival in Croatia. Over two weeks, pageants, street dances, concerts, masked balls, exhibitions and parades take place. **February**

The small village of Galičnik, in North Macedonia, sees thousands of visitors attend its **traditional wedding festival** (p256) to see one or two lucky couples wed here and to enjoy eating, drinking, traditional folk dancing and music. **July**

SNOWFALLS

Mid-winter, many attractions and coastal towns all but close – time to hit the ski slopes!

 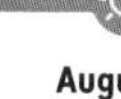    

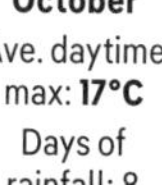

July	August	September	October	November	December
Ave. daytime max: **29°C**	Ave. daytime max: **29°C**	Ave. daytime max: **23°C**	Ave. daytime max: **17°C**	Ave. daytime max: **10°C**	Ave. daytime max: **5°C**
Days of rainfall: 8	Days of rainfall: 7	Days of rainfall: 9	Days of rainfall: 8	Days of rainfall: 9	Days of rainfall: 8

LEFT: ILIJA ASCIC/SHUTTERSTOCK ©; RIGHT: PHOTO 12/ALAMY STOCK PHOTO ©

GET PREPARED FOR THE WESTERN BALKANS

Useful things to load in your bag, your ears and your brain.

Clothes

On the coast The Adriatic coastline has lots of pebbly stretches, and beach shoes are a necessity. In summer, a swimming suit also comes in handy away from the beach, as you can cool off in lakes and rivers.

In the mountains If you're planning on hitting the trails, bring hiking boots or sturdy shoes. It gets cold in the mountains even in summer, so you'll need layers.

Going out in the cities The Balkans are laid-back, but people tend to dress up for swankier restaurants and clubs – it's worth bringing at least one smarter outfit for these occasions.

Visiting religious sites When entering monasteries and mosques, both men and women should be dressed modestly, with legs and shoulders covered. In mosques, a loosely wrapped headscarf is recommended for women.

Manners

Thorny topics Approach discussions of regional politics and history with caution – these topics are best avoided unless locals bring them up.

Language Bosnian, Croatian, Montenegrin and Serbian speakers will appreciate it if you don't confuse their languages (although they're essentially the same).

Splitting the bill Not done in the Balkans – the person who initiated dining out or drinks will always insist on paying.

READ

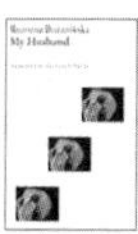

My Husband (Rumena Bužarovska; 2014) Macedonian short stories, narrated by honest, sharp, provocative female characters.

Quiet Flows the Una (Faruk Šehić; 2016) Personal account of the trauma of the Bosnian war, awarded with the EU Prize for Literature.

Catherine the Great and the Small (Olja Knežević; 2019) A generational tale of Montenegrin women, equal parts humorous and tragic.

The Masterpiece (Ana Schnabl; 2021) Love affair and political drama intertwine in this debut from an award-winning Slovenian writer.

Words

Make an effort to get familiar with the Cyrillic alphabet. Macedonian uses Cyrillic; Albanian, Croatian and Slovene use Latin. In Serbia and Montenegro, Cyrillic and Latin are employed interchangeably. In Bosnia and Kosovo, Cyrillic is found in Serbian-majority areas and Latin elsewhere.

BCMS (Bosnian, Croatian, Montenegrin, Serbian)

Ćao – all-purpose casual greeting (hi/bye) adopted from Italian (note the local spelling).

Zdravo – works as 'hello' in BMS, while in Croatia *Bok* is the phrase to use.

Doviđenja – the everyday 'see you later'; *Zbogom* is a more formal 'goodbye'.

Molim/Hvala – please/ thank you

Izvinite/Oprostite – used as both 'excuse me' and 'sorry' (the former in BMS, the latter in Croatian)

Živjeli/Živeli – 'cheers'; the former in BCM, the latter in Serbian (pronounced 'zheev-ye-lee' and 'zhee-ve-lee')

kava/kafa – 'coffee'; the former in Croatia, the latter in Serbia and Montenegro, while both come up in Bosnia along with *kahva*

Macedonian & Slovene

Zdravo – 'hello'

Do gledanje/Na svidenje – 'goodbye' in Macedonian/ Slovene

Molam/Blagodaram – 'please/thank you' in Macedonian

Prosim/Hvala – 'please/ thank you' in Slovene

Na zdravje! – 'cheers!'

Albanian

Tungjatjeta/Mirupafshim – 'hello/goodbye'

Ju lutem/Faleminderit – 'please/thank you'

Gëzuar! – 'cheers!'

WATCH

We Are Not Angels (Srđan Dragojević; 1992) Angel and Devil fight for the soul of a Belgrade playboy in this comedy.

Before the Rain (Milcho Manchevski; 1994; pictured) Lyrical Macedonian movie featuring three fated-love stories.

Consequences (Darko Štante; 2018) Slovenian film exploring youth criminality and LGBTIQ+ issues.

Murina (Antoneta Alamat Kusijanović; 2021) Psychological family drama unravels on a Dalmatian island.

Hive (Blerta Basholli; 2021) Kosovan woman defies societal expectations; three Sundance awards.

LISTEN

Dnevnik jedne ljubavi (Josipa Lisac; 1973) Acclaimed conceptual album of Croatia's long-lasting pop avant-garde diva.

Svjat dreams (Mizar; 1991) North Macedonia's cult darkwave band whose songs incorporate Byzantine folk influences.

20th Century – Selected Works (Borghesia; 2009) A retrospective of works from Slovenia's electro/industrial music legends.

Zemlja snova (Kralj Čačka; 2016) Serbia's most authentic new voice mixes blues, jazz and chanson with noir, humour and poetry.

HAREXAPE/SHUTTERSTOCK ©

Turkish-style coffee and baklava

THE FOOD SCENE

The regional cuisines reflect the area's mishmash of cultural heritage. Expect great food made from top-notch, seasonal ingredients.

Being a region rich in diverse cultural influences, the cuisines of the Western Balkans work with a wealth of different flavours. Depending on the area, you'll find ingredients being prepared in ways reflecting Mediterranean, Ottoman and Greek, Central European and Highland tastes.

For hundreds of years, Venice dominated the coast as far as Montenegro – leaving a legacy of excellent risotto, gnocchi and pasta. This is also where you'll find high-quality olive oil and wine.

The countries where the Ottoman influence is most pronounced are North Macedonia, Albania, Kosovo, Serbia and Bosnia, and as well as the ubiquitous *burek/byrek*, you'll find excellent baklava, *lokum/ratluk* (Turkish delight) and Turkish-style coffee throughout the region.

The Austrian influence is strongest in Slovenia and the Zagreb and Zagorje regions of Croatia. However, strudel and Wiener schnitzel have made their way across the Western Balkans. In the mountains, food is traditionally more stodgy and meaty, providing comfort and sustenance on those long winter nights.

Coastal Cuisine

The food of the coast is typically Mediterranean. You'll find a wealth of risottos, while the flavoursome fish soup *(riblja čorba)* is a must-try, as is octopus (*hobotnica*; either carpaccio, in a salad or cooked under a *peka* – a domed baking lid). Lamb from the islands of Cres and Pag is deemed Croatia's best; try *paški sir*, a pungent hard sheep cheese from Pag. Istrian cuisine is known

Best Western Balkan Dishes

AJVAR
A roasted red-pepper condiment at its best in North Macedonia, Serbia and Bosnia and Hercegovina.

BUREK/BYREK
A ubiquitous filo-pastry pie with a cheese, spinach, potato or meat filling.

ĆEVAPI
Grilled kebab-style meat served with bread and raw onions, loved by all.

for its quality ingredients and unique specialities. Typical dishes include *maneštra* (thick vegetable-and-bean soup similar to minestrone) and *fuži* (hand-rolled pasta often served with *tartufi* (truffles). Truffles and wild asparagus are an Istrian obsession.

Ottoman & Greek Influences

Grilled meat – *ćevapi* – is king here, usually served with bread and raw onions. Dolma (vegetables such as eggplant and peppers stuffed with meat and rice) is a must; a similar filling wrapped in a cabbage or vine leaf is called *sarma* and *japrak*.

Tomatoes grow abundantly and feature prominently in salads such as North Macedonia's and Serbia's *šopska salata* (with peppers, onion, cucumbers and feta-style cheese). These two countries are also the home of *ajvar* (pronounced 'eye-var'), a condiment made from red peppers and oil.

Wine Tasting

The Western Balkans has an array of localised indigenous grape varieties on offer. Most wineries are small, family-run affairs which welcome visitors but usually require a little notice. Slovenia has three main regions: Podravje, Posavje and Primorska. Croatia produces some of the Balkans' best wine; the top regions to tour are Istria, Dalmatia (particularly the Pelješac Peninsula and the islands) and Slavonia (especially around Baranja). In Bosnia, head to Hercegovina to sample *žilavka* (white) and *blatina* (red). Most of Montenegro's grapes are grown around Lake Skadar and the plains leading to Podgorica; try *vranac*, their signature red. In North Macedonia, the Tikveš Wine Region is worth a visit for its scenery as much as its top-notch wines.

YARUNIV STUDIO/SHUTTERSTOCK ©

Dolma/sarma

EYE UBIQUITOUS/ALAMY STOCK PHOTO ©

FOOD & WINE FESTIVALS

Kavadarci Wine Carnival The wine harvest in North Macedonia's Tikveš Eine Region is celebrated with a costumed parade, public wine tasting and merrymaking.

Cow's Ball Slovenia's weekend of folk dancing, music, eating and drinking in Bohinj marks the return of the cows from their high pastures to the valleys in typically ebullient Balkan style.

Martinje St Martin's Day is celebrated in all the wine-producing regions across Slovenia and Croatia on 11 November. There are wine celebrations and lots of feasting and sampling of new wines.

Istria Truffle Festival (pictured) In October, the truffle is celebrated in the town of Buzet, in Croatia, with producers from across the country showing their delicacies.

Good Food Festival Dubrovnik hosts an array of events across the city, with workshops, dinners and gastronomic tours.

FUŽI	PAŠKI SIR	PRŠUT	ŠOPSKA SALATA	DOLMA/SARMA
Istria's delicious hand-rolled pasta, often served with *tartufi* (truffles).	A pungent hard sheep cheese from the island of Pag.	Dry-cured ham, very much like the Italian prosciutto.	A juicy salad with peppers, onion, cucumbers and feta-style cheese.	Aubergines, peppers, cabbage or vine leaf stuffed with minced meat, spices and rice.

Local Specialities

Taste the staples and the unusual.

Total Treats

Truffle The signature taste of Istria. It makes its way into most things.

Meat roasted 'ispod sača/peka' A traditional cooking method, with meat or fish slow-cooked with potatoes under a dome-shaped metal lid, covered with charcoal.

Spit-roasted meat The tantalising scent of the spit-roast wafts throughout the Balkans.

Pršut This dry-cured ham is every bit the equal of Italian prosciutto.

Olive oil Istrian olive oil regularly wins international awards, and the region has plenty of boutique producers offering tastings and tours.

Cheap Treats

Burek/byrek This savoury filo-pastry pie is the consummate Balkan snack, available from bakeries or speciality *buregdžinica/ byrektorë* throughout the region.

Ćevapi/ćevapčići

Ćevapi/ćevapčići Small minced beef, lamb or pork kebabs – hugely popular throughout the Western Balkans but particularly in Bosnia and Serbia, where they're considered national dishes.

Ražnjići Chunks of grilled meat (often pork) on a skewer.

Pizza You're never far from Neapolitan-style pizza anywhere in the Balkans.

Palačinke Thin pancakes are the default sweet offering.

MEALS OF A LIFETIME

Iva New Balkan Cuisine (p275) Reinventing Belgrade's gastronomy in a fusion of flavours and organic ingredients.

Foša (p141) Zadar's Michelin-star restaurant is famous for its excellent and imaginative fish dishes.

Konoba Ćatovića Mlini (p206) A historic mill hides one of Montenegro's top restaurants, with masterfully prepared traditional dishes.

Nadžak (p240) Very basic and very good, serving North Macedonia's traditional dishes, perfectly prepared.

Agroturizam Grubinjac (p162) Korčula's most charming place to eat has a seasonal home-caught and homemade menu.

Gostilna Pri Lojzetu (p338) A Slovenian Slow Food bastion, with a master chef, a Michelin star and incredible local ingredients.

THE YEAR IN FOOD

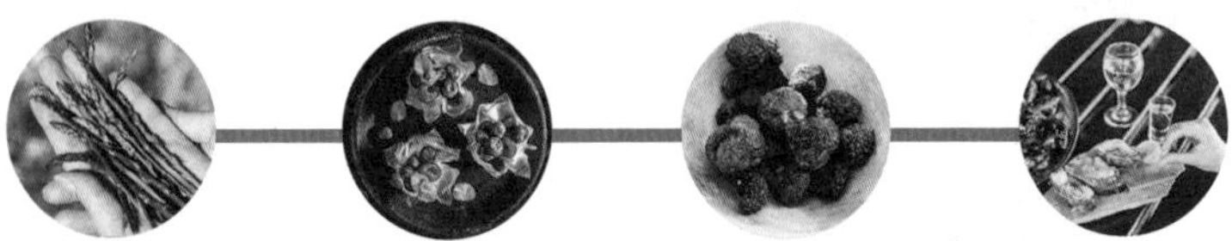

Spring

Wild asparagus comes into season in Istria (Croatia) and gets its own festival. In April, restaurants in Korčula (Croatia) show off signature dishes. Istrian winemakers throw open their cellar doors in late May.

Summer

Berries and stone fruits are in season. Dine al fresco on freshly caught seafood along the coast, especially during the Isola (Slovenia) fishing festival.

Autumn

Mushroom-hunting shifts into high gear. Festivals showcase truffles (Istria), chestnuts (Kvarner, Croatia), cheese (Pljevlja, Montenegro) and the olive and wine harvests (almost everywhere).

Winter

Start the season with the wine and fish festival at Lake Skadar (Montenegro), then prepare for hearty Christmas and Carnival treats.

TOP LEFT: ALEKSANDAR BLANUSA/SHUTTERSTOCK ©; RIGHT: OLGA GONT/GETTY IMAGES ©

Burek/byrek

FOTO MATEVZ LAVRIC/SHUTTERSTOCK ©

Hiking, Krk (p133), Croatia

THE OUTDOORS

The Balkans' varied landscape makes it ideal terrain for endless outdoor pursuits – whether on mountains, lakes, rivers, canyons or the sea.

A wide range of outdoor activities is available across the Western Balkans and enthusiast local crews have stepped in to make them possible. Spring and autumn are the best seasons for rock climbing, rafting, whitewater kayaking, and spotting migratory birds in the various wetlands, and the weather is great for hiking, cycling and windsurfing. Summers are ideal for swimming, diving, kayaking, sailing, horse riding and more sedate rafting and kayaking, while winter is best for skiing and snowshoeing.

Hiking

Every country in the region offers excellent hiking, with marked trails through forests, mountains and national parks. But be aware: they're not all well maintained or well marked (Slovenia is the exception). The best months for hiking are from May to September, especially late August and early September, when summer crowds have largely disappeared.

There are long-distance, cross-border hiking tracks, such as the 192km Peaks of the Balkans and the 495km High Scardus Trail. The Via Dinarica (viadinarica.com) is ever developing, with plans for three themed paths following the Dinaric Alps.

Diving & Snorkelling

The clear waters and varied marine life of the Adriatic support a vibrant diving industry, and snorkelling is worthwhile just

Challenge Yourself

CYCLING
Bicycle touring is increasingly popular, both independently or with organised groups; try the spectacular scenery at Đerdap Gorge (p297).

SKIING
Most ski areas, such as the two near Sarajevo (p92) are small, but they are affordable and easy to access.

SAILING
Zadar in Croatia (p138) and Montenegro offer plenty of affordable opportunities for both day sails and organised multiday tours.

FAMILY ADVENTURES

Step into an underground wonderland Even the littlest ones can enjoy the natural underground wonderland that is **Lipa Cave** (p218) near Cetinje.

Explore a Danube marshland Go cycling, canoeing and birdwatching in Vojvodina province's **Gornje Podunavlje** (p284), aka 'the Amazon of Europe'.

Row around a castle island Rent a kayak on **Lake Bled** (p317), Slovenia's picture perfect spot.

Visit an arcadian paradise The whole familywill be in awe of the water beauties in **Plitvice National Park** (p142).

Get a bird's eye view of the city The nine-minute **Sarajevo Cable Car ride** (p90) is fun for kids.

about everywhere. Visibility ranges from 10m to 25m but is usually around 15m. The best times to dive are from the middle of May until September, when the surface water is up to 25°C, dropping to 16°C under 30m (you'll need a 7mm neoprene wetsuit).

The area's history has bequeathed it numerous underwater sights, from wrecks dating to antiquity through to a downed WWII plane, plus there are plenty of reefs, drop-offs, springs and caves.

There are diving centres all along the Croatian and Montenegrin coasts and throughout the islands. Cave diving takes place at Postojna, Škocjan and in the tunnel at Wild Lake (Divje Jezero) near Idrija. Another unusual diving tour delves into North Macedonia's Lake Ohrid to check out the remains of a Neolithic settlement at the Bay of Bones. 'Speed river diving' is an activity invented in Una National Park (Bosnia) involving scuba diving in fast-flowing waters.

BEST SPOTS

For the best outdoor spots and routes, see map on p42.

Tara River (p225), Montenegro

Rafting & Kayaking

Whitewater rafting is offered from around April to October. The biggest thrills are in spring, when the melting snow speeds up the flows.

Commercial rafting is well established on the Tara River in Bosnia and Montenegro. The Montenegrin section includes the spectacular 1300m-deep Tara Canyon – best viewed on a two-day wilderness rafting trip. Elsewhere in Bosnia there's wonderful rafting through the Vrbas Canyon and on the Una and Neretva Rivers.

Slovenia's centre for kayaking and rafting is the Soča River at Bovec, famed as one of the best and least spoiled whitewater routes in the European Alps. Croatia's prime rafting locale is the Cetina River, which spills through a steep gorge and into the Adriatic at Omiš. In Albania, the key spots are the Vjosa and Osumi Canyons.

As for sea kayaking, there's nowhere more dramatic to paddle than at the foot of the mighty walls of Dubrovnik at sunset – although Montenegro's fjord-like Bay of Kotor comes close.

WINDSURFING & KITESURFING
Brač (p158) offers ideal conditions for windsurfing; kitesurfers head to Montenegro's Velika Plaža (p214).

ROCK CLIMBING
Excellent spots for rock climbing are available in Slovenia – Mt Triglav's north face (p322) is spectacular – and Croatia, as well as Montenegro.

HORSE RIDING
Slovenia is a nation of horse riders. Serbia and Galičnik (p254) in North Macedonia also have good riding options.

ZIP LINING
There are many zip lining opportunities across the region, such as Zipline Dolinka (p320) at Lake Bled.

AUSTRIA
HUNGARY
SLOVENIA
CROATIA
BOSNIA & HERCEGOVINA
ITALY
Mura
Jesenice
Triglav
Bled
Maribor
Medvednica Nature Park
Gorizia
LJUBLJANA
Monfalcone
Postojna
ZAGREB
Trieste
Kočevje
Koper
Karlovac
Lonjsko Polje Nature Park
Sava
Slavonski Brod
Osijek
Rijeka
Crikvenica
Plitvice Lakes National Park
Vrbas
Brčko
Krk Town
Banja Luka
Bosna
Pula
Bihać
Tuzla
Mali Lošinj
Veli Lošinj
Paklenica National Park
Jajce
Zenica
SARAJEVO
Zadar
Krka National Park
Bjelašn
Split
Mostar
Biokovo Nature Park
Blagaj
Neretva
Hvar
Korčula Town
Adriatic Sea
Dubrovnik
Naples
Tyrrhenian Sea
0 250 km
0 150 miles
Skiing & Snowboarding
1 Kopaonik Ski Resort (p294)
2 Bjelašnica (p93)
3 Jahorina (p92)
4 Kolašin (p226)
5 Mavrovo National Park (p256)
6 Kanin Ski Centre (p325)
Walking & Hiking
1 Uvac Canyon (p294)
2 Accursed Mountains (p65)
3 Peaks of the Balkans (p188)
4 Durmitor National Park (p223)
5 Via Dinarica (p109)
6 Sutjeska National Park (p97)

ACTION AREAS

Where to find the Western Balkans' best outdoor activities.

Subotica
Tisa
Zrenjanin
Novi Sad
Fruška Gora National Park
Dunav
Sava
BELGRADE
Pančevo
Šabac
Bijeljina
Smederevo
ROMANIA
Danube
Negotin
SERBIA
Drina
Kragujevac
Čačak
Kraljevo
Kruševac
Tara National Park
Kopaonik National Park
Stara Planina Nature Park
Durmitor National Park
Novi Pazar
Leskovac
Biogradska Gora National Park
MONTENEGRO
Mitrovica
Peja (Peć)
Nikšić
Prokletije National Park
PRISTINA
Vranje
KOSOVO
PODGORICA
Valbona
Prizren
Shar Mountain National Park
Kumanovo
Cetinje
Lake Koman
Lake Fierza
Shkodra
Lake Shkodra
Tetovo
SKOPJE
Ulcinj
Mavrovo National Park
NORTH MACEDONIA
Mat
ALBANIA
Prilep
Durres
TIRANA
Lake Ohrid
Ohrid
Bitola
Elbasan
Lake Prespa
Pelister National Park
Berat
Vlorë
GREECE
Ionian Sea

Cycling

1. Parenzana Bike Trail (p335)
2. Fruška Gora (p279)
3. EuroVelo 6 (p284)
4. Amazon of Europe Bike Trail (p284)
5. Novi Sad (p276)

Kayaking & Canoeing

1. Tara Canyon (p225)
2. Bovec (p324)
3. Canyon Matka (p242)
4. Osumi Canyon (p71)
5. Dubrovnik (p166)
6. Bay of Kotor (p205)

Vineyards & Wineries

1. Hvar (p157)
2. Korčula Island (p162)
3. Crmnica Wine Region (p222)
4. Fruška Gora Wineries (p279)
5. Vipava Valley (p337)
6. Negotin Region (p300)
7. Popova Kula (p261)

WESTERN BALKANS

THE GUIDE

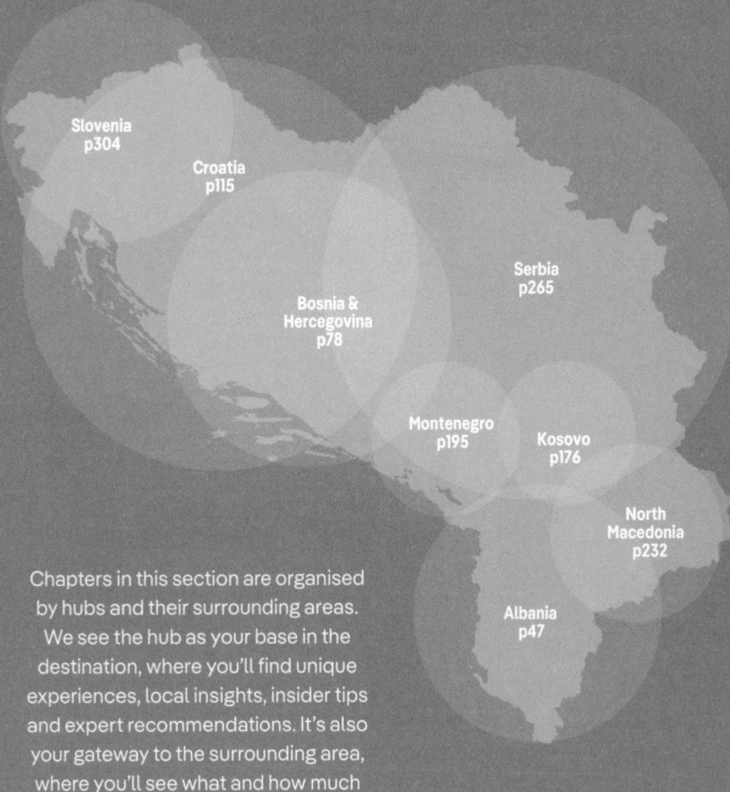

Chapters in this section are organised by hubs and their surrounding areas. We see the hub as your base in the destination, where you'll find unique experiences, local insights, insider tips and expert recommendations. It's also your gateway to the surrounding area, where you'll see what and how much you can do from there.

Plitvice National Park (p142), Croatia

VICTOR CARDONER/GETTY IMAGES ©

Above: Theth Church (p66). Right: Shkodra (p63)

Albania

STILL UNDERRATED, SOMEHOW

Limestone-painted seas, spectacular mountain hiking and thousands of years of history etched into crumbling ruins. It's hard to understand why some still skip Albania.

Albania's borders were shut for much of the 20th century due to a brutal strain of communism steered by the iron fist of leader Enver Hoxha. Even its own residents couldn't get out. But in 1991, communism fell and Albania's doors swung open. What travellers discovered back then was an enchanting land where the wind whistled through shattered remnants of half-forgotten Roman and Greek ruins and azure water drifted gently up empty beaches. These days, the secret's out, as Instagram reels of dreamy beaches rivalling any in the Mediterranean have put Albania at the top of many a travel list. Albanians, for the most part, haven't adjusted. They're still as honest and friendly as ever. The prices aren't close to nearby Greece or Croatia. And you can still find quiet beaches and authentic towns.

In Tirana, cranes and stylish bars are evidence that this European capital is on the upswing, while the Albanian Riviera's cool blue water is a refreshing respite from the summer heat. Inland, Berat and Girokastra's genius Ottoman architecture and alleyways graciously remain intact ,and bike-friendly Shkodra is a perfect gateway to breathtaking Accursed Mountain trails. Strangely, some still avoid Albania due to the infamous reputation of its mafia abroad, memories of communism and ethnic discrimination. Ignore them and go now before this amazing country gets well and truly swarming.

THE MAIN AREAS

Find Your Way

Albania is a nearly 30,000 sq km stretch of land made up largely of mountains and coastline. Travelling with public transport is doable, but not without its headaches. Fly into Corfu if the beach is your target.

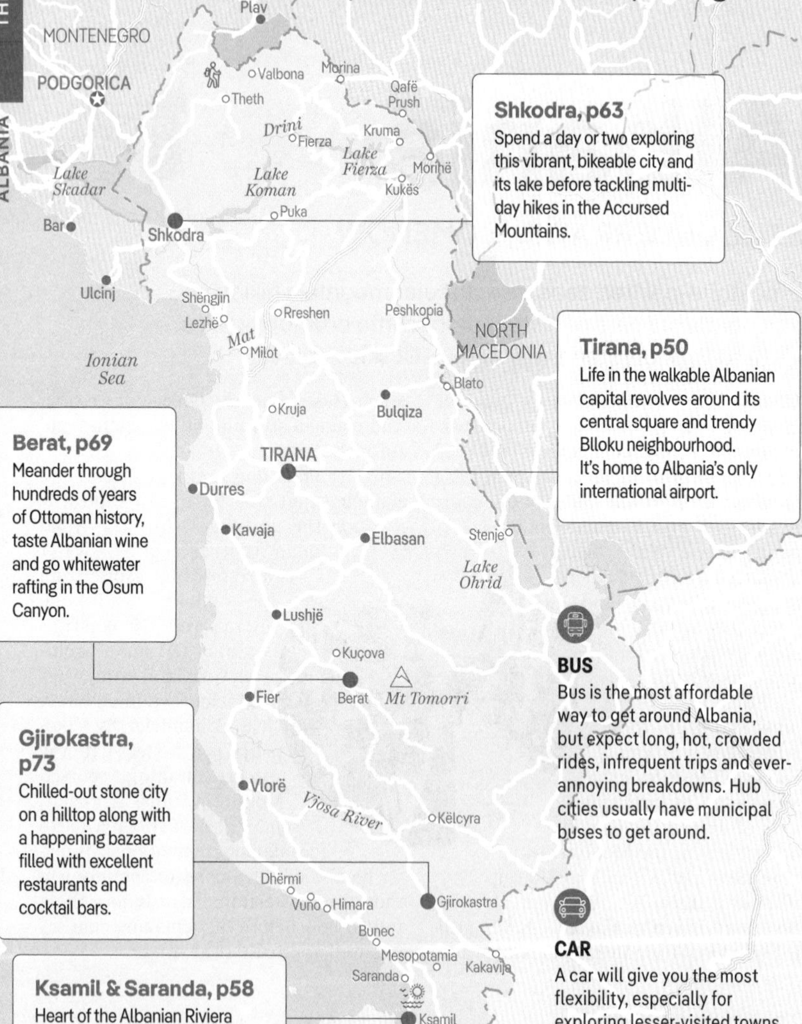

Shkodra, p63
Spend a day or two exploring this vibrant, bikeable city and its lake before tackling multi-day hikes in the Accursed Mountains.

Tirana, p50
Life in the walkable Albanian capital revolves around its central square and trendy Blloku neighbourhood. It's home to Albania's only international airport.

Berat, p69
Meander through hundreds of years of Ottoman history, taste Albanian wine and go whitewater rafting in the Osum Canyon.

Gjirokastra, p73
Chilled-out stone city on a hilltop along with a happening bazaar filled with excellent restaurants and cocktail bars.

Ksamil & Saranda, p58
Heart of the Albanian Riviera close to busy beaches and the unmissable Butrint ruins. Go up the coast for quieter beaches near Himara.

BUS
Bus is the most affordable way to get around Albania, but expect long, hot, crowded rides, infrequent trips and ever-annoying breakdowns. Hub cities usually have municipal buses to get around.

CAR
A car will give you the most flexibility, especially for exploring lesser-visited towns, beaches and hiking spots. But car hires can be pricey and roads off the major highways dicey. City driving is also pretty aggressive. Traffic cops are common.

National History Museum (p53), Skanderbeg Sq, Tirana

Plan Your Time

Much of Albania's hubs can be visited in a day or two, but you should leave padding for missed, delayed and infrequent buses if taking public transport.

A Week to Explore

Start in **Tirana** (p50) around Skanderbeg Sq and the trendy Blloku neighbourhood. Then off to the Ottoman-era town of **Berat** (p69) and continue down the coast beach hopping to **Dhermi** (p62), **Himara** (p61), **Saranda** (p58) and busy **Ksamil** (p58). Leave time for **Butrint's ruins** (p59) before wandering the charming stone bazaar in **Gjirokastra** (p73).

Slow Travel & the North

Follow the one-week itinerary, then head into Albania's incredible Accursed Mountains. In Italian-flavoured **Shkodra** (p63), get transport to Koman for the morning ferry to **Fierza** (p65). Spend the night in charming **Valbona** (p66), then hike to **Theth** (p66) on the **Peaks of the** Balkans Trail. Dip in the near-freezing **Blue Eye** (p67) and admire the rainbow-touched waterfall.

Seasonal Highlights

SPRING
Enjoy the perfect Mediterranean climate for mountain hikes and no beach crowds, though the water is very chilly.

SUMMER
The beaches may be packed and the mountains and cities scorching, but summers in Albania are fun.

AUTUMN
Possibly the best time to visit Albania, with few visitors and warm weather until December.

WINTER
Visit Tirana's museums and warm up with a cocktail in Blloku. The intrepid can snowshoe in the Accursed Mountains.

Tirana

CULTURE | CUISINE | NIGHTLIFE

Lively Tirana has come a long way from its grey, communist era (1944 to 1991). The Albanian capital is bursting with colour, from parks and thoroughfares flourishing with foliage to apartment buildings painted in vibrant hues. Busy traffic rolls past captivating mosque minarets and dome churches, as Tirana's chic locals stroll through clean, safe streets to sprawling patios for an espresso, *raki* (fruit brandy) or fancy cocktail in the dapper Blloku neighbourhood. Look at the skyscrapers popping up everywhere, especially around the shiny new Skanderbeg Sq, for more evidence that this aspiring European Union capital is on the rise.

Spend a day or two visiting Tirana's communist bunker museums and former spy centre as well as its religious buildings before spending a night out in Blloku. If there's time, take the cable car up Dajt Mountain for sprawling views over the city.

GETTING AROUND

An airport bus runs every hour from near Skanderbeg Sq on Rr Luigj Gurakuqi between the two parks. The trip takes 30 minutes. Tirana also has more than 20 public bus lines. To get elsewhere, Tirana has no central bus terminal – buses stop in different places outside the centre depending on where you're going.

With no Uber or Bolt, Tirana's taxis are pricey and drivers rarely speak English. Electric car taxis like Do Taxi tend to be cheaper. WhatsApp them for a ride or airport pickup (067 490 0000).

TOP TIP

Albanians are still firmly committed to cash and few businesses accept card payments. Prices are posted in Albanian lek, but you can usually pay with euros if you prefer. There are plenty of ATMs around town that dispense lek, but expect a high transaction fee of €6 or more.

Eat & Drink Like a Local

Out on the town

Like its formerly Ottoman-occupied neighbours, Albanians salivate for savoury grilled meats, flaky pastries and strong *rakija* (grape or plum brandy known here as *raki*). Traditional *zgara* (barbecue restaurants), found across Tirana but especially around the **Pazari i Ri** (New Bazaar) and along Rr Kavaja, specialise in *qofta* (round or log-shaped minced meatballs also known as *kernacka*). Eat it with bread, *tarator* (yoghurt dip akin to *tzatziki*) and a raw vegetable salad. Try qofta at **Met Kodra**, a budget-priced local institution that has been grilling *qofta* with the same recipe since 1957. *Burek* (meat, cheese or spinach-stuffed filo pastry spelt *byrek* here), a satisfying snack best washed down with a *dhallë* (yoghurt drink) or *ayran* (the same but salted), is found at *byrektorë* and *furre buke* (bakeries) across Tirana. Also, try *tavë* (a casserole with mixed cheese and liver) and, if you're brave, *kokë* (sheep's head either cooked and split or in a *pacë* soup) at a midrange white-tablecloth restaurant like **Oda Garden** or **Era**.

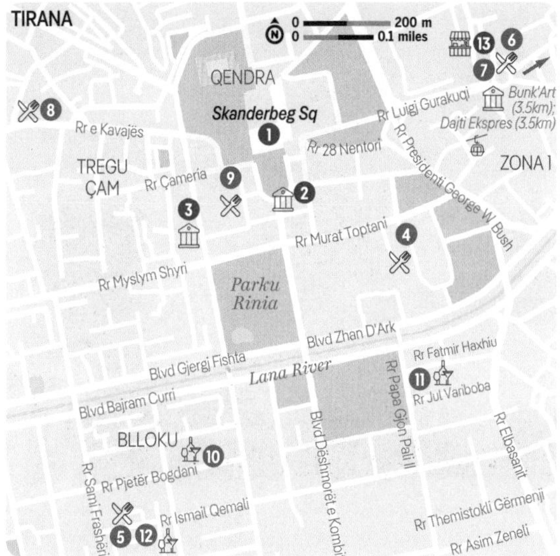

South of the Lana River, Tirana's stylish Blloku neighbourhood has a plethora of superb bars for your drinking pleasure. Blocked off for nearly half a century as a heavily guarded home to Communist Party officials, the neighbourhood was reopened in 1991 and populated with trendy plant-filled patio bars frequented by high-heeled locals. Try 35 flavours of *raki* including quince, saffron, cinnamon and coffee amidst funkadelic decor at **Komiteti - Kafe Muzeum** and have creative cocktails with an Albanian twist surrounded by vintage audio devices at **Radio Bar**. End the night at **Charl's Bistro** to join Albanians in coordinated line dancing to popular songs.

Albania's Grim Communist History

Nearly 50-year dictatorship

Born in Gjirokastra and a former teacher, 34-year-old Enver Hoxha was 'elected' in March 1943 in a contest with no challengers. To be fair, Albania had most of its infrastructure destroyed by fascist Italy during World War II and had a self-anointed monarch before that. Hoxha went on to rule Albania with an iron fist until his death in 1985 due to natural causes at the age of 76. Six years

HOXHA'S HOMETOWN

Despite being where Enver Hoxha was born, the central Albanian town of Gjirokastra (p73) has little to do with the former dictator today. Check out its charming Ottoman-era bazaar and hilltop castle, and explore creepy bunker tunnels.

WHERE TO STAY IN TIRANA

Trip'n'Hostel
Chill, clean and social hostel with a great breakfast in the leafy garden. €

Bujtina e Gjelit
An oasis outside the centre with a pool, comfy mattresses atop wooden platforms and a traditional restaurant. €€

Rogner Hotel
Luxurious Blloku hotel that feels like a country club with an enclosed tropical garden and lobby bar. €€€

ALBANIA ALONE

When Albanian communism kicked off in 1944, it could rely on its comrades in the Soviet Union if anyone dared to invade. But when Joseph Stalin died, Albanian leader Enver Hoxha broke ties with the USSR and turned east to Mao Zedong's Communist China, getting yuan, grain, weapons, infrastructure projects and soldier training out of the friendship.

But Hoxha soon broke ties with China as well and Albania was left all alone. Paranoid Hoxha went on to launch a bunker blitz: one mushroom-shaped concrete shelter or tunnel for every adult male in Albania. An estimated 170,000 were built across Albania, and today many are still visible and even visitable, with a few being reused as tourist attractions in Tirana and Gjirokastra.

Skanderbeg Sq

later, student-led protests erupting from Shkodra and Tirana toppled the communist regime in favour of the parliamentary democracy it is today.

It's hard to conclude with exact numbers, but around 30,000 people were held as political prisoners and between 6000 and 25,000 were executed. To stifle dissent, paranoid Hoxha used a vast network of spies, brutal prisons throughout the country, rigid border security and torture. Some of these inhumane practices were coordinated from the **House of Leaves**, a former obstetrics hospital turned into an interrogation (read: torture) centre. Named after the dense trees that obscure it from the busy street, the House of Leaves is now a sombre museum highlighting the extent of communist spying. Inside, you can see tiny mechanical 'bugs' (spy devices that were implanted into jackets, brooms, phones and other innocent-looking objects to tip off authorities) and watch what you say – the bugs are on and listening.

Grim communist education continues in **Bunk'Art 2**, one of an estimated 170,000 bunkers built across Albania as protection if the isolated country was attacked. Throughout bunker rooms and tunnels, the dark and dingy museum tells the story of the communist Sigurimi state police and restrictive policies.

WHERE TO DRINK COFFEE IN TIRANA

Hana Corner Cafe
Who is Hana? Who knows, but this hip corner cafe and cake shop is a delight.

Mulliri i Vjetër
Beloved local chain filled with locals day and night having an espresso and a pastry.

Café Botanica
Skanderbeg Sq-facing cafe with a big terrace, good wi-fi and healthy food.

TIRANA WALKING TOUR

Take a walk through tiny Tirana's best sites starting at ❶ **Skanderbeg Sq** (Sheshi Skënderbej), a fantastic new city square surrounding a statue of the 15th-century Albanian hero, Skanderbeg. Now Tirana's beating heart, the square was a busy traffic roundabout as recently as the last edition of this book. In the northwest corner, beneath the vivid mosaic depicting Albanian historical icons, is Albania's ❷ **National History Museum**, with the country's best collection of Illyrian and Roman artefacts. Briefly exit the square to see ❸ **Resurrection of Christ Orthodox Cathedral**, a modern mosque-like round church built in 2012; observe the concrete candles that noodle their way up the clock tower.

Walk back through the square to ❹ **Et'hem Bej Mosque**, a small but striking 18th-century mosque painted with delicate flowing frescoes. Walk south to ❺ **Bunk'Art 2**, one of tens of thousands of bunkers built during communist rule now turned into a museum. Continue to a pedestrian street lined with shops and restaurants leading to ❻ **Tirana Castle**. Walls are all that remain of this 4th- and 5th-century castle, but the inside has been turned into an attractive shopping and wine bar strip. Continue to the ❼ **Shën Pali Catholic Cathedral**, which is graced by a statue of Albanian-Macedonian philanthropist Mother Teresa, and cross the Lana River to ❽ **Piramida**, a pyramid originally devoted to communist dictator Enver Hoxha and now a selfie spot and mall.

Turn right on Rr Ismail Qemali to reach ❾ **Enver Hoxha's Former Residence**, which remains empty though well maintained by its gardener and housekeeper. Walk south along Rr Ibrahim Rugova to visit Tirana's beautiful ❿ **Grand Park** with well-maintained cobblestone paths and cafes overlooking an artificial lake.

TIRANA'S BEST RESTAURANTS

Tirana Free Tour (@tiranafreetour) guide **Aurora Çelanji** shares her favourite restaurants in Tirana.

Tymi Restaurant
The best *zgara* (grilled meat) restaurant in town. Very popular with locals. **€**

Oda Garden
Go here to understand traditional food and how much Albanians like to eat and chat through the meal. **€€**

Era Restaurant
Tirana classic that gives you options between traditional and modern food at reasonable prices. **€€**

Ceren Ismet Shehu
The decor and atmosphere give you a taste of traditional cuisine. Find it at Tirana Castle and near Mt Dajti with great views. **€€**

Ulliri City Center
The prices are a bit higher than the others, but of course they are justified by the food, the service and the restaurant itself. **€€€**

Dajti Express

Contrary to the sentiment of the name, Bunk'Art 2 is heavy on text and light on art, but at least it keeps you cool on a hot day.

Five kilometres east via public bus 11 is a similar, though much larger bunker museum, **Bunk'Art**. Inspired by North Korean communists, Bunk'Art focuses on external factors that led to communist rule (ie, Italy's invasion) and includes plenty of archival photos and communist clothing over its 106 rooms. A combo pass for both Bunk'Arts, available at either, will save you some lek.

Cable Car Up a Mountain

Views over Tirana

Five kilometres from central Tirana and a block from Bunk'Art is the **Dajti Express**, a cable car station with gondolas that loop passengers 4350m up the 1613m-tall **Dajti Mountain**. The Austrian-built cable car is the longest in the Balkans and the 15-minute trip (each way) has stunning views over the city – at least it would if the plexiglass in the cable cars wasn't so scratched up. Once you get to the top, there are unobstructed views and a grab-bag of touristy attractions like a mini-putt course, caged rabbits, toy machine gun practice and horseback rides through a garbage-filled patch of grass. The most interesting thing up here is straight ahead after you leave the station, where you'll find a yellow **abandoned hotel** (be careful of broken glass). You can also try your hand at the hiking trails, but they aren't maintained.

For the best views of Tirana, a few local operators offer **paragliding** experiences from the top of Dajti.

Beyond Tirana

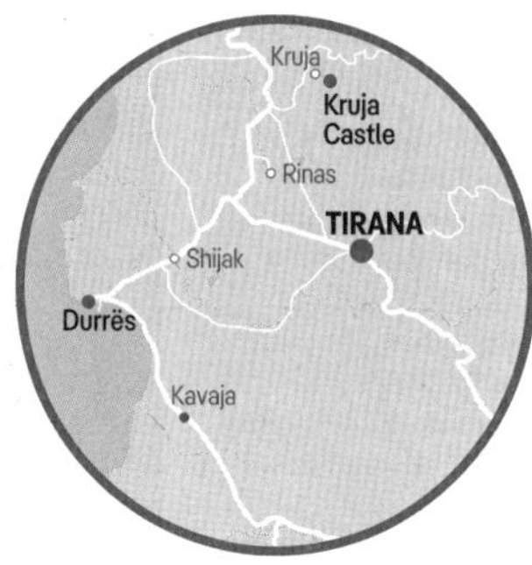

Escape to the mountains to see a hiiltop fortress entrenched in Albanian lore and see Roman ruins on the coast.

A short *furgon* (bus) ride away from Tirana are two towns that have played pivotal roles in the country's mesmerising history. On the western coast is Durres, the country's main port and a former capital that has ruins of a Roman amphitheatre, busy beaches as well as terrific seafood. Northeast in the mountains you'll find Kruja, the base from which Albania's greatest hero took on the powerful Ottoman Empire – and won – until his lands were finally taken over a decade after his death. Kruja also has idyllic views over the valley, a bazaar that's the best place in Albania to shop for souvenirs and a Bektashi shrine carved into the mountainside.

Durres

See a Roman Amphitheatre

Durres was once – albeit briefly – Albania's capital. It's now virtually an extension of Tirana, joined to the capital by a ceaseless urban corridor of hypermarkets and car dealerships. Blessed with a reasonable 10km stretch of **beach**, Durres is a pleasant – if rather built-up – escape from Tirana. It has a charmingly Mediterranean air once you get off the seafront, which can be very crowded and noisy during the summer months. The main reason for coming to Durres isn't for the beaches (for those, you're better off going south to the Albanian Riviera), but for the interesting Roman amphitheatre and superb archaeological museum.

Imagine you're Spartacus battling a lion in front of thousands of screaming fans by walking around Durres' **Roman Amphitheatre**, which was built on the hillside inside the city walls in the early 2nd century CE. In its prime, it had the

Places

GETTING AROUND

Catch the *furgon* (bus) to Durres in Tirana from the Dogana roundabout, 5km from the city centre. To get to Dogana, take a bus labelled Tirana e Re or Kamez from behind the Opera, east of Skanderbeg Sq. For Kruja, take either bus from the same stop to the South and North Albania Bus Terminal. Make sure the *furgon* is going to Kruja proper, not just Fushë Krujë, the modern town well below.

ILLYRIAN ORIGINS

Albanians call their country Shqipëria (Land of the Eagles) and trace their roots and language (a European linguistic oddity) to the ancient Illyrian tribes that occupied the Western Balkans during the 2nd millennium BCE. Illyrians built fortified cities, mastered silver and copper mining and became adept at sailing the Mediterranean.

The Greeks arrived in the 7th century BCE to establish self-governing colonies at Epidamnos (now Durres), Apollonia and Butrint. Rome defeated the Illyrian kingdom in 229 BCE and slotted Albania into its eastern Byzantine empire in 395 CE. Invasions were led by the Visigoths, Huns, Ostrogoths and Slavs before the Ottoman Empire took control over Albania in 1389. It would have stayed Ottoman if not for a guy named Skanderbeg.

STEVEN.JPG/SHUTTERSTOCK ©

Inside Durres' Roman Amphitheatre

capacity to seat 15,000 to 18,000 spectators, but these days it's little more than tunnels and ruins with few signposted explanations. A visit won't take longer than 30 minutes or so.

Nearby and just back from the seafront, the **Durres Archaeological Museum** was undergoing major renovations during research, but it usually has a breathtaking collection of historical artefacts, including amphoras recovered from the seafloor, delicate gold jewellery and beautifully preserved vases and pots. The museum was already more modern than most in Albania, so it will be exciting to see what they do with it.

WHERE TO EAT BEYOND TIRANA

Meison Bistro
Tasty market-fresh seafood with a chic ambience close to the Durres coast. **€€**

Restaurant Panorama
Tuck into a mix of modern Albanian and international favourites with stellar views at this Kruja hotel. **€€**

Bar Restaurant Horizont
Superb panoramic views and traditional Albanian mezze plates high above Kruja. **€€**

Kruja Castle

Climb to a hero's stronghold

After wandering around Tirana's Skanderbeg Sq and seeing the statue, learn about the warrior who marks its name (and the country's lek currency) by visiting the citadel where the Albanian version of Braveheart or Alexander the Great and his army of rebels held off Ottoman forces from 1444 until 1478, 10 years after his death.

High in the mountains, 30km northeast of the capital, Kruja Castle has an impressive number of remaining ruins for a castle built in the 5th or 6th century, especially one so battle-hardy. It also has a stone **clock tower** and breathtaking views towards the Adriatic Sea. Enter the white-stone **Skanderbeg Museum**, which while meant to look old, was actually designed by Enver Hoxha's daughter and son-in-law and opened in 1982. Inside are invigorating sculptures and murals, especially the chaotic *Endurance* mural, which depicts scenes from the three Ottoman-led sieges on Kruja in 1450, 1466 and 1467. The castle grounds are also home to Kruja's **Ethnographic Museum**, an Albanian and Ottoman home built in 1764, though it was closed for renovations during research.

Below the castle, Kruja's Ottoman-style **Bazaar** has the best collection of souvenirs you'll find in Albania, including carpets, wooden spoons, delicately painted plates and antiquities like military helmets and working gramophones.

If you have a car, drive up Rr e Malit to visit **Sari Salltik**, a shrine in honour of the man credited with bringing Bektashism (a form of Islamic Sufi mysticism) to the Balkans in the 13th century. The green and white shrine has steep steps down into the cliff face, where believers light candles and rinse in spring water. Yes, the hooks outside are used for exactly what they look and smell like – animal sacrifices.

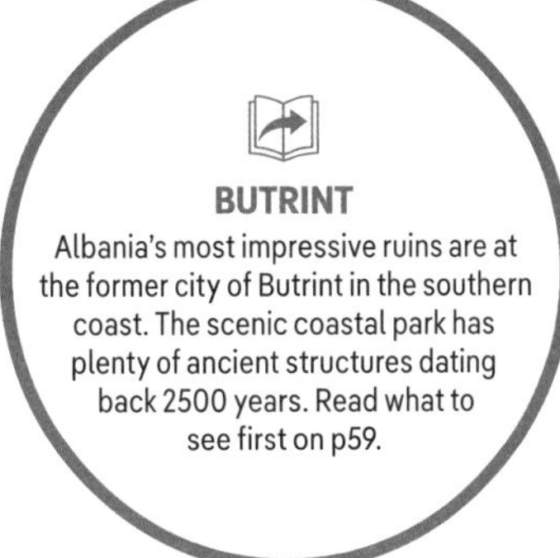

BUTRINT

Albania's most impressive ruins are at the former city of Butrint in the southern coast. The scenic coastal park has plenty of ancient structures dating back 2500 years. Read what to see first on p59.

TOP TIP

The bus stops for Kruja and Durres are west of downtown Tirana. Take a public bus or taxi to get there.

SKANDERBEG'S SIGNIFICANCE

Born Gjergj Kastrioti in 1405 to Emathian royalty, Albania's greatest hero was given to the Ottoman Empire by his father as a hostage and trained as a warrior. Named Iskander after Alexander the Great and awarded the honorary title *bey*, Skanderbeg led Ottoman forces before the Empire turned on his ancestral lands. Bad idea. United under a red-and-black flag with a two-headed eagle (a nod to the Byzantine Empire) and with funding from Italian kingdoms, Skanderbeg and his group of Albanian rebels shocked the Ottomans by resisting them for 25 years. Skanderbeg's forces finally lost in 1478, a decade after he died from either illness or poison. This led to 439 years of Ottoman rule, but Skanderbeg and his flag are national symbols for Albanians today.

Ksamil & Saranda

BEACHES | ANCIENT RUINS | HISTORY

TIRANA

GETTING AROUND

A public bus runs between Saranda, Ksamil and Butrint with several stops in Saranda. Driving along the main road is a nightmare in summer due to sudden stops from other drivers and few parking spots. Getting into Saranda is quicker from the Greek island of Corfu than Tirana. The Port of Saranda has frequent ferries to Corfu with two companies: Ionian and Finikas. Both offer slow ferries that take just over an hour as well as slightly pricier, fast ferries that take just over 30 minutes.

TOP TIP

Saranda's Lekuresi Castle is the place to be for sunset as locals dress up for photos and dine in the classy restaurant (the food is just okay, but the ambiance is unparalleled). Go at least an hour before the actual sunset before a mountain obscures the sun.

A decade and a half ago, Saranda was a sleepy beach port in proximity to a vast stretch of pristine beaches over cobalt-coloured water that few outside of Albania knew existed. The cat is now out of the proverbial bag and both Saranda and Ksamil – a narrow arm of land 17km south of Saranda between sea and a sparkling lagoon famed for its mussels – are overrun with tourists in high season. Still, the unofficial capital of the Albanian Riviera is a lot of fun with its bumping boardwalk, party ships and quality Italian-inspired seafood dishes. While most people come for the beaches, don't miss Butrint, Albania's finest archaeological site.

Staying in busy Ksamil will be twice the price of Saranda, and you'll be subject to the crime of paying for beach access, but it's got better beaches – just don't expect to find much peace and quiet.

Go to the Beach

Busy but beautiful

You might have seen Ksamil's crisp turquoise beaches on Instagram or TikTok as some sort of secret European alternative to the Maldives. Well, others have seen the same videos, and Southern Albania has been on the travel radar for a decade or so. That means Ksamil's beaches are usually filled with beachgoers throughout the summer and prices for food and accommodation are twice what they are elsewhere in Albania. That said, the water really is beautiful and refreshing on a hot day, and Ksamil's coarse-sand beaches are better overall than the busy, larger-pebble urban beaches you'll find in Saranda.

Technically, Ksamil's beaches are for everyone, but private restaurants or hotels often charge an inflated fee of €15 or €20 for the use of a sunbed and an umbrella. The government struggles to enforce the public nature of its beaches, but even if it did, beaches here are so packed with sunbeds that there's no room to put a towel down. **Paradise Beach** is the only one technically considered public. A highlight is **Ksamil Beach**

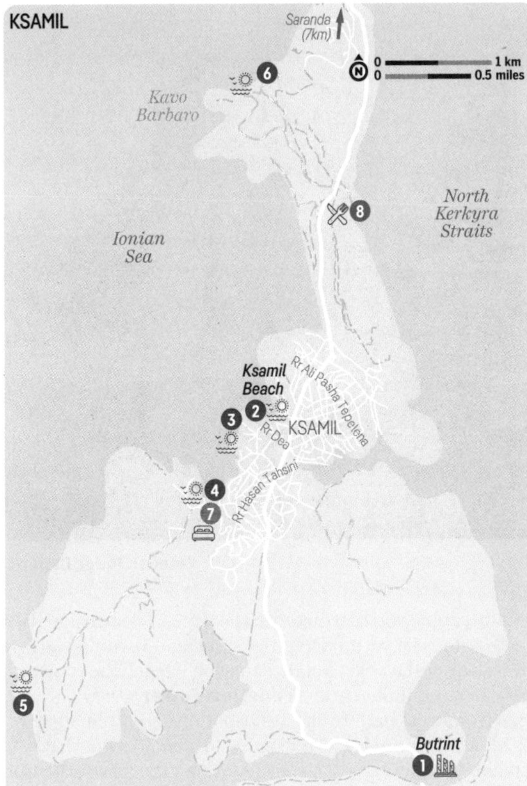

HIGHLIGHTS
1 Butrint
2 Ksamil Beach

SIGHTS
3 Bora Bora Beach
4 Paradise Beach
5 Pema e Thatë
6 Pulëbardha Beach

SLEEPING
7 Hotel Luxury

EATING
8 Mussel House

across from four forested islands that you can reach by swimming or renting a boat. If you're looking to party, follow the music to **Bora Bora Beach**. Outside the centre, **Pema e Thatë** on the southern Corfu-facing tip is a more peaceful, private beach but you'll have to drive on dirt roads to get here. Similarly, **Pulëbardha Beach** has a wilder, more natural coastal energy as waves brush up against jagged rocks.

If you're a diver, underneath Ksamil's water are five communist-era shipwrecks. See them on a dive guided via **Saranda Dive Center**.

Explore an Ancient City

Over 2500 years of history

South of Ksamil is **Butrint**, a great fortified city that had long stretches as a stronghold for various empires including Greeks from Corfu, Romans and Byzantines, for over 2500 years. Abandoned when Italian archaeologists arrived in 1927, the ruins, which are plentiful, are in a fantastic natural setting that's part of a 29-sq-km national park.

BEST RESTAURANTS IN KSAMIL & SARANDA

Taberna Labëria
This lovable family-run restaurant serves terrific, generous portions of seafood and meat over its two busy terraces. €

Green Life Market
Saranda's only vegan restaurant has creative, ever-changing meals made by its Canadian and Argentine owners. €€

Haxhi
Fishing-themed upper-floor restaurant with cool rope lighting, excellent seafood and a celebratory atmosphere. €€

Mussel House
Overlook Butrint's lagoon and mussel beds while eating shellfish and excellent grilled fish. €€

Manxuranë
French, Albanian and Italian fusion with Albanian wines and friendly service from devoted owner Fatmir. €€€

BEST DAY TRIPS FROM KSAMIL & SARANDA

Vënçe tour coordinator **Gazmir Galanxhi** (WhatsApp +355 69 897 8100) shares his favourite day trips.

Qeparo
It's such an experience to visit and appreciate life in a rural Unesco-protected village 600m above sea level. It hasn't changed much since communism.

Hadrianopolis
Most people don't know Roman Emperor Hadrian lived in the area. A brilliant day out for anyone interested in Albanian rural life joined with archaeological facts.

Permet
Known as the town of flowers, it's such a drive from Saranda in terms of scenery and there are amazing thermal baths.

Boat Trip
Visit some of the very few remaining rural beaches in Albania. The journey offers snorkelling, swimming and just the feeling of being blessed.

Venetian Tower, Butrint

Many people whizz straight to the Greek Theatre, but save the best for last by ignoring the signs and turning right at the fork after the ticket booth. Soon you'll reach the comparatively modern 16th-century **Venetian Tower**. Carry on along a narrow forest path to the atmospheric and often quiet ruins of the **Triconch Palace**, a grand Roman villa that was expanded in the early 5th century. Along the same path and deeper in the forest is the 6th-century paleo-Christian **Baptistry**, which was once the largest such building between Rome and Constantinople. Its floor is made up of one of the finest mosaics in Albania (as seen in the brochure), but it's covered with sand for its own protection. To the left is a **wall with Greek inscriptions** and a gymnasium with intact mosaics. Turn back towards the water to the impressive arches of the 6th-century **Basilica**, then follow the massive **Cyclopean wall** (dating back to the 4th century BCE) along the lake shore until you get to the imposing **Lion Gate**, which has a relief of a lion killing a bull above the gate. By slowly following the shady path to the top of the hill, you'll come to a **Venetian castle** that today houses an informative artefact-filled museum. Head back down the hill to marvel over Butrint's show-stoppers: the 3rd-century-BCE **Greek Theatre**, which could seat about 2500 people, the **Forum** and **public baths**.

WHERE TO STAY IN KSAMIL & SARANDA

Wallaby Hostel
Wild, Australian-owned party hostel with nightly activities, awesome rooftop views and free breakfast. €

Hotel Titania
Fairly priced hotel above the boardwalk with modern, sea-facing rooms that feel like a giant goldfish bowl. €€

Hotel Luxury
Very clean, business-like Ksamil hotel with a nice front terrace. No beach access. €€€

Beyond Ksamil & Saranda

Jump into water as clear as a swimming pool and dance your worries away at a music festival.

The Albanian Riviera was a revelation 15 years or so ago, when backpackers discovered the last virgin stretch of the Mediterranean coast in Europe, flocking here in droves, setting up ad-hoc campsites and exploring scores of little-known beaches. Since then, things have become significantly less pristine, especially around Saranda where overdevelopment has blighted once-charming beachside villages (see: Ksamil). But worry not; drive north on the mountain coastal road and you'll find plenty of space to throw down a towel and while away a day under the beaming sun. There are ample beaches to choose from, but if you're looking for a party and cool vibes, head to Dhermi for a summer electronic festival.

Places

GETTING AROUND

Minibuses leave Saranda and connect towns along the coast, though they're irregular and often full. Plus, beaches are usually several kilometres downhill, which can be a slog under summer heat. Another option is to take a day tour or rent a car and cruise the winding coastal road, ideally with the windows down. There are plenty of private car-hire agencies in Saranda. Ferry boat service is available to Himara, Vlora and Saranda from Corfu.

North of Saranda

Find your vibe with a beach-hop up the coast

Are the beaches of Ksamil and Saranda too busy for your liking? Don't despair. Hop in a car or bus north along the stunningly beautiful coastal road to find beach bliss.

Borsch Beach is a huge, sweeping white-stone beach that's several kilometres long. While it's still far from over-run with development, it's hardly undiscovered either. There are plenty of summer-only bars and restaurants, plus a few places to stay.

Himara is the biggest town between Saranda and busy Vlora, with a bustling promenade, a couple of main beaches and **castle** ruins on the hilltop with enchanting frescoes and views. Tour operators on Himara's boardwalk sell boat trips to isolated beaches with crystal-clear water and few, if any, other beachgoers. The boats can leave you at the beach for up to five hours before picking you up in the afternoon. Himara is a backpacker hot spot as well, with budget lodgings at the ever-fun **Sun Bakers Hostel** as well as campgrounds with ready-to-sleep-in tents, **Sea Cove** and **Pine Side**.

TOP TIP

If you want true peaceful beach bliss, book a boat tour from Himara, the Riviera's biggest town.

DHERMI MUSIC FESTIVALS

Dhermi, a town about 70km up the coast from Saranda, has become Albania's unofficial electronic music festival capital. **Kala**, which lasts a week on Dhermi Beach in early June, has asserted itself as one of Europe's best beach parties. Shortly after Kala, heal your body and mind at **Anjunadeep**, a wellness-focused electronic music festival.

In late July, **Turtle Fest** at Drymades Beach has been going strong for a decade. To cap out the festival season, newcomer **ION Festival** brings the party one more time in mid-September until everything restarts the next season.

ZM_PHOTO/SHUTTERSTOCK ©

Gjipe Beach

Gjipe Beach, at the mouth of a canyon, is gorgeous but a hike to get to without a car. Turn off the main road for the Monastery of St Theodor and follow signs for the one-hour (3.5km) hike down to the beach, or drive down until the paving ends and walk the last kilometre.

BLUE EYE

Really want to cool down? Take a dip in a Blue Eye – a refreshing mountain stream that drops to as low as 7°C. There's one near Saranda, but you're not supposed to swim there, so go to Theth National Park instead (p66).

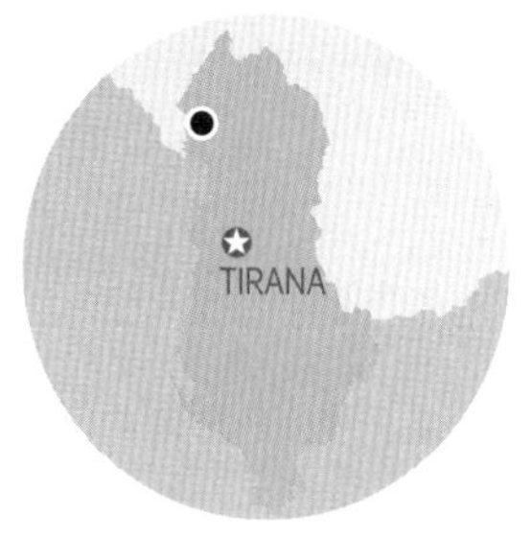

Shkodra

CASTLE | CYCLING | PHOTOGRAPHY

One of the oldest cities in Europe, dating back to Illyrian times, Shkodra is a lively city enriched by its students and bike culture – you'll be hard-pressed to find another city in Eastern Europe with this many locals whizzing around on two wheels. Many travellers rush through Shkodra while travelling between Tirana and Montenegro or en route to the Accursed Mountains, but it's worth spending a couple of nights to soak up this pleasant and welcoming city. Check out the interesting photography and communist-era prison museums – Shkodra was harshly repressed during Hoxha's reign and sparked the first pro-democracy protests – and rent a bike to see the ancient hilltop fortress and codfish-filled lake, which is the biggest in the Balkans. If you do plan to hike in the mountains, accommodation in Shkodra can book your transport and store your bags.

GETTING AROUND

If your guesthouse doesn't rent bikes there are several shops around town that do – scooters and electric bikes are also often available. Otherwise, Shkodra has taxis and a public bus service, which can take you to the lake or castle. Catch the bus from the stop at the northeastern side of the Sheshi Demokracia roundabout.

Photography, Communist Prison, Cycling & a Castle

Shkodra in a day

Do as Shkodrans do and explore this wonderful city on two wheels. But first, pop into the **Marubi National Photography Museum**, the country's only photography museum highlighting the work and influence of Pjetër Marubi, an Italian who travelled throughout Albania documenting life in the mid-19th century. Upstairs, the permanent Marubi exhibit includes the first-ever photographs taken in Albania in 1858, as well as fascinating portraits, street scenes and early photojournalism. There's also an interesting exhibit of camera equipment over the decades and changing temporary exhibitions.

Walk or bike to the **Site of Witness and Memory Museum**, which highlights Shkodra's role in the overthrow of communism as the location of the first student protests on 14 January 1990. Walk through the museum's red-painted

TOP TIP

Hikes in the Accursed Mountains, including the ever-popular Valbona to Theth circuit (p66), take at least two nights – one in Valbona after taking the Lake Koman Ferry and another in Theth. Allow more days for a blissful escape from society, as well as a couple more to explore Shkodra.

SIGHTS
1 Marubi National Photography Museum
2 Site of Witness and Memory Museum

SLEEPING
3 Hotel Tradita
4 Rose Garden Hotel
5 Wanderers Hostel

EATING
6 Fisi Restaurant

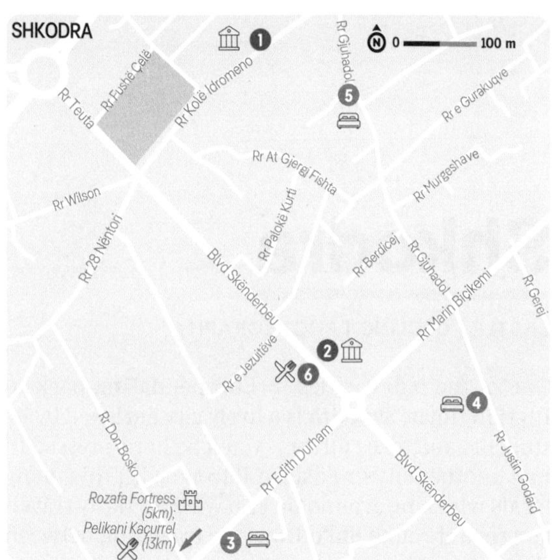

BEST PLACES TO STAY & EAT IN SHKODRA

Wanderers Hostel
Make travel friends in the garden before embarking on organised trips to the Accursed Mountains. €

Rose Garden Hotel
Mix of modern decor and Victorian-style furniture around a lovely hidden courtyard that has more than roses. €

Hotel Tradita
Shkodra's best accommodation is a museum dedicated to pan-Albanian artefacts, along with the city's best traditional restaurant. €€

Fisi Restaurant
Hearty portions and fair prices for mixed grilled meats, as well as friendly service. €

Pelikani Kaçurrel
Make this your cycling destination: a lovely fish restaurant and beach near the Montenegro border with Lake Shkodra. €€

tunnel and inside actual prison cells used to hold political detainees.

Now pedal about 30 minutes along the main street and walk your bike up a steep hill to the **Rozafa Fortress**, which has been inhabited since the 4th century BCE during Illyrian times, though the 3.6ha structure you see today was built by the Venetians and Ottomans. The main reason to visit the fortress is for its sweeping views over Shkodra's waterways and brightly painted homes, though it's peaceful to walk around the courtyards and atop the stone walls as well.

Bike back down to the Buna riverfront and cross the pedestrian bridge to cruise alongside the largest lake in the Balkans: **Shkodra Lake**. The paved, slightly hilly road meanders past gravel beaches and restaurants specialising in lake fish like grilled carp, which Shkodrans prefer as fresh and large as possible.

VISIT KOSOVO'S CAPITAL

Shkodra was a major destination for Kosovars escaping the 1998–99 war with Serbia. Learn more about Kosovo's wrenching history and see how the newborn nation has been developing since the war by visiting Pristina (p180).

Beyond Shkodra

Accursed Mountains
Valbona
Dragobija
Valbona Pass
Boga
Theth
Bajra Curri
Brida
Ducaj
Fierza
Zagora
ALBANIA
Kopljik
Shkodra
Koman
Puka

See what the buzz is all about by hiking Albania's jaw-dropping Accursed Mountains and plunging into crisp turquoise pools.

Places

Names don't come much more evocative than the Accursed Mountains (Bjeshkët e Namuna), also known as the Albanian Alps. But the dramatic peaks of northern Albania truly live up to the wonder in their name. Sure, at 3000m they might not be as tall as the Swiss Alps, but these snow-sprinkled mountain pinnacles, deep green valleys and thick forests northeast of Shkodra are nothing to scoff at. Mountain villages here feel graciously stuck in time, cultivating their crops with a sickle, eating yoghurt and cheese from chiming cattle and horned sheep, commemorating ancient Kulla (Code) traditions and remaining happily hospitable despite the swell of visitors from June through September. This might become your favourite destination in Albania.

Accursed Mountains

Hiking them is not even that hard

Most people come to the Accursed Mountains for one spectacular **hike** between Valbona and Theth, which takes between five and seven hours depending on where in either village you start or end. It's not a particularly tough hike and is attempted by many first-time mountain walkers. Even so, it's quite long and steep and can get very hot, especially on the longer Valbona-facing slope. You can walk it either way, though the majority of people go from Valbona to Theth as this allows for a neat circle from Shkodra via the Lake Koman Ferry. The Theth side of the mountain is also steeper and shadier, so many choose to take it on the way down.

The **Lake Koman Ferry** cruises for three hours past spectacular mountain scenery from its terminal in **Koman** to **Fierza** or vice versa. The ride is a fun, sociable affair with many

GETTING AROUND

Aside from SH 21 from Shkodra to Theth and Valbona's main road, roads can be rough here, so take the bus from Shkodra and walk instead of driving if you have the time. Both Theth and Valbona are very spread out, so expect to walk a long way to the trailheads depending on where your accommodation is located. Taxis are available to get to the Blue Eye trailhead, and there are usually shared buses waiting there at the end of the day.

buying beers on board and sharing snacks. Any accommodation in Shkodra can buy inclusive tickets for you, which includes minibus pickup at 6.30am in Shkodra, ferry transport and another minibus trip to Valbona for a 1.30pm arrival. Alternatively, book bus and ferry tickets on the Berisha ferry company's website, but you won't save any money by doing so.

Valbona is a long strip of guesthouses, many owned by the Selimaj family, surrounded by daunting peaks. Guesthouses can advise on alternative treks if you want to avoid the Valbona–Theth crowds, but it's a good idea to hire a guide if you take a less-frequented route, as they aren't well-marked. Many stay a night in Valbona after the ferry before tackling the trail to Theth the next morning before it gets too hot.

The main trail begins at the end of the road in Valbona, so get a lift from the guesthouse to the trailhead – otherwise, it's a tiring and monotonous walk over a dry, often very hot, stone riverbed. It's possible to hire a horse or mule to carry your stuff to the next town, but most pack light and leave the rest of their gear in Shkodra. On the whole, the trail itself is decently marked with red and white markings and there are a few teahouses where you can get refreshments and fill up your bottle with potable spring water (you'll get told off if you take water without buying anything).

The path up from Valbona is mostly underneath the beaming sun but is capped up with spectacular vistas from the **Valbona Pass** about 7.5km from Valbona and 1800m up. The way down to Theth is steep and with loose dirt, but at least it's mostly under the shade of old-growth forest. In autumn, a less busy and cooler time to hike, these trees are ablaze in reds and oranges. A confusing part comes as you pass the final tea shop – if you find yourself at a pretty stream and wooden bridge, turn back to the cafe and walk beneath its patio. It's a long but fairly gentle descent into the spread-out village of Theth, where it's common to spend another night or two before heading back to Shkodra.

☑ TOP TIP

Leave your car in Shkodra or don't hire one at all, as accessing the Accursed Mountains by bus and ferry is easy.

WHY I LOVE ALBANIA'S NORTH

Joel Balsam, Lonely Planet writer

Many are infatuated by Albania's turquoise beaches, but the north is where I fell in love with this country – and I reckon you will, too. Cycling to Lake Shkodra was the freest I'd felt in a long time, and while the Accursed Mountains are compared to the Alps, they're a refreshing throwback to a time without ski resorts. Set aside at least a few days to hike, swim and relax here. Warning: it may be tough to return to busy city life.

Theth

Mountain village and chilly dips

After a sun-soaked hike, get wet-soaked around the mountain village of Theth about two hours from Shkodra. Theth works as an overnight trip from Shkodra, or stay for another night or two after hiking from Valbona, before returning via the 11am bus back to Shkodra.

In town is the beautiful 19th-century stone-and-shingle **Theth Church** and 400-year-old **Reconciliation Tower**, a

WHERE TO STAY IN VALBONA

Hotel Rilindja
This fairy-tale wooden house has been a traveller-favourite since opening in 2005. It's 3km from Valbona's centre. €

Jezerca
Freestanding pine cabins that sleep two, three or five people, and guesthouse rooms. €€

Oda N'bjeshkë
Guesthouse mixing traditional and modern. Ask English-speaking owner Artemis to share some stories. €€

MATTHEW FIGG/SHUTTERSTOCK ©

Valbona Pass

stone tower where blood feuds were negotiated according to the Kanun (Code) that instructed 15th-century life. You can enter the three-storey tower, where costumed guides recount stories of Kanun days in Albanian – ask the great-grandchildren of a tower judge outside to explain in English.

The **Theth Waterfall** is the best quick hike from town. To get there, walk along the eastern bank of the river and turn left up the mountain instead of crossing the red bridge. Then hop over a slippery cascade up to the waterfall. The whole trip takes about 30 minutes depending on where you started. The water is chilly yet refreshing and you may see an afternoon rainbow if the sun hits it right.

For a longer hike, head to the **Blue Eye**, a natural pool of turquoise water fed by a small but gushing waterfall. It's a

THE FALL OF COMMUNISM

As word spread across Lake Shkodra that the Berlin Wall had fallen, a few hundred people, mostly students, took to the streets to topple the bust of Joseph Stalin in Shkodra. The January 1990 protests, about five years after the death of Enver Hoxha, quickly spread to Tirana and across Albania. In March 1992 the country voted in favour of parliamentary democracy in national elections.

But the transition was far from smooth. Finally free to leave, Albanians fled to neighbouring countries and across Europe, even swimming to Corfu and hijacking a ship. Organised crime families filled the power vacuum and a pyramid scheme in 1996–97 emptied Albanians' savings, leading to violent protests. Albanian politics have calmed down since then as the country vies for EU membership.

WHERE TO STAY IN THETH

Guesthouse Dreni
Dorms and privates in a sweeping farm at the southern tip of Theth. Wanderers Hostel (p64) sends you here. €

Vila Zorgji
Gorgeous stone guesthouse, camping and shady restaurant terrace offering respite from the heat. €€

Guesthouse Marashi
Guesthouse facing the water with an Instagrammable standalone tub in the penthouse suite. €€€

BEST HIKES IN ALBANIA

Guide **Erenik Selimaj** (067 323 0951) shares his top hikes.

Radomirë
Hike up Mt Korab, Albania and North Macedonia's tallest peak for scenic views and huge diversity of flora.

Langarica Canyon
Breathtaking views of the canyon reaching 100m in depth, waterfalls and virgin, untouched scenery.

Llogara National Park
Do the loop from the top of Llogara Pass to Qafa e Thellë and to the restaurants. You'll definitely have the best sea views.

Vajush Peak in Lepushe
Absolutely one of the best hikes. Easy to do and super rewarding views on the top of the peak.

Tujani Tirana
The walk goes through beech forest and opens to have splendid views towards Tirana and almost all of Albania.

Blue Eye (p67)

half-day (17km) hike from Theth, but well worth it as it crosses a variety of enchanting terrain and body-numbing pools. To get there, take the red bridge south of Theth before crossing the dry riverbed at the village of Nderlysaj. Turn right on the main road to the restaurant where you can stop for a dip before walking up rocky trails and across a bridge (which you can jump off) to the Blue Eye. The temperature at the mouth is a chilly 7–10°C and gets warmer downhill. It's possible to taxi from Theth to Nderlysaj, but you'll still need to walk uphill 2.5km to the Blue Eye.

PEAKS OF THE BALKANS

The Theth to Valbona hike is part of the recently developed Peaks of the Balkans Trail, a 192km transnational trek that spans Kosovo, Montenegro and Albania. The trail can last two days to two weeks, and several companies offer tours. Learn more on p188.

Berat

UNESCO HERITAGE | WINE | RAFTING

Wander through 2500 years of history in beautiful Berat, a mountain town in central Albania with a very special kind of magic. Berat, which started as an Illyrian settlement around the 5th century BCE, is crowned by its town-sized fortress more than 200m up. Cascading down from the castle are preciously preserved 14th- and 16th-century stone neighbourhoods and photo-deserving white houses that give the city its name of 'one above the other windows' or 'town of a thousand windows'. A Unesco World Heritage city since 2008, Berat's historic centre is heavily visited (locals live in adjacent modern and crumbling communist neighbourhoods), though prices remain fair and the dynamic owners of its charming guesthouses and traditional restaurants friendly.

Stroll Berat's historic neighbourhoods for a day or two, then enjoy tasting wines made with Albanian grapes and go whitewater rafting in the nearby Osum Canyon.

GETTING AROUND

Berat's bus terminal (Terminali Autobusave) is nearly 3km from the tourist centre. There are occasional public buses into town, or you can take a taxi or walk 3km. The town is walkable, but taxis are available too, which is especially helpful for the steep climb up to the castle.

Castle, Neighbourhoods & Windows

Like one big museum

Look up and you can't miss Berat's **Kalaja** (Castle) peeking out over the mountain. The castle is a town in and of itself with more than 100 residential houses, dozens of towers and churches, two mosques and a stone wall more than a kilometre long. In spring and summer, the fragrance of chamomile is in the air (and underfoot), and wildflowers burst from every gap between the stones, giving the entire place a magical feel. There are shops, restaurants and hotels inside the castle walls as well as terrific views up here, so leave at least an hour to explore or spend the night. Don't climb on the ancient structures for your safety and the castle's longevity.

Below the castle is the **Mangalem Quarter**, a neighbourhood that dates back to the 16th century. Get lost in its winding

TOP TIP

Despite what Google Maps tells you, you cannot drive between Berat and Gjirokastra on any road except the main highways (unless you want to destroy your rental car as this writer did). Roads are treacherous from the Osum Canyon Bridge to Ballaban and south to Piskova and Permet. Instead, take highways SH73 and SH4 to Gjirokastra.

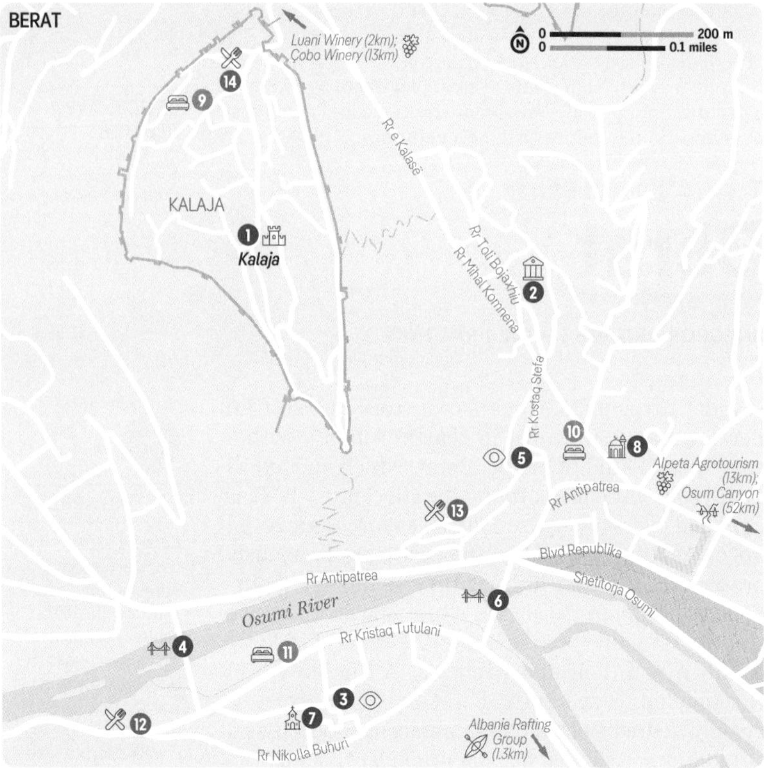

BERAT

HIGHLIGHTS

1 Kalaja

SIGHTS
2 Ethnographic Museum
3 Gorica
4 Gorica Bridge
5 Mangalem Quarter
6 New Bridge
7 St Spyridon
8 Xhamia Mbret

SLEEPING
9 Hotel Klea
10 Hotel Mangalemi
11 Maya Hostel

EATING
12 Eni Traditional Food Berat
13 Lili Homemade Food
14 Onufri

BEKTASHI CAVE SHRINE

Visit a Bektashi shrine carved directly into the mountain high above Kruja, a mountain town dedicated to Albania's greatest war hero. See what else to do in Kruja and how to get there from Tirana on p57.

stone alleyways and visit its three mosques, including the 15th-century **Xhamia Mbret** (Sultan's Mosque) completed by Berat's pasha, who ended up getting poisoned by the Ottomans. The **Ethnographic Museum** in a beautiful 18th-century Ottoman house was closed for renovations during research, though it usually has displays of traditional clothes and tools used by silversmiths and weavers as well as traditionally styled rooms. Mangalem is also where you'll find Berat's famous windows, but the best views are from the river boardwalk or in the **Gorica** neighbourhood on the other side. Take either the 1780 **Gorica Bridge**, which was rebuilt with stone by the Pasha, or the **new bridge** which was built in 2002, though probably won't last long from the looks of it. Gorica, which is about 200 years older than Mangalem, has only a few main stone thoroughfares, though plenty of great photo spots, and the **St Spyridon** church, which was painted over during communist days but still has unique Orthodox paintings.

Taste Albanian Wines

Berat's tasty terroir

Albanian wine is making a name for itself on the international oenology circuit and **Çobo Winery**, 20 minutes from Berat, is leading the charge. The lovely vineyard does tastings in its peaceful garden and family-built cottage surrounded by chirping birds and the smell of fruit and flowers. Do a tasting or bring home a bottle with wines made from Albanian grapes including *shesh i zi* (a red with strong tannins) and *puls* (orange wine). The show-stopper is the Shendeverë label, meaning 'joyful' in Albanian. It's a sparkling wine made in the Champenoise method. Tastings come with fruit, olives, cheese and crackers and you may visit the cellar underground to learn how Çobo's wine is produced and aged. A 10-minute documentary about how the winery was founded in 1998 is on loop inside and on YouTube. Bus tours are available from Berat if you don't have a car.

Closer to Berat across from the bus stop, **Luani Winery** does tastings in the basement below its Hotel Belagrita. Tastings include three or four wines plus two *rakis* and a visit to the vineyard behind the hotel.

Or instead of a tasting, do a wine-drinking tour in the **Alpeta Agrotourism** region. The distinction here is that while you get to taste and learn about Albanian wine, you'll probably get drunk with the amount you're offered. Ask your hostel or hotel or a tour office about one of these tours, which run from 7pm to midnight. It's a good idea to eat dinner beforehand so you don't get too wasted.

Rafting in the Canyon

Thrilling adventure

South of Berat, the Osum River snakes down to become the most impressive gorge in southern Albania. **Albania Rafting Group** hosts fun whitewater rafting excursions through **Osum Canyon** lasting 3½ hours on the water plus time for the two-hour drive from Berat. The experience is both peaceful and exhilarating as tall marble cliffs tower up to 100m on

RELIGION IN ALBANIA

After the arrival of Christianity during Byzantine times, many Albanians converted to Islam when the Ottomans moved in. During communism, Albania was declared a secular state, then banned religion altogether in 1967 – some say leader Enver Hoxha was the country's only sanctioned god. Today, religion is accepted in Albania, with the majority identifying as Sunni (Islam), followed by Catholicism, Eastern Orthodox Christianity and Bektashi (also Islam).

In daily life, though, many Albanians are only nominally religious and you'll rarely see symbols such as hijabs or crosses. When a religious holiday like Easter or Eid hits, Albanians will happily take the day off to celebrate, even if the tradition isn't their own.

WHERE TO STAY IN BERAT

Maya Hostel
A traditional white windowed house along the river with good breakfast, front garden and friendly staff. **€**

Hotel Klea
Hilltop hideaway near the castle gates with five compact, wood-panelled rooms and pretty patios. **€**

Hotel Mangalemi
The first post-communism hotel built over the Pasha's 1764 palace is Berat's most charming accommodation. **€€**

NATURE TRIPS OUTSIDE BERAT

Albanian artist **Nevila Muka** (@nevi_paints) shares her favourite adventures outside Berat.

Osum Canyon
If not rafting, it's still worth visiting this spectacular canyon, and you can sunbathe on the riverbanks.

Bogova Waterfall
It is a 30-minute hike but it's worth it. If you're brave enough, jump in the ice-cold water.

Tomorri Mountain National Park
The best time to visit is 20–25 August when Bektashis make a pilgrimage to where Imam Abbas Ali rests in a small shrine. It's traditional to buy a sheep and bake it on a spit while setting up your tent.

Shpirag Mountain
Hike up this 1200m peak, which has a few traditional restaurants cooking delicious food. It's all worth it after the hike, believe me.

DAMIAN RYSZAWY/SHUTTERSTOCK ©

Osum Canyon (p71)

both sides, narrowing to barely the size of the raft. Look out for oddly shaped rocks that look like a nose or dragon and be prepared to get soaked (perhaps while kissing your love) in gushing waterfalls.

Rafting season lasts from February through June, with the highest rapids following the winter rains. In May and June, the rapids dial down to Class I or II and you may have to jump up and down to move over the rocks by the end of the season. It's worth paying the extra €20 for the van ride from Berat and lunch in Skrapar as the drive is a challenging zigzag even for the most experienced drivers. It's also worth re-emphasising that you cannot drive south from the canyon to Permet or Gjirokastra unless you have an off-road vehicle or want to destroy your car.

It's possible to drive to the canyon for views and to jump in the turquoise water. Accommodation in Berat can organise tours.

THE ACCURSED MOUNTAINS

If canyons and cool cliffs are your thing, head up to northern Albania to hike in the Accursed Mountains from Valbona to Theth or vice versa. Follow a detailed guide on p65.

WHERE TO EAT IN BERAT

Eni Traditional Food
Small, affordable menu, made with heart. Try Berati speciality *vienez* (schnitzel-like fried meat and cheese roll). €

Onufri
Castle-top restaurant akin to an Albanian feast, especially with a mixed platter for two. €

Lili Homemade Food
Leave with a smile on your face, a full belly and a new friend in English-speaking owner Lili. Reserve ahead. €€

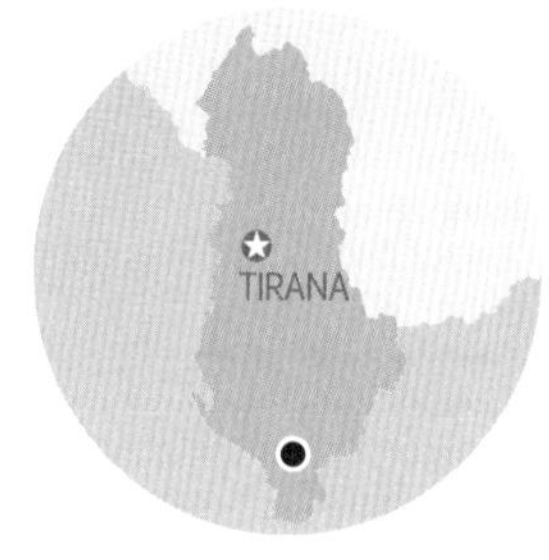

Gjirokastra

UNESCO HERITAGE | ARCHITECTURE | OLD BAZAAR

On a mountain range overlooking the fertile Drino Valley, Gjirokastra is a Unesco World Heritage site and was a museum town (along with Berat) under the communists. Its massive castle, inhabited by plenty of leaders over more than five centuries, stands commandingly over a stone town made up of some 600 Ottoman-style houses with extremely heavy rock slab roofs as well as a shoddily-built new town in the floodplains. Wander the quaint Qafa e Pazarit (Old Bazaar) alongside enticing traditional restaurants, souvenir shops and, since the pandemic, hip cocktail bars. As you walk around, be sure to stay on the lookout for archways with metal doors – they're probably bunkers built by paranoid Gjirokastra-born Enver Hoxha. The municipality also offers tours of the biggest, complete with hilarious dry-humoured guides.

If driving to or from Berat, take only the major highways (marked yellow on Google Maps) to avoid shoddy mountain roads.

GETTING AROUND

Intercity buses stop on the highway in the newer town at the bottom of the hill. From there you can walk up (warning: it's a workout!) or take a local public bus. Times vary. There are also taxis. Consult with your accommodation beforehand about the best way to climb up.

Castle & Bazaar

Stones etched with history

The hilltop where **Gjirokastra Castle** overlooks the valley has been inhabited since as far back as the 4th century, though much of what you can see today was built about 500 years ago. In that time, this strategic complex has been a medieval fortress, a base for Ottoman Ali Pasha before he challenged the sultan (and ended up losing his head), a prison during Albania's monarchy and communist periods and an army barracks. Today, the castle is a refreshing respite from the summer heat and filled with antique artillery and a sprawling terrace that hosts a clock tower and US fighter jet allegedly abandoned at the Tirana airport. The castle also hosts two **museums** – one contains dozens of communist weapons and tools (though no English explanations), the second is a wonderful exhibition

TOP TIP

There isn't a tremendous amount to do in Gjirokastra, but there's a magic here that beckons you to stay a few days or longer to meander the bazaar and explore the surrounding goat paths. That's the case especially if you're a backpacker, as Gjirokastra is home to Albania's best hostel.

HIGHLIGHTS
1 Gjirokastra Castle

SIGHTS
2 Bazaar Mosque
3 Cold War Tunnel

SLEEPING
4 Gjirokastra Hotel
5 Stone City Hostel

EATING
6 Argjiro Patisserie
7 Odaja Restaurant
8 Taverna Tradicionale Kardhashi

DRINKING & NIGHTLIFE
9 Bukowski Bar
10 Hangover Cocktail Bar

SHOPPING
11 Te Kubé

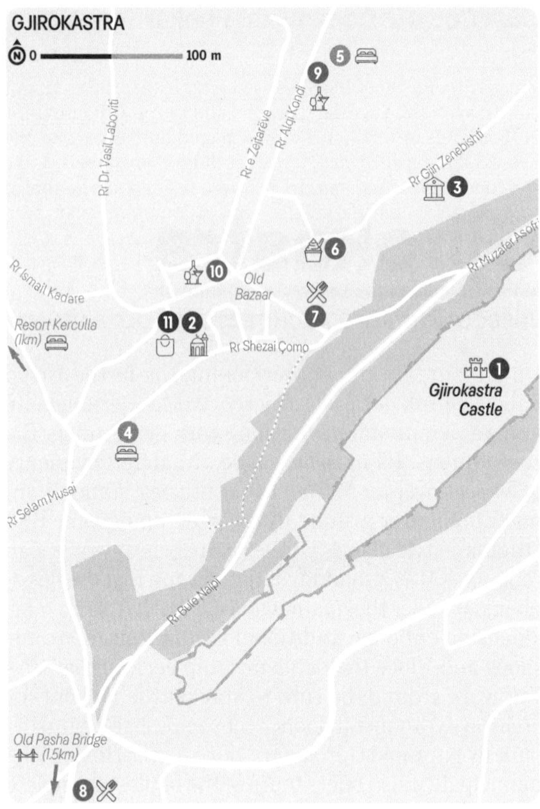

ISMAIL KADARE

Born in Gjirokastra in 1936, Ismail Kadare is Albania's greatest author and one of the world's most renowned scribes of the 20th century. Both celebrated and threatened during communist times, prompting an escape to France in 1990, Kadare has written more than two dozen books, many of them translated into English. His novels often touch on the history of Albania. Usually, his novels have a grotesque and surrealist bent. Kadare won the first Man Booker prize in 2005, has been nominated for 15 Nobel literature awards and continues to publish into his late 80s.

delivering the most thorough history of Albania in the country. The museums cost an extra 200 lek on top of the castle's entrance fee. Every five years, the castle's terrace also hosts the **National Folk Festival** where Albanians from far and wide sing quivering iso-polyphony songs and dance in choreographed performances. The last event happened in 2023, so the next should be in 2028.

Below the castle is Gjirokastra's **Old Bazaar**, which dates back to the 17th century but was kept up during communist times at the behest of former hometown hero and now heretic Enver Hoxha, who was born here. Have a fancy cocktail and people-watch on the main promenades. Look at the thick stone walls which hold up roofs layered with heavy stone slabs from the mountains. Oddly shaped thin metal fences around town are made from moulds of a now-defunct communist cutlery factory.

It's worth catching the sunset at the **Old Pasha Bridge**, a steep walk up through the village on the other side of the hilltop.

Cool Down in Communist Bunker Tunnels

Cold in various ways

When Albania found itself isolated after leader Enver Hoxha cut ties with the Yugoslavs, Soviets and Chinese, it built tens of thousands of small mushroom-shaped bunkers across the country in case of attack. It also built bunker tunnels, some of which hosted frequent drills where residents were forced to sit on cold, damp benches before commanding comrades told them they were free to return home. Locals understandably have little interest in hanging around this grim slice of Cold War history, but there are a few abandoned bunker tunnels around Gjirokastra that you can explore (claustrophobes beware). The most pristine is the **Cold War Tunnel** above Çerçiz Topulli Square. There, a municipality tour guide will take you around the tunnel's 80 rooms, built by prisoners housed in the castle through the 1960s. See the decaying conference room, kitchen, and generator, and learn about Albania's communist period. Even if you've been to Tirana's Bunk'Arts (p52), the history comes alive here, especially if you're lucky enough to be hosted by a guide with deadpan humour. Tours are led every hour during high season.

Beneath the **Bazaar Mosque** (Xhamia e Pazarit), find another bunker tunnel transformed into an auditory experience. Found inside **Te Kubè**, a bookshop and laptop-friendly cafe, the colour-lit tunnel plays the sounds of traditional Albanian folk songs. Outside the tunnel, play a documentary and hear sound-enriched explanations of Albanian iso-polyphony music and its unique instruments like the lute, *dajre* (tambourine), bagpipes and *kaval* (oblique flute).

BEAUTIFUL BERAT

Despite both being museum towns in the mountains with castles and Ottoman architecture, Berat and Gjirokastra look completely different and both are worth visiting. See what to do in Berat on p69.

BEST FOOD & DRINK IN GJIROKASTRA

Odaja Restaurant
Delightful, honest Albanian cooking since 1937 with plenty of vegetarian options. €

Taverna Tradicionale Kardhashi
A tad pushy, though eminently generous top-of-the-hill restaurant with plenty of outdoor seating. €

Argjiro Patisserie
Try Gjirokastra's traditional dessert, *oshaf* (pudding made with sheep's milk, sugar, and dried fig). €

Bukowski Bar
Laid-back novelist-themed bar with comfy chairs for people-watching and good snacks.

Hangover Cocktail Bar
Trendy bazaar bar with elaborate cocktails served in funky glassware.

WHERE TO STAY IN GJIROKASTRA

Stone City Hostel
Dutch owner Walter runs Albania's best hostel, with modern-meets-traditional decor and daily activities. €

Gjirokastra Hotel
Lovely family-run hotel inside a 300-year-old house with huge balconies and gorgeously carved wooden ceilings. €€

Resort Kerculla
Luxury hotel overlooking Gjirokastra with exquisite poolside views. Day pool passes are available. €€€

ALDO91/SHUTTERSTOCK ©

Tirana International Airport

Arriving

Albania's only international airport is in Tirana, but it's closer to fly to the Greek island of Corfu and take a ferry if going to the Albanian Riviera. Albania also has ample land crossings and bus connections with Montenegro, Kosovo and North Macedonia as well as Greece. Travel to Albania is visa-free for 90 days for Europeans, North Americans, Australians and New Zealanders.

By Air

Tirana International Airport, 17km from the city centre, is a seamless experience for EU, Canadian and US passport holders with fully automated scanning gates. The quickest way to get to Saranda or Himara is with an air/ferry combo from Corfu.

By Land

Albania has land crossings with Montenegro, North Macedonia and Greece and an open border with Kosovo. There are no passenger trains into Albania, so your options are bus, *furgon* (minibus), taxis or walking through to pick up transport on the other side.

Money

Currency: lek

CASH

Cash is still king nearly everywhere in Albania. Both Albanian lek and euro are accepted, and most businesses will give you the actual conversion rate. You'll find ATMs dispensing lek in all major towns and cities, just expect to be slapped with a 600–850 lek fee and possibly a conversion percentage in addition to what your home bank charges. Unfortunately, Credins Bank, which used to be fee-free, now charges as well. Keep smaller bills and change handy, especially if taking the bus, as splitting the 5000 lek bills usually dispensed at machines can be a challenge.

CARDS

Bank or credit cards are almost never accepted in Albania beyond upscale hotels. Even car hires want cash or bank transfer, and online bookings won't require a credit card if you used one to reserve. If cards are accepted, at pharmacies in Tirana for instance, expect a transaction minimum and a plea to pay cash instead.

Getting Around

Buses have a notorious reputation in Albania. They're often too small, crowded and hot, and have a nasty habit of breaking down. Driving has its own issues, with bold drivers as well as confusing and rocky roads off the main highways. Plus car hires can be expensive, especially for automatic cars. Choose based on budget, time and will to explore beyond the hubs.

DRIVING

Fears of driving in Albania are often exaggerated, especially on major SH highways, but you will see other drivers make bold manoeuvres like blind passing on mountain corners and parking in the middle of the road to grab a coffee. Keep your distance from other cars and stand your ground.

HELGE LINDAU/SHUTTERSTOCK ©

Tirana

BUS

Bus and *furgon* (minibuses) are the main forms of public transport in Albania. Fares are low, and you either pay the conductor on board or before you hop off, which can be anywhere along the route. Municipal buses operate in all major cities.

TIMING YOUR TRAVEL

Prepare to be loosey-goosey with your schedule if travelling by *furgon*. Timetables aren't always accurate, and trips often take longer than expected. Consult your accommodation for the most up-to-date timetable.

TAXI

Rideshare services like Uber aren't available in Albania. Official taxis are common in cities and Tirana has electric taxis that are often cheaper. Drivers in Tirana rarely speak English, but you can punch in your destination on their phone.

HIRING A CAR

International car hire brands are rare beyond the Tirana airport, and are much more expensive than local operators. If going with a local operator, expect to pay cash or bank transfer and be sure to verify the level of coverage for accidents as well as fees for cross-border travel.

DRIVING ESSENTIALS

City driving is chaotic.

Maps.me is more accurate than Google Maps

Traffic stops are common

Bosnia & Hercegovina

RICH HISTORY, WILD NATURE, WARM WELCOME

Bosnia and Hercegovina has stunning natural beauty, charming cities, and a fascinating history. Make sure you engage with its friendly people.

Bosnia and Hercegovina's dramatic natural beauty is only matched by its history. The meeting point of Byzantine and Roman Christianity and Islam, via the Ottoman and Austro-Hungarian Empires, and socialist Yugoslavia, is still associated in most people's minds with the heartbreaking war of the 1990s. And while the scars from that time remain deep and visible, today's visitors are likely to remember the country for its deep, unassuming human warmth, its incredible mountains, numerous medieval castle ruins, raftable rivers, impressive waterfalls and bargain-value skiing.

Major drawcards include the reincarnated historical centres of Sarajevo and Mostar, counterpointing splendid Ottoman stone architecture with quirky bars, inviting street-terrace cafes, traditional barbecue restaurants and vibrant arts scenes.

Sutjeska National Park, in Eastern Bosnia, has an actual rainforest that visitors can explore, as well as the country's highest mountain peak and many lakes.

Hercegovina's incredible Kravice waterfalls and the Ottoman mini-towns of Počitelj and Blagaj are like tiny miracles on the landscape with their beauty, while Western Bosnia's town of Jajce manages to pack waterfalls, lakes and rivers into its centre, together with fascinating historical sights.

Following the valley of the gorgeous River Una and tracing its fascinating swimming and rafting spots is an unforgettable experience.

The fact that it's relatively crowd-free and the prices are affordable makes this one of Europe's best-value destinations.

THE MAIN AREAS

SARAJEVO
Bustling Ottoman centre, nation's best food. p84

HERCEGOVINA
Magnificent Mostar, pretty Počitelj, leafy Trebinje. p99

WESTERN BOSNIA
Incredible waterfalls and rivers, and verdant towns. p107

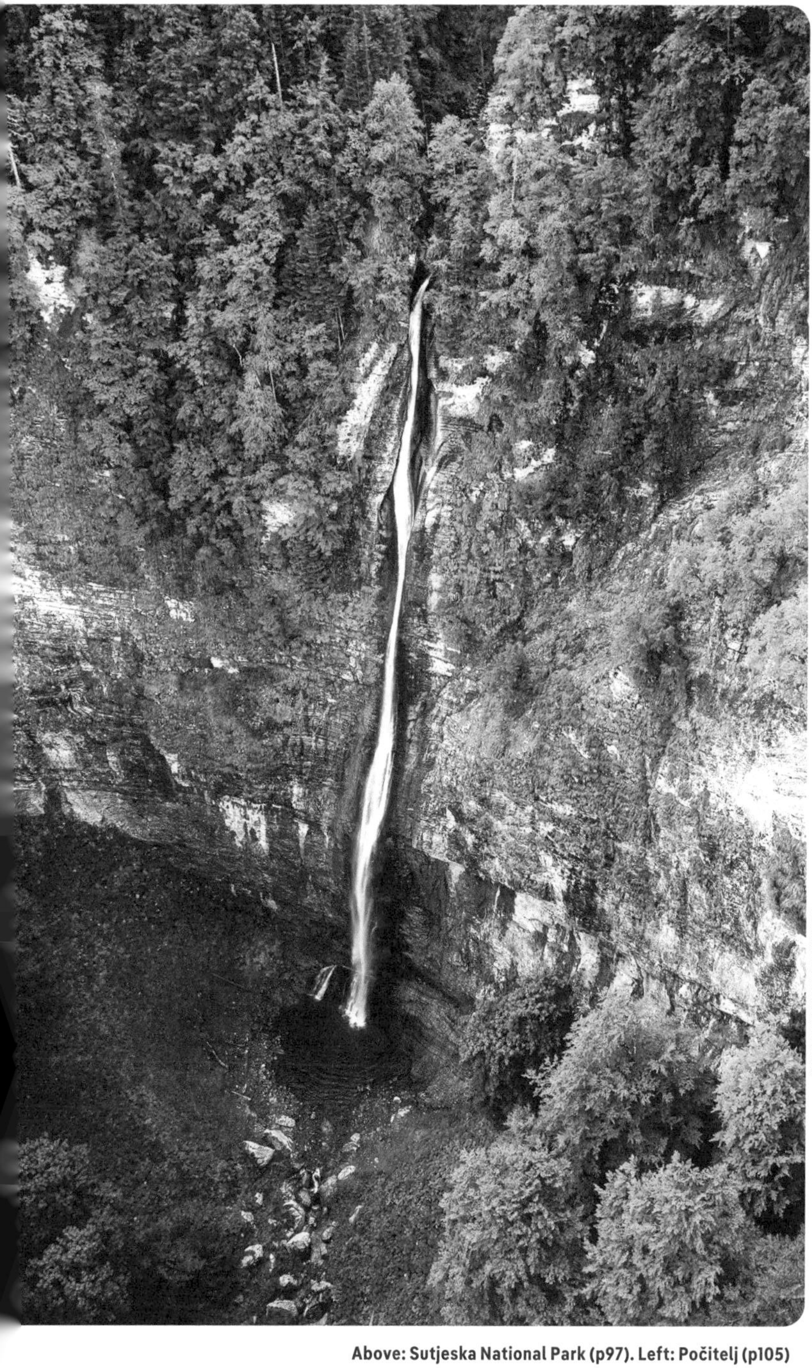

LUKAS_VEJRIK/SHUTTERSTOCK ©

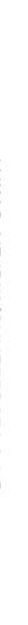

Above: Sutjeska National Park (p97). Left: Počitelj (p105)

Find Your Way

Getting your own car is the best way to explore Bosnia and Hercegovina, but for those not wishing to drive, the bus service network is reasonably priced and efficient. Trains are limited but pleasant.

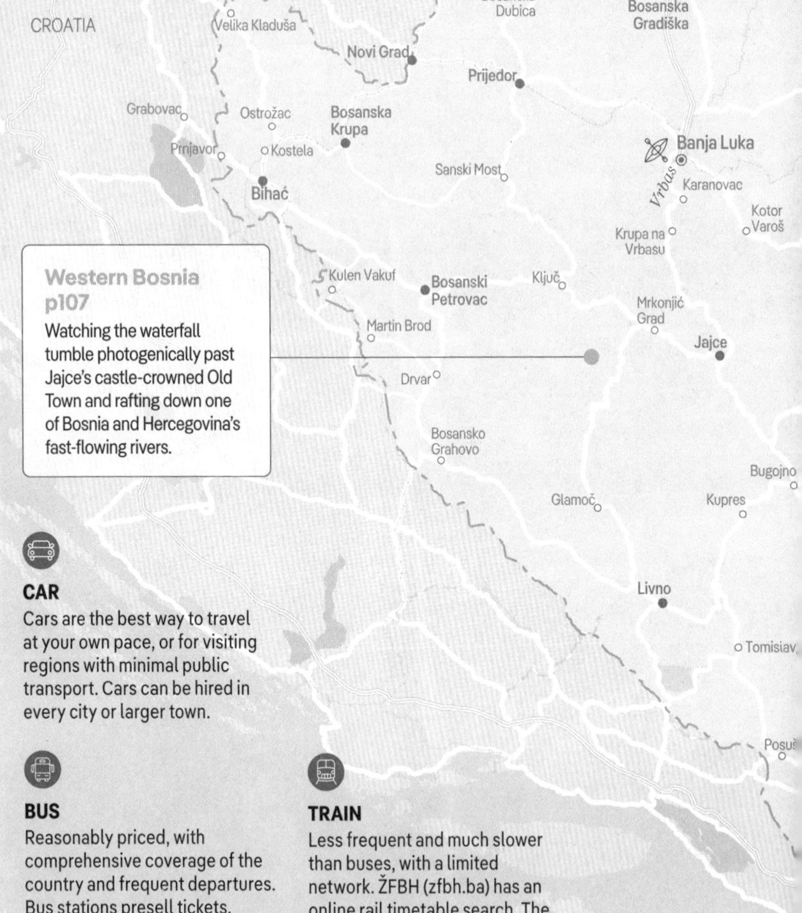

Western Bosnia p107

Watching the waterfall tumble photogenically past Jajce's castle-crowned Old Town and rafting down one of Bosnia and Hercegovina's fast-flowing rivers.

CAR

Cars are the best way to travel at your own pace, or for visiting regions with minimal public transport. Cars can be hired in every city or larger town.

BUS

Reasonably priced, with comprehensive coverage of the country and frequent departures. Bus stations presell tickets. Between towns it's normally easy enough to wave down any bus en route.

TRAIN

Less frequent and much slower than buses, with a limited network. ŽFBH (zfbh.ba) has an online rail timetable search. The main routes are Sarajevo–Visoko and Sarajevo–Konjic–Mostar.

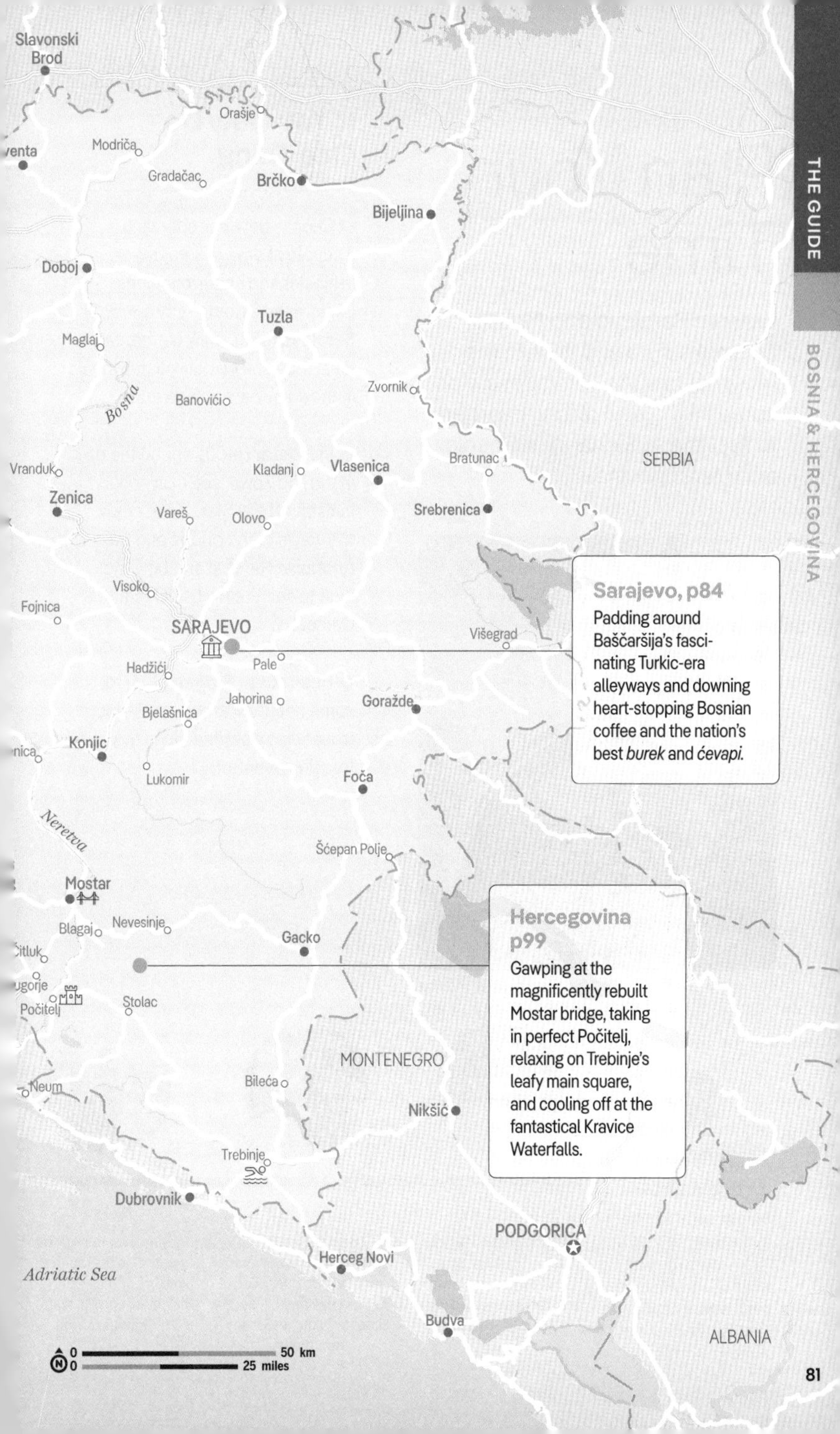

Slavonski Brod
Orašje
Modriča
Gradačac
Brčko
Bijeljina
Doboj
Tuzla
Maglaj
Bosna
Banovići
Zvornik
Vranduk
Kladanj
Vlasenica
Bratunac
SERBIA
Zenica
Vareš
Olovo
Srebrenica
Visoko
Fojnica
SARAJEVO
Višegrad
Hadžići
Pale
Jahorina
Goražde
Bjelašnica
Konjic
Lukomir
Foča
Neretva
Šćepan Polje
Mostar
Blagaj
Nevesinje
Gacko
Stolac
Počitelj
MONTENEGRO
Neum
Bileća
Nikšić
Trebinje
Dubrovnik
PODGORICA
Herceg Novi
Adriatic Sea
Budva
ALBANIA
0 50 km
0 25 miles

Sarajevo, p84

Padding around Baščaršija's fascinating Turkic-era alleyways and downing heart-stopping Bosnian coffee and the nation's best *burek* and *ćevapi*.

Hercegovina p99

Gawping at the magnificently rebuilt Mostar bridge, taking in perfect Počitelj, relaxing on Trebinje's leafy main square, and cooling off at the fantastical Kravice Waterfalls.

Plan Your Time

Explore Sarajevo and Mostar, but make sure you go into the mountains and river valleys, do some hiking and rafting in order to feel the real charm of Bosnia and Hercegovina.

NERMIN K/SHUTTERSTOCK ©

Stari Most (p100), Mostar

If You Only Do One Thing

- Choose between spending a couple of days in Sarajevo or in Mostar and its surroundings. Explore the Ottoman city centre in **Sarajevo** (p84), drink coffee, eat local food and go out with the locals in the many bars around town.

- In **Mostar** (p100), spend the day in the Old Town, see a diver hurl himself off the Stari Most, enjoy the views of the bridge and the turquoise Neretva and take the time to see the Partisan Memorial Cemetery.

- Head out to **Blagaj** (p103) for some beautiful architecture, local trout and a possible dip in the freezing river Buna.

Seasonal Highlights

Spring, early summer and autumn are ideal for a visit. The first week of September is best: high season has just finished but the autumn rains haven't yet set in.

JANUARY

Skiing gets cheaper after the New Year holidays and snow mostly lasts all the way to mid-March.

MAY

Beat the heat in Hercegovina; flowers bloom in Bosnia; rivers are at peak flows – best time for hiking the many mountains.

JUNE

It's almost summer; the weather is perfect for walking and exploring the cities, and it's warm enough for rafting.

FROM LEFT: EVRONPHOTO/SHUTTERSTOCK ©, VEDAD.CERIC/SHUTTERSTOCK ©, PHOTOPANKPL/SHUTTERSTOCK ©

Four Days

- If you're coming from the coast, you might enter the country from leafy **Trebinje** (p105), where you can sip coffee on the relaxing central square.

- Alternatively, take the road to **Metković** (in Croatia) and make a detour to the spectacular **Kravice Waterfalls** (p105) and the hill town gem of **Počitelj** (p105).

- The next day, choose between a stop in **Blagaj** (p103) and **Stolac** (p106) via the Radimlja Necropolis, en route to **Mostar** (p100) and its famous Ottoman bridge and Old Town.

- Head down the gorgeous Neretva Canyon road, to spend your last two days exploring **Sarajevo** (p84).

Seven Days

- After following the four-day itinerary, spend day five soaking up the sights of the **Una River Valley** (p110) and day six exploring the lakes, waterfall and historical old centre of **Jajce** (p108).

- Split day three between **Travnik** (p109) and **Visoko** (p94), pushing back to **Sarajevo** (p104) in time for bed.

- If you're heading back towards the coast, stop at **Konjic** (p105), where you can stop to admire the rebuilt Ottoman bridge.

JULY

Hot and sweaty, but great for rafting, river and lake swimming and enjoying the evenings outdoors.

AUGUST

Gets sweaty and accommodation fills up, but events like the **Sarajevo Film Festival** (p95) keep things lively.

SEPTEMBER

The heat lessens, the nights are cooler, the high season is done and the rains haven't yet set in – an ideal time.

DECEMBER

Snowfall in the mountains or Bosnia proper, good skiing and winter holidays.

Sarajevo

CULTURE | HISTORY | NIGHTLIFE

GETTING AROUND

Sarajevo has an extensive network of trams, buses, trolleybuses and minibuses, all operated by GRAS. You can pre-purchase tickets from kiosks, or buy from the driver; they must be stamped once aboard, and inspections are common. Tram 3 (every four minutes during the day) leaves from Ilidža and passes the National Museum, then loops one-way (anticlockwise) around Baščaršija. Tram 1 (every 17 minutes during the day) starts at the train station, then does the same loop as Tram 3.

TOP TIP

The best way to get a feel for the city is to stroll the old town's pedestrian lanes and grand avenues, then climb the picturesque slopes of Vratnik for sweeping views. Seeking out museums is likely to take you into modern, businesslike Novo Sarajevo and beyond to park-filled Ilidža.

Ringed by mountains, Sarajevo is a singular city with an atmosphere all of its own – meander around the Ottoman quarter of Baščaršija and savour the smoking barbecue restaurants and local coffee, peek into the mosques, churches and synagogues, and marvel at the dilapidating socialist architecture, before joining the locals in the lively and stylish bars and restaurants.

Once renowned as 'the Jerusalem of Europe' for its religious diversity, Sarajevo is now majority Bosniak, with most of the Orthodox Christians living in newly built Istočno Sarajevo (East Sarajevo) on the Republika Srpska side. The 20th century thrust Sarajevo into the world's consciousness via the assassination which precipitated WWI, the 1984 Winter Olympics, and sadly, by the brutal almost-four-year siege of the city in the 1990s.

Sarajevo is once again a wonderful place to visit – war scars visible as they are. Enjoy its intriguing architectural medley, vibrant street life and irrepressible spirit.

Explore the Heart of Sarajevo

Atmospheric alleys and architecture in Baščaršija

Centred on **Sebilj fountain**, Baščaršija (pronounced barsh-char-shi-ya) is the very heart of old Sarajevo. The name is derived from the Turkish for 'main market' and it's still lined with stalls, a lively (if tourist-centric) coppersmith alley, grand Ottoman mosques, *caravanserai* (inn) restaurants and lots of inviting little cafes. The east–west lane, Sarači, broadens out into the wide pedestrian boulevard Ferhadija, where Austro-Hungarian–era buildings take over. Some particularly grand examples line the waterfront.

Starting right there, the storybook neo-Moorish striped facade makes the triangular **City Hall** (Vijećnica, 1896) Sarajevo's most beautiful Austro-Hungarian–era building. Seriously damaged during the 1990s siege, it reopened in 2014

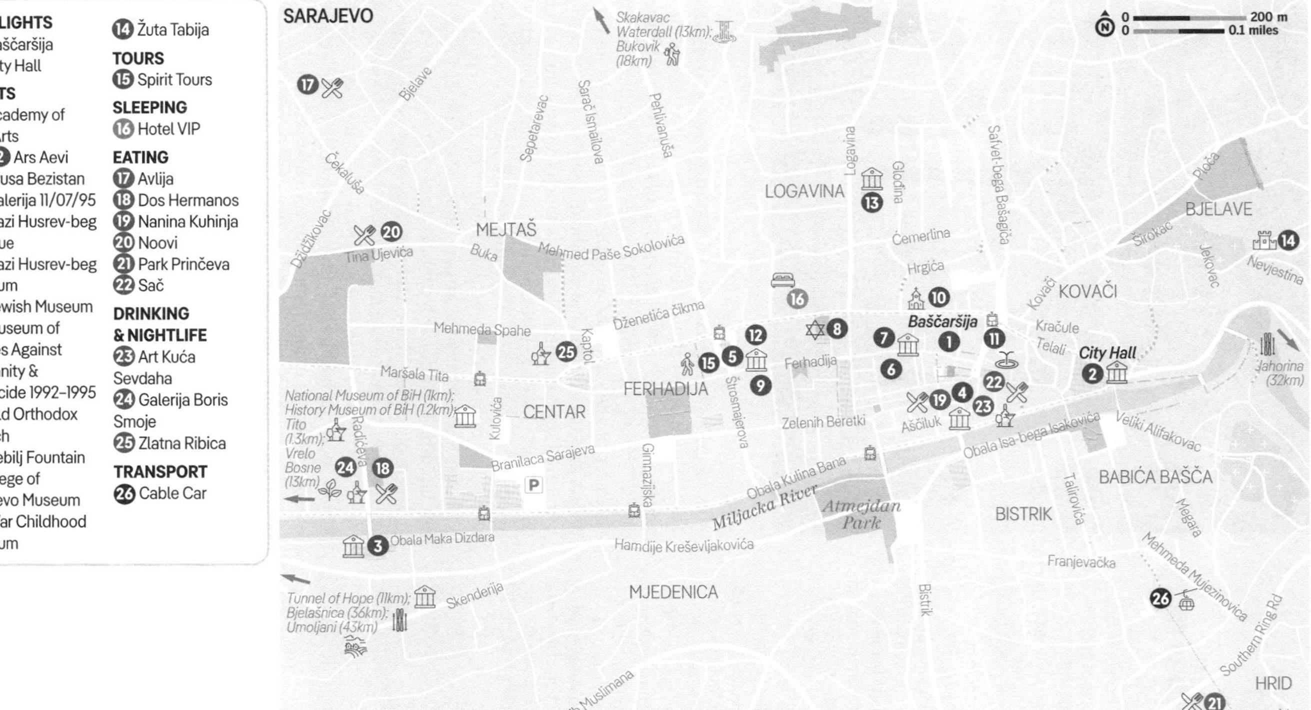

HIGHLIGHTS
1 Baščaršija
2 City Hall

SIGHTS
3 Academy of Fine Arts
see 2 Ars Aevi
4 Brusa Bezistan
5 Galerija 11/07/95
6 Gazi Husrev-beg Mosque
7 Gazi Husrev-beg Museum
8 Jewish Museum
9 Museum of Crimes Against Humanity & Genocide 1992–1995
10 Old Orthodox Church
11 Sebilj Fountain
12 Siege of Sarajevo Museum
13 War Childhood Museum
14 Žuta Tabija

TOURS
15 Spirit Tours

SLEEPING
16 Hotel VIP

EATING
17 Avlija
18 Dos Hermanos
19 Nanina Kuhinja
20 Noovi
21 Park Prinčeva
22 Sač

DRINKING & NIGHTLIFE
23 Art Kuća Sevdaha
24 Galerija Boris Smoje
25 Zlatna Ribica

TRANSPORT
26 Cable Car

NATIONAL MUSEUM OF BIH

Bosnia's biggest and best-endowed museum of ancient and natural history is housed in an impressive, purpose-built quadrangle of neoclassical 1913 buildings. It's best known for housing the priceless Sarajevo Haggadah illuminated manuscript (p89), but there's much more to see. Along with the Haggadah, the main building houses extraordinary Greek pottery and Roman mosaics. Behind this, the central courtyard has a pretty little botanical garden and an exceptional collection of medieval *stećci* (grave-carvings).

MEHDI33300/SHUTTERSTOCK ©

Gazi Husrev-beg Mosque

after laborious reconstruction. Its colourfully restored interior and stained-glass ceiling are superb. Your ticket also allows you to peruse the excellent **Sarajevo 1914–2014 exhibition** in the octagonal basement. This gives well-explained potted histories of the city's various 20th-century periods and insights into fashion and music subcultures.

In 1914 Franz Ferdinand and his much frowned-upon wife Sophie (she had been his mother's former lady-in-waiting) were on their way back from this very building when they were shot by Gavrilo Princip, a member of Young Bosnia, a secret group resisting the Austro-Hungarian rule. From 1949 the building became the National Library but in August 1992 it was deliberately hit by a Serbian incendiary shell. Around two million irreplaceable manuscripts, books and documents were destroyed. Those that survived might one day return, but for now the building is used as the council chamber, for events and occasionally for concerts. Various exhibitions are staged in the upper level and an **International Criminal Tribunal for the former Yugoslavia** (ICTY) information centre sits on the ground floor, including the contents of the original courtroom, which were shifted here from the Hague.

WHERE TO EAT IN BAŠČARŠIJA

Željo
The legendary spot for *ćevapi*, where locals brave the tourist throngs for the best grilled meat. €

Mrkva
Considered by some locals to be old Sarajevo's classic place for *ćevapi*. €

Dveri
A 'country cottage' eatery with an enchanting atmosphere, serving goulash and inky risottos. €€

The **Museum of Crimes Against Humanity and Genocide 1992–1995** covers the many atrocities of the 1990s war in unsparing visual detail. Video footage combined with photographs, artefacts and personal testimonies illustrates the horror and brutality of the times. We wouldn't recommend bringing children.

Bosnia's second Ottoman governor, Gazi Husrev-beg, funded a series of splendid 16th-century buildings, of which the 1531 **Gazi Husrev-beg Mosque**, with its 45m minaret, is the greatest. The domed interior is beautifully proportioned and even if you can't look inside, it's worth walking through the courtyard with its lovely fountain, chestnut trees and the *turbe* (tomb) of its founder.

If you'd like to learn more about the colourful life and philanthropic legacy of Husrev-beg, visit the **Gazi Husrev-beg Museum**. It is situated inside the 1537 **Kuršumlija Madrasa building**, distinctive for its pointed chimneys and the lead roof from which it takes its name. There's little in the way of artefacts but the video is well worth watching.

Brusa Bezistan was built in 1551 as a silk-trading bazaar, and it is an elegant two-storey building topped with six green-metal domes and encircled by shops. It's now a branch of the **Museum of Sarajevo**, providing an overview of the city from prehistoric times up until 1914. At its centre is a scale model of Sarajevo as it looked in 1878. The only concession to recent history is a series of grisly large-scale photographs of the mass-grave excavations from the 1990s genocide.

More religiously open-minded than most of Western Europe in its day, the Ottoman Empire offered refuge to the Sephardic Jews who had been exiled en masse from Spain in 1492. While conditions varied, Bosnian Jews mostly prospered until WWII, when most of the 14,000-strong community fled or were murdered. The community's story is well told in the **Jewish Museum**, housed in a 1581 Sephardic synagogue that still sees active worship during Jewish New Year.

While the final form of the outwardly austere stone **Old Orthodox Church** dedicated to the archangels Michael and Gabriel dates to 1730, it was founded considerably earlier – possibly as long ago as the 5th century. Inside, under a star-spangled night-blue ceiling, is a superb gilded iconostasis from 1674 fronted by a pair of 3m-high candlesticks. The cloister museum displays manuscripts, vestments and icons, the oldest of which were painted in the 15th century.

BEST PLACES TO STAY IN SARAJEVO

Isa-Begov Hamam Hotel
An ornate 19th-century *hammam* with 15 luxurious rooms designed to evoke the spirit of the age. Guests get free use of the *hammam*. €€€

Hotel Colors Inn
As the name suggests, this is a hotel that likes colour – it's stylish, comfortable, neat and very central, with a lush breakfast. €€

Hotel VIP
On a quiet lane in the centre of town, with great rooms (some with balconies), excellent bathrooms and a good breakfast. €€

War Hostel
Sleep here only if you are ready to engage with the wartime experience. Weird, and certainly memorable. €

Hostel Franz Ferdinand
A spot for those wanting to meet fellow travellers, this is a popular, good quality hostel in the centre of town. €

WHERE TO SLEEP IN SARAJEVO

Halvat Guest House
The six rooms at this friendly, family-run guesthouse are clean, spacious, quiet and central. **€€**

Hotel Aziza
An extremely comfortable and friendly family-run hotel, with a daily sauna included. **€€€**

Colors Inn
Modernist decor and photos of 20th-century Sarajevo give way to comfortably stylish rooms. **€€€**

A SARAJEVO STROLL

Start at the ❶ **Eternal Flame**, a Yugoslav-era symbol of togetherness. Stroll past the cafes and shops of ❷ **Ferhadija**, and go up Gajev trg to reach Mula Mustafe Bašeskije street, where you will find the Austro-Hungarian-era market hall ❸ **Gradska Tržnica** – pop in to get some local goodies. After another block, go down Trg Fra Grge Martića and back on Ferhadija you'll reach a central square dominated by the ❹ **Catholic Sacred Heart Cathedral**, built in 1889 in the neogothic style. Continue east down Ferhadija to reach the first significant Ottoman building on your right, the ❺ **Bezistan**. Enter and walk past the stalls selling tourist tat as far as the first exit on your left.

As you get back to Ferhadija and carry on, the street name becomes Sarači. You'll see ahead of you the 1529 ❻ **Clock Tower** – topped with an Islamic prayer clock – and the elegant minarets of the ❼ **Gazi Husrev-beg Mosque** (p87). Cut through the mosque courtyard and exit by the gate nearest the fountain. Opposite is the 1537 Islamic school which houses the ❽ **Gazi Husrev-beg Museum** (p87). Continue east along Sarači to the square at the very heart of ❾ **Baščaršija** (p84) – ahead is the ❿ **Baščaršija Mosque**, while to the left is the gazebo-like 1891 ⓫ **Sebilj** drinking fountain. Take the tiny lane, Luledžina, to the right by the fountain, and cut past the water-pipe bars. The first lane on your right brings you out onto ⓬ **Kazandžiluk**, the atmospheric coppersmith alley. Turn left and follow it around until you hit ⓭ **Bravadžiluk**, Baščaršija's main eating strip. At its eastern end, take a right towards the river and Obala Kulina Bana, where you will see the exuberant red-and-yellow striped ⓮ **Sarajevo City Hall** (p84).

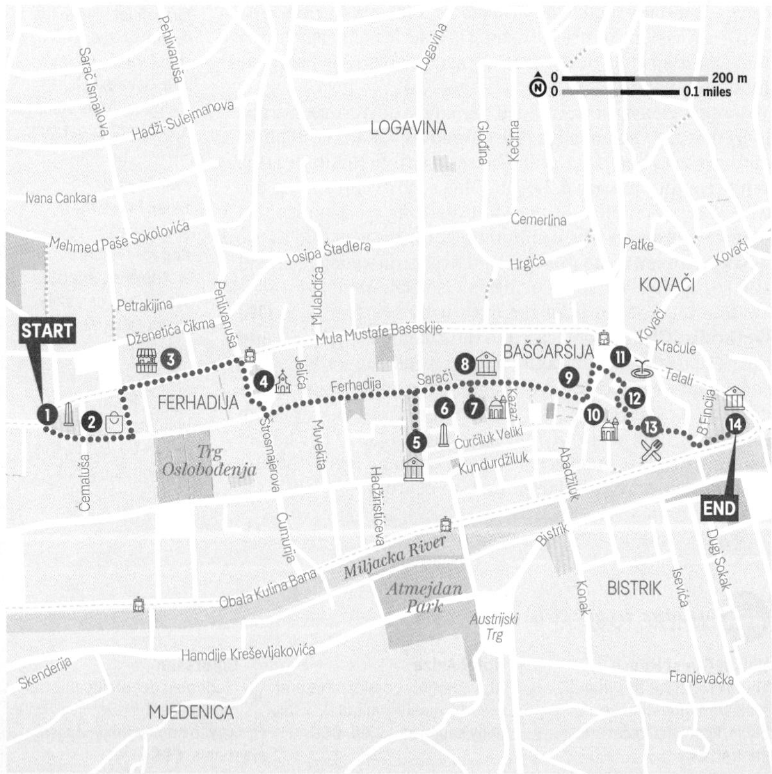

Sarajevo Haggadah, National Museum

Learn about Sarajevo's Recent History

Sarajevo war sites

Start with the **War Childhood Museum**, an affecting place that had its genesis in a 2013 book edited by Jasminko Halilović, in which he asked a simple question of survivors of the Sarajevo siege: 'What was a war childhood for you?' Of the hundreds of replies received, 50 short written testimonies are presented here, each illustrated by personal effects donated by the writer, such as diaries, drawings, toys and ballet slippers. It's a lighter, less gore-filled approach to the conflict than you'll find elsewhere, but equally devastating.

Many of the works in the thought-provoking **Ars Aevi** contemporary art gallery were collected as donations for Bosnia during the 1990s conflict. The collection includes works by the likes of Anish Kapoor, Nan Goldin and Marina Abramović; a rotating selection of them is displayed in a factory-esque interior of metal ducts and polished chipboard within the lumpy Skenderija Centar.

Somewhat misleadingly named, the **History Museum of Bosnia and Herzegovina**, is a small yet engrossing museum. It occupies a striking, still partly war-damaged 1960s socialist-modernist building originally dubbed the Museum of the

THE SARAJEVO HAGGADAH

Arguably the greatest treasure of the National Museum of Bosnia and Herzegovina (p86) is the world-famous Sarajevo Haggadah, a priceless 14th-century illuminated codex (used during Passover) filled with beautiful hand-painted illustrations – a rarity in Jewish texts. The story of its survival is marvellous.

Presumably created in Barcelona and taken from Spain during the expulsion of the Sephardic Jews, it turned up in Venice and was saved from destruction in 1609 by a Catholic priest. It was sold to Sarajevo's museum in 1894 and survived the Nazis thanks to a Muslim librarian and cleric, who hid it in his mosque. During the 1990s siege, it was saved from the bombardment, again by a Muslim curator, who interred it in the vaults of the National Bank.

WHERE TO HAVE TEA & COFFEE IN SARAJEVO

Čajdžinica Džirlo
Minuscule Džirlo brews 29 types of tea, many of them made from distinctive Bosnian herbs.

Franz & Sophie
A temple to tea, with just three tables and knowledgeable staff.

Caffe von Habsburg
A shoebox cafe-bar, with original brick-arched ceilings, full of Austro-Hungarian memorabilia.

SARAJEVO'S NATURE SITES

Reopened in 2018 after being destroyed during the war, Sarajevo's **cable car** once again shuttles people on a nine-minute ride, climbing 500m to a viewpoint 1164m up on Mt Trebević. From here it's a short walk to the wreck of the Olympic bobsled track, seemingly held together by layers of graffiti.

Ever popular with local families, **Vrelo Bosne** is an extensive park, home to a patchwork of lush mini-islands at the cliffed mouth of the Bosna River. The classic way to get there is to stroll or take a horse-drawn carriage ride (20KM) for 3km along elegantly tree-lined Velika Aleja, starting near Ilidža's Hotel Aleja.

Tunnel of Hope

Revolution. It regularly hosts high-profile international exhibitions but the main attraction is the permanent Surrounded Sarajevo display, which charts local people's life-and-death battles for survival between 1992 and 1995. Alongside some heartbreaking photographs are personal effects such as self-made lamps, examples of food aid, stacks of Monopoly-style 1990s dinars and a makeshift siege-time 'home'. Also interesting is the collection of 1996–2011 before-and-after Sarajevo images in the hallway. Directly behind the building, the tongue-in-cheek Tito bar is a museum in its own right.

During the 1992–95 siege, when Sarajevo was surrounded by Bosnian Serb forces, the only link to the outside world was an 800m-long, 1m-wide, 1.6m-high tunnel between two houses on opposite sides of the airport runway. Walking through a 25m section, now called the **Tunnel of Hope**, is the moving culmination of a visit to the shell-pounded house that hid the western tunnel entrance. The story of the siege and the tunnel's construction is told via video, information boards and an audioguide accessible via free wi-fi.

Although the airport was supposedly neutral and under tenuous UN control during the conflict, crossing it would have been suicidal. The solution was to secretly build the tunnel,

WHERE TO DRINK IN SARAJEVO

Birtija
Popular with an artsy, bohemian crowd, this wonderful wee bar has a great vibe.

Cinemas Sloga
A cavernous club in an old cinema with themed nights, a young crowd and cheap beer.

Male Daire
One of the Old Town's best hookah bars, with outdoor tree-shaded seating and no booze.

which was eventually equipped with rails to transport food and arms. That proved just enough to keep Sarajevo supplied during nearly four years of siege.

Galerija 11/07/95 is a powerful memorial to the 8372 victims of the Srebrenica massacre. You'll need well over an hour to make the most of a visit, and it's worth paying the extra for the audioguide to gain more insight. The gallery uses stirring photography, video footage and audio testimonies of survivors and family members of the Srebrenica genocide.

The **Siege of Sarajevo Museum** opened in 2023, on the 31st anniversary of the siege of Sarajevo, housing many objects, photographs and testimonials of the extraordinary circumstances under which the city's inhabitants survived the longest siege in Europe's history.

Sarajevo for Culture Vultures

The country's best film and music

Sarajevo has a good cultural life but the cream of the culture crop is the **Sarajevo Film Festival**, featured annually in mid-August. It is an excellent time to visit the city. The globally acclaimed eight-day film festival turns the whole city into a giant party with countless concerts and many impromptu bars opening on street corners.

The next best is the **Jazz Fest Sarajevo**, taking place in early November, with three days of concerts at major venues, and plenty of fringe events in the pubs and clubs around town. You can see international and local names and have yourself a great time.

Throughout July, make sure you see some of the events of **Baščaršijske Noći**, a wide-ranging arts festival that sees music, theatre and all kinds of performance arts hosted in the city centre.

The best place to hear traditional Bosnian music is **Art Kuća Sevdaha**. Sit in the intimate fountain courtyard of an Ottoman-era building sipping Bosnian coffee, juniper or rose sherbet, or herb-tea infusions while nibbling local sweets. The experience is accompanied by the lilting wails of *sevdah* (traditional Bosnian music) – usually recorded, but sometimes live. Within the building is a museum celebrating great 20th-century *sevdah* performers along with a store selling CDs.

Originally built in 1899 as an evangelical church, the **Academy of Fine Arts** is a riverfront academy that resembles a mini version of Budapest's magnificent national parliament building. Inside, the small **ALU Gallery** hosts occasional exhibitions.

BEST PLACES TO DRINK IN SARAJEVO

Zlatna Ribica
The tiny and eccentric 'Golden Fish' is a cosy treasure trove of antiques and kitsch.

Galerija Boris Smoje
Local micro-brewery beer, plentiful choice of rakija. Small and cosy inside, it has a garden and a loyal local clientele.

Tito
Behind the History Museum, this is an homage to President Tito, with many photos and a garden with WWII 'memorabilia'.

Pivnica Sarajevo
The city's most famous beer house, where you can also eat and hear live music.

Art Kuća Sevdaha
Drink and listen to *sevdah* – usually recorded, but sometimes live.

WHERE TO HAVE FUN AT NIGHT IN SARAJEVO

Kino Bosna
This historical cinema hosts Bosnian *sevdah* parties, Yugo New Wave nights and other themed parties.

Pivnica Sarajevo
Local live music, a garden drinking area and a restaurant – all in one offering.

Jazzbina
A great place for drinks, live jazz and all kinds of other genres. A local favourite.

BEST PLACES TO EAT IN SARAJEVO

Avlija
Locals and a few in-the-know expats cosy up at painted wooden benches in this colourful, buzzing covered yard, dangling with trailing pot plants, strings of peppers and the odd birdcage. Local specialities are served. €€

Dos Hermanos
A neat, stylish and central restaurant with delicious salads, pastas, risottos and meat served on a lovely terrace. Great wine selection too. €€

Noovi
A gorgeous little courtyard with a small but eclectic menu of steaks, pizzas and vegetarian dishes, plus a good wine list. A local favourite. €€

Sač
Sač bakes everything *ispod sača*, meaning under a domed metal lid covered in charcoal. Our pick for Sarajevo's best *burek* and *sirnica*. €

Best Bosnian Food

Taste the local delicacies

Rich, meaty stews dominate home cooking – don't miss trying all kinds of dolmas – stuffed peppers, tomatoes, onions, in a delicious sauce, often served with mashed potato. Second national favourite is *sarma* – mostly cooked in winter time – consisting of meat and rice and spices wrapped in pickled cabbage leaves. Summer alternatives are *zelena sarma* (or *japrak* in Hercegovina), which uses green cabbage leaves to create these delicious parcels. The best place to try these is **Nanina Kuhinja**, in Baščaršija.

The favourite barbecue staple and the reason behind all the smoke wafting out of Baščaršija restaurants are *ćevapi* (barbecued, cylindrical spicy beef 'fingers'. Taste these at **Željo**, Sarajevo's most famous *ćevabdžinica*. They are served in a fabulously soft *somun* (pita bread) in portions of five or 10, and come with or without (you decide) fresh onions, *ajvar* (a sweetish pepper paste), *kajmak* (cheese curdle) and a fresh cabbage salad.

Do not miss the *burek* and pita experience – this is fillo pastry that is filled with meat, cheese, potato or spinach. Step into a *buregdžinica* and don't forget to order a yoghurt alongside your pita. *Burek* is the name for the meat option, *sirnica* is filled with cheese, *krompiruša* with potato and *zeljanica* with spinach; in season, try the *tikvenica* – a pita with pumpkin.

Local dessert favourites are baklava, *tufahije* (baked apples stuffed with walnut paste and topped with whipped cream), and *hurmašice* (syrup-soaked sponge fingers), all found in a good *slastičarna* (cake shop).

Skiing in Sarajevo

Slalom down majestic mountains

Sarajevo is surrounded by some amazing mountains – and it's an excellent idea to explore them, summer or winter.

Of Sarajevo's two Olympic skiing resorts, multi-piste **Jahorina** (26km southeast of the city, on the Republika Srpska side) has the widest range of hotels, each within 300m of one of seven main ski lifts. The ski season usually starts in mid-November and continues through to late March. The best skiing is in mid-February.

In summer the settlement becomes a semidormant cool-air retreat from the city, with some well-heeled locals escaping here for day-spa relaxation at the upmarket **Termag Hotel**.

Beside the longest slope, **Rajska Vrata** is a charming ski-in alpine chalet which sets diners beside a central fire with a

WHERE TO FIND ACTIVITIES IN SARAJEVO

Toorico Tours
Free (tip-based) two- to three-hour walking tours depart from in front of the Eternal Flame (p88) on Maršala Tita.

Spirit Tours
Free (tip-based) 90-minute walking tours depart from their office at 10am daily.

Sarajevo Funky Tours
A wide range of offerings in and around Sarajevo, plus longer multiday tours around the country.

Jahorina

VIEWS FROM YELLOW FORTRESS

One of the most appealing yet accessible viewpoints gazing over Sarajevo's red-roofed cityscape is from this bastion, known as **Žuta Tabija**. Built in the 18th century as part of the walls encircling Vratnik, it is now full of lovely old trees and has a cafe. It's a popular place for picnickers and canoodling lovers. By tradition, the end of the Ramadan fast is formally announced by a canon shot from here.

giant metallic chimney or on the piste-side terrace. Specialities include double-cheese *uštipci* (Bosnian dough balls) and homemade juices (elderberry, rosehip, raspberry etc). Upstairs, six Goldilocks-esque pine-walled guest bedrooms have handmade beds fashioned from gnarled old branches.

The modest ski resort of **Bjelašnica**, around 25km south of Sarajevo, hosted the men's alpine events during the 1984 Winter Olympics. There's usually enough snow to ski from around Christmas, and New Year is the busiest time, though February is more reliable for good piste conditions. Floodlit night skiing is offered, and the main lift also operates May to October, allowing walkers easy access to high-altitude paths.

In summer there are magical mountain villages to explore – **Umoljani** is one.

WHERE TO SHOP IN SARAJEVO

Bazerdžan
A stylish spot to find local designers for clothing, accessories, wood pieces and all kinds of beautiful creations.

Thara Concept
Great Sarajevo-themed jewellery pieces and unique souvenirs and clothing by local fashion designers.

Isfahan Gallery
Specialising in high-quality Persian and Afghani rugs, along with glass lamps and richly glazed ceramic work.

Beyond Sarajevo

The area around Sarajevo has some gorgeous, diverse landscapes and interesting towns, all a day trip away.

Places

GETTING AROUND

Sarajevo is the country's main transport hub, with an international airport, good bus connections and trains heading northwest and south. Visoko and Višegrad are reachable from Sarajevo on public transport, but you'll need your own car to explore Sutjeska National Park.

Aside from the extraordinary capital city, Sarajevo, Eastern Bosnia is largely off the radar for most travellers. The sad legacy of ethnic cleansing has cast a pall over much of the region, although many stop to pay their respects at Srebrenica, the most notorious site of all. Other places of interest include magnificent Sutjeska National Park and Višegrad, with its Unesco-listed bridge and literary connections. Most sights can easily be reached on a day trip from Sarajevo, which has an excellent selection of accommodation in every price range. Višegrad has modest but acceptable options, and there are atmospheric bungalows at a rafting camp on the Tara River near Sutjeska National Park.

Visoko

Witness an alleged archaeological wonder

An hour away from Sarajevo, by bus or regular train service, Visoko is a curious spot. Once the capital of medieval Bosnia and the spiritual centre of the long-suppressed Bosnian Church, by the 20th century it had become an unremarkable leather-tanning town. Then came an audacious claim: that the partly wooded triangular hill that looms distinctively above Visoko is in fact the world's largest **pyramid**, attracting tourists and New Age mystics. The Pyramid of the Sun Foundation has since expanded the theory to incorporate a whole series of other hill-pyramids, a subterranean labyrinth and a web of energy fields focused with 21st-century stone circles.

The Bosnian pyramid theory has been discredited by archaeologists and geologists who deplore Bosnia's concentration of efforts on Visoko when so many credible historical sites remain little investigated. But even so, many find the 'pyramid' claim fascinating.

Visoko's most popular tourist draw is a guided tour through the **Tunnel Ravne**. At this highly commercialised site, a dozen or more kilometres of tunnels supposedly form a labyrinth that dates back many millennia. Believers assert that

Pyramid, Visoko

ALEKSANDAR TODOROVIC/SHUTTERSTOCK ©

monoliths found here give healthy vibrations, that the water inside is unusually pure (small bottles are sold for the princely sum of 10KM) and that 'negative radiation' probably made the site a place of healing. A half-hour hard-hat tour through the ever-growing network of accessible tunnels is a curious experience.

In the meadow below the tunnel entrance is **Ravne 2 Park**, full of features designed to focus what Pyramid-ists believe to be powerful energy fields.

TOP TIP

Having a car to get to Sutjeska National Park is a good idea – Visoko and Višegrad are reachable by public transport.

VISOČICA HILL EXCAVATION SITE

Excavations of the superhard slabs of 'concrete' on Visočica Hill show what American-Bosnian businessman Semir Osmanagić claims as 'proof' of the pyramid's human hand. The diggings are a five-minute climb up a steep track past the ticket booth, situated at the end of a narrow lane with limited parking. There are three main dig sections with a couple of information boards. A path to the right continues way up into the forest but doesn't pass any further dig sites.

WHERE TO EAT AND SLEEP IN VISOKO

Pyramid Lodge
This immaculate hotel gives a sense of urban, artistic style that contrasts deliciously with the peaceful rural setting. **€€**

Ćevabdžinica Ihtijarević
Churning out Bosnian-style grills since 1931, this place looks like a 1950s diner. **€**

Restaurant No.1
Serves meat as well as a decent vegetarian and vegan selection catering to visiting pyramid chasers. **€€**

Andrićgrad

THE GRAND ARCHITECT

Mimar Sinan was the chief Ottoman architect, engineer and mathematician for sultans Suleiman the Magnificent, Selim II and Murad III. He built more than 300 major structures in the former empire, such as the Selimiye Mosque in Edirne, and the Sultan Ahmed Mosque in İstanbul – among many others. The Mehmed Paša Sokolović Bridge in Višegrad is his one definitive structure in Bosnia and Hercegovina; his apprentice Mimar Hayruddin later designed the Old Bridge in Mostar.

Višegrad

Literary connections and a magnificent bridge

Famous for the Unesco-listed 'Bridge on the Drina' immortalised in Ivo Andrić's classic novel, Višegrad has parlayed this identity into a niche tourist industry by building Andrićgrad, a small but likeable mock-historical city nominally celebrating the author. The city is a three-hour ride from Sarajevo.

A majority Bosniak town before the 1990s war, Višegrad suffered a brutal campaign of ethnic cleansing resulting in the deaths of at least a thousand Bosniaks in and around it. The population is now 88% Serb.

Višegrad's faux-antique Old Town – **Andrićgrad** – is a walled historical fantasy and custom-built tourist trap that is well worth a stroll. Although named after author Ivo Andrić, it's a project of Sarajevo-born Serbian film director Emir Kusturica. Completed in 2014, it incorporates accommodation,

WHERE TO SLEEP AND EAT IN VIŠEGRAD

Hotel Višegrad
Spacious rooms and a perfect riverside location with terrace bridge views between trees. €€

Restoran Kruna
Succulent veal, lamb or pork cooked *ispod sača* (roasted under a metal dome) is the speciality here. €

Ćevabdžinica Kasaba
Go for the *ćevapi* or the thinly sliced liver steaks topped with garlic and parsley – delicious. €

cafe-bars, souvenir shops, a gallery, a cinema and an Orthodox church. The architecture is a medley of Byzantine, Ottoman and Renaissance styles, and there are images of Serbian heroes (Andrić, Tesla, Njegoš, Princip) liberally scattered around.

The city's real beauty, however, is the **Mehmed Pasha Sokolović Bridge**. Built in 1571, and named after the grand vizier who commissioned it, the glorious 11-arch bridge is the only structure in Bosnia confirmed as being designed by Mimar Sinan, chief architect for the Ottoman Empire. The bridge rose to international fame after WWII when it played the starring role in Nobel Prize-winner Ivo Andrić's classic novel, *The Bridge on the Drina*. Declared a Unesco World Heritage site in 2007, it has been fully restored and is tastefully floodlit at night.

Sutjeska National Park

A magnificent monument and nature park

Even from the road, it's easy to admire the magnificent tree-dappled grey-rock crags that flank the Sutjeska canyon like scenes from a classical Chinese painting. This splendid national park is a place to leave the asphalt behind, whether hiking or on a mountain bike. Tracks include a section of the multi-country **Via Dinarica** megatrail. You will need a car to get here – it's a two-hour drive from Sarajevo.

You can organise guides and more in Tjentište, the park's only settlement and the site of the **Memorial Complex to the Battle of Sutjeska**.

The park has a network of **mountain-bike and hiking trails**. While these are waymarked, indications aren't as thorough or as frequent as you might hope, though you can arrange guides (preferably in advance) through the National Park Information Office or a specialist adventure agency such as Encijan. Rafting is possible on the Tara River, just outside the national park.

One of the most popular treks leads to **Maglić** (2386m), Bosnia's highest mountain. However, as it briefly crosses the (unguarded) Montenegrin border, be sure to carry your passport. Another popular trail winds among the numerous upland lakes of **Zelengora**. Reaching the **Perućica rainforest** requires you to employ a guide as a condition of entry to what is a more strictly protected zone.

It's worth noting that many of the major trails start with as much as a 20km trip along rough jeep tracks that you could drive if you have a suitable 4WD. There are four trekkers' huts in the mountains for those who want to take longer routes without camping.

TJENTIŠTE: SUTJESKA BATTLE MEMORIAL HOUSE COMPLEX

The Sutjeska Battle Memorial House Complex was built in honour of the Battle of Sutjeska – one of the most difficult and bloodiest WWII battles in Yugoslavia. Designed by sculptor Miodrag Živković in 1971, it is considered one of the best and most complex sculptural memorials in the former Yugoslav region.

The structure consists of a pair of two massive 19m-tall white concrete fractal walls soaring into the sky at a sharp angle, like a pair of wings – almost as if defying gravity. The inner base of the sculpture is made of a series of tightly arranged concrete honeycomb structures that vary in density, which gives it the illusion of floating. It is one of the most popular and widely visited WWII memorial sites in the entire country.

BACKGROUND

The Srebrenica Genocide

The Bosniak Muslim–majority town and municipality of Srebrenica had already been under constant attack by Bosnian Serb forces for a year before the town was declared a 'safe area' by the UN in April 1993, with the support of UNPROFOR troops. As the siege tightened around the town, Srebrenica drew thousands of refugees fleeing from Bosnian Serb assaults on nearby Bosniak villages.

There were an estimated 45,000 desperate people crammed into Srebrenica when, on 11 July 1995, Bosnian Serb forces entered the town following a week-long major offensive. Roughly 400 Dutch peacekeepers proved powerless to influence events, as the victorious forces of Bosnian Serb commander General Ratko Mladić marched another 7km north to the Potočari battery factory, then used as the local UN base. Some 5000 Bosniaks had taken temporary refuge within the base, with many thousands more gathering outside hoping in vain for protection. Instead, the Bosniak women and girls were separated from their menfolk and were eventually bussed out in convoys; many were raped. Over the following days, more than 8000 men and boys were summarily executed at various sites and buried in mass graves.

In 2007 the International Court of Justice upheld earlier rulings by the International Criminal Tribunal for the former Yugoslavia (ICTY) that the massacre, along with mass deportations of more than 20,000 women and elderly, constituted genocide, though a UN vote accepting that definition was vetoed by Russia in 2015. In 2004 the government of the Republika Srpska issued an official apology for the crimes that took place in Srebrenica, based on its own report into what had happened. In 2018, the Republika Srpska government annulled the 2004 report and called for a new probe, and this controversy has yet to be resolved.

Srebrenica Genocide Memorial, Potocari

The old UN base in Potočari now houses the Srebrenica-Potočari Memorial Centre, incorporating a major display entitled Srebrenica Genocide – The Failure of the International Community. You could easily spend hours here, starting by watching a 30-minute film and then examining the photographs, in-depth displays, graffiti left by Dutch peacekeepers and video testimonies of survivors. The deeply moving experience is made all the more intense when accompanied by a guide – likely a survivor whose own family was decimated in the events.

The main focus of the complex is the extensive cemetery directly across the road, with row after sentinel row of pointed white Islamic-style gravestones, each commemorating a reburied victim. More are added each year as the painstaking examination of bone fragments, rotted clothing and DNA samples slowly reveals the identities of more individuals. Within the cemetery, a one-room subterranean photographic gallery powerfully evokes the trauma of this heart-breaking identification process.

Hercegovina

SARAJEVO

MEDITERRANEAN CLIMATE | WINE | ARCHITECTURE

Hercegovina ('hair-tse-go-vi-na') is the sun-scorched southern part of the country, shadowing Croatia's Dalmatian coast. It takes its name from 15th-century duke (*herceg* in the local lingo) Stjepan Vukčić Kosača, under whose rule it became a semi-independent duchy of the Kingdom of Bosnia.

Its arid Mediterranean landscape has a distinctive beauty punctuated by barren mountain ridges and photogenic river valleys. Famed for its fine wines and sun-packed fruits, Hercegovina has beautiful historical towns and fantastic rivers.

These days Western Hercegovina is dominated by Bosnian Croats, while Eastern Hercegovina is part of the Republika Srpska. Bosniak Muslims maintain an uneasy position between the two, especially in the divided but fascinating city of Mostar. Not counting the Catholic pilgrims who flood Međugorje, Mostar is far and away Hercegovina's biggest tourist drawcard. Trebinje is lesser known but has an appealing Old Town.

GETTING AROUND

While Mostar has its own airport, only serving occasional flights to Zagreb, those of Dubrovnik and Split (both in Croatia) are far busier and very close to the border.

The only railway line runs from Čapljina to Mostar and on to Sarajevo through the Neretva Canyon, but the main centres are all well connected by bus.

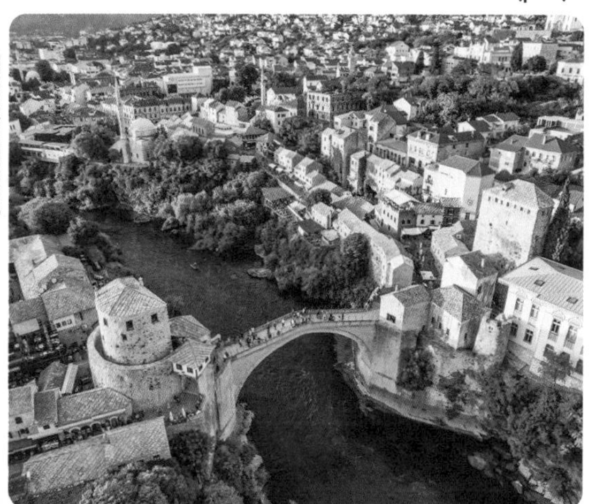

Mostar (p100)

TOP TIP

Between November and April most tourist facilities go into hibernation, while summer here is scorchingly hot. Spring and autumn are ideal times to visit.

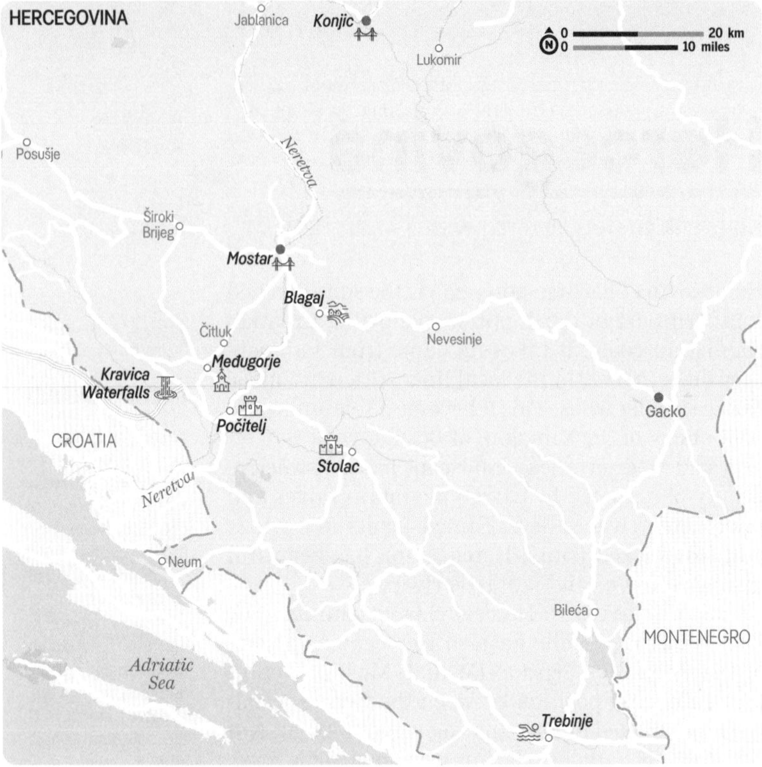

HERCEGOVINA

Jablanica
Konjic
Lukomir
0 20 km
0 10 miles
Posušje
Neretva
Široki Brijeg
Mostar
Blagaj
Čitluk
Nevesinje
Međugorje
Kravica Waterfalls
Počitelj
Gacko
CROATIA
Stolac
Neretva
Neum
Bileća
MONTENEGRO
Adriatic Sea
Trebinje

Wander the Country's Prettiest City

The Balkans' most celebrated bridge

Mostar is the largest city in Hercegovina, with a small but thoroughly enchanting Old Town. At dusk the lights of numerous millhouse restaurants twinkle across gushing streams, narrow **Kujundžiluk** bustles joyously with trinket sellers and, in between, the Balkans' best-known bridge forms a majestic stone arc between medieval towers.

The world-famous **Stari Most** (meaning 'Old Bridge') is Mostar's indisputable heart. Its pale stone magnificently reflects the golden glow of sunset or the tasteful night-time floodlighting. The bridge's swooping arch was originally built between 1557 and 1566 on the orders of Suleiman the Magnificent. An engineering marvel of its

WHERE TO EAT IN MOSTAR

Tima-Irma
Very very very popular for *ćevapi* and grilled meat, in the heart of the Old Town. €

Hindin Han
This highly atmospheric old mill cottage efficiently serves a mixture of local dishes – sit on the terrace. €€

Niđe Veze
One of Mostar's better breakfast spots, a riverside cafe with a lovely shaded terrace. €

age, the bridge was pounded into the river during a deliberate Croatian artillery attack in November 1993.

The current structure is a very faithful 21st-century rebuild, painstakingly reconstructed using 16th-century building techniques and stone sourced from the original quarry. It reopened in 2004 and is now a Unesco World Heritage site. In addition to its perennial **bridge divers**, you can watch the annual diving competition if you're here in late July. In any case, sit in one of the numerous well-positioned cafes and restaurants and savour the splendid view.

Entered from a gated courtyard, the **Koski Mehmed Pasha Mosque** was first built in 1618 and substantially rebuilt after the war. It has a dome painted with botanical motifs and punctuated by coloured-glass windows. You can climb the claustrophobic minaret for sweeping town views. Access to the charming courtyard is free but there is a ticket for the river and Stari Most view.

Mostar's biggest and most beautiful, the **Karadjoz-bey Mosque** was built in 1557. Heavily damaged during the war, it has since been completely renovated with a distinctive lead-roofed wooden veranda and a four-domed madrasa annex.

The late 16th-century **Hammam Museum** is an Ottoman bathhouse that has been attractively restored with white-washed interiors, bilingual panels explaining *hammam* (Turkish bath) culture and glass cabinets displaying associated traditional accoutrements.

Hidden behind tall walls, Mostar's most interesting old house, **Kajtaz House**, was once the harem (women's) section of a larger homestead built for a 16th-century Turkish judge. Full of original artefacts, it still belongs to descendants of the original family but is now under Unesco protection. A visit includes a very extensive personal tour.

Ring the bell to be ushered into **Muslibegović House**, a walled Ottoman courtyard house, built in the late 17th century and extended in 1871. Its main function today is as an atmospheric hotel, but several of the sitting areas are decorated with museum-like collections of artefacts and costumes.

Don't miss the **Partisan Memorial Cemetery**, a 20-minute walk from the Old Town. Although sadly neglected and badly vandalised, fans of 20th-century socialist architecture should seek out this magnificent memorial complex, designed by leading Yugoslav-era architect Bogdan Bogdanović and completed in 1965. Paths wind up past a broken bridge, a no-longer-functioning water feature and cosmological symbols to the upper section made of stone, which contains the gravestones of 810 Mostar Partisans who died fighting fascism during WWII.

MOSTAR'S HISTORY

Mostar means 'bridge-keeper'. In the 16th century, the construction of the iconic stone Stari Most marks the time when Mostar was booming within the Ottoman Empire. Under Austro-Hungarian rule in the 19th century, the city's centre of gravity shifted north to Trg Musala with lovely neo-Moorish buildings.

Before the 1990s conflict, Mostar had one of Yugoslavia's largest proportions of mixed marriages. When the Yugoslav army started bombarding Mostar in April 1992, the city's Bosniaks and Croats banded together, but on 9 May 1993 a conflict erupted between the former allies. A front line emerged north–south along the Bulevar, with Croats to the west and Bosniaks to the east. Every building in the city suffered war damage and around 2000 people lost their lives.

WHERE TO SLEEP IN MOSTAR

Muslibegović House
An extremely charming boutique hotel that mixes modern and Ottoman traditional. **€€**

Pansion Čardak
An old stone house on a central lane has seven spacious en-suite rooms. **€€**

Shangri La
A grand facade, eight individually themed rooms and a fine roof terrace. **€€**

MOSTAR'S SCARS

Start at ❶ **Španski trg**, where a monument honours Spanish peacekeepers killed during the 1990s war. This square was right on the front line. Several shell-pocked buildings remain in ruins, though the main street is slowly being restored, including the apricot neo-Moorish ❷ **Stara Gimnazija** (Old Grammar School, 1902).

Head towards the river and cross over to ❸ **Trg Musala**. The City Baths building (1914) has been restored, and the once-splendid ❹ **Hotel Neretva** (1892) has had scaffolding put around the ruins.

Turn right past the mosque onto the Braće Fejića street. Stop to admire the stonework of the ❺ **Roznamedži Ibrahimefendi Mosque**. Built before 1620, it was the only mosque to survive the war intact. Further along is the beautifully rebuilt ❻ **Karadjoz-bey Mosque**.

Take the next street to the left, past grand ruins, then turn right onto Maršala Tita. Cut through the wartime cemetery. Take the steps up to the 17th-century ❼ **Ottoman clock tower**, which was commissioned by a woman.

Walk back down towards the domed 1564 ❽ **Nesuh-aga Vučijaković Mosque**. Cross the road and take the cobbled lane nearly opposite and turn left past the two tombs onto ❾ **Mala Tepa**. The entrance to the ❿ **Koski Mehmed Pasha Mosque** is to your right.

Continue through the ⓫ **Kujundžiluk Bazaar** to the ⓬ **Stari Most**. After crossing the bridge, take the first lane to your right and enter the ⓭ **Tabhana**, an old tannery complex where the central tanning pond is now a swimming pool. Head out onto the little square for the ⓮ **Hammam Museum** and the ⓯ **Tabačica Mosque**. Cut through to cobbled Oneščukova and the lane heading down to the ⓰ **Crooked Bridge**.

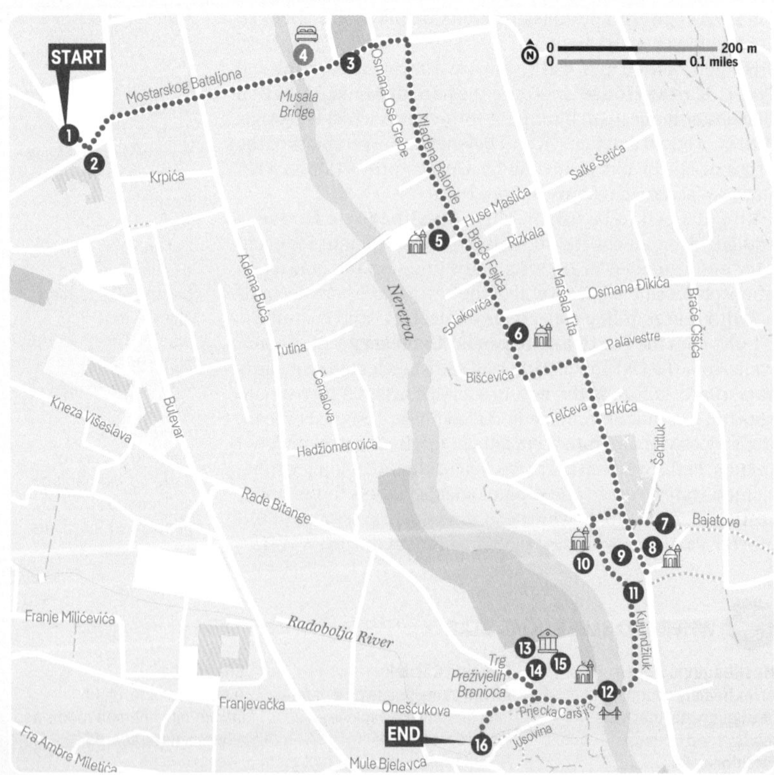

Visit Blagaj's Historical Tekke

A pretty town and turquoise river

An easy day trip from Mostar, pretty Blagaj hugs the turquoise Buna River at its source – it gushes out of a cave past a historical *tekke* (Sufi dervish spiritual house), several enticing restaurants and Ottoman-era homesteads.

Forming Blagaj's signature attraction is **Blagaj Tekke** (Blagajska tekija), and the centrepiece of this complex of traditional stone-roofed buildings is a very pretty half-timbered dervish house with wobbly rug-covered floors, carved doorways, curious niches and a bathroom with star-shaped coloured glass set into the ceiling. The dervishes follow a mystical strand of Islam in which the peaceful contemplation of nature plays a part; hence the idyllic positioning of the *tekke* above the cave mouth from which the Buna River's surreally blue-green waters flow forth. The last sheikh died in 1923 and the *tekke* was inactive for a long period since before WWII. It is now once again a venue for dhikr praise-chanting three nights a week.

In summer you can take a five-minute **boat ride** pulled along on a rope, into the Buna Cave from a landing directly opposite the *tekke*; it is the spring of the Buna, and you can drink the water.

High above Blagaj and accessible only on foot are the hefty ruins of **Stjepan Grad**, a powerful medieval fortress. Although it's been fortified since Roman times, it's named after 15th-century *herceg* (duke) Stjepan Kosača, who had his residence here and from whom the name Hercegovina is derived. A garrison was stationed here up until 1835 when it was abandoned. Allow an hour for the walk up (less back) and wear sturdy shoes.

The Pilgrimage Destination of Međugorje

Honest faith and cash-in tackiness

Međugorje is a Catholic pilgrimage town in the mould of Lourdes (France) or Fatima (Portugal) – although, unlike these, it has never been officially approved by the Vatican. Apart from the affecting Resurrected Saviour statue and the piety of the faithful streaming around St James Church, there's little of beauty here and nonpilgrims generally find a one-hour visit enough to get the idea.

Međugorje's central focus is **St James Church complex**, a rather functional double-towered 1969 church and the parklike

THE HOLY CONTROVERSY

Before it was transformed into a bustling pilgrimage centre, Međugorje was a poor winemaking village. On 24 June 1981 six local teenagers claimed to have experienced a vision of the Virgin Mary on what is now known as Apparition Hill. Three of the six claim to have daily apparitions, while the other three claim at least one a year. The core messages relayed by the visionaries are uncontroversial, calling for peace, prayer, penance and reconciliation.

The Vatican does not officially accept the veracity of the apparitions. A Franciscan priest, Father Tomislav Vlašić, became the children's main advocate and spiritual director, but was subsequently defrocked after allegations of sexual misconduct with a nun. Tensions between the local Franciscans and the broader church are rife.

WHERE TO EAT AND SLEEP IN BLAGAJ

Hotel Blagaj
This neat hotel contrasts white- and lavender-wash walls with sepia scenes of old Mostar. €€

Restoran Vrelo
Across the river from the *tekke*, taste the local trout on terraces overlooking the river rapids. €€

Lax
A 15-minute walk from the *tekke*, Lax has excellent trout, a gorgeous garden and campsite. €€

WHY I LOVE HERCEGOVINA

Vesna Maric, Lonely Planet writer

Hercegovina is where I was born and grew up, until the 1990s war, and I have returned as often as I could for its remarkable nature and cultural flavour. Despite the war and divisions, it remains a diverse region, full of local life. But what I love best about Hercegovina is its nature, and its beautiful light and warmth. There are numerous wild rivers where one can go swimming, excellent mountains for hiking, and more spectacular waterfalls than one can imagine for such a small area.

ROLF E. STAERK/SHUTTERSTOCK ©

Source of the Buna River, Blagaj Tekke (p103)

grounds behind it. The main daily service is a 6pm rosary followed by a 7pm Mass, which in summer is celebrated in the huge outdoor arc behind the church.

A white statue of the Queen of Peace marks **Apparition Hill**, the site of the original 1981 visions on the hillside, 2km from central Međugorje. The trail is rough rock-studded red earth, but a few walk barefoot in deliberately painful acts of penitence. Sculptures representing the rosary's Joyful Mysteries lead straight to the statue, or you can continue with the Sorrowful Mysteries on a longer loop leading up and over the crest of the hill.

Erected in 1933 for the 1900th anniversary of Christ's crucifixion, the **giant cross** on the top of this 520m mountain has been a place of Catholic devotion since well before Međugorje became famous. Although it's marginally more shaded, the climb is tougher than Apparition Hill. The views from the summit are extraordinary, stretching north over Međugorje and west all the way to the Croatian town of Vrgorac.

WHERE TO BOOK A RAFTING TRIP IN KONJIC

RaftKor
Reliable, recommended outfit for rafting. Trips start with a visit to Boračko Lake.

Visit Konjic
Handy central agency offering rafting and canyoning.

Konjic Rafting
Package includes rafting, meals and hostel overnight stay.

Look out from a Hilltop Fortress

A picture-perfect architectural ensemble

The medieval fortress village of **Počitelj** is one of the most beautiful spots in the country. Cupped in a steep rocky amphitheatre, it's a warren of stairways climbing between ramshackle stone-roofed houses and pomegranate bushes.

The village was badly damaged by Bosnian Croat forces in 1993, including the beautiful **Hajji Alija Mosque**. This 1563 structure has now been restored, although photos show a great loss of the decorative paintwork. There are good views from the terrace area, where you'll also see various salvaged fragments of carvings from the original structure.

Nearby is a 16m **Ottoman clock tower**, while further up the hill is a partly ruined fortress, capped by the octagonal **Gavrakapetan Tower**. You can climb up the tower. There are even better panoramas from the uppermost rampart bastions.

Rafting & Surprise Bunker Art in Konjic

Green river and historic town

The small town of Konjic was battered in both WWII and the 1990s war, but has revived its compact historical core centred on a beautiful six-span **Old Stone Bridge**. Originally built in 1682, it was dynamited at the end of WWII by the Nazis and accurately reconstructed in 2009.

Don't miss the extraordinary D-0 ARK, otherwise known as **Tito's Bunker**, designed to keep Yugoslav president Tito and his high command safe from a 25-megaton blast. Built in secret between 1953 and 1979, it is now used for art biennales. It's located 4km southeast of Konjic.

Rafting downstream on the Neretva is extremely popular. RaftKor or Visit Konjic are reliable outfits for rafting and canyoning trips.

All buses and trains going between Sarajevo and Mostar pass through Konjic.

Trebinje Strolls & Coffee Culture

Leafy squares and a rushing river

By far the prettiest city in Republika Srpska, Trebinje has a compact centre with a tiny walled Old Town flanked by a leafy market square. The **Trebišnjica River** is slow and shallow as it passes through, its banks lined with **swimming spots** and replicas of waterwheels. Mountains provide a sunbaked backdrop. It is a three-and-a-half-hour drive from Mostar.

KRAVICE WATERFALLS

There's a slightly unreal Disney-esque quality to this outstanding natural attraction, where the Trebižat River plummets in a broad 25m-high arc into an emerald pool. In spring, this gorgeous mini-Niagara pounds itself into a dramatic, steamy fury. In summer it's a more gentle cascade, but the basin offers an idyllic respite from the sweltering heat for hundreds of locals and tourists. Further downstream, kayaks can be hired. Admission tickets include access to two nearby sights: a monastery museum in Humac and the Koćuša waterfall.

The falls are a 15-minute walk from a car park that's 4km down a dead-end road which is well signposted from the M6 (Čapljina–Ljubuški Rd). There's no public transport

WHERE TO SLEEP AND EAT IN TREBINJE

Hostel Polako
A much-loved hostel with dorms and two private doubles, and shared bathrooms. €

Hotel Platani
On Trebinje's pretty, central square, evoking Austro-Hungarian-era elegance. €€

Sesto Senso
One of Trebinje's best international restaurants, serving everything from local grills to chicken curries. €€

STOLAC & ANCIENT TOMB STONES

Well worth a stop if you're driving from Mostar to Trebinje, Stolac is one of Hercegovina's prettiest castle towns, with a history going back to Roman times. Near Stolac are two sets of classic *stećci* (grave-carvings), listed as World Heritage sites by Unesco since 2016. Beside the Mostar road, 3km west of Stolac, is the famous **Radimlja Necropolis** with around 110 white stone blocks intricately carved.

While less celebrated than the *stećci* at Radimlja, the 270 **Boljuni Stećci** – arranged in two groups under venerable oak trees – feature the cross-shaped tombstone of warrior-hero Vlatko Vuković. Boljuni is 12km from Stolac, 4.2km off the Stolac–Neum road, itself a narrow, rural delight passing right beside the **Hutovo fortress** ruins.

ELDAR NURKOVIC/SHUTTERSTOCK ©

Radimlja Necropolis

It's barely 30km from Dubrovnik, but in tourist terms, it's a world away – not to mention vastly cheaper. Some canny travellers base themselves here and 'commute'.

Trebinje's central point is **Trg Slobode** (Freedom Sq) with chestnut trees and stone-flagged pavements, old stone buildings with wrought-iron overhangs, and appealing street cafes. Directly to the southeast, shaded by mature plane trees, is **Dučić Trg**, the site of a morning vegetable market.

The **Arslanagić Bridge** is a unique double-backed structure built in 1574 under the direction of Grand Vizier Mehmed Pasha Sokolović. It was originally 10km further upstream from its present location but in 1965 it disappeared beneath the rising waters of the Gorica reservoir. Rescued stone by stone, it took six years to reassemble.

Offering phenomenal views, **Hercegovačka Gračanica** is a hilltop complex comprising a bell tower, gallery, cafe-bar and bishop's palace, but most notably the compact but eye-catching **Presveta Bogorodica (Annunciation) Church**. The latter's design is based very symbolically on the 1321 Gračanica Monastery in Kosovo, a historically significant building that's considered sacred by many Serbs. The Trebinje version was erected in 2000 to rehouse the bones of local poet-hero Serb nationalist Jovan Dučić.

SARAJEVO

Western Bosnia

NATURE | CASTLES | HISTORY

Travelling through this region of green wooded hills, river canyons, rocky crags and mildly interesting historical towns, you'll find yourself constantly passing in and out of Federation of Bosnia and Hercegovina territory and the Republika Srpska. You'll always know when you're in the latter by the red-blue-and-white Serbian flags that sprout in profusion whenever you enter it. Prominent towns include the old Ottoman administrative capital Travnik, the gorgeous hilltop settlement of Jajce, and Republika Srpska's quasi-capital Banja Luka. In the west, the Una River gushes flamboyantly over a series of waterfalls before joining the Sava on its rush to the Danube and, ultimately, the Black Sea.

Waterfall, Jajce (p108)

GETTING AROUND

Banja Luka is the region's biggest city and transport hub, though Bihać is also well connected.

Bus-hopping from Sarajevo via Visoko, Travnik and Jajce to Banja Luka is relatively straightforward and the last leg takes you through the Vrbas Canyons. Jajce to Bihać is also easy by bus.

Visiting the Una River Valley is more complicated without a vehicle, though buses do run to Kulen Vakuf. Various Una rafting companies offer client pickups from Bihać.

TOP TIP

Visiting the Una River Valley is complicated without a vehicle, so you're best advised to rent a car to really take in the best of the region.

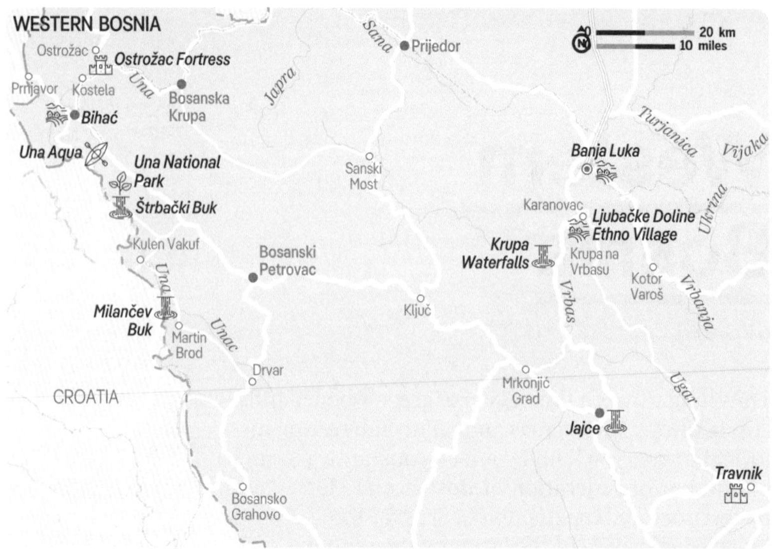

CATACOMBS OF JAJCE

Jajce was the capital of the medieval Kingdom of Bosnia until it fell to the Ottomans briefly in 1459 and more permanently in 1527. The ruins of the church where the Bosnian kings were crowned can still be seen; it was converted into a mosque but fell into disrepair after a fire in the 1830s.

Built around 1400 CE for the aristocratic Hrvatinić family, this two-level crypt is small and roughly hewn but artfully half-lit and notable for the boldly sculpted cross, sun and crescent moon motifs (downstairs), a rare surviving memorial to the independent Bosnian Church. Tito is said to have hidden here during 1943.

The Historic Capital of Bosnian Kings

History, two rivers, and a waterfall

Jajce is a historical gem, with a highly evocative walled Old Town clinging to a steep rocky knoll with rivers on two sides. The Pliva River tumbles into the Vrbas River by way of an impressive 21m high **urban waterfall** right at the very foot of the town walls. Immediately to the west, the Pliva is dammed to form two pretty **lakes** that are popular with swimmers, strollers, bikers and boaters.

A **viewing platform** (adult/child 4/2KM) has been built opposite the waterfall's base, accessed from stairs that start between the bus station and the petrol station. In the first week in August, daredevils leap from the waterfall in an **annual competition** featuring around 30 professional divers.

Jajce's **fortress ruins** have a powerful aspect when seen from afar, but inside is mostly bald grass. The ramparts offer sweeping views of the valleys and crags that surround Jajce's urban sprawl, though views of the fortress are generally more memorable than views from it. The castle's most photographed feature is the partially conserved Kotromanić stone crest beside the entrance portal, and you don't have to enter to see that.

Two idyllic **lakes**, west of Jajce, reflect the surrounding wooded mountains in their clear waters and are popular for boating and simply strolling or cycling around. Between them lie the **Mlinčići**, a cute collection of 20 tiny wooden watermills. At the bottom of the lower, smaller lake, boardwalks cross a pretty set of rivulets spilling into a dam basin, which is a popular swimming spot.

Travnik, the Birthplace of Ivo Andrić

Castle, cheese and Nobel author

Once the seat of Bosnia's viziers (Ottoman governors), the castle town of Travnik is now best known for its sheep's cheese and as the birthplace of Nobel Prize–winning author Ivo Andrić, who set his classic novel *Bosnian Chronicle (The Days of the Consuls)* here. It's a pleasant place to spend a couple of hours while travelling between Sarajevo and Jajce.

Travnik's 15th-century **Old Town Fortress** surveys the city from a shoulder of hillside. The stone walls gleam so brightly in the sunshine that they appear to have been scrubbed. The fortress looks over **Plava Voda** ('Blue Water'), a convivial gaggle of restaurants flanking a merrily gurgling stream, crisscrossed by small bridges – you should definitely have your lunch here.

Although officially called Sulejmanija Mosque, everyone in Travnik calls this **Šarena Džamija** (Many-Coloured Mosque), a longstanding nickname that references its famous frescoed facade. The colours have since faded but the building remains notable for the *bezistan* (mini-bazaar) built into the stone arched arcade. There's been a mosque here, at Travnik's

VIA DINARICA: THE WHITE TRAIL

The Bosnian section of the White Trail enters the country south of Buško Lake in Hercegovina and cuts east between Konjic and Mostar before heading northeast through Bjelašnica and then southeast through Sutjeska National Park.

The supporting infrastructure is still being developed, so you're wise to seek advice before setting out; refer to the official website or to that of the Via Dinarica Alliance (via-dinarica.org), which arranges tours and promotes tourist activity along the way.

The best of the Bosnian sections is the well-established and beautiful path through Sutjeska National Park, taking in **Maglić** (2386m), Bosnia's highest mountain.

Plava Voda

WHERE TO SLEEP AND EAT IN JAJCE

Hotel Stari Grad
This comfortable little hotel has wood beams and panelling and a heraldic fireplace. **€€**

Kod Asima
Central Jajce's most atmospheric eatery has soup, goulash, and the usual grills. **€**

Konoba Slapovi
This magical tavern is perched above a horseshoe weir. Serves fish and slow-roasted veal. **€€**

RAFTING THE UNA

Rafting is a draw here; in addition, there's kayaking and 'speed river diving', a sport invented here involving scuba diving in fast-flowing waters. Each activity centre has its own campsite and provides transfers from Bihać.

Various companies offer rafting, particularly on the 15km stretch from Štrbački Buk to Lohovo within the national park. The best months for white water are April and May, after the spring melts, when it's graded level 3 to 5. **Una Aqua** rafting centre is an attraction in itself, comprising five small islands interlinked with wooden bridges. There's a good swimming spot, a restaurant, a campsite and a tree house cabin raised on stilts above a super-comfy waterside hammock. Three different rafting routes are offered.

centre point, since the 16th century. Its current form dates from 1757, although it was largely reconstructed after a major fire in 1815.

Don't miss the **Viziers' Graves**, a collection of finely carved *turbe* (tombs) of Bosnia's Ottoman governors, clustered at the western end of the main shopping strip, along with those of prominent court officials and poets.

See the Cascades of the Una River Valley

A lush river of greens and opals

The adorable **Una River** goes through widely varying moods. In the lush green gorges to the northeast, some sections are as calm as mirrored opal, while others gush over widely fanned rafting rapids. The river broadens and gurgles over a series of shallow falls as it passes through the unassuming town of **Bihać**. Occasionally it leaps over impressive falls, notably at Štrbački Buk, which forms the centrepiece of the 198-sq-km **Una National Park**.

Ostrožac Fortress is one of Bosnia's most photogenic castles, a spooky Gothic place high above the Una Valley. There's plenty to explore from various epochs, ramparts to walk, towers to climb and a manor house on the verge of collapse. Off-season you might have to call the caretaker to get in, but it's only officially closed if it's snowing.

A strong contender for the title of the nation's most impressive waterfall, **Štrbački Buk** is a seriously dramatic 40m-wide cascade, pounding 23.5m down three travertine sections, including over a superbly photogenic 18m drop-off, overlooked by a network of viewing platforms. The easiest access is 8km along a graded but potholed unpaved road from Orašac on the Kulen Vakuf road. There are swimming spots to stop at along the way.

Collectively, **Milančev Buk** is a group of cascades that tumbles down a vertical height of more than 50m, with a wide arc of rivulets pouring into a series of pools surrounded by lush, green foliage. Make sure you check out the view from the red footbridge near the car park.

Banja Luka, Bosnia's Second City

A fascinating mosque and church

Banja Luka is the second-biggest city in Bosnia and the de facto capital of Republika Srpska, but there's very little here to detain travellers for long. After Serb nationalists systematically destroyed most of the city's historical and cultural heritage – including mosques, Catholic churches, a historical

WHERE TO EAT AND DRINK IN TRAVNIK

Garbun
Within the fortress walls, this is a lovely place to observe Travnik over a coffee. €

Lutvina Kahva
This Moorish cube of a cafe was the Lutvo's Cafe featured in Ivo Andrić's *Bosnian Chronicle* novel. €

Konoba Plava Voda
This tavern's tempting summer terrace occupies a perfect spot above a gurgling stream. €€

UTA SCHOLL/SHUTTERSTOCK ©

Ferhadija Mosque

clock tower and various 16th-century buildings – a rather bland, soulless place was left.

Two rebuilt religious buildings are now the city's biggest drawcards. The first is the beautiful **Ferhadija Mosque**, Banja Luka's standout sight, built in 1579 at the behest of Ottoman district commander Ferhat-paša Sokolović. It was under Unesco protection when, in 1993, it was deliberately destroyed as part of a brutal campaign which saw non-Serbs expelled from the city. A meticulous reconstruction commenced in 2001, using 16th-century techniques and incorporating around 60% of the original masonry rescued from various dumps. It was completed in 2016.

Banja Luka's Orthodox **Cathedral of Christ the Saviour** is an impressive structure of layered gold-brown and crab-pink stones, golden domes and an unfeasibly tall free-standing bell tower. The interior has a splendid iconostasis and a dazzling image of Christ on the main dome. The church was damaged by Nazi bombers, then demolished by the Ustaša (Croatian fascist) regime. The reconstruction commenced in 1993 and was completed in 2004.

Aside from these two, you can wander around the chunky walls of **Kastel Fortress**, though it's mainly unremarkable parkland. It's thought there's been a fort here since Neolithic and Roman times, but Kastel's current look is largely 16th century.

WATERFALLS & VILLAGES: AROUND BANJA LUKA

Secluded in the Vrbas River Valley, between Banja Luka and Jajce, **Krupa Waterfalls** are exceedingly pretty, with a set of log-built mill huts with their own millraces. A path follows the stream up through mossy woodland beyond the mills. The waterfalls are a short stroll from a car park lined with cafes, 700m off the main M16 road.

The **Ljubačke Doline Ethno Village** consists of around 30 rescued and reconstructed historical rural buildings, packed with rustic artefacts on a pretty hillside meadow. The inviting 'museum' section, with a little room of Yugoslav nostalgia, doubles as bar-restaurant with forest juices and traditional meals (when available); it also offers accommodation. It is 20km south of central Banja Luka.

MOHD EDZWAN KAMARUZMAN/SHUTTERSTOCK ©

Sarajevo International Airport

Arriving

Bosnia has four main international airports, although only Sarajevo has an extensive range of flights. Depending on where in the country you're heading to, it's often worth comparing prices on flights to Dubrovnik, Split or Zagreb in Croatia, then connecting to Bosnia by land. Belgrade (Serbia) and Podgorica (Montenegro) are also options.

By Air

Sarajevo International Airport is Bosnia's busiest, with flights all over Europe and the Middle East. Tuzla International Airport is tiny but a hub for budget airline Wizz Air, with flights to Austria, Switzerland, Germany, the Netherlands and Sweden.

By Land

Bosnia has multiple border crossings with Croatia, Serbia and Montenegro. Direct bus connections link Bosnia to all of its neighbours and to as far afield as Sweden.

Money

Currency: Bosnian Convertible Mark (KM)

ATMS
ATMs accepting Visa and Mastercard are ubiquitous in city centres and towns, but will charge around 10KM for withdrawals. Before withdrawing money, check the different ATM charges to find the cheapest bank.

CREDIT CARDS
Top-end hotels, airline offices and upmarket boutiques and restaurants generally accept major credit cards, and you will be able to pay by card at most restaurants nowadays. Cash is safest in budget options across the board, in eating, sleeping or drinking spots.

DIGITAL PAYMENTS
You can use digital payment in fancier restaurants and hotels, and many shops, but it can be unreliable, so make sure you always have cash with you.

Getting Around

Transport in Bosnia and Hercegovina is reasonably priced and generally efficient. Bus services are excellent and relatively inexpensive, while trains are slower, less extensive and cheaper. Driving is the best way to really explore the country – cars can be hired in every city or larger town. Cyclists who can handle the hills will find Bosnia and Hercegovina's secondary routes helpfully calm.

TRAIN

Trains are slower and far less frequent than buses, but generally slightly cheaper. ŽFBH (zfbh.ba) has an online rail timetable search. The main routes are Sarajevo–Visoko–Bihać and Sarajevo–Konjic–Mostar.

MARCIN JUCHA/SHUTTERSTOCK ©

Rural Steppe, Bosnia

BUS

Bus services are excellent and relatively inexpensive. There are often different companies handling each route, so prices can vary substantially. Luggage stowed in the baggage compartment under the bus costs extra (around 2KM a piece). Bus stations presell tickets.

BICYCLE

There are off-road trails for mountain bikers, notably around Bjelašnica, but beware of straying from them in areas where landmines remain a danger.

PUBLIC TRANSPORT IN SARAJEVO

Sarajevo's public transport consists of trams, trolley buses and city buses. As a visitor, if you go to places that are outside of the city centre, make sure you buy a ticket at a kiosk before boarding, and validate it onboard as you enter.

CAR

Driving makes sense to reach the country's more remote areas. There are a few toll motorways in the centre of the country; collect your ticket from the machine at the set of booths where you enter, then pay at the booths where you leave the motorway.

DRIVING ESSENTIALS

Drive on the right.

It's compulsory to carry a first-aid kit, warning triangle, reflective vest and spare-bulb kit.

Speed limits are 130km/h on tolled motorways, 100km/h on other dual carriageways, 80km/h on rural roads, 60km/h or less in town.

CLEMENT LEONARD/GETTY IMAGES ©

Above: View of Dubrovnik from Fort Minčeta (p171). Right: Hvar (p153)

Croatia

LIVING UP TO THE HYPE

A must-visit destination since *Game of Thrones* showcased the country's magnificent architecture and coastline, Croatia is still having its moment in the sun.

Dazzling ancient cities and medieval towns, eight national parks, famous lakes and waterfalls, rugged mountain ranges, islands for days (and days) and mesmerising crystal-blue waters at sun-drenched beaches – Croatia quite literally has it all, meaning myriad holiday opportunities await. The question is – what trip are you looking for?

Tourism to the country is nothing new, mind. The Habsburg Empire set up shop on the coast 140 years ago and opened bijou health resorts, many of which are still open, with updated approaches to wellness. Later came President Josip Broz Tito's push for international guests in the 1960s and '70s, pouring funding into impressively modern hotel architecture that lined the coast and creating Croatia's first tourism industry.

This came to a halt during the Homeland War from 1991 to 1995, when the nation was engaged in battles with its fellow ex-Yugoslavia neighbours. While the country recovered, it took a couple of decades for travellers to return in significant numbers – but today they're most certainly back, with 19.6 million visitor arrivals in 2019. Not bad for a country with a population of four million. And with a nascent gastronomy scene, natural wonders galore, endless beaches to laze on and millennia of history to explore, Croatia's popularity isn't set to wane any time soon.

THE MAIN AREAS

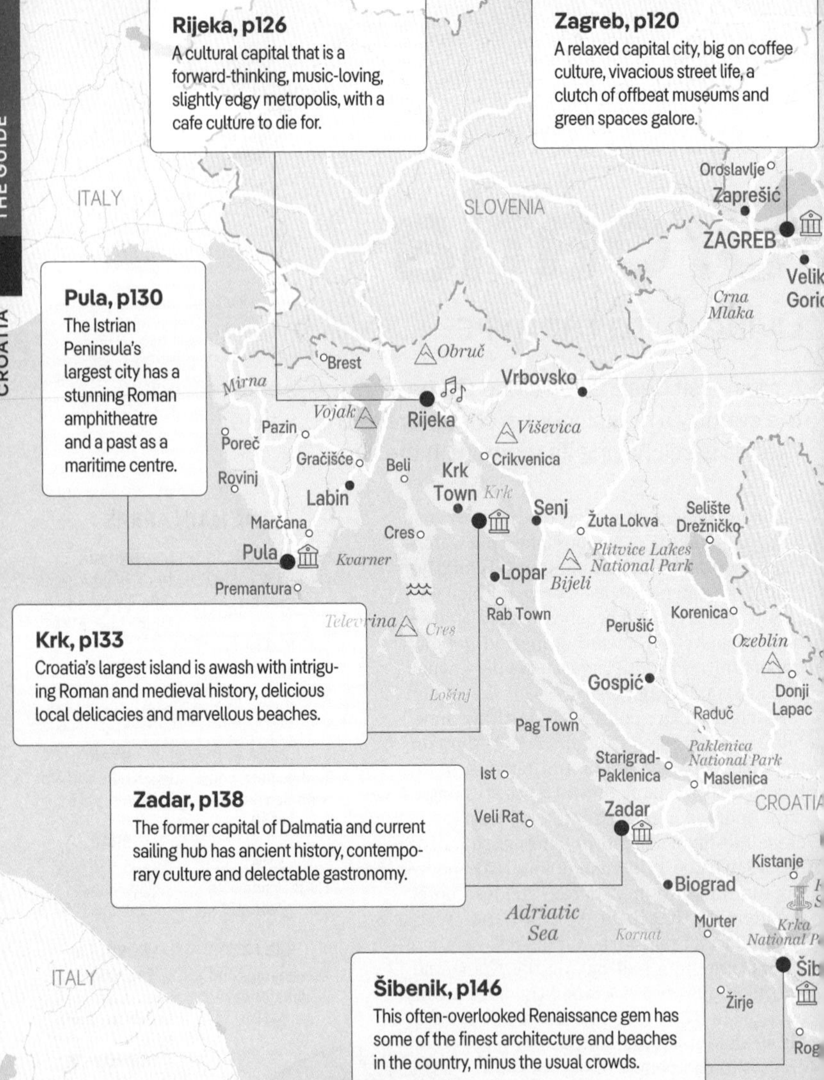

Find Your Way

Smooth, winding coast roads with incredible views link the mainland villages, towns and cities of this long, thin, predominantly coastal country – but the rural inland areas are just as scenic and peaceful to explore.

FERRY

Ferry links in Croatia are cheap and efficient, so reaching the islands is entirely doable DIY, no matter your transport situation. National ferry company Jadrolinija connects the mainland to all of the inhabited islands throughout the year.

CAR

Driving a car is the easiest way to explore Croatia, particularly if you plan to visit some of the rural, off-the-beaten-path gems. Best rental prices are found in Zagreb or Rijeka.

BUS

Croatia has a vast bus network, operated by local companies such as Arriva and international fleets like the Flixbuses that often travel the length of the country and are the quickest intercity option.

Split, p148

Croatia's second city was built around the walls of its Roman-era palace. Its other main draws are a lively seaside promenade and sandy beaches.

Brač, p158

A vast and mountainous isle famous for extraordinary Zlatni Rat beach, exceptional white stone and high-quality olive oil.

Hvar, p153

Hvar Island entices with its pretty port towns, a Unesco site and superb beaches.

Korčula, p160

Many will tell you this is Croatia's most heavenly island and, with Korčula's wine, beaches and good life, they'd be right.

Dubrovnik, p166

Outstanding architecture, magical beaches, seafood for dinner and kayaks galore.

Plan Your Time

Timing is everything in Croatia, a country with 48 inhabited islands to explore and seasonal ferry and flight schedules, so plan in advance.

A Quick City Break

- Top of everyone's city break list is busy **Dubrovnik** (p166), which deserves the notoriety; wide, marble-paved boulevards lined with monumental baroque churches and gothic palaces dazzle visitors, while glorious beaches neighbouring the old city are the perfect place to rest after a few days sightseeing.

- Laid-back **Zadar** (p138) has an up-and-coming food scene, national parks nearby and sailing companies just waiting to whisk you away to the islands.

- And of course **Zagreb** (p120) is a city to visit all year round – the capital is packed with lively cafes, museums and music venues to dive into.

FRANK FELL MEDIA/SHUTTERSTOCK ©

St Anastasia's Church and Belltower (p140), Zadar

Seasonal Highlights

Croatia gets undeniably busy in the summer. If you can, visit during spring or autumn for the same gorgeous scenery but fewer fellow travellers. The country has lots of traditional events:

FEBRUARY

The bombastic **Rijeka Carnival** (p128) is usually in early to mid-February. Or head to Dubrovnik for the mighty **Feast of St Blaise**.

APRIL

Spring is the time to wade through the forests of **Istria** foraging for wild asparagus and garlic, both local delicacies.

MAY

Split celebrates its patron, Sv Duje (St Domnius) during **Sudajma**, a festive week-long blow-out culminating on 7 May.

FROM LEFT: MADRUGADA VERDE/SHUTTERSTOCK ©, GORAN_SAFAREK/SHUTTERSTOCK ©, WALTER9X, CC BY SA 3.0, VIA WIKIMEDIA COMMONS ©

A Week to Spare

● The winning first-timers' trip to Croatia begins with a couple of nights in **Split** (p148), taking in the ancient Roman city centre inside Diocletian's Palace, the local beach bars and cool restaurants, before taking the ferry to one or two of the Dalmatian islands.

● After a couple of nights in **Hvar** (for partying; p153), **Brač** (for beaches; p158) or **Korčula** (for wineries; p160), depending on your priorities, ferry onwards for a final few days in **Dubrovnik** (p166), the 'Pearl of the Adriatic', whose awesome architecture, lovely sands and all round elegance make the crowds worthwhile.

Slow Travel Sojourn

● If you're location-independent or travelling long term, renting a place for a month as a base to explore from can save a lot of euros and ease the pace of travel. **Split** (p148) is the most popular place for digital nomads, but **Zadar** (p138) and **Dubrovnik** (p166) also have expat scenes worth discovering.

● If you're looking for an extended break to switch off and relax, a month on an island like **Korčula** (p160) or at a mainland spot like rural Istria rewards long-stay visitors with quaint, less-frequented villages steeped in local culture, food and tradition – as well as incredible wineries.

JULY

Don't miss the three day **žlahtina wine festival** in the idyllic small village of Vrbnik (p135) in Krk, where the vineyards are based.

AUGUST

The **Light is Life Festival** in Šibenik (p146) shines on 28 August every year.

SEPTEMBER

The annual **rowboat regatta** in Mali Lošinj (p136) and **barrel regatta** in Veli Lošinj (p136) celebrate the island's strong nautical traditions.

DECEMBER

Advent festivities have done much to extend Zagreb's season, bringing droves of visitors to the capital for its now famous **Christmas markets**.

Zagreb

MUSEUMS | CAFE CULTURE | MARKETS

GETTING AROUND

Zagreb Electric Tram, better known as ZET, runs through the Upper and Lower Towns in the centre, and buses then cover where trams don't go, meaning you can easily take public transportation to most places in the capital. Buy tickets from kiosks, the driver or via the Moj ZET app.

The oldest part of Zagreb, the Upper Town (Gornji Grad), is a storybook maze of cobblestone streets and squares wonderful for roaming around. Spread across two hills, Gradec and Kaptol, connected by a string of staircases and passageways, this area is where the city originally began back in medieval times. When the two settlements merged in 1850, Zagreb was officially born.

Today, the Upper Town streets are speckled with landmark buildings that range from baroque palaces, neoclassical mansions, medieval towers and neogothic churches, all from various stages of Zagreb's history. While pockets of the Upper Town may appear sleepy and abandoned, its feast of historic architecture features dashes of vibrant life – from perennially full cafe-bars along buzzy Tkalčićeva street to quirky museums and leafy viewpoints. It's also the location for many events, from wintertime advent markets to festivals throughout spring and summer.

TOP TIP

Brace yourself for a loud blast at noon sharp. You'll likely get startled but fear not: it's just the Grič cannon being fired from the Lotrščak Tower to mark midday, as it has for the last 100 years. Locals set their watches by it.

Capital Museum Hopping

Discover the city's cool collections

The **Museum of Broken Relationships** explores the mementoes left over after a relationship ends, with displays of items donated from around the globe ranging from the hilarious to the heartbreaking. Each comes with a story attached. The **Museum of Illusions** is heaps of fun and a fantastic little sensory adventure that started in Zagreb in 2015 and has since spread with franchises across the world. The Slanted Room and Mirror of Truth are among 70+ intriguing exhibits, hologram pictures and puzzles. For a more traditional but extremely interesting collection, the **Ethnographic Museum**, housed in a domed 1903 building on Mažuranićev trg, has vast displays, including ceramics, jewellery, musical instruments, tools, weapons and folk costumes, from Slavonia

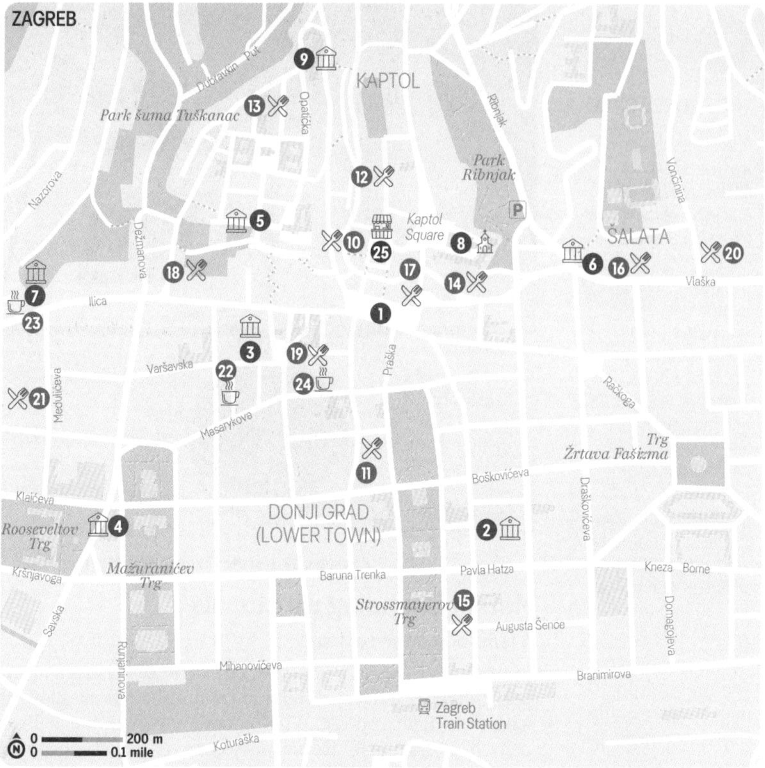

ZAGREB

HIGHLIGHTS
1 Trg Bana Jelačića

SIGHTS
2 Cannabis Museum
3 Chocolate Museum
4 Ethnographic Museum
5 Museum of Broken Relationships
6 Museum of Hangovers
7 Museum of Illusions
8 Zagreb Cathedral
9 Zagreb City Museum

EATING
10 Amfora
11 Bistro Fotić
12 Curry Bowl
13 Didov San
14 Gajbica
15 Lari & Penati
16 Mali Bar
17 Pod Zidom
18 Stari Fijaker
19 Submarine
20 Vegehop
21 Zrno

DRINKING & NIGHTLIFE
22 Cogito Coffee
23 Eliscaffe
24 Quahwa

SHOPPING
25 Dolac Market

and the island of Pag. Though the whole of central Zagreb is like an open-air museum, another actual museum worth popping into is **Zagreb City Museum**, inside the 17th-century Convent of St Claire, which presents the history of the city, including archaeological finds unearthed during the building's restoration in the 1990s, and socialist-era paraphernalia. Finally check out the interactive exhibits at the **Chocolate Museum**, learn the difference between hemp, cannabis and marijuana (very much illegal in Croatia) at the **Cannabis Museum** and take in a bunch of drunken tales and play inebriated darts at the **Museum of Hangovers** (best with a group).

THE ZAGREB CARD

Purchase this card for free transport all around the city, entry to five museums (Museum of Broken Relationships; Chocolate Museum; Zagreb City Museum; Museum of Contemporary Art; Nikola Tesla Technical Museum) and the Zagreb Zoo. You can choose the 24-hour (for €20) or the 72-hour card (€26), available from the visitor centres as well as from a number of hotels, and online. Find out more at zagrebcard.com.

ZVONIMIR ATLETIC/SHUTTERSTOCK ©

Zagreb city statute, Zagreb City Museum (p121)

Market Shopping with locals

A feast of food and colours

Indulge your senses at busy, central **Dolac farmers' market**, dotted with red parasols and countless stalls overflowing with fresh fruit and veg. With its pops of colour, the 'belly of Zagreb' offers a field day for photo ops. This place has been trader-central since the 1930s when the city authorities set up a market space on the 'border' between the Upper and Lower Towns. Vendors from all over Croatia descend here on a daily basis to hawk their garden-fresh produce. The main part is on an elevated square; the street level has indoor stalls selling meat, dairy and flowers. The stalls at the northern end of the market are packed with locally produced honey, oil, handicrafts and fast-food kiosks.

The Buzz of Trg Bana Jelačića

Mingle with locals on the main square

Zagreb's main orientation point, the separation line between the Upper and Lower Towns and its geographic heart is **Trg Bana Jelačića**. If you enjoy people-watching, sit in one of the cafes and observe the tramloads of people getting on and off,

WHERE TO EAT IN ZAGREB

Submarine
Great choice for yummy burgers, with several locations around the city centre. Their plant-based options are tops. €

Bistro Fotić
Cosy bistro that dishes out pizzas, pastas and quiches, in eclectically decorated interiors. €€

Gajbica
Great salads, soups and stews, loads of gluten-free options and delicious raw cakes. Tiny space; lunch time only. €

greeting each other and dispersing among the newspaper kiosks and flower stalls along the strip towards Dolac Market. The square's name is a tribute to Ban Jelačić, the 19th-century *ban* (governor) who led Croatian troops into an unsuccessful battle with Hungary in the hope of winning more autonomy for his people. Today, the equestrian statue of Jelačić and the clock tower nearby are the main rendezvous points for city inhabitants meeting up.

Zagreb's Coffee Culture

From bean to cup to ritual

Coffee in Croatia has always been deeply ingrained in its culture, with a strong social aspect. Pretty much everything happens over *kava* (coffee), from business and gossip to catching up and first dates. If a Zagreb local has time on their hands, chances are you'll find them sipping a cup of joe at a cafe.

This love of coffee provided the perfect setting for the rise of speciality brews in the capital, which have become one of the city's top draws. Among the first to kick off the movement was **Eliscaffe** on Ilica, right off Britanac, roasting their own 100% arabica beans and serving a mean *triestino* (a Trieste-style large macchiato in a glass). Then came **Cogito Coffee**, Croatia's top boutique roaster adjacent to the artsy Café U Dvorištu, devoted to sourcing in-season fresh coffee beans and seeing the process through all the way to that delicious cup of coffee you'll drink at one of their Zagreb locations (they have four, plus two in Dubrovnik and one in Philadelphia). Another roastery and coffee shop worth checking out is **Quahwa**, tucked away in a courtyard off Teslina; it serves up some of the finest arabica in Zagreb, from superstrong lattes to traditional Turkish coffee. Other places not to miss for fantastic speciality coffee are Express Bar on Petrinjska, Luta on Bauerova off Martićeva, Monocycle on Kneza Mislava and Filteraj, a plant-based zero-waste cafe on Vlaška.

Take a Tour

See Zagreb with a twist

If you don't feel like traipsing up and down the cobblestones of the Upper Town and traversing the sights of the Lower Town on foot, you can get on a hop-on, hop-off **Zagreb City Tour Panoramic Bus** (zagrebcitytour.com). These depart from Palmotićeva 2 several times a day and make seven stops around the city centre.

For walking tours with an edge, book with **Secret Zagreb** (secret-zagreb.com), led by the inspiring storyteller Iva Silla.

ZAGREB CATHEDRAL

The twin spires of Zagreb Cathedral, Croatia's largest religious building, have soared over the city for eight centuries. It was closed and under lace-like scaffolding at the time of research for repairs after a 2020 earthquake, which tore off the top of the southern spire and caused other damage.

WHERE TO TRY TRADITIONAL DISHES IN ZAGREB

Didov San
Rustic tavern serving cuisine of the Neretva River delta, including grilled eel and prosciutto-wrapped frog. €€

Stari Fijaker
Sample old-school Croatian and central European staples while soaking up the atmosphere of yesteryear. €€

Amfora
Right by the fishmonger's in Dolac, an unexpected frozen-in-time spot serving fresh seafood from next door. €

PUTTING THE 'FUN' IN FUNICULAR

The iconic blue Zagreb funicular, said to be the world's shortest cable railway used for public transport, has connected the Lower and Upper Towns since 1890. The ride takes 64 seconds, has fun views and costs just €0.66. Catch it from Tomićeva street, just off Ilica, up to the Lotrščak Tower.

MIROSLAV POSAVEC/SHUTTERSTOCK ©

Varying in theme, tours range from the Badass Women of Zagreb and Sleeping Dragon & Other Legends to The Real City tour, which involves a tram ride to Novi Zagreb. You can also sign up for a historical figure-themed walking tour, following in the footsteps of Tito (more at walkwithtito.com) or Tesla, learning what inspired the brilliant inventor and visionary as you stroll through the city checking out the sites (teslatourcroatia.com).

On a self-guided tour, keep your eyes peeled for the results of Zagreb's booming street art scene, including some amazing murals and stencils. Or for a curated experience, book a walking tour with graffiti artist Krešimir Golubić aka **Leon GSK** (via leongsk.com).

Lakeside Fun at Jarun

Explore the 'sea of Zagreb'

Located in south Zagreb, **Jarun** is a popular getaway for residents at any time of the year, but especially in summer, when the clear waters of its artificial lake are ideal for swimming. Although part of the lake is marked off for boating

WHERE TO GO VEGGIE IN ZAGREB

Zrno
Airy bistro serving vegan and vegetarian meals, with many of the ingredients from their nearby organic farm. **€€**

Vegehop
Small eatery dishing out tasty lunches that change daily; in a courtyard off Vlaška. **€**

Curry Bowl
Spicy Sri Lankan favourites on Tkalčićeva, with good veggie options among them. **€**

Jarun

competitions (rowing, kayaking and canoeing), there is still plenty of space to enjoy a leisurely dip.

Other recreational options include biking on its many paths, rollerblading and kids' playgrounds. On arrival, head left to Malo Jezero for swimming and canoe or pedal-boat rental, or right to Veliko Jezero, where there's a pebble beach and windsurfing.

Wander Croatia's Biggest Flea Market

Take a trip out to Hrelić

Croatia's largest and most colourful flea market, **Hrelić** is a huge space packed with everything from car parts and antique furniture to clothes, records and kitchenware – or 'from needle to a locomotive', as their tagline goes. It's a side of Zagreb you don't see anywhere else in the city – expect lots of Roma people, music and grilled meat smoking in the food section. It's way out of the centre, but there are bus connections to get there. It's open until 3pm on both Wednesdays and Sundays.

Ride Sljeme Cable Car

Hit the heights

The new cable car from the station in Dolje, accessible by tram from the centre, whisks you up to Sljeme, the top of Medvednica Mountain, in 20 minutes. The gondola ride can be shaky but the views of the city along the way are striking. Once at the summit, visit the newly opened lookout at Sljeme Tower, at an altitude of 1118m, for the best panorama over the capital. A rotating restaurant and a zip line are in the pipeline too.

TOP FOR PANORAMAS

The Upper Town is the most scenic vantage point for catching wide views of Zagreb spread out below. Among the best spots to do so is the Strossmayer promenade or Stross, as locals call this leafy promenade that was the city's first public walkway, today filled with chestnut trees and benches.

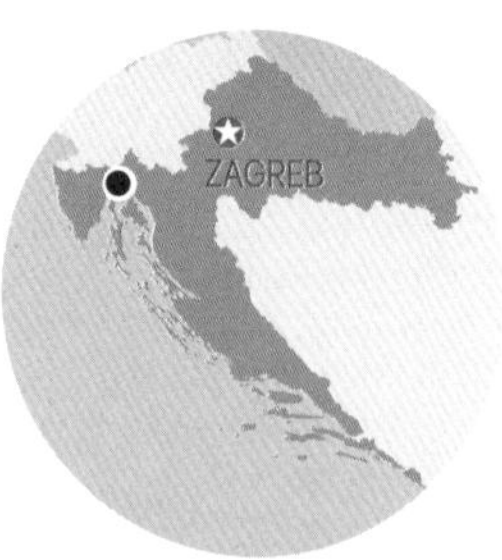

Rijeka

AUSTRO-HUNGARIAN HERITAGE | CARNIVAL | MUSIC

GETTING AROUND

Rijeka is a walkable, compact city with cultural venues and restaurants all in close proximity to each other, transected by a large pedestrianised boulevard lined with cafes and shops. It's also a transport hub with international and domestic buses pulling up right in the centre, and seasonal flights landing at Rijeka Airport, a short bus ride away.

Rijeka (meaning 'river' in Croatian) is often overlooked in favour of its Dalmatian counterparts. But this underrated cultural metropolis has nothing to prove. Its left-leaning residents enjoy their coastal city without the crowds of mass tourism, making it one of the most affordable places to live like a local and enjoy the thriving music and food scenes while being just a five-minute drive from a beach. The city has a tumultuous history. Its strategic location and deep waters made it a desirable port for empires to capture, including the Romans and Austro-Hungarians – the latter were in town for 450 years until 1918. Things got complicated in the 20th century, when Rijeka was occupied by Italian Fascists and then German Nazis, before being reclaimed for the Socialist Republic of Croatia and in turn Yugoslavia in 1945.

Rijeka's Gritty Grandeur

Ornate architecture in Croatia's largest port

The Rijeka we know and love (and can see) today is a product of some enduring town planning by the Austrian Habsburgs who rebuilt their biggest seaport following a devastating earthquake in the 1750s. Most of the grand, ornate architecture in the town centre dates to the late 1800s though, when the city housed the Habsburg navy and cultural institutions to boot. Some prime ones to look out for: the baroque **clock tower** above the arched city gate, designed by Filbert Bazarig in 1876; the **Croatian National Theatre**, which was reconstructed

WHERE TO DRINK IN RIJEKA

Book caffe Dnevni boravak
Understated and effortlessly cool, this cafe by day/bar by night hosts great live music.

Celtic Caffe Bard
Very fun and popular Irish bar with live music most nights of the week.

Nemo Pub
Down to earth, al fresco drinking by the river, at very reasonable prices.

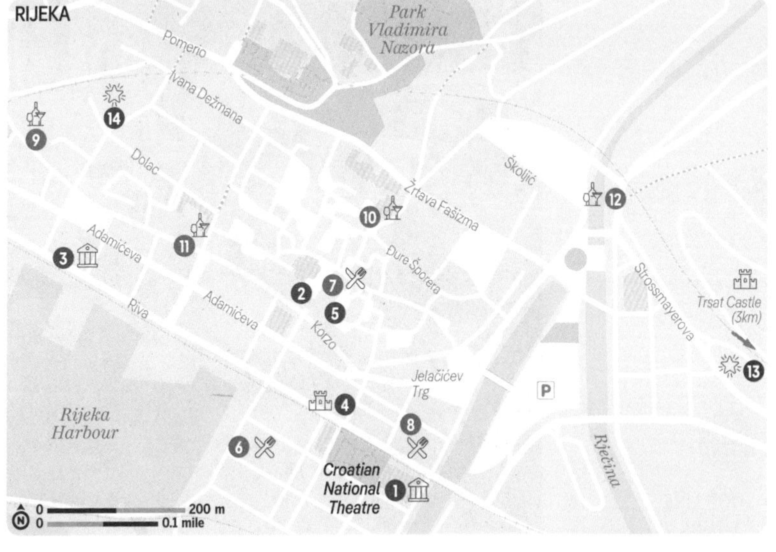

HIGHLIGHTS
1 Croatian National Theatre

SIGHTS
2 Clock Tower
3 Jadrolinija Building
4 Palace Modello
5 St Barbara's Square

EATING
6 Bistro Mornar
7 Maslina
8 Seafood Restaurant Feral

DRINKING & NIGHTLIFE
9 Book Caffe Dnevni Boravak
10 Celtic Caffe Bard
11 Filodrammatica
12 Nemo Pub

ENTERTAINMENT
13 Pogon Kulture
14 Youth Club

in 1885 and is home to some early work by Gustav Klimt; **Palace Modello**, designed by Buro Fellner & Helmer and built in 1885; and the colossal **Jadrolinija** building, a neorenaissance layer cake completed in 1897 for the Austro-Hungarian government who ruled the city from here.

A Street by Any Other Name

Six names are better than one

To coincide with Rijeka's tragically timed turn as European Capital of Culture in 2020, a second set of signage was produced for the old town centre's alleys, squares and thoroughfares. You can spot the small silver plaques, giving a subtle but poignant nod to the turbulent history of these paved streets, displaying all the previous names each site has ever had. The narrow **St Barbara's Square**, for example, has had multiple titles, depending on the language of the occupiers of Rijeka at the time, including Piazza di Santa Barbara, Piazza delle Erbe, Ulica Janeza Trdine and finally back to the Croatian language incarnation of its original name, Trg Svete Barbare.

KLIMT'S IN TOWN

It turns out that Rijeka can proudly make the claim of liking Klimt before he was famous. Gustav Klimt, his brother Ernst and their colleague Franz Matsch worked on a series of nine canvas paintings for the ceiling of the then newly built Croatian National Theatre in the 1880s, three of which were by the 23-year-old Gustav himself. The paintings were made in Vienna then transported down to Rijeka, where you can now see them from a newly installed viewing platform when they're at home – the originals do go on tour a lot.

Carnival, Rijeka

SHOP LIKE A LOCAL

Rijeka's elaborate Central Market was built in 1913 and over a century later is still going very strong indeed, packed full of the best local produce and freshly caught fish. If you're staying in an apartment in the city and have your own little kitchen, do what the locals do and grab your seasonal fruit, vegetables, nuts, honey, olive oil and, of course, seafood right here, delivered to the city directly from the countryside and Adriatic that surround it. You'll wish you'd stocked up on more delicious supplies once you've left.

Croatia's Biggest Carnival

Giving Venice a run for its money

Every year on the last Sunday before Christian Lent commences, Rijeka holds a gargantuan **carnival**. A parade of 10,000 costumed people dance, march and party down the length of the main boulevard, Korzo, led by the city's official mayor, the carnival queen and the honorary mayor of the day, 'Meštar Toni', a local who is chosen and handed the keys to the city for the duration. The highlight of the parade is saved until last; the *halubajski zvončari* bell ringers, a group of 100 men who appear in their striped shirts, masked as imaginary but very ferocious animals, bells on their belt, bouncing to ring them, making a cacophony of sound as they go. The noise scares away bad spirits, the winter and, as legend would have it, the Ottoman army. Local tales suggest that when the Ottomans tried to invade, men put real animal heads on and fought off the attacking soldiers who were scared by the masks. You don't have to be a member of a parade group to dress up, though. The motto of Rijeka carnival is: be whatever you want to be. After the parade, parties go on until the small hours, with young locals making the most of the opportunity to down as much alcohol as possible.

WHERE TO EAT IN RIJEKA

Seafood Restaurant Feral
Quirky fish restaurant with nautical decor and a homey vibe. €

Bistro Mornar
Best seafood (and indeed menu in general) in the city at this Rijeka institution. €€

Maslina
Great Italian restaurant with squid ink spaghetti to die for and the best pizza around. €

Trsat's Castle in the Sky

The best views over the city

Peering down over Rijeka in the hilltop suburb of Trsat sits a 13th-century Frankopan-family fortress, which has origins dating back as far as Roman times. The majestic views from **Trsat Castle** span the horizon and sea in one direction, and the river and gorge behind it. It's absolutely worth the slog up the 560 steps as you'll be rewarded with the breathtaking panorama and a drink at **Vintage Cafe**, which sits within the walls.

Rijeka Rocks

The musical legacy lives on

There's a number of theories as to why Rijeka was Yugoslavia's music capital. It could have been the Liverpool effect; a busy port city with ships coming and going from the USA bringing the latest rock music albums here first, meaning everything from rock 'n' roll to punk was more accessible for the youth of Rijeka. Or it could be all the empty warehouses following the city's industrial decline, just begging to be used as rehearsal spaces and impromptu gig venues. Whatever the reason, Rijeka poured out Yu-Rock band after Yu-Rock band (short for Yugoslavian Rock) across decades and genres and is still considered as Croatia's music capital, with new wave punks Paraf, synth outfit Denis i Denis and noise rockers Grč being revered today.

But it's local institution Let 3 who continue belting out their raucous punk after 30 years. Selected as Croatia's entry in the 2023 Eurovision Song Contest with the oh-so-enjoyably-provocative track 'Mama ŠČ!' performed by the band as they launched faux nukes into the audience, berating the Belarusian president Alexander Lukashenko for aiding Russia in the invasion of Ukraine (although through thinly coded lyrics, as political sentiment is banned at the Eurovision.) Legendary punks aside, Rijeka's music scene is still thriving, nourished by the brilliant, award winning **Ri Rock Festival**, which puts on the biggest annual rock festival in the city. It also manages Ri Rock Academy music school and Music Box, very low-cost but top-quality rehearsal studios at which young people can jam and get advice from the festival team.

A LOCAL SCENE TO RECKON WITH

Vinko Golembiowski, Vice President of Ri Rock Festival. *rirock.hr*

I'm always telling people how cool Rijeka is and what's going on here. The city is full of little bars that the locals like to visit to see which musicians are playing. Everyone in Rijeka loves music; we wouldn't call it a rock city – people here are humble – but it is really. Go to as many shows as you can and you'll soon figure out the scene; just talk to people and they'll tell you what's happening.

Most of the live music organisations here also run associations to support LGBTIQ+ causes or shelters for those escaping domestic abuse.

Now that Let 3 are internationally known, Rijeka's music is coming for you. It's here. You can't avoid it.

WHERE TO CATCH LIVE MUSIC IN RIJEKA

Youth Club
This cafe and bar space maintains a very welcoming, studenty vibe but is attended by locals of all ages.

Pogon Kulture
One of the larger venues, it's a bit of a dive, but if you're lucky to catch a show, it's a legit Rijeka punk experience.

Filodrammatica
An Italian-era ballroom that's hidden in plain sight, tucked away up some stairs off the main square.

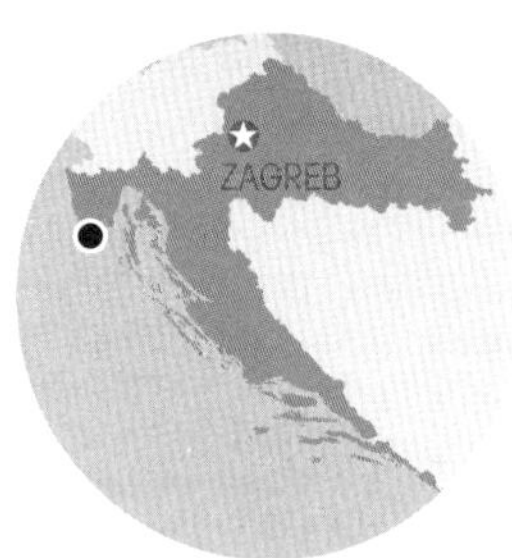

Pula

ROMAN ARCHITECTURE | GASTRONOMY | NIGHTLIFE

GETTING AROUND

A regular shuttle bus runs from Pula's airport to the main bus station during the peak summer season. Taxis from the airport tend to be overpriced. An intercity and suburban bus service is run by Pulapromet (pulapromet.hr/en); buy tickets from newsagent kiosks or from the driver. E-scooters and e-bikes can be rented by the hour via the NextBike app (nextbike.hr). Cammeo is an app-based taxi service similar to Uber (cammeo.hr/en/cities/pula).

Seaside Pula is Istria's largest city, occupying the southwestern tip of Croatia's largest peninsula. Its well-preserved 1st-century Roman amphitheatre is the city's symbol and main drawcard. Other remnants of its ancient past live on in the Roman street plan of the old town and other architectural highlights, from millennia-old arches and mosaics, to temples and theatres.

During Austro-Hungarian times, Pula was an important naval base as well as a centre for shipbuilding for over 150 years. Bilingual street signs are a reminder that this is one of the Istrian cities where Italian is an official second language. Since 1953, the city has also been the host of the annual Pula Film Festival during which the old amphitheatre becomes a makeshift open-air cinema.

A favourite pastime for residents is strolling along the beloved *lungomare* from Valkane to Valsaline beaches, a path that traces the rocky coastline, fringed with fragrant pine trees.

Pula's Architectural Highlights

On the Roman trail

Any visit to Pula starts at its harbour-facing amphitheatre, known locally as the **Arena**. Built in the 1st century, this beloved architectural icon made of limestone is one of only six remaining Roman amphitheatres in the world. 20,000 spectators were once entertained here by battling gladiators while today it seats 5000 for open-air concerts and the annual Pula Film Festival.

A few steps away is the fascinating **House of Istrian Olive Oil** (Kuća istarskog maslinovog ulja). Stop in to learn about the history of olive growing in Istria, a tradition dating back to the Romans, and a guided tasting of award-winning local olive oils.

TOP TIP

Catch a concert in the Pula amphitheatre when it becomes the atmospheric stage for big ticket artists during the summer. Sitting under the stars among the ancient stones of this unique venue is an unforgettable experience.

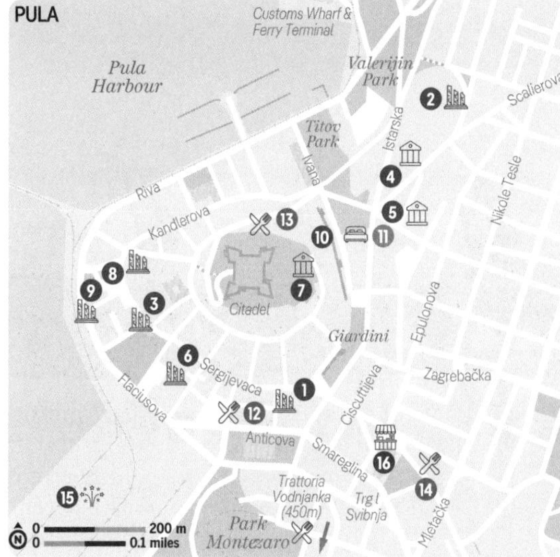

SIGHTS
1 Arch of the Sergii
2 Arena
3 Forum
4 House of Istrian Olive Oil
5 Memo Museum
6 Roman Floor Mosaics
7 Small Roman Theatre
8 Temple of Augustus
9 Town Hall
10 Zerostrasse

SLEEPING
11 Rock Hostel

EATING
12 Fresh Sandwiches & Salads
13 Jupiter
14 Pjero Istrian Gourmet

ENTERTAINMENT
15 Lighting Giants

SHOPPING
16 City Market

Nearby lies the 1st-century **Small Roman Theatre** (Malo rimsko kazalište), revived in 2023 when the stage and semicircular seating area of ancient stones got a much-needed upgrade. Today it's an atmospheric venue for concerts and cultural events seating up to 1700.

The **Arch of the Sergii** (Slavoluk Sergijevaca), the triumphal arch on Trg Portarata, dates to around 27 BCE. Walk through the gate and follow Sergijevaca, a cobblestone lane lined with shops and restaurants, looking out for signs pointing to the **Roman Floor Mosaics** on the left. These well-preserved 3rd-century mosaics depict the Punishment of Dirce and were once the intricate floors of a Roman villa.

Head back to Sergijevaca to continue on to the **Forum**, a handsome square that was the civic heart of the Roman city. The 13th-century palace embellished with an arched colonnade is the **Town Hall** (Zgrada gradske vijećnice), while next to it stands the magnificent **Temple of Augustus** (Augustov Hram) supported by six tall Corinthian columns; it was built between 2 BCE and 14 CE.

Exploring Contemporary Pula

New life for old sites

The place to rub shoulders with Pula residents is at the **City Market** (tržnica). At its heart is a beautiful building of wrought iron and glass, opened to the public in 1903 during Austrian rule. You'll find the fish market on the lower level, while staircases wind upstairs to a clutch of shops and small restaurants. The delightful fruit and vegetable market extends outdoors on a line of original stone tables set under the shade of soaring chestnut trees. This is a popular spot for an early morning cup of coffee.

BEST PLACES TO EAT

Fresh Sandwiches & Salads
A popular snack bar serving freshly made sandwiches, toasted panini, wraps and smoothies, including veggie options. €

Jupiter
A busy pizzeria with an atmospheric terrace and a big selection of pizza, pasta and grilled meat dishes. €

Pjero Istrian Gourmet
Dig into Istrian favourites in a fabulous setting under a canopy of chestnut trees near the city market. €

Trattoria Vodnjanka
A casual, family-run restaurant with a menu of traditional Istrian dishes prepared homestyle. €

BEST CAFES & BARS

Lorena Boljunčić, entrepreneur and founder of the House of Istrian Olive Oil (@museumoleihistriae), reveals her favourite bars and cafes in Pula.

The Shipyard Pub
Has a beautiful courtyard – a hidden space easy to miss. In the evening there's a buzzing vibe.

Boca Wine Bar
Always has a great atmosphere and jazz bands often play here.

Pomidor Beach Bar
Just off the *lungomare*. I go here for the surroundings: it's near the sea but tucked among old pine trees.

Uliks
Right next to the Arch of the Sergii, it is famous for its statue of James Joyce on the patio. It's open all year round.

Dvojka
On Giardini, Pula's tree-lined promenade. It has a cultural vibe, great music and good service.

ANTONYPHOTO/SHUTTERSTOCK ©

Lighting Giants light show, Uljanik shipyard

Next take a nostalgia trip at the quirky **Memo Museum**, where everyday objects from the '50s to late '80s provide a peek into life during socialist times. Kids especially love getting hands-on with the interactive displays of early computers, typewriters, cassette recorders, rollerskates and toy train sets, but the star attraction is the Zastava 750, a diminutive but beloved automobile that symbolises the 'good old times' of Yugoslavia.

Head underground to experience **Zerostrasse**, a surprising maze of subterranean tunnels dating back to WWI. Wander through eerie passageways once used as air raid shelters and ammunition warehouses. This dark underworld is also the unexpected venue for cultural events and electronic music concerts.

At dusk, take in **Lighting Giants**, a spectacular light show on from June to September at the 19th-century Uljanik shipyard, an important economic symbol of the city. On the hour, eight towering cranes come alive for 15 minutes in an explosion of 16,000 different colour schemes created by renowned lighting designer Dean Skira.

WHERE TO STAY IN PULA

Rock Hostel
Clean and cosy rock-themed rooms and dorms at a top location in the centre of town. **€€**

Boutique Hotel Valsabbion
Tasteful rooms, an outdoor pool and dedicated beach bar are draws at this small hotel on a quiet bay, south of town. **€€€**

Grand Hotel Brioni Pula
A luxury hotel boasting plush rooms with sea-facing balconies, a spa and wellness centre. **€€€**

Krk

ROMAN HERITAGE | BEACHES | ORGANIC PRODUCE

Croatia's largest island is known for its sprawling sands, gorgeous seaside towns and rich cultural heritage thanks to ancient Liburnians, industrious Romans, dynastic Frankopan lords and Glagolitic-writing Slavic priests. It's the folklore and intangible history here that really add to the wonder, though, with the practice of haunting flute tunes and scent of herbal remedies wafting through the air. Krk is a hugely popular destination for both international tourists (around 100,000 visit every summer) and Croatian visitors alike; the highway bridge connecting the island to the mainland makes a trip here very easy, as does Rijeka airport, which is actually in the northwest corner of Krk and has a busy international schedule from April to October. The island's vineyards produce Vrbnička žlahtina, a fabulous dry white wine, and olive oil is abundant too, making this a top destination for organic produce and healthy living.

GETTING AROUND

Krk is linked to the mainland by a free bridge. Arriva buses run from Rijeka down to Krk old town, passing through Omišalj, Njivice and Malinska on the way. From there services run to Baška in the far eastern corner of the island. Buses also run from Rijeka to Krk's southern ferry port Valbiska, where Jadrolinija runs a regular service over the narrow straight to Cres island. The buses are not regular but they are reliable, so you can easily work your trip around them.

The Most Beautiful City

Ancient Roman retirement resort?

The ancient Romans loved to relax by the sea as much as anyone. Krk Town, or Curicum as it was known 2000 years ago, was home to not one but two thermal baths, a rare temple to the goddess Venus, a large forum marketplace, and villa homes with beautiful mosaic floors – some of which are still intact in the town today, featuring god of the sea Triton, surrounded by dolphins. A **Roman plaque** displayed on a building in **Vela Placa** shows Latin inscriptions referring to *splendidisimi Civitatis Curictarum* – the most beautiful city of Krk. It's on the base of a sculpture of a rich retired military general (whose name has been lost) who after serving three emperors

TOP TIP

Grape brandy or *lozovača* is produced on Krk, with fermented noble vine grapes distilled to make one of the strongest alcohols in the world at 55%. Historically Krk locals offer a shot with a few dried figs to their guests on arrival and it's a very tasty combo. Raise a glass and *živjeli*!

DRAGONCELLO/SHUTTERSTOCK ©

Vela Placa (p133)

BIG NIGHTS OUT

One of Krk's biggest celebrations of the year is **Lovrečeva**, an annual festival dedicated to the island's patron, St Lawrence. Taking place annually in mid-August, Lovrečeva celebrates its 500th year in 2024 so it's definitely the time to visit if you can. A great food market backdrops historical reenactments, live music and folk dances at sites in and around Krk old town. Keep an eye on the local tourism board's website for updates: tz-krk.hr/en.

retired here to enjoy *splendidisimi* living. This proves Krk was a prosperous outpost with a good quality of life in Roman times, much like it is today. There's also a huge garden full of **Roman ruins** in the backyard of nearby snazzy bar **Volsonis**, who named their spot after Volson, a Roman ruler of Krk. His tombstone was found alongside the other remains in the garden, after 700 trucks of debris were removed. And don't miss the remains of the **Temple of Venus**, which can be seen through the glass floor in the shop **Memento**. Venus, the Roman goddess of love and beauty, had a limited number of temples dedicated to her in the Roman Empire, as only the noble Julia family (as in Julius Caesar's lot) were allowed to do so, making its presence here very special indeed.

BEST OLIVE OIL PRODUCERS

OPG UTLA, Malinska
The award-winning olive farmers at UTLA are happy to give you a tour of their olive groves, followed by a tasting.

NONO Oleoteka, Krk Town
The proprietors of one of the best restaurants on the island make their own olive oil at an oil press in their tavern.

Krk Olive Oil 10-30-10, Vrh
Life-affirming olive oil grown and pressed by David Mrakovčić outside the quaint village of Vrh.

A Real Song and Dance

Folk music and medieval dance is alive and well

Intangible heritage is plentiful across Croatia's islands, with most having their own traditional dances, dress and music, so of course the country's biggest island has some of the most interesting. The stand-out feature is the otherworldly tunes played on the *sopile* flute which was, in ancient times, crafted from the twisted bark of a mulberry tree. These days there's one last artisan on the island making them: Marijan Orlić Senkić, who carves them at his workshop in the village of Kras. The accompanying *Tanac po staro*, Krk's traditional dance, is on the Unesco World Heritage list and you can watch it on Easter Monday in the town square of Omišalj. Other villages such as Kornić, Poljica and Vrh also have their own folk dance groups, performing throughout the year at events like Krk Music Fest and Lovrečeva, or St Lawrence Day, in mid-August.

Glagolitic Krk

Spot the medieval Slavic script across the island

The ever-so-mysterious-looking Glagolitic script was used across Croatia in medieval times and is considered to be the oldest known Slavic alphabet. Not hugely dissimilar in form to Cyrillic, linguists have also traced Armenian, Greek and Hebrew influences. It was designed in the 9th century by St Cyril and his brother Methodius, two missionaries from Thessaloniki in Greece, who used their Glagolitic alphabet to spread Christianity to the Slavic people to the north of them. Krk was a Glagolitic stronghold; the earliest known Glagolitic inscription, the **Baška Tablet**, from the town of Baška in Krk, was carved in the 11th century. It's an 800kg stone slab inscribed with details of how Croatian king Zvonimir gave land to the local community (the original tablet is displayed in the Strossmayer Gallery of Old Masters, Zagreb).

While on Krk keep your eyes peeled as an impressive number of the churches have Glagolitic words carved into their altars, doors and shrines – or you can request to visit the library in the idyllic, artistic northern hilltop village of **Vrbnik**, which is housed within the tourist information office and has a large collection of Glagolitic scripts.

ISLAND PARADISE

Slanica Peričić, Storyteller and Krk Guide

I couldn't live anywhere else; we have such a good quality of life in Krk. We're a very green island, with self-sufficient water use, and are working towards being zero waste. The nature is incredible: we have the richest biodiversity of any island in the Mediterranean, so we're mindful to preserve it and to consume biodynamic produce, like our sheep's cheese or olive oil. It's so safe and peaceful here, and ideal for families; our children and elderly are well taken care of. And it's very easy to drive a scooter or walk to find a secluded corner of coast and peace for yourself.

WHERE TO EAT ON KRK

Konoba NONO, Krk Town
Delicious calamari, delectable mussels and the best *pljukanci* pasta on the island; it's hard to choose what to order. **€€**

Restaurant Konoba Nada, Vrbnik
Go big with the octopus or tuna, or just sample the local wine and sheep's cheese. **€€**

Restaurant Rivica, Njivice
Overlooking the little port, this family-run spot serves fish straight from the sea. The langoustine is life-changing. **€€**

Lošinj

PORT TOWNS | DOLPHIN-WATCHING | WELLNESS

GETTING AROUND

Arriva buses (arriva.com.hr/en-us/) from Cres run through Osor on the way down to Mali Lošinj. The rest of the island isn't served by public transport so you'll need a car, moped or taxi to get between Mali Lošinj and Veli Lošinj.

There is something very ethereal about Lošinj; the warm microclimate, the healing forests and the iconic ancient Greek treasure in situ make this island feel particularly blessed. Naturally connected to neighbouring Cres island until the Romans cut the lengthy landbridge in two by building a canal at Osor, Lošinj is the island to head to for some rest and recuperation, with a wellness tourism industry that dates back to the 1880s. And while there are other villages on the island, it's Mali Lošinj and Veli Lošinj that people gravitate to. These pretty towns appear similar at first glance (particularly in off-season or shoulder-season), their cute ports lined with colourfully painted buildings, but money has driven a distinction between them as Veli Lošinj retains its old world charm and Mali Lošinj has been revamped for the very wealthy traveller.

Dolphin Watching Done Right

Croatia's leading light in marine biology

Founded in 1999, the researchers at the Blue World Institute study the bottlenose dolphin population of the Adriatic from three sites, Veli Lošinj, Vis and Murter, using non-invasive photo identification methods, setting the example of ethical ways to interact with our favourite finned mammals. Since opening the **Lošinj Marine Education Centre** in Veli

WHERE TO EAT ON LOŠINJ

Konoba Mandrac, Veli Lošinj
Great spot on the waterfront, where the excellent chef serves grilled fish to die for and incredible *pljukanci* pasta. **€€**

Restaurant Za Kantuni, Mali Lošinj
A very local vibe, locally sourced fish or lamb dishes and service with a smile. **€€**

Konoba Bonifacic, Osor
Book one of the seaview tables at this garden restaurant that specialises in grilled fish steak, mussels and langoustines. **€**

Dolphin-watching tour

Lošinj, the passionate team have been running daily dolphin-watching tours at 1pm (from spring to autumn) that cruise the east coast of Lošinj to see if any of the 200 local bottlenose are in the mood to socialise. To find a pod, skippers use binoculars (as the institute does not allow tracking devices at all, the dolphins are completely wild) and follow fishing trawler ships, just as the dolphins do. As well as covering your excursion, the fee (€50 for kids and €60 for adults) goes towards supporting the great work of the marine biologists, who also run a turtle rescue centre that's not open to the public.

Clear Your Lungs

Forest bathing is so hot now

The 'Island of Vitality', as Lošinj is nicknamed, has been a wellness destination for over 100 years, with the first Habsburg-era health resorts built on the island in the 1880s. But something new is brewing these days – forest bathing. The Japan-originating therapy *shinrin-yoku* is proven to help the immune system and lower blood pressure, reducing stress and promoting relaxation. And with the dense pine forests across Lošinj, the island couldn't be a better place for it. Qualified therapists are now offering forest bathing sessions as part of their health programmes at Boutique Hotel Alhambra and Villa Elizabeth, so give it a go. The trees are calling.

SEARCHING FOR DOLPHINS

Barbara Sucich, Educator at Lošinj Marine Education Centre

When you choose a dolphin-watching trip, ask a few questions. Nobody can guarantee 100% that you will see dolphins, so that's a sign not to go with them if they do. They'll be chasing dolphins and that's not good.

We're not against companies running dolphin watching – there are quite a few people here in Lošinj who do it – but do it the right way! We print code of conduct leaflets that we give out at the beginning of the summer: boats should always approach dolphins sideways, not directly head on or from the back; keep a minimum distance of 50m; maintain gentle behaviour; turn off the engine when near; and stay no more than 30 minutes with a pod.

Zadar

ROMAN OLD TOWN | AWARD-WINNING SCULPTURE | GASTRONOMY

GETTING AROUND

Whether arriving in Zadar by plane or bus, both airport and bus station are served by local buses (or cheap taxi apps) that deliver you to the old town where you will no doubt be staying. Once dropped off at your pad, the old town is fully pedestrianised and enjoyably walkable.

One of Zadar's biggest fans, the director Alfred Hitchcock wrote in his old town hotel guest book that the city has the best sunsets he'd ever seen. Evening after evening the sky over the waterfront of this ancient city dazzles visitors and locals with its deep reds, pinks and purples that you just won't find anywhere else in Croatia. The biggest draw of Zadar though is its magnificent Roman old town, still populated by a bustling community of locals, not yet pushed out by mass tourism. Pop to the markets, enjoy the coffee shops and dance the nights away in the park-based nightclub and you'll feel like a local yourself. With a growing food scene, nature galore at your fingertips and sailing companies just waiting to whisk you away to the glorious islands of the straits, you'll only wonder why you didn't visit Zadar sooner.

Zadar's Really Seen It All

Millennia of history, one vibrant city

Probably best known these days as the sailing hub of Croatia, this ancient city also has charm by the bucket-load for those willing to seek it out. The old town is an absolute treasure trove of living history. Where else are you going to find a cafe-bar in an 11th-century church, a bank in a medieval church and a tiny Romanesque church that now serves as souvenir shop, Galerija Sv. Petar, selling gorgeous pieces by local artisans? What's left of old Zadar (80% of it was flattened in WWII) is meticulously preserved. Consequently you've got stunning 1970s modernist architecture in the form of the **Archaeology Museum Zadar** overlooking the best preserved, 2000-year-old **Roman forum**

WHERE TO STAY IN ZADAR

Almayer Art & Heritage Hotel
A gorgeous option at the end of the old town's peninsula. The elegant rooms with park views are a real treat. **€€**

Hotel Bastion
Historic hotel with an excellent spa and views of the marina. Relax on the terrace over their delicious breakfast. **€€**

Teatro Verdi Boutique Hotel
This minimalist modern stay, intimate and comfortable, is in the heart of the old town with luxurious rooms. **€€**

Painter, Zadar

Croatian architect Nikola Bašić. They not only serve as a serene spot to end the day, but also have a place in the hearts of locals. Before their creation, the promenade area here had fallen on bad times, having been bombed during WWII and again in the Homeland War of the 1990s, leaving it in a slum state for generations. Aiming to regenerate the waterfront, the city put out a tender for a sculpture and Bašić's beautiful concept of an organ played by the sea not only won the bidding but in 2006 was proclaimed installation of the year by Barcelona Institute of Architecture. Summer sees Zadar University students relaxing here between lectures, alongside sunbathing and swimming tourists, so the architect's dreams of bringing life back to this part of town have been a melodic success.

Knock-Out Flavour

Seafood is just the start

Delicious cuisine has always been a Zadar selling point thanks to the city's unique *mare monte* position, between the sea and the mountains of Velebit. But now with two Michelin-recommended restaurants and myriad mind-blowing seafood *konobe* (traditional restaurants), Zadar is finally getting the recognition it deserves as a culinary hotspot. Head to **the open-air food market** *(pijaca)*, the core of the city's identity, time a trip for one of the food festivals such as the Tuna, Sushi, Wine Festival in April or the Street Food Festival in September, and book in advance for the top restaurants.

LOCAL LIFE

Šime Botica, Tour Guide, art-and-nature-travel.com

Zadar is the greenest city on the coast. It's such an enjoyable place to live in, partly thanks to its large parks. The first, Queen Jelena Madijevka Park, was opened in 1829. There's a bar and nightclub there called Ledana, which means 'ice land' because historically the space was used by the rich to store ice. Near that park there's an even bigger one, Vladimir Nazor, where you see a lot of locals with their dogs and can get a sense of the local community. Finally our city walls from the 16th century have small green areas and benches on which to sit and chill. A spot not to miss.

WHERE TO EAT IN ZADAR

Foša
Chef Saša Began serves his famous approach to fish in ingenious presentations both raw and cooked. **€€€**

Kaštel
Named for its castle location, it's a treat whether you go for the exceptional seafood or local lamb. **€€**

The Botanist
Zadar's only plant-based restaurant takes a fine-dining approach, with every plate beautifully presented. **€€**

ZAGREB

Plitvice National Park & the Lika Region

SCENERY | HIKING | TESLA'S BIRTHPLACE

TOP TIP

You won't spot brown bears in Plitvice National Park, but if you do want to see some of Europe's largest animals, the wonderful team at Kuterevo Bear Sanctuary gives refuge to young orphaned cubs who are endangered due to hunting and poaching, which is sadly still legal in Croatia.

Aside from its famous Plitvice Lakes, the Lika region is very much off-the-beaten-path, with only the most dedicated hikers coming here for the opportunity to connect with the wilds of Croatian nature. Most visitors stop off at Plitvice National Park on a day trip from Zagreb or Zadar, on tours or one of the public buses, and some culture vultures swing by Smiljan, the town where Nikola Tesla was born; his birthplace is now a museum. But stay a few nights in the Lika region and you'll find a lot more to explore than Plitvice. From rafting or canoeing on the River Gacka, horse riding or cycling along the country roads with the Velebit Mountains in view, or even spelunking in the Grabovača cave complex near Perušić, there's heaps of activities to get stuck into, before or after you visit Croatia's famous turquoise lakes.

Loving Lakes at Plitvice National Park

A true wonder of nature

The country's oldest national park (1949) and its most popular (over one million visitors every year), **Plitvice National Park** is an arcadian paradise – if you go off-peak or in shoulder season, that is. It gets busy here all summer and for good reason: the 16 dazzling, aquamarine lakes are as stunning as the interconnecting waterfalls, one of which, **Veliki Slap**, is Croatia's highest at 62m. Calcium carbonate in the rushing waters and the bed of tufa karst underneath make this an unforgettable spectrum of turquoise blues and greens that truly make your jaw drop. The lakes make up less than 1% of the total park area, which is also home to brown bears (don't worry, you'll never see one), over 300 species of butterflies, 150 different breeds of birds and 1200 plant varieties. Exploring the

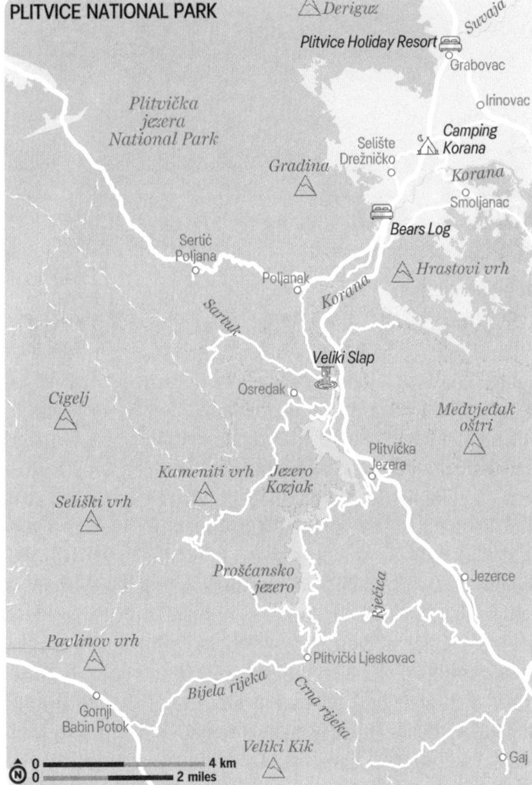

shores of these lakes on foot takes six hours but, if that sounds like too much trekking, you can shave a couple of hours off by taking the park's free, electricity-powered boats and connecting buses; both services leave every half hour from April through October from near entrance two. If you're in a rush and just in the park for half a day, prioritise the lower lakes canyon, known as Route A, which gets you to Veliki Slap, aka the Great Waterfall, which you must see from above, as well as a loop of the boardwalks through the lakes and beside the waterfall below. There are seven different trails of differing lengths suggested and signposted, which you can check out in advance: np-plitvicka-jezera.hr/en/plan-your-visit/istrazite-jezera/activities/lake-tour-programmes.

LIKA'S BOOMING GREEN SCENE

From ecotourism to local green initiatives, Lika is blossoming and just waiting for nature lovers to catch on. It's by no means a new thing – for 20 years the GTF Initiative for Sustainable Growth has run an annual permaculture project every June, with volunteers of all ages coming together to work on vegetable gardens in Perušić – but the tourism industry has certainly gotten behind it in recent years. Places like Linden Tree Retreat & Ranch near Gospić offer tepees or wooden chalets in the thick of the forest, while Tree House Lika 1 in Raduč has, well, a treehouse.

WHERE TO STAY

Plitvice Holiday Resort
Close to Entrance 1, this resort has fun treehouses around a little lake, to get you in the mood for the national park. **€€**

Camping Korana
This campervan park and campsite has very cute bungalows right in the middle of the national park. **€€**

Bears Log
A log cabin in a beautiful spot close to the park, full of rustic charm with an outdoor hot tub for post-lakes relaxation. **€€€**

Krka National Park

WATERFALLS | SWIMMING | NATURE

TOP TIP

There are five entrances to Krka National Park but for your first visit prioritise the famous waterfall, Skradinski Buk, and enter from the lovely village of Skradin where you can buy your ticket at the park kiosk. Journey up river by boat, which leaves hourly and is included in the price of your pass.

The star of Croatia's second most famous and visited national park is its namesake, the River Krka, a 73km-long waterway that courses through Dalmatia and has been the lifeblood of the region for millennia. Declared a national park in 1985, the area includes seven waterfalls that cascade over 17 levels and provides sanctuary to 46 types of mammal, including deer, otters and badgers, as well as lots and lots of ducks. You can't miss them. With cycling and hiking trails, as well as boats that link the upper and lower ends of the river, Krka National Park is marvellous to visit in any season. Spring and autumn are best for hikers, temperature-wise; summer is glorious (if busy) and the time to go for a swim; and the winter months are fascinating too, as the geomorphological forms in the rocks and tufa are visible in the dazzling blue waters.

Do Go Chasing Waterfalls

Hues of water like nothing you've seen

The highlight of Krka National Park, **Skradinski Buk** waterfall is likely what you've come for. Its turquoise, greens and blues take centre stage in all and any social media posts and press about the park – but nothing prepares you for seeing them in person. The breathtaking waters rushing 800m before crashing 46m down over the tufa rock formations truly are picture-perfect. A loop of boardwalk takes you around

OTHER SIGHTS

Mother of Mercy Franciscan Monastery
In the middle of Lake Viskovac, this serene monastery was built by Franciscan monks in 1445.

Orthodox Monastery
Still functioning monastery founded in 1345. Enthusiastic guide Mihajlo explains the history of the catacombs and the rare iconostasis.

Burnum Roman Ruins
Just off the road from Kistanje to Knin are the remains of the only Roman military amphitheatre in Croatia, as well as two arches from an aqueduct.

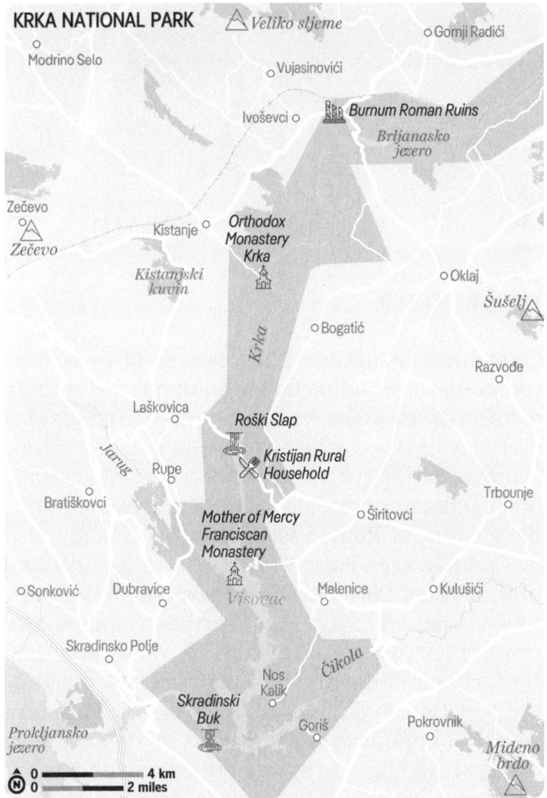

HIDDEN KRKA

Nikolina Lučić, Educator & Interpreter at Krka National Park

One of my favourite hiking trails in the whole park is the path around the Manojlovački waterfall; it's a hidden gem. You can walk to the bottom of the waterfall and see so many different green colours in the water, and the remains of the old water mills. It's like a fairytale.

It's up in the north of the park, near the Orthodox Monastery. If you're renting a car, it's easy; we have signs on the road. I see it as a place for people who are real nature lovers, who like to wander around and visit isolated, secret places.

this, the largest and last waterfall, before the river flows out to sea. Note that swimming in the lower lake beneath the fall has been out of bounds since 2020, when, as park visitor numbers reached over a million, conservationists realised it was time to protect the travertine karst forms in the water, which grow just 2mm per year, from damaging feet. Around Skradinski Buk, beautifully restored historic water mills have been converted into a small museum, souvenir stores and eateries; in summer, locals sell their homegrown wares of figs, olive oil and honey at a small market. Recognising visitors' need for a dip, particularly in the heat of summer, the park has now opened up the lake under **Roski Slap** waterfall for swimmers. The water here is lovely and also surrounded by old water mills, one of which, **Kristijan Rural Household**, is a restaurant, bar and delightful family-run time capsule of life on the river from decades past.

Šibenik

HISTORY | GASTRONOMY | FESTIVALS

TOP TIP
Don't be fooled by your maps app – there are a lot of stairs in Šibenik's old town. Many hotels and hosts will offer to come and meet you so don't carry your suitcases if you don't have to. It's a walkable place, though. Once in town there's no need for transport, as the bus station is just a few minutes away, right on the seafront.

Charming Šibenik lacks the crowds of its coastal counterparts, meaning that in addition to the beauty of its medieval architecture, there's still the sense of everyday life here, with a welcoming vibe in the air complementing the fresh sea breeze. Unlike many other Dalmatian seaside communities, Šibenik was not a Greek or Roman settlement but was founded by Croatian king Petar Krešimir IV in the 11th century, selected for its defensive position, nestled between Zadar and Split. The tiny city certainly shares similarities with its neighbours: it was a successful trading hub in the Middle Ages, was conquered by the Venetian Republic and contains a plethora of beautiful architecture. Its marble, old town streets transport you back to bygone eras, while its delectable food scene and lively festivals place it very firmly in the 21st century.

Architecture So Fine

Marvel at the wonderful buildings

From the **Riva**, Šibenik's seaside promenade, stairs sweep up to one of the undisputed jewels of Dalmatian architecture, **St Jakov Cathedral**. This masterpiece by Juraj Dalmatinac, who was brought into the construction project in 1441 after ten years of failed attempts by other builders, is a wonder of bright white stone, mined entirely from the neighbouring islands of Brač and Korčula. Now a Unesco World Heritage Site, you'll see a montage of architectural styles from different

WHERE TO EAT

Pelegrini
A tasting menu full of modern twists on Dalmatian cuisine earned local Chef Rudolf Štefan a Michelin star. €€€

Peperoncino Kitchen & Bar
With exceptional local wines and a modern menu, this charming restaurant on a terrace is one not to miss. €€

KOKA Pizza
Wonderful family-run restaurant serving arguably the best pizza in Croatia. Try the truffle pizza. €

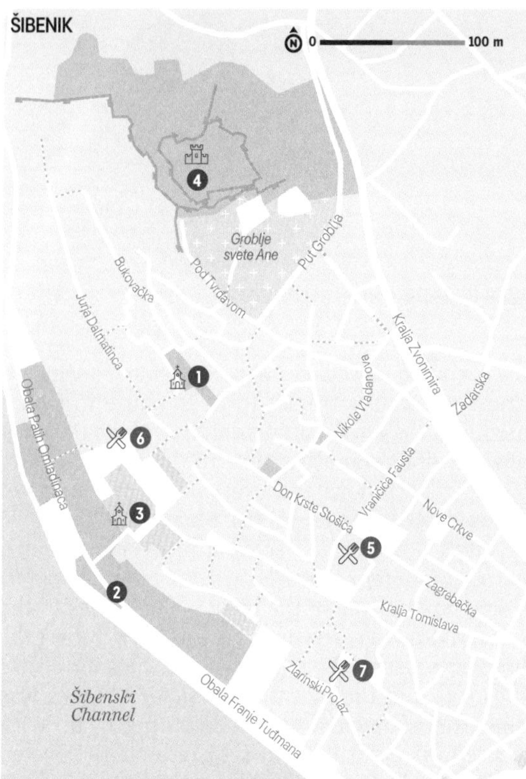

SIGHTS
1 Church & Monastery of St Lawrence
2 Riva
3 St Jakov Cathedral
4 St Michael's Fortress

EATING
5 KOKA Pizza
6 Pelegrini
7 Peperoncino Kitchen & Bar

eras, with both gothic and renaissance features piled on top of one another like a layer cake, as the cathedral was only completed in 1536. Its most fascinating feature is the frieze of 71 heads that adorn the outer walls at the city end of the building. The portraits pull all manner of funny faces, from the hilarious to downright scary, and were all based on local 15th-century citizens, albeit caricature versions.

Beyond the cathedral, the compact centre is home to 22 elegant churches – the **Church and Monastery of St Lawrence** is an unmissable one, with a very zen garden in its churchyard. It's **St Michael's Fortress** you'll want to make your way to before leaving, though; narrow alleys and passageways connecting wider lanes all flow up toward the peak of the hilltop fortification. Destroyed and rebuilt numerous times over the centuries, this citadel was first recorded as a church in 1066 and is now home to an open-air auditorium where Bryan Ferry, Róisín Murphy and The National have all performed in recent years.

DON'T KNOCK THE HAT

Šibenska kapa, or the Šibenik cap, is one of the most prominent features of St Michael's Day. Every year on 29 September, the city's patron saint is celebrated in a procession through the streets and by locals proudly donning traditional costume, including the unmistakable orange cap with two rows of black embroidered decorations called *bule* in Croatian. The Šibenik cap has even been listed on the national intangible heritage list since 2008.

Brilliant tour guide and culture expert Zvonimira Krvavica (instagram.com/kzvonimira) is one of a handful of locals running workshops for the next generation on how to make *Šibenska kapa*, ensuring the tradition is not forgotten.

Split

OLD TOWN | HISTORIC PROMENADE | ROMAN PALACE

GETTING AROUND

Split is a city that's easy to explore on foot. Promet, the public bus system, has wide coverage – download their excellent app to your smartphone to buy tickets, check schedules and even see a bus' location in real time. Local taxis tend to be overpriced – try Uber or Bolt instead.

Just a couple of decades ago, Split was considered little more than a transit town to pause in before catching a ferry to Croatia's islands. Despite the magnificence of its star attraction, the huge Diocletian's Palace stood forlorn and overlooked, with parts of it even described as a ghetto. Meanwhile the Riva, the city's now beloved seaside promenade, was a thoroughfare for car traffic.

Today Split is one of the most visited cities in the country, drawing crowds of visitors even during the shoulder seasons. This is a popular halt for cruise ships too, and the fact that *Game of Thrones* was filmed here may also have something to do with its rise in popularity. Split is also the most coveted destination for Croatia's growing tribe of digital nomads. No longer a mere launchpad to the islands, the city has finally attracted the attention it so deserves – though native Splićani are still learning to adjust to their home's new star status.

TOP TIP

Look out for the NextBike bike-sharing scheme and its handy app that lets you rent bicycles and e-bikes at a budget-friendly hourly rate.

An Exploration of Split's Old Town

Tracking architectural highlights

When nearby Salona fell in the 7th century, its people first settled in Diocletian's Palace and then in newer constructions which sprung up beyond its walls. The Iron Gate is the former's western boundary: here you leave behind the emperor's abode and step onto **People's Square** (Narodni trg). The handsome gothic **Town Hall** with its loggia of peaked arches is one of the square's only remaining medieval buildings, along with **Cambi Palace**, adorned with arched windows and a trifora on its upper floor. A few doors away is the restored art nouveau shopfront of Morpurgo bookshop, founded in the 1860s and now occupied by a newsagent chain.

Next, visit **Braće Radić Square**, better known as Fruit Square (Voćni trg), to marvel at the **statue of poet Marko Marulić**, another creation of Ivan Meštrović. Dominating the

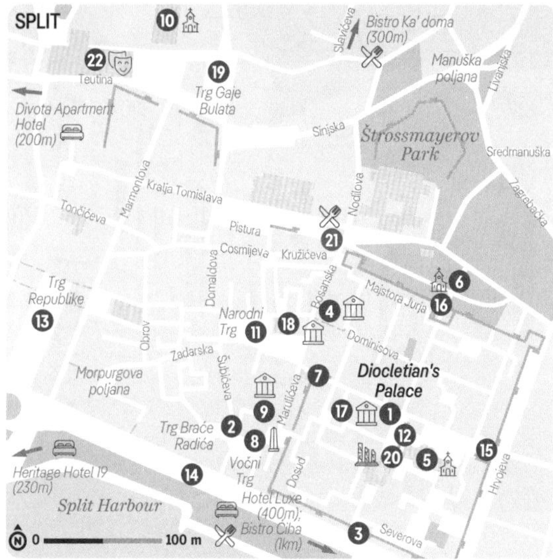

square is the striking 17th-century baroque **Milesi Palace** and the Venetian Tower, all that remains of a medieval castle.

Move on to the fish market, where on a corner of pedestrian-only Marmontova you'll stumble on an example of Croatian art nouveau. Embellished with decorative figures and faces, the **Sulphur Spa** (Sumporne Toplice) was built in 1903 atop some therapeutic springs – the smell supposedly keeps flies away from the fish stalls.

Continue north along Marmontova to Trg Gaje Bulata and its imposing modernist church of **Our Lady of Health**, dating from 1937. The canary yellow building nearby is the **Croatian National Theatre** (Hrvatsko Narodno Kazalište) – at the cafe upstairs, snag a table next to the balcony doors for a view over the square.

Walk the Riva

See and be seen

A favourite pastime for Split residents is enjoying a coffee and a long chat or a relaxed stroll on their much-loved seaside promenade. Quay of the Croatian National Revival (Obala hrvatskog narodnog preporoda) is the official name of this 250m-long stretch of waterfront. But for Splićani locals, it's the **Riva**.

At its eastern end, look for a bronze 3D model of the old town and, a few steps away, a similar model of Diocletian's Palace in the 4th century. Take a ramble along the white stone walkway and browse the wooden stalls hawking souvenirs made of wood, handmade jewellery, locally produced wine or honey and other goodies like dried figs, herbal teas and natural soaps.

Continued on p152

BEST BEACHES

Bačvice
A sandy beach with buzzing bars and a favoured spot for players of *picigin*, a local ball game.

Firule
This popular horseshoe-shaped sandy beach has cliffside cafes and a scene that continues way past sundown.

Žnjan
One of the bigger beaches with several bays of white pebbles and views of the mountainous coastline.

Kašjuni
A narrow pebble beach and sunset party spot curving around a bay on the south side of Marjan.

There's no entry fee but the cathedral complex and museums are ticketed. Scan here for information on opening times.

Peristyle

TOP SIGHT

Diocletian's Palace

Protected by Unesco since 1979, Diocletian's Palace is one of the world's biggest and most complete Roman edifices. The fortress-like palace was built in the 4th century as Emperor Diocletian's swanky retirement home, covering a rectangular area of 38,700 sq metres. This huge complex of 200 or so ancient buildings has been inhabited for the past 1700 years, but only a few hundred tenants remain today.

DON'T MISS

- The Four Gates
- Peristyle
- Cathedral of St Domnius
- Bell tower
- Temple of Jupiter (Baptistery)
- Vestibule
- Palace substructures

Golden Gate (Zlatna Vrata)

Set in its northern wall, the **Golden Gate** (one of four) was the palace's main entrance. Hovering outside is the gigantic bronze statue of Gregory of Nin by renowned sculptor Ivan Meštrović. Rub his shiny big toe for good luck before heading down the steps and through the gate. Once beyond, look for a staircase around the corner to the right ascending to what was once a guardhouse. Tucked above the gate, in a 1.64m-wide space, is 7th-century **St Martin's Church**, the city's oldest and smallest.

Peristyle (Peristil)

At the heart of the palace, where its two main thoroughfares intersect, you'll find the handsome **Peristyle**. Framed by soaring columns on three sides, this imperial square has been guarded by a black granite sphinx for millennia. At

Lvxor Cafe, pause on one of the red cushions laid out on the steps encircling the square and admire the ancient stone buildings and Cathedral of St Domnius. In summer, live music is hosted by the cafe each evening in this atmospheric open-air setting.

Cathedral of St Domnius (Katedrala Sv Duje) & Bell Tower

The octagonal dome of the **Cathedral of St Domnius** was originally built as Emperor Diocletian's mausoleum, and converted into a church in the 5th century. This is the world's oldest working Catholic cathedral that still has its original structure. Have a peek at the elaborate interiors before tackling the steep and slightly scary climb up floating metal stairs to the top of the 12th-century bell tower. Your reward is expansive views covering the palace complex, the mountains to the north and the shimmering Adriatic Sea dotted by islands to the south.

Temple of Jupiter (Baptistery)

A narrow alley opposite the cathedral's entrance leads to its baptistery, occupying the only remaining Roman temple of the palace's original three, the **Temple of Jupiter**. This 6th-century building is surprisingly intact, while the headless sphinx on its porch is less so. Pop inside to see the sculpture of St John the Baptist by Ivan Meštrović posing under vaulted ceilings. To the baptistery's left is the palace's narrowest passageway, dubbed by locals *Pusti Me Proć* (Let Me Pass) as it's only wide enough for one person.

Vestibule

A few steps at the southern end of the Peristyle ascend to a porch where Diocletian would address his subjects. This opens onto the **Vestibule**, a domed rotunda that led to the imperial corridor and the emperor's apartments. The large open dome has excellent acoustics put to the test each morning by professional *klapa* singers. Linger a while for a free concert of this a cappella tradition recognised by Unesco.

Palace Substructures

More stairs descend under the Vestibule to the palace's massive cellars where goods were stored after being unloaded from arriving ships. A corridor lined with stalls selling artwork and souvenirs leads to the **Bronze Gate**, opening onto the seafront. Doorways to its left and right hold a small museum of Roman relics, including remains of an ancient oil and wine press. But most impressive are the massive barrel-vaulted ceilings. Fans of *Game of Thrones* will recognise these cellars as the place where Daenerys Targaryen kept her three dragons.

LABYRINTH OF ROMAN LANES

Stone-slabbed Decumanus (Krešimirova) is the palace's thoroughfare, bookended by the **Silver Gate** in the east and the **Iron Gate** in the west. It marked the separation of the emperor's residence from the military quarters, and cuts north-south through Cardo (Dioklecijanova) at the Peristyle. Between lies a labyrinth of passageways lined with centuries-old buildings.

TOP TIPS

- Head out early to roam the palace first thing in the morning before the guided tour groups crowd the cramped lanes.
- The cathedral can be accessed for prayer and contemplation before its official opening at 8am.
- Look up to spot quirky details hidden in the ancient stones, such as the head of a sphinx or a 15th-century sculpted moor's head peering at you from a stone wall on Dominisova, just opposite a leafy courtyard garden.
- The best spot to capture a great shot of the cathedral and bell tower is just inside the Silver (eastern) Gate.

BEST PLACES TO EAT IN SPLIT

Sara Dyson, founder of Expat in Croatia (expatincroatia.com), an informational website and consultancy, shares her favourite places to eat in Split.

Bistro Ka' doma
A very affordable lunch place with a small menu that changes every day. You'll find typical Dalmatian cuisine but also more unusual dishes like bulgur salad. **€**

Villa Spiza
Watch chefs at work in this palace option. The menu is seasonal and I've never had a bad meal here. They don't take reservations so go off-peak. **€€**

Bistro Ćiba
Another favourite for their excellent meat and fish dishes. It's not a fancy place but you have to reserve because they're popular. **€€**

Republic Sq

Continued from p149

Then do like the natives and sit yourself down for a cup of coffee. Saturday morning is when people go to town in their Sunday best, and the long row of cafes (ranging from unfussy to fancy) buzzes with chitchat and the clinking of cups on saucers.

Next continue to the Riva's western end, where you may catch the distinctive whiff of sulphur from the healing waters that have been bubbling up in this spot since Diocletian's time. Some believe these therapeutic springs are the reason he built his retirement home here. Venture into handsome Venetian-inspired **Republic Sq** (Trg Republike Hrvatske) to admire its vibrant red facade and the elegant arches of its three-sided colonnade.

Come early evening, chattering swallows swoop between the Riva's neat rows of palms while families amble up and down the footpath. Park yourself on one of the sea-facing benches to watch the ferries glide in and out of Split's port.

WHERE TO STAY IN SPLIT

Heritage Hotel 19
An elegant boutique hotel set in a heritage property with a courtyard garden and romantic vibe. **€€€**

Hotel Luxe
A modern hotel in a top location next to the old town and port, and rooms with sea views. **€€€**

Divota Apartment Hotel
Apartments and guest rooms in restored stone houses in charming Veli Varoš neighbourhood. **€€€**

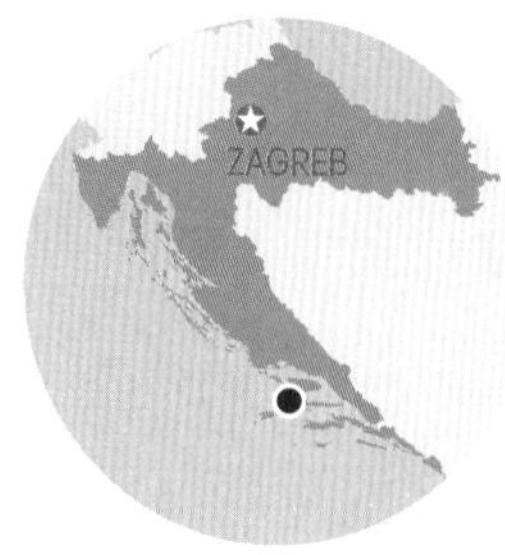

Hvar

GLAMOUR | BEACHES | NIGHTLIFE

Hvar has become synonymous with swank, thanks to Hvar Town's image as a posh destination for the jet set who sail in on their luxury yachts and drop anchor in this picturesque port. The island's capital is also known for its lively nightlife and beach bars where parties go on until the small hours. But if you're not a fan of the glitterati or all-nighters, fear not, there's the rest of Hvar island to enjoy. Lovely Stari Grad, one of the oldest Croatian towns, is charming and easier on the wallet. Then there's the other delightful port towns of Jelsa and Vrboska, and the lush Stari Grad Plain – a Unesco World Heritage Site. Other highlights include the scenic bays ribboned by gorgeous beaches, fields of fragrant lavender and the superb wines produced here. Most tourist attractions are concentrated on the western side of the island, meaning few venture further east than Jelsa – except to maybe catch the ferry to the mainland from easternmost Sućuraj.

GETTING AROUND

A regular bus service connects Hvar Town, Stari Grad port, Stari Grad and Jelsa. Car and scooter rentals are available, as well as e-bikes – a convenient way to negotiate hilly roads for sporty types. Look out for taxi boats in the port towns – they provide a convenient way to access beaches and nearby islands. You can also rent your own boat with a 5HP engine without requiring a boat licence.

Tour Historic Hvar Town

Cathedrals and castles

At the heart of **Hvar Town**'s religious, public and social life is long, rectangular **St Stephen's Square** with its namesake, baroque St Stephen's Cathedral and its soaring bell tower looming at the eastern end. On the southwest corner sits the boxy 14th-century **Arsenal**, a former Venetian shipyard and now an exhibition space; the upper floor is home to Europe's oldest theatre. Climb the external staircase to the balustraded terrace for a view of the square's elegant facades of white stone, the renaissance clock tower and loggia, tiny port and pavement cafes which fill early with people-watchers.

TOP TIP

Hvar Town is only serviced by passenger ferries (listed as *katamaran* on sailing schedules), while car ferries *(trajekt)* arrive at Stari Grad port, 3km from Stari Grad and 16.5km from Hvar Town.

HVAR

SIGHTS
1 Dubovnica
2 Maslinica
3 Mlini
4 Pakleni Islands
5 Palmižana
6 Pokonji Dol
7 Stari Grad Plain

DRINKING & NIGHTLIFE
8 Beach Club Hvar
9 Falko
10 Hula Hula Hvar
11 Laganini

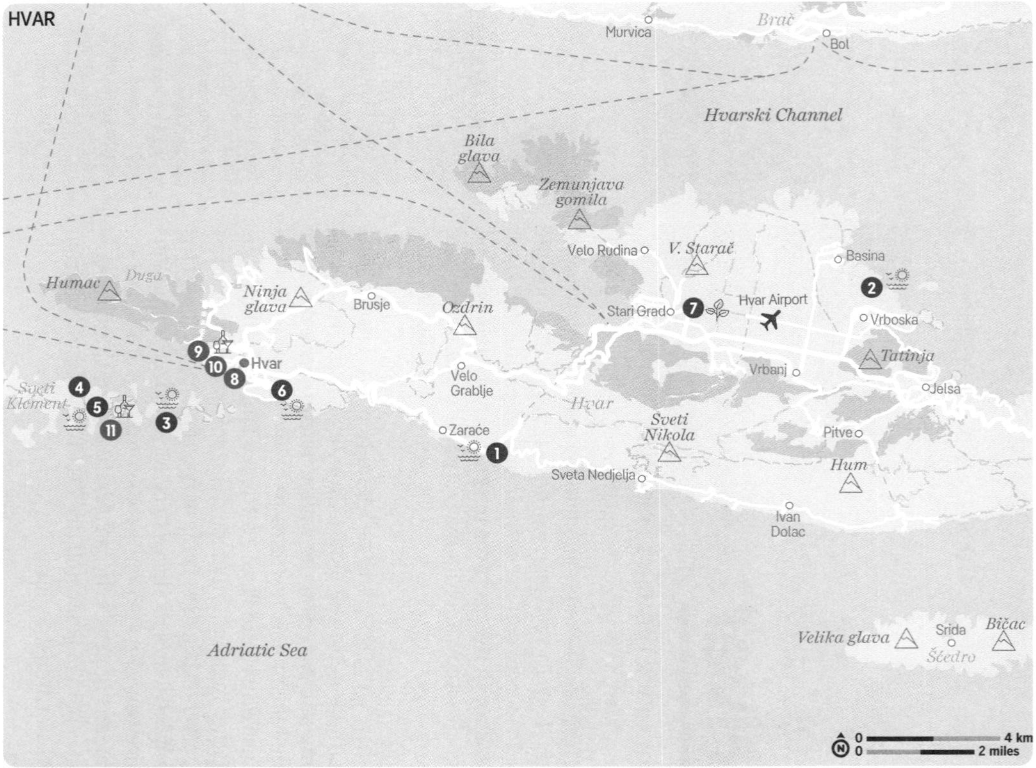

Murvica
Brač
Bol
Hvarski Channel
Bila glava
Zemunjava gomila
Velo Rudina
V. Starač
Basina
Humac
Duga
Ninja glava
Brusje
Ozdrin
Stari Grad
Hvar Airport
Vrboska
Hvar
Velo Grablje
Tatinja
Vrbanj
Jelsa
Sveti Klement
Zaraće
Sveti Nikola
Pitve
Sveta Nedjelja
Hum
Ivan Dolac
Adriatic Sea
Velika glava
Srida
Bičac
Šćedro
0 4 km
0 2 miles

Plavac Mali grapes
(p157)

View from Hvar over Pakleni Islands

Continue past the cathedral and up a short staircase on the left and you'll soon reach the colour and bustle of the daily fruit and vegetable market. Next, wander along the narrow stone streets climbing upwards and follow the signs to **Fortica**, the town's Venetian castle. From its ramparts, pause to take in the dazzling views over terracotta rooftops and the Pakleni Islands bobbing in the sparkling Adriatic.

Pakleni Islands

Coves, caves and beaches

Scattered in the waters facing Hvar Town are just over a dozen small uninhabited islands that look tantalisingly close. The car-free **Pakleni Islands** scream adventure: there are secret coves, dazzling beaches and crystal-clear bays to explore. Some beaches like Palmižana on Sveti Klement island and Carpe Diem on Marinkovac island have a long-established beach bar and club scene. Jerolim island is known for its nudist beach, while Mlini Beach on Marinkovac is for those looking for a quiet and scenic swim spot. Regular boats set off from Hvar Town port to all of these for €10 return.

BEACH-BUMMING ON HVAR

Dubovnica
Arrive by taxi boat or brave the steep downhill path to this beautiful cove of white pebbles.

Mlini
A quiet pebble beach on Marinkovac island overlooking an islet and lapped by waters of two-tone blue.

Pokonji Dol
Set on a pretty bay just 2km from Hvar Town, this pretty pebble beach can be reached on foot.

Palmižana
This gorgeous beach on Sveti Klement is pebbly and partly rocky but the seabed is surprisingly sandy.

Maslinica
Set on a stunning cove 1km from Vrboska, this beach of pebbles and rocks is surrounded by soaring pines.

WHERE TO STAY ON HVAR

White Rabbit Hostel
Cheery private rooms and mixed dorms with lockers, air-con and a kitchen, smack in the centre of town. **€**

Palace Elisabeth Hotel
A chic 5-star in a period building with sea-facing rooms, fine-dining restaurant, pool and spa. **€€€**

Hotel Antica, Stari Grad
A small seafront hotel with outdoor pool near the ferry terminal and walking distance to Stari Grad. **€€€**

STARI GRAD PLAIN ON TWO WHEELS

From ❶ **Stari Grad bus station**, cycle east along Put Gospojice where asphalt quickly gives way to a gravel road. You'll be zipping past stone walls enclosing neat patches of vineyards and olive groves that make up the Stari Grad Plain, recognised by Unesco as a World Heritage Site for its significance as a 'cultural landscape'. The Greeks arrived here in the 4th century BCE, creating a geometric grid of land division made up of 73 rectangular plots demarcated by dry stone walls (built without mortar) that has remained largely intact. Once past the tiny 16th-century ❷ **Church of Our Lady**, continue for 1km, looking out for two towering cypresses where a well-preserved example of a ❸ **trim** still stands. This circular shelter of neatly stacked flat stones provided farmers with cover from sun and rain.

At the next left, leave the main road and cycle 1.5km along ❹ **Mathio's Path** to a sign pointing to ❺ **Maslinovnik**. A rocky footpath through bushes of rosemary and laurel leads to the ancient remains of this rectangular watchtower, once part of the 4th-century defence system. Returning to the main road, you'll spot a signboard for ❻ **OPG Dionis**, a rustic family-run tavern with a welcoming tree-filled courtyard. Stop in for natural juices, homemade cheese and cured ham, or a home-cooked meal of grilled fish or meat. Once refuelled, continue on to ❼ **Vrboska**, an atmospheric town of canals and arched bridges, and follow the delightful pine-scented road hugging the shoreline all the way to ❽ **Jelsa**. Spend some time taking in the lively ambience of its harbour lined with cafes and bars before heading back to Stari Grad via the picturesque village of ❾ **Vrbanj**.

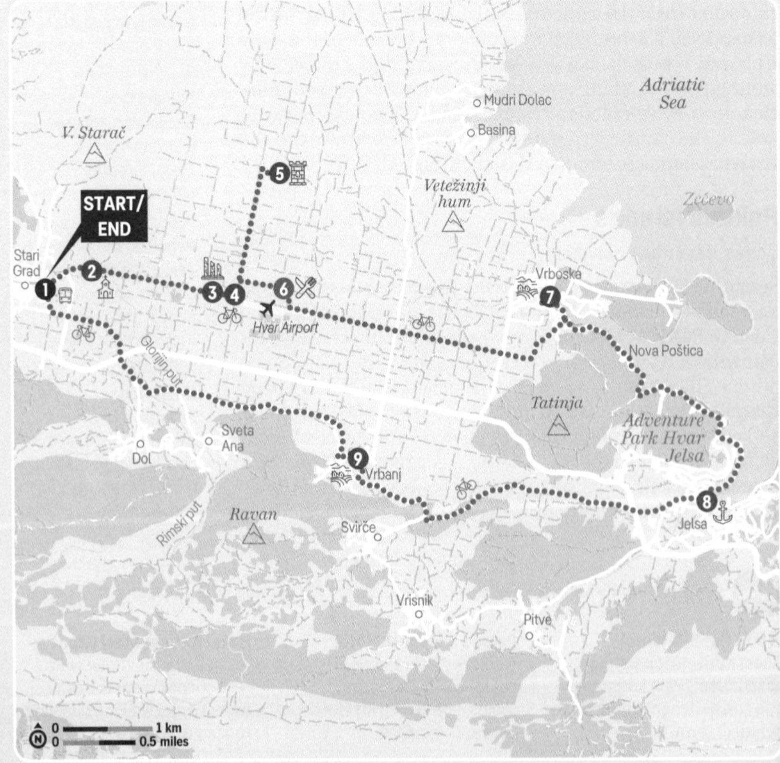

Marinkovac, Pakleni Islands (p155)

Historic Stari Grad

Outdoor spaces and inner sanctuaries

Stari Grad means 'old town' – fitting for Croatia's oldest settlement, but its original name was Faros, given by the Greeks who founded it in 384 BCE. Take in the ancient atmosphere on its quaint squares of renaissance buildings and Venetian palazzos, and in its labyrinthine lanes.

The town's most notable landmark, **Tvrdalj Castle**, was built in the 16th century by the celebrated poet and philosopher Petar Hektorović, as his summer residence. Inside, you'll find a rectangular fish pond surrounded by a lovely arcade of vaulted stone, and a romantic walled garden full of fragrant herbs and medicinal plants. You can imagine the poet drawing inspiration from this ethereal inner sanctuary.

The high stone walls of the 15th-century **Dominican Monastery of St Peter the Martyr** hide another otherworldly refuge that invites contemplation. Delight in the beautiful cloister garden filled with orange trees, and browse the medieval library of age-old books and collection of paintings that includes Tintoretto's *Lamentation of Christ*.

A Wine-Tasting Tour of Hvar

Flavours of the soil

Hvar's homegrown grape varietals pack a punch. White wines have an alcohol content of 11% to 14.5%, while reds hover b etween 12% and 18%. In addition to Plavac Mali, Zinfandel's older Dalmatian cousin which grows here, a number of other grapes are indigenous to Hvar's soil: Bogdanuša, Prč, Kuč and Maraština are pressed into white wines, while Drnekuša is a rare red variety.

Some of the island's best-known wineries include **Duboković** in Jelsa, **Pavičić** in Vrbanj and **Zlatan Otok** in Sveta Nedjelja. Sign up for a private or group vineyard tour and guided tasting with Secret Hvar (phone 095 805 9075).

HVAR'S BEACH CLUBS & BARS

Hula Hula Hvar
A buzzing all-day party spot where people come to eat, drink, swim and be merry.

Falko
Hammocks strung between pines, bean bags and sun loungers make this a perfect chill-out zone.

Laganini
A lounge bar and seafood restaurant with a wonderful rustic vibe on Sveti Klement island.

Beach Club Hvar
Upscale waterside cabanas and sunbeds for a spot of relaxation away from the party scene.

Carpe Diem
A legendary Ibiza-like but overpriced beach club on Stipanska Beach on Marinkovac island.

Brač

BEACHES | OLIVE OIL | MOUNTAIN LANDSCAPES

GETTING AROUND

Brač has a limited bus service between the main ferry port of Supetar and Milna, Škrip, Pučišća and Sumartin, the ferry port at the island's easternmost tip. The most convenient way to get around this vast island is by renting a car, scooter or ATV. A network of 25 bicycle trails covers a total distance of 1026km across the island.

Brač, Croatia's third biggest island, is all about picture-postcard-perfect beaches, dramatic mountain landscapes, delightful fishing villages and rustic stone hamlets seemingly frozen in time. The island is also home to Vidova Gora, the highest mountain peak in the entire Adriatic archipelago, and the country's best-known beach, Zlatni Rat.

Brač's history has been shaped by its exceptional natural resources. First planted by the Romans, the olive tree is a symbol of this Mediterranean isle whose rocky landscape is blanketed with olive groves of over a million trees, growing alongside neat rows of vineyards.

The island is also famous for its high-quality limestone, quarried here since Roman times and used to build many of Croatia's most notable architectural treasures: Diocletian's Palace in Split, St Lawrence Cathedral in Trogir and Šibenik's St James Cathedral were all built of Brač's white stone. Some even claim the columns of the White House in Washington originate from here.

TOP TIP

Brač has its own airport (airport-brac.hr) with seasonal flights to Zagreb, Graz, Linz, Bolzano, Munich, Bratislava and Košice. .

Otherworldly Beaches

White pebbles and turquoise waters

Zlatni Rat is Croatia's best-known and most-photographed beach, and it doesn't disappoint. Its long V-shape (about 370m long on its western side and 470m on its eastern edge) magically shifts and changes with the waves and tides. Its fine white pebbles are soft on the soles of the feet and don't stick to your skin. Then there's the astonishingly turquoise water as clear as a bath, making swimming a true delight. It can be reached from the town of **Bol** along a 2km-long shady promenade lined with umbrella pines. A taxi boat also makes the trip from Bol's port.

Around 850m east of Zlatni Rat is lovely **Borak Beach**, another pebbly stretch that's also a popular windsurfing spot. And 500m further east is an accessible beach that can be reached via ramps and a special chairlift.

East of Bol's port lie two more exceptional swimming spots. Follow the shoreline past rustic-looking Ribarska Kućica restaurant to arrive at **Kotlina Beach**, a pebbly cove stretching towards the Dominican Monastery. East of here lies equally lovely **Martinica Beach**.

Zlatni Rat

BRAČ'S BEST EATING EXPERIENCES

Marino Franinović, owner of heritage hotel Villa Giardino (@villa.giardino.bol) and renewable energy expert, recommends a few of Brač's best eating options.

Konoba Kopačina, Donji Humac €€
The panoramic views and traditional dishes made of wholesome ingredients guarantee a memorable dining experience.

BioMania, Bol €€
A vegan restaurant with two locations: a bistro in Bol, and streetfood stand at Zlatni Rat beach.

Agroturizam Kaštil Gospodnetić, Dol €€
A delightful place for excellent local cuisine on a rustic terrace overlooking Dol's terracotta rooftops.

Apinelo, Supetar €€
A favourite for its delicious cuisine but also for the ambience and impeccable service.

Mali Raj, Bol €€
A charming restaurant in a garden setting highly recommended for their fresh seafood.

Korčula

VENETIAN WALLS | FOOD AND WINE | ORGANIC PRODUCE

GETTING AROUND

You can get to Korčula by taking Jadrolinija or Krilo ferries to either Vela Luka at the far west end of the island or Korčula old town at the east. From Korčula old town bus station (next to the ferry port) local buses take you onwards to Blato, Lumbarda or Vela Luka. Check the Arriva bus webpage for times as they vary from season to season: arriva.com.hr/en-us/dalmatia/korcula

TOP TIP

Book accommodation outside of Korčula's old town; the island is awash with fantastic holiday apartments with warm, welcoming hosts and prices that are significantly cheaper than at the hotels and guesthouses within the walls of the eponymous town centre.

A firm favourite in the hearts and minds of Croatians and Croatia lovers, the island of Korčula sits between Split and Dubrovnik but has had closer links with the latter in recent centuries, with many referring to its old town as 'mini Dubrovnik'. That's to oversimplify. Korčula has Iron Age sites and Mesolithic caves that stem back to 20,000 BCE, significantly more ancient than the 'Pearl of the Adriatic', but you can understand why parallels are drawn when you see its old town walls and marble-paved lanes. It was the Venetian Republic who kept a firm grip on Korčula from 1420 until 1797, leaving some fantastic gothic buildings behind them. Beyond the impressive old town, the island is a wonderful mix of vineyards, wineries, olive groves and small villages packed with niche, vivid local culture, much of which goes unexplored – so stray out west and you'll be handsomely rewarded.

The Old Town: Your First Port of Call

A stunning island capital

The grand old town we know and love today was built in the 15th century, to ensure this far-flung outpost of the Venetian Republic, was defended from invasion by fortress-dotted walls. The sweeping main entrance to the old city is through a majestic tower, **Korčula Town Gate**, complete with a huge lion, the emblem of Venice, carved above it. The original drawbridge is long gone but the wide, imposing stone steps that replaced it give an impression, even if they aren't the easiest to traverse with a heavy suitcase. Once inside, the streets are densely packed with gothic and renaissance beauties that line the cleverly laid-out centre; the fishbone formation was designed to allow in the breezy summer Maestral winds but keep out the punishingly forceful winter Bura gales. Must-sees are the soaring 15th-century **St Mark's Cathedral** and the **Korčula Town Museum** in the 16th-century Gabriellis

KORČULA

Mostir
Bičac
Šćedro
Adriatic Sea
Neretva Channel
Lovište
Duba Pelješka
Goč
Sveti Ilija
Korčula Channel
Viganj
Podgorje
Orebić
Račišće
Prigradica
Babina
Vela Luka
Kupa
Žrnovska Banja
Korčula
Pupnat
Zeča brdo
Veli vrh
Badija
Hum
Kom
Blato
Čara
Postrana
Vrnik
Kula
Potirna
Smokvica
Pupnatska Luka
Zmija brdo
Karbuni
Korčula
Istruga
Zavalatica
Rasohatica
Prižba
Brna
Lastovo Channel
0 4 km
0 2 miles

SIGHTS
1 Blato
2 Čara
3 Korčula
4 Lumbarda
5 OPG Komparak
6 Smokvica
7 Vela Luka
8 Žrnovo

ACTIVITIES, COURSES & TOURS
9 Kočje Forest
10 Vela Spila

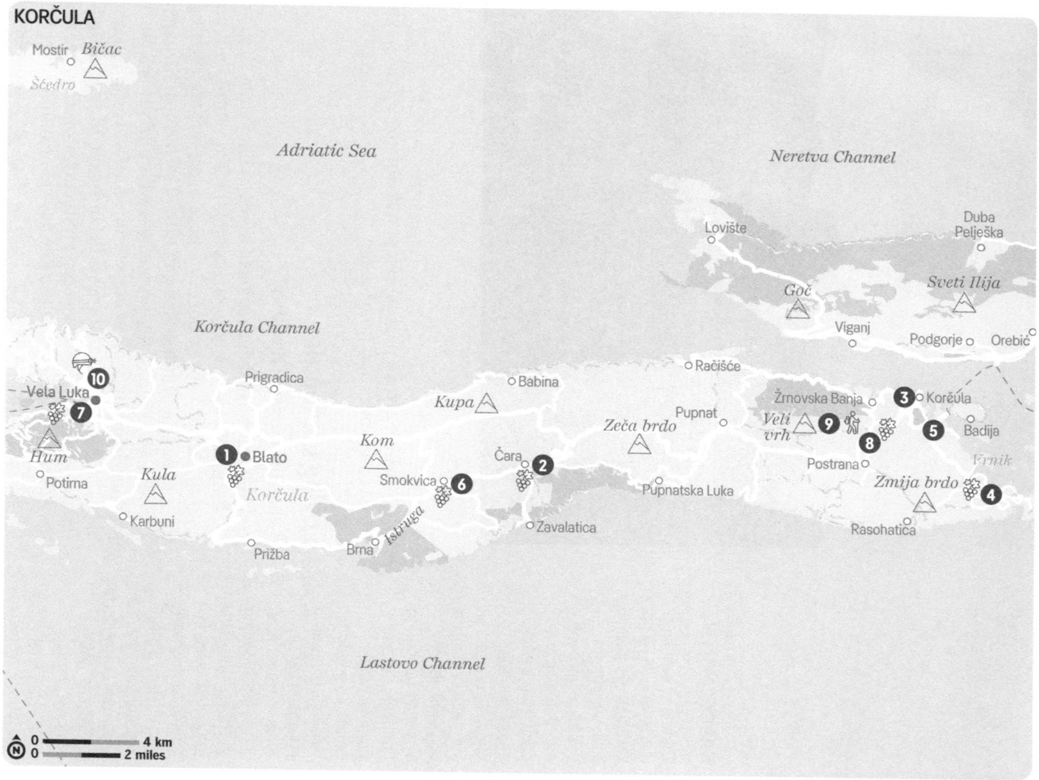

Korčula Town Gate

NARVIKK/GETTY IMAGES ©

Palace, which gives a neat overview of the history of the town via its arts, crafts and archaeology.

Loving Lumbarda

A peaceful corner of the island

Probably the most idyllic region of Korčula, Lumbarda stretches southeast of Korčula town, its small town centre built up around an old fishing port. It's here every Friday evening throughout the summer you can attend Fishermen's Nights, a food market along the promenade where locals sell their produce, hang out and eat everything on offer. The unmistakable Lumbarda area feature is its landscape of vineyard after vineyard. Families have been producing homemade wines here for centuries, and quite a few have gone public in recent decades, opening wineries of varying sizes for the public to visit. The region is so densely populated with incredible viticultural options you'll be hard pressed to choose one, but do bear in mind that as all of the outlets are selling just their

MARCO? POLO?

There's no avoiding this myth if you visit Korčula's old town, so listen without prejudice because they might have a point. Marco Polo, one of the most famous explorers and storytellers of all time, was undoubtedly Venetian, but during his lifetime so was Korčula. While there's no concrete evidence of his birth in Korčula per se, there are records of a Polo family selling the house (the house promoted as his, in the old town today) and the man himself was buried in the Slavic area of Venice's graveyard, which suggests he was indeed Schiavone – the term for Venetians of Dalmatian origin. So, you never know. Just don't mention it in Italy.

WHERE TO EAT ON KORČULA

LD Restaurant, Old Town
Korčula's Michelin-starred restaurant is a treat. Dine on seasonal fish, local beef and its famed gyoza. **€€€**

Atrij Žrnovo Simple Cuisine, Žrnovo
Traditional Croatian dishes done to perfection; the *žrnovski makaruni* is a must. **€**

Agroturizam Grubinjac, Žrnovo
Everything on the seasonal menu here is freshly caught and homemade. **€€**

Vineyards, Lumbarda

own wines, if you come too late in the season (late September onwards) some are likely to be sold out. Once it's gone, it's gone until next year.

One Organic Island

No modern farming here on Korčula

You see the term 'agrotourism' bandied about readily in the Balkans, but in Korčula they really mean it. Farming and agriculture were never modernised on this island so wines, olive oils, honey and even gin are all made using traditional age-old methods; grown without pesticides and produced without large factory facilities. Locals are glad of this and are happy to explain it to you; particularly the team at **OPG Komparak** who offer olive oil, honey and gin tasting at their brilliant education space just between Korčula old town and Lumbarda. Trust us, you won't leave empty handed.

WHY I LOVE KORČULA

Lucie Grace, Lonely Planet writer

I had the good fortune to work on Korčula in 2021, a lovely job in Lumbarda, a town which will always have a special place in my heart. What I've found in the three summers I've visited is an island of innovative, deeply enthusiastic but humble people. Korčulans know they live in one of the most special places on the planet but they're not going to boast about it; they're just happy to share it with you any way they can.

Nautical artisans studio Atelier/Studio Korčula or the beekeeping gin makers at OPG Komparak are what makes Korčula for me, although I have been known to laze on a beach or two here and there.

WHERE TO DRINK ON KORČULA

Mariola Wine Bar, Korčula Old Town
Marija has got the best wines of the island here in her bar and is happy to share her expertise.

Do-Bar, Vela Luka
Enviable harbourside location, cocktails, and wine tasting and wine pairing with chic platters of local charcuterie.

Caffe Bar Prvi žal, Lumbarda
This seaside bar makes excellent cocktails to enjoy between dips in the cool water.

KOČJE FOREST

Kočje Forest, a preferred location for locals to go for a hike, is a truly special, unspoilt stretch of rugged, serene nature with thin, clean, rubble paths and information boards around so you can wander easily and not get lost. A sad but romantic tale is associated with the forest. In WWII there was a lot of political division, fascists versus communists, and many residents were killed by the opposing side. A husband and wife were murdered in the forest and on that very spot two trees have grown, twisted and intertwined, leading people to believe it's the couple united in death as they were in life.

XBRCHX/SHUTTERSTOCK ©

Vela Spila

Wine So Fine

Korčula is all about the wine

Viticulture has been the first and foremost agricultural industry on Korčula since the 4th century BCE when the Greeks brought winemaking with them to this fertile island whose mild climate is ideal for vineyards. And vineyards there are, many of which grow varieties of grape that are only available here: Grk is a crisp fruity white, grown in Lumbarda and the eastern end of the island, while Pošip is a bolder and faintly spicy white, cultivated in **Čara** and **Smokvica**. And of course the pride of Dalmatia, Plavac Mali, a divinely robust red, grows across the island as well as the mainland too. While Čara, Lumbarda and Smokvica are the famous wine regions, you'll spot small vineyards in practically every village on the island, so do keep an eye out for family-run wineries in Blato, Vela Luka and **Žrnovo** too.

WHERE TO TRY WINE ON KORČULA

Popić Winery, Lumbarda
Family-run for 300 years, Popić pairs delicious Grk wine tasting with views of the vineyards and the sea from their terrace.

Pošip 'PZ', Čara
This agricultural cooperative sees the whole village of Čara join forces to produce the best Pošip in Croatia.

Tasovac Winery, Žrnovo
Intimate spot where welcoming host Sanja serves award-winning Pošip and newly cultivated Grk.

Oliver's Vela Luka

The fishing village immortalised in song

Croatia's answer to Sinatra, Oliver Dragojević, known lovingly as Oliver, wooed the Balkans with his pop, jazz and bluesy hits for over 40 years, and was equally popular with the diaspora of Croats who had emigrated to other corners of the world, selling out huge gigs at the Sydney Opera House, London's Royal Albert Hall and New York's Carnegie Hall. Born and raised in **Vela Luka**, the small port and fishing town at Korčula's far western corner, Oliver immortalised his hometown in moving, heartfelt songs. You can visit his grave, which is always covered in flowers, in Vela Luka's hillside St Roka Cemetery and keep your eyes peeled for his memorial house and ferry-facing statue, which are planned to open soon. To sample his music, listen to 'Kad Mi Dođeš Ti' and 'Nije htjela'.

Blato Has Some Ancient Secrets

Tiny town, lots of Korčula culture

Often overlooked, **Blato** is a real gem of a town with a fascinating history that makes it well worth a visit. Start with the easy to spot Venetian era **Loggia and Church of All Saints**, before delving into the **Blato Culture Centre** – and prepare to be amazed. This place houses pottery, jewellery and weapons from an Iron Age burial site just northwest of the town, known as the Kopila Hillfort. The ancient Illyrians who built this site ceremonially buried these items with hundreds of children here, for reasons unknown – there's never been a necropolis for infants like this one found anywhere else in the Mediterranean. The site itself was open for tours while Croatian and international archaeologists worked to find answers, but it's currently covered up to protect the incredible structure; photographs are on display in the culture centre, though.

Then bounce forward two thousand years to the simply charming house museum, the **Barilo Ethnographic Collection**. This time capsule is a love letter to Blato of the past, with over 60% of the household artefacts (from the late 19th and early 20th century) being family heirlooms from the owners' childhoods. Meeting the two ladies who are the owner-curators is half the fun as they walk you round the house they were born in, which now has additional elements of the collection, displaying noble life in Blato in the past too, thanks to donations from locals. Also be sure to say hi to their dog Juro, who is a very good boy.

VELA SPILA, THE BIG CAVE

The mind-boggling mysteries of Vela Spila, which translates as 'big cave', will captivate even the most reluctant historian. Who lived there? How did they live there? What we do know is that humans occupied this cave high up on a hillside that overlooks Vela Luka from as far back as 20,000 BCE. Excavations from 2006 found 17,500-year-old ceramic artefacts, which are the only examples of ceramic figurative art in southeastern Europe from the Palaeolithic period. You can visit the cave, then go to see these artefacts in the small Centre for Culture, Vela Luka (due to reopen in 2024).

Dubrovnik

FAMOUS WALLS | GASTRONOMY | ARCHITECTURE

GETTING AROUND

From Dubrovnik airport shuttle buses leave around 30 minutes after every flight, stopping at Ploče Gate in the old town centre. If you arrive by ferry at Gruž port, a number of local bus routes (1, 1A, 3) regularly head into the old town. Dubrovnik has fantastic pay-as-you-go mopeds called Mynt bikes; simply download the app, top up your credit and drive yourself around. The old town itself is pedestrianised so wear comfy shoes for lots of walking.

TOP TIP

Aim for shoulder season; a visit in May or late September/October misses the mega-peak and you'll get a spot on the beach and a table for dinner. Visit in June, July and August and all bets are off. If that's unavoidable then just be sure to reserve your restaurants, hotels and day trips well in advance.

Catapulted to international popularity by HBO's hit show *Game of Thrones,* Dubrovnik is busier than it's ever been before. Swathes of tourists come to marvel at the 16th-century walls that protect the magnificent streets of the old town below, where steep narrow steps and winding alleys lead to the busy thoroughfare, the Stradun. Those tourists have all come to be dazzled by the well-preserved gothic, renaissance and baroque architecture, which is some of the finest in the world. There's so much more to this city of 28,000 people than its old town though: it's a regional hub for education, employment and cultural events, so take your time and get to know Dubrovnik outside of its walls, as well as within.

Old Town Glory

She's a beauty, make no mistake

With over 1000 years of culture to absorb, Dubrovnik's walled town can seem overwhelming, particularly on a summer's day in peak season. The crowds, the heat and the generally exorbitant prices on the Stradun – the main thoroughfare that links the **Pile Gate** to the protected harbour – are enough to defeat even the most seasoned traveller. But don't let that beat you. There's an incredible jewel of a city to get to grips with and if you plan it right, avoiding peak season if possible, there's stunning architecture to see in this unique, Unesco-listed destination.

The former seat of government for the whole of the Ragusan Republic (as Dubrovnik was formerly known) and one of the most impressive buildings standing in the old town, the gothic-renaissance **Rector's Palace** is now a Cultural History Museum, with beautifully restored rooms where portraits, coats of arms and coins are displayed, bringing the history of Dubrovnik to life.

SIGHTS
1 Buža Gate
2 Fort Bokar
3 Fort Minčeta
4 Fort St John
5 Maritime Museum
6 Pile Gate
7 Ploče Gate
8 Rector's Palace
9 Sponza Palace
10 St Blaise Church
11 Stradun
12 War Photo Limited

EATING
13 Lady Pi-Pi
14 Restaurant 360°
15 Trattoria Carmen

DRINKING & NIGHTLIFE
16 Caffe Bar Salvatore
17 Glam Bar
18 Soul Caffe & Rakhija Bar

ENTERTAINMENT
19 Club Revelin

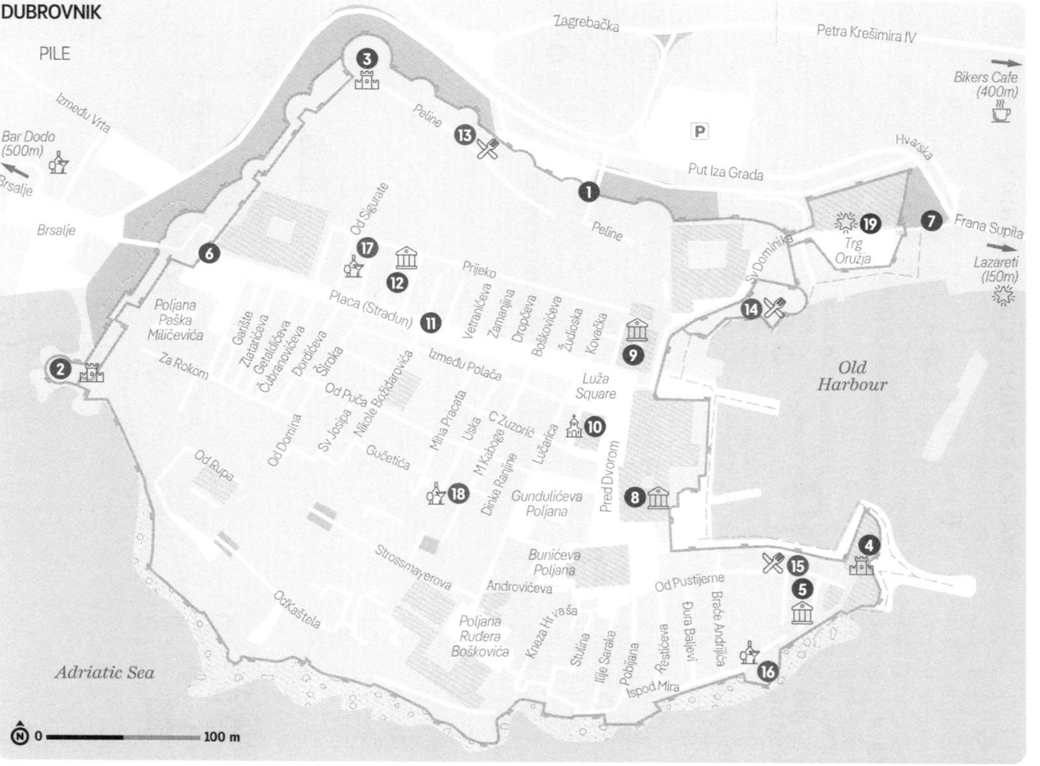

A WALK AROUND OLD DUBROVNIK

Start your stroll at scenic ❶ **Ploče Gate**, the eastern entrance to the city. As you pass through, take a few steps left and enjoy the ❷ **Old Town Harbour viewpoint**, looking down over the port. Keep following the Ploče Gate path as the lane gets narrower and make your first stop at the ❸ **Dominican Monastery**, a peaceful 13th-century oasis with a wonderful museum of holy relics and silver. After, head down the steps and pause at ❹ **Peppino's Gelato** for the best ice cream in town, then continue into the heart of the city, Luza Square, to see its emblem ❺ **Orlando's Column** and the majestic ❻ **St Blaise Church**, which honours Dubrovnik's patron saint. Veer to the left of the church and you'll soon reach the gothic marvel ❼ **Rector's Palace**, which is a fab local history museum today.

Turn left after the palace to reach the ❽ **Maritime Museum**, before moving up into the city to ❾ **Church of St Ignatius** and the famous Jesuit stairs. The stairs lead down to ❿ **Gundulićeva Poljana Market** and its local produce and wares. Cross over the Stradun to the remarkable ⓫ **Dubrovnik Synagogue**, a beautiful museum of rare artefacts. Then it's time to tackle ⓬ **the Stradun**, the town's main artery. Go slowly and take it all in with stops at the ⓭ **War Photo Limited** and the ⓮ **Franciscan Church and Monastery**, both off the Stradun to the right. Finally splash your face and refill any water bottles at ⓯ **Onofrio's Large Fountain** on the left, before ending at the ⓰ **City Walls Pile Gate Entrance**, the best place to start walking the walls.

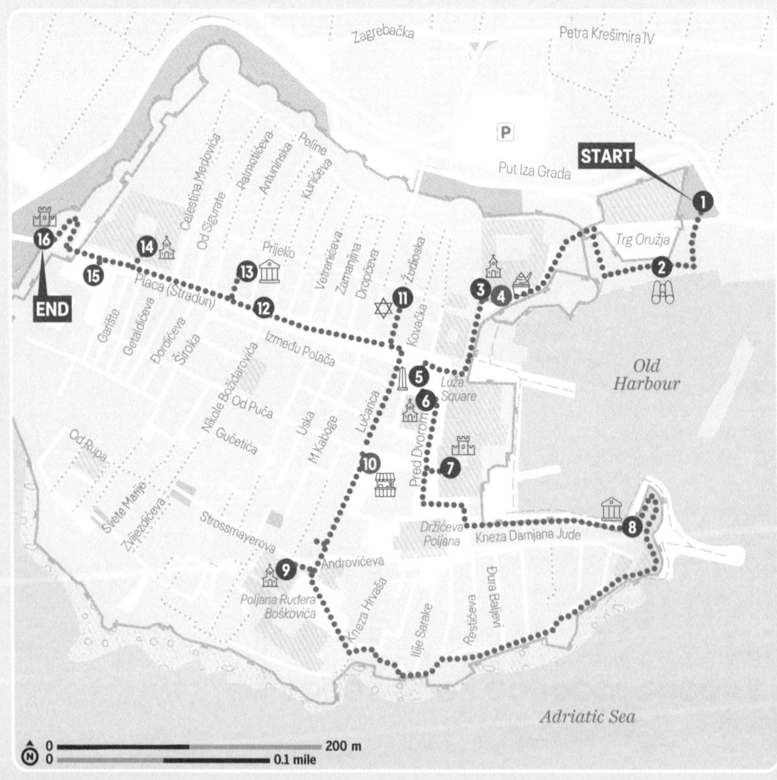

Pile Gate, city walls

The humble renaissance-era **Sponza Palace** is one of the oldest buildings in Dubrovnik, having survived a devastating earthquake in 1667. It's free to pop your head in and admire the sweeping, column-lined cloister hall within, and the Memorial Room of the Defenders of Dubrovnik, a very moving exhibition honouring those who died defending the city during the Homeland War. Opposite is the baroque marvel, **St Blaise Church**, a delightfully ornate structure dedicated to Dubrovnik's patron saint, which was built in 1715. The interior houses sumptuous marble altars and a 15th-century statue of St Blaise, who holds a model of the city.

Dubrovnik Like a Local

Get the inside scoop

You really won't meet locals more passionate about their hometown than *Dubrovčani*, as Mihaela Skurić, Director at the Institute for the Restoration of Dubrovnik summarised beautifully for us: 'What's specific here is it's not just a place where you live, it's part of you. Every individual is made of the city, and

Continued on p172

THE DUBROVNIK PASS

Unlike many city passes around the world, the Dubrovnik Pass is actually very worthwhile. Available for one, three or seven days, it includes entry to the City Walls (which alone are €35 to visit) as well as admission to museums, galleries, a palace and a monastery. And if that's not enough, you get free public transport too – very useful for trips to the beach or exploring the lovely local suburb of Gruž. For nomads and long-stay visitors, a 30-day Dubrovnik pass is being trialled too, if you can prove you're staying for 28 days or longer. Email the tourism board to enquire.

IHOR PASTERNAK/SHUTTERSTOCK ©

Scan this QR code for the official site of the charity that maintains the walls:

TOP SIGHT

Dubrovnik's City Walls

Croatia's number one tourist attraction, Dubrovnik's walls are majestic, impressive and truly unforgettable. Circling the old town in one unbroken loop, the walls present visitors with resplendent views of the palaces, churches, streets and alleys within, and the azure hues of the Adriatic Sea without.

DON'T MISS

- Fort Minčeta
- Fort St John
- Fort Bokar
- Caffe Bar Salvatore
- Basketball courts
- The Foundry Museum
- Fort St Lawrence

The Mighty Walls

Stretching a monumental 1940m in length, Dubrovnik's old town walls are the largest and best-preserved in Europe. The current fortifications have been standing 25m tall for over 500 years. You can thank Dubrovnik locals for that. Any time modernisation or development was mooted by fleeting municipal governments, the old towners doggedly refused, fighting back against numerous suggestions that sections be pulled down. So much so that, in 1952, the Society of Friends of Dubrovnik Antiquities was formed, a charitable organisation that restores, manages and maintains the walls to this day.

History of the Walls

Defensive walls were first built around Dubrovnik in the 9th century, but it was the Middle Ages that saw proper fortifications pop up using 1.5m-thick stone, with 15 turrets built to line the perimeter. Ragusa (as the city was known then) was under constant threat of attack, even after allying with the Ottoman Empire (rather than the Venetians) in 1382, so the barriers were

ANSHARPHOTO/SHUTTERSTOCK ©

Fort Minčeta

made thicker, higher and stronger until the town was completely fortified by the 15th century. The following centuries saw the walls constantly being updated with the best warfare tech possible. They were permanently guarded until the Republic of Ragusa ended following Napoleon's conquest in 1808.

Highlights of the Walls

At the walls' northern edge lies Fort Minčeta's round tower, the highest point of the walls, originally built in 1319 as a square tower to protect the landward edge of the city from attack. It was expanded to its current form in 1464 following a design by Juraj Dalmatinac, an architect most famous for Šibenik's extraordinary cathedral (p146). In TV's *Game of Thrones*, its exterior doubled as the House of the Undying in Qarth. Standing at the walls' eastern edge is Fort St John, whose massive battlements guard the entrance to Dubrovnik's old harbour; the cannons on the upper terrace are a popular photo opportunity. Fort Bokar is the westernmost tower of the city walls, built to protect the approach to the Pile Gate.

The Foundry Museum & Fort St Lawrence

Under Fort Minčeta, one of the most picturesque highlights of the City Walls, sits a hidden little gem Gornji Ugao (which means upper corner) aka The Foundry Museum, which lay covered up for centuries until remains were unearthed in 2008. All sorts of metalwork weaponry were produced here until the earthquake that hit Dubrovnik in 1667, when it was sealed over and forgotten about, making it one of the best preserved examples of a medieval foundry in the world.

Dubrovnik's patron and protector St Blaise adorns the colossal Fort St Lawrence, overlooking the sea-facing walls of the old town. Built in 1301 to keep watch over the city's western side and stand guard for either land or sea invasion, it's a huge building with walls that are up to 12m wide. It's pretty empty inside but worth a look for the incredible views of the old town over the bay. Entry to both is included in your walls ticket.

RESTORING THE WALLS

Mihaela Skurić, Director at the Institute for the Restoration of Dubrovnik

The City Walls have been restored constantly since the 1950s. Deterioration comes from weeds, sea salt and earlier restorations. Profits from tickets pay for the work, so by walking them you're supporting their restoration at the same time.

TOP TIPS

- The route around the walls runs anticlockwise only and takes around an hour if you don't stop for breaks.
- There are three entrance points: the Pile Gate; the Ploče Gate; and the Maritime Museum. You can buy your ticket there if you haven't already done so in advance or invested in the Dubrovnik pass.
- Visit during golden hour, the hour before sunset, when it's cooler and the light is incredible.
- Take refreshments with you (Caffe Bar Salvatore, on the route, is great but expensive).
- Avoid the heat of the day in the summer – there's little to no shade.

DUBROVNIK FOR VISITORS 101

Old town survival tips from **Ivan Vuković**, photographer and tour guide *dubrovnik-tourist-guides.com*

Wake up and get out early to beat the crowds. Enter the old town by the quieter Buža and Ploče Gates if possible. Walk around the side streets: there are lots of steps but it's worth it to see where locals still live. Dining-wise, if there's someone outside the restaurant with a menu, inviting you in, it's probably not going to be good. Especially if the menu has pictures. You can play basketball with the locals every afternoon from 6pm; there's a tiny door by the entrance to the Foundry Museum (p171) leading to a magnificent court.

IMAGEDOC/ALAMY STOCK PHOTO ©

Continued from p169

the city is made of us.' It's easy to wander round the old town in awe, not really taking it in, but chatting with locals in their favourite bars or even staying in the city for a longer stretch if possible, will reveal the unsung treasures hidden in plain sight. Checking out **War Photo Limited**, a really important museum that gives insight into what the city went through in the Homeland War of the 1990s. Then **Bar Dodo**, **Glam Bar** and **Bikers Cafe** are good places to grab a coffee, or go for evening beers in Gruž, northwest of town; **Dubrovnik Beer Company** here is a local favourite. Get around on the handy Mynt pay-as-you-go mopeds and go for a swim under **Hotel Belvedere**, southeast of town. Check out the exhibitions and events at the beautifully restored old quarantine centre, now an event space, **Lazareti**, and if you're a party animal, **Club Revelin** is where to find the ravers.

WHERE TO EAT IN DUBROVNIK

Trattoria Carmen
Fantastic option for incredible seafood, steaks and pasta at the most reasonable prices in town. €€

Lady Pi-Pi
Take a seat on the terrace overlooking the old town (get here early) and order the incredible seafood platter. €€

Restaurant 360°
Michelin-listed experience offering tasting menus, a la carte and great seafood, particularly oysters. €€

Game of Thrones tour

Game on!

Wandering Westeros

Game of Thrones is unavoidable in Dubrovnik. The walls, steps and forts stood in for King's Landing from Series 2 onwards, and pretty much every old town local you meet was an extra in the show. There's no resentment, only love. *Game of Thrones* tours of varying quality loop the old town every day; you can join a group tour to get the basics of what happened where, or go with a film specialist such as Ivan Vuković: dubrovnik-tourist-guides.com

WHERE TO DRINK IN DUBROVNIK

Glam Bar
A local favourite, tucked away down a quiet side street; it stocks a sweet selection of craft beers.

Soul Caffe & Rakhija Bar
Excellent wines, beers and *rakhija* are lovingly poured while you listen to the live jazz musicians (most nights).

Bar Dodo
Open all day for beers, burgers and chilled vibes under the watchful eye of Fort Lovrijenac next door.

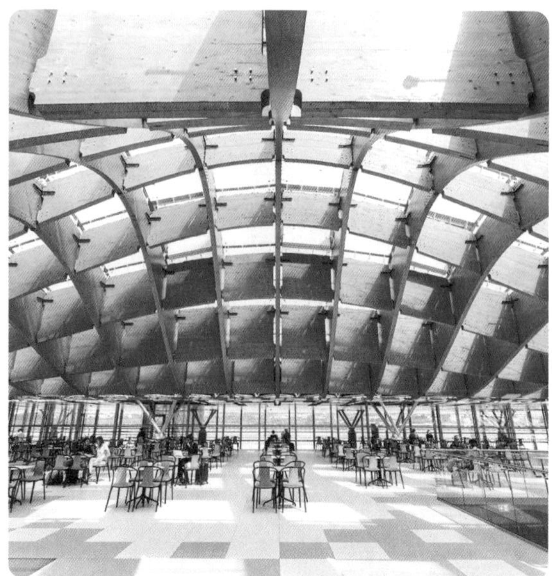

Split Airport

Arriving

It's always thrilling to arrive in Croatia, whether landing at one of the nine airports, coming in by sea at a port, or even by bus or car, as the verdant landscapes sweep by. It's busier during the high summer season (July/August) but with vistas this stunning, a trip any time of the year is heavenly.

By Air

Zagreb International Airport is Croatia's main hub. From spring through autumn, the regional airports come alive, with swathes of international arrivals heading for Dubrovnik, Pula, Rijeka, and Zadar.

By Land

With limited train services in the Balkans, many travellers find the long haul (and affordable) buses run by companies like Flixbus and Arriva to be the best way of getting to Croatia, with regular international services into Zagreb and Rijeka.

Money

Currency: Euro (€)

CASH

Like most countries in the Balkans, cash is very much still king in Croatia, especially in the villages and smaller towns on the islands where cafes and restaurants are likely to take cash only. It's also wise to check with your accommodation in advance, particularly if staying in rural or remote spots.

CREDIT CARDS

You can pay by card (or phone) in all large chain stores in Zagreb, Zadar, Split, Dubrovnik and other metropolitan areas. Have small change ready though for small purchases, bus tickets and the like. Most hotels will take card payment, but do check with hostels.

TIPPING

A tip of 10% is recommended in cafes, bars and restaurants – and preferred in cash. Most hospitality staff in Croatia are seasonal workers who are employed for the summer only, so tips make a big difference to their income.

Getting Around

Croatia is relatively small – it takes just 7 hours to drive from one end to the other if you stick to the highways. That being said, a lot of your journeys are likely to involve ferries if you plan to visit the islands, so don't rush and do allow slow travel days.

FERRY

National ferry company Jadrolinija links the mainland to the islands (and islands to islands) all year. Their schedule ramps up come peak season, and other companies like Krilo run services on useful routes like Split to Dubrovnik during the summer too.

MOREIMAGES/SHUTTERSTOCK ©

Mountain biking, Istria

BUS

Arriva, Autotrans and Flixbus all serve the mainland cities Zagreb, Pula, Rijeka, Zadar, Split and Dubrovnik where you can change to cheap, punctual, local buses from Arriva and Autotrans, which journey onwards to the major islands and more rural destinations.

TRAIN

Croatia is not well served by train. Arriving from Slovenia, Hungary, Austria and other neighbours into Zagreb Glavni Kolodvor (main train station), the only onward route you're likely to use is the Zagreb-to-Split train, which is best booked in advance.

BICYCLE

Long-distance cycling is popular with tourists to Croatia. One favourite route, the Parenzana, runs 123km between Trieste in Italy to Poreč in Croatia, while another choice is taking on the Dalmatian coast: Šibenik to Split is a nice option to start with.

CAR

Renting a car is undoubtedly the best way to explore Croatia if you can drive. Best rental prices are found in Zagreb or Rijeka; expect to pay double in Split or Dubrovnik. The highways are modern and smooth but have tolls in parts.

DRIVING ESSENTIALS

Drive on the right.

While Croatians are courteous drivers, do not expect locals to stick to the speed limits.

Speed limit is 50km/h on urban roads, 90km/h on main roads and 130km/h on highways.

Kosovo

A YOUNG AND BEAUTIFUL NATION

See history being written in this excited new nation filled with Ottoman history, marvellous medieval monasteries, breathtaking hiking trails and spirited locals.

Many who've never been to Kosovo will warn you not to visit. That's their loss. Europe's newest country has the energy of an excited teenager, both curious and aspirational, and it's perfectly safe to visit outside the north. Walk the capital Pristina's pedestrian boulevards with young, beautiful locals who have a glimmer in their eye when they talk about their new nation. See an ancient fortress, mosques and churches in Prizren's charming old town. Visit fresco-filled Serbian Orthodox monasteries and hike the Peaks of the Balkans, one of Europe's most buzzworthy trails.

Kosovo declared independence from Serbia in 2008, and while it has been diplomatically recognised by the majority of countries, there are still many – notably Serbia, Russia and Spain – that see its borders as a dotted line. Memories of the 1998–99 war that killed more than 13,000 and displaced hundreds of thousands remains top of mind, and NATO forces – which intervened to protect Kosovo's Albanian majority during the war and maintain a peacekeeping force – frequently scuffle with ethnic Serbs close to the northern border. Yet Kosovo is ready to grow into adulthood. See in real time how this once-traditional society is modernising (with help from international aid), learn about its heart-wrenching history and wander its serene mountains. And go now before this off-the-beaten-track destination sees the same crowds as its neighbours.

OPIS ZAGREB/SHUTTERSTOCK ©

THE MAIN AREAS

PRISTINA
Maturing capital city. **p180**

PRIZREN
Historic cultural core. **p185**

PEJA
Adventure hub for the Accursed Mountains. **p188**

JUSTIN FOULKES/LONELY PLANET ©

Above: Rugova Canyon (p189). Left: Pristina (p180)

Find Your Way

Kosovo is small at under 11,000 sq km. If you're not on a tight schedule and don't mind some walking, taking the bus is a no-brainer. A car, as always, will give you more control.

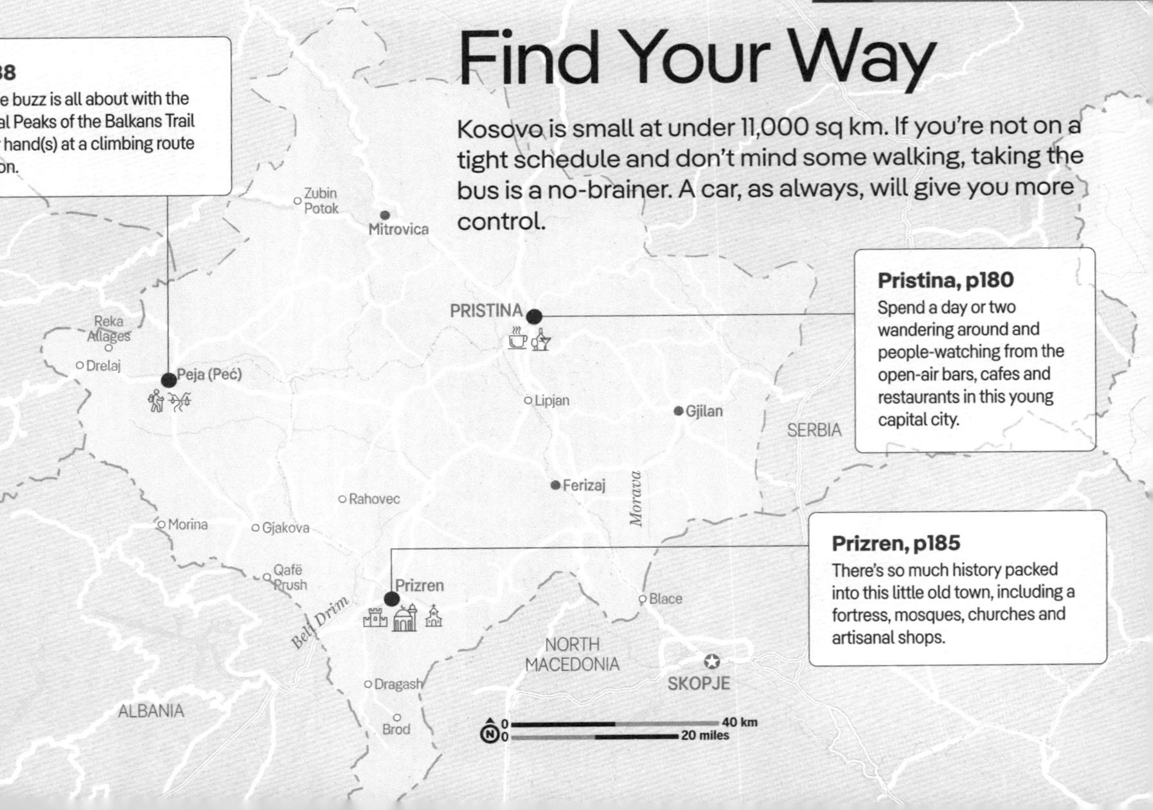

Peja, p188
See what the buzz is all about with the transnational Peaks of the Balkans Trail and try your hand(s) at a climbing route over a canyon.

Pristina, p180
Spend a day or two wandering around and people-watching from the open-air bars, cafes and restaurants in this young capital city.

Prizren, p185
There's so much history packed into this little old town, including a fortress, mosques, churches and artisanal shops.

MONTENEGRO
Zubin Potok
Mitrovica
PRISTINA
Reka Allages
Drelaj
Peja (Peć)
Lipjan
Gjilan
SERBIA
Ferizaj
Moravа
Rahovec
Morina
Gjakova
Qafë Prush
Beli Drim
Prizren
Blace
NORTH MACEDONIA
SKOPJE
Dragash
Brod
ALBANIA
0 40 km
0 20 miles

BUS

Buses in Kosovo are frequent and most sites are centralised around the three main cities, so you can easily save money and avoid chaotic urban drivers by taking public transport.

CAR

Go off the beaten track and have more mobility if doing day hikes in the mountains. Just do yourself a favour and park your car when exploring the cities, as urban driving can be a nightmare.

Prizren Fortress (p185)

Plan Your Time

Kosovo is small and contains few attractions. It's easy enough to get around, though, and certainly worth spending a week to explore before crossing into nearby Western Balkans countries.

A Few Days

Spend a day soaking in the energy of Kosovo's capital, **Pristina** (p180). Next visit the **Visoki Dečani Monastery** (p191) and its medieval frescoes, then head to the cultural capital, **Prizren** (p185), to watch the sunset from its fortress. Head back to Pristina the next day, stopping if you can at the 14th-century **Gračanica Monastery** (p183) and nonprofit **Bear Sanctuary** (p183).

An Active Week

Head over to historic **Prizren** (p185) to see its sacred buildings and outstanding archaeology museum. The next day, visit the **Visoki Dečani Monastery** and **Patriarchate of Peć** (p191) in **Peja** (p188) before heading to the Rugova Valley. Spend a couple of days hiking the **Peaks of the Balkans Trail** (p188) and dangling from a *via ferrata* over **Rugova Canyon** (p189).

Seasonal Highlights

SPRING
Cash in on lower prices and avoid the summer heat by visiting before high season.

SUMMER
Explore Kosovo while it's still off many visitors' radars and attend DokuFest in Prizren.

AUTUMN
Great weather for hiking in the Accursed Mountains along the transnational Peaks of the Balkans Trail without the crowds.

WINTER
Snowshoe Kosovo's untouched slopes and warm up with a glass of red from the Rahovec wine region.

Pristina

COFFEE CULTURE | CUISINE | NIGHTLIFE

GETTING AROUND

Bus 1A connects the airport with Pristina's main bus station. Check the city bus schedule at Trafik Urban's website (not in English) or via its smartphone app. Taxis are common and can take you to the outskirts. Pay a little extra if you want the driver to wait.

Europe's newest capital is full of optimism and potential, though a little rough around the edges. A mix of bland communist apartment blocks (some are thankfully being painted with vibrant murals), a busy walkable boulevard and trendy cocktail bars tucked behind storefronts, Pristina has a lot going on but little to do from a visitor's perspective besides soaking in the vibe. Eat at its ambience-filled restaurants, people-watch while drinking a Turkish coffee or stylish cocktail, and hop from one monument to the next, stopping to visit its two worthwhile museums and ugly-beautiful library. If nothing else, witness how Pristina is shifting from its traditional Kosovo Albanian roots westward to Europe and the US (and we're not just talking about the streets named after US presidents, though there's that too).

Before you leave, see a fascinating Serbian Orthodox Monastery and a sanctuary for bears liberated from tiny restaurant cages.

TOP TIP

Pristina can get scorching hot in the summer, so cool off in the city's peaceful Gërmia Park. The huge 62 sq km space has plenty of forested trails as well as a big pool with a slide. For a gourmet lunch or dinner, slice into a farm-fresh meal at Soma Slow Food in the park.

Eat Kosovar Cuisine

Get a taste of local culture

Like other Western Balkans nations, Kosovar cuisine is heavily influenced by its five centuries under Ottoman Empire rule. A day in Pristina kicks off with Turkish coffee (food isn't served in most cafes). For nourishment, have a *burek* (heavy pastry stuffed with meat, cheese or spinach) from a *burektore* or *furra buke* (bread shop). *Fli* (layered crepe pie) is a common snack or dessert, especially in the mountains.

For lunch or a cheap early dinner, head to a *qebabtore* for a plate of mixed meats, some spicy some not, including *su-juk* (thick-crusted sausage) served with fluffy bread, cabbage,

EATING
1 Baba Ghanoush
2 Gjakova e Vjetër
3 Liburnia
4 Renaissance

TRANSPORT
5 Pristina Main Bus Station

onions and *ayran* (salted yogurt drink). Doner places are where you'll find Turkish-style kebabs. For a great local *qebabtore*, try the family-run **Gjakova e Vjetër** – the meats are delicious and always served with a smile. Vegetarians should check out **Baba Ghanoush** tucked behind shops off Rr Johan V. Hahn. It has pretty meze platters of Mediterranean dips along with lentil patties and falafel balls, which are alternatively served inside wraps. For dinner, try *tavë* (clay pots filled with meat, veggies, or dairy and served straight from the oven). **Liburnia** is a great dinner option with homemade bread to die for, plus a romantic ambience with tangled vines and flowering plants dripping from the twisted roof beams. Or, try **Renaissance**, a stone-and-wood seasonal organic restaurant tucked into a quiet side street south of Pristina's centre. There's no menu – just a delicious three-course meal including local wine and rakija. Eating there is just magical.

Bear Sanctuary

Cute bears for a cause

Before 2010, 13 beautiful European brown bears were locked up in tiny cages across Kosovo as restaurant mascots. Thankfully, that inhumane practice was made illegal that year and in 2013 Austrian nonprofit Four Paws took the bears into its 16-hectare **Bear Sanctuary**. Now with 20 bears plus a rescued lion, the sanctuary, about 20km south of Pristina, is a fun day trip in support of a worthy cause.

From the gorgeous visitor centre, walk the trails and say hello to the adorable bears and lion. Yes, the bears are still behind metal, but they have much more space than the

SERBIA-KOSOVO RELATIONS TODAY

Fifteen years after enacting its constitution, Kosovo is still not recognised by Serbia and relations are tense. Kosovo Prime Minister Albin Kurti, who was elected in 2021, has cracked down on alleged Serbian gangs in the north, to the dismay of Western allies tied up in Ukraine. This led to clashes in June 2023 that left more than 50 Serbs and 40 NATO Kosovo Force (KFOR) troops injured. Serbia responded by sending troops to the border, and KFOR did the same.

For Kosovars, this type of flare-up is par for the course and nothing to worry about. From a travel perspective, Kosovo remains safe at the time of writing, though it's a good idea to avoid Mitrovica and the north.

BEST BARS IN PRISTINA

After dark, the modern and progressive nature of Pristina's young population shines bright in spaces that are casual yet experimental and full of chatter against the backdrop of electronic beats. **Isa Myrseli** (@isssssmyrseli), a cultural worker in Pristina, shares where to experience the city's vibrant nightlife.

Rakia Street (Rr 2 Korriku)
There are a bunch of bars on this street. Sit outside and people-watch whilst drinking a Peja beer or eating *qebaba* (grilled meat).

FARË Bar
This bar delights vegan enthusiasts with plant-based dishes and fruity cocktails.

Servis Fantazia
A music bar with a DJ every night, often hosting legendary parties.

Bubble Pub
This place shines as Pristina's first queer bar.

Gračanica Monastery

tiny restaurant cages and the Bear Sanctuary says they wouldn't survive in the wild now that they've been fed by humans and would be a danger to nearby towns. The sanctuary has some information posted, as well as a little labyrinth where a correct answer to a bear fact will take you in the right direction.

To get here via public transport, take a frequent regional bus towards Gjilan from Pristina's Plepat bus stop and ask to get off at the Bear Sanctuary or the gas station by the road that leads to Mramor. It's a 3km walk from there, which can be accompanied by a dip in the artificial **Badovc Lake**, or you can wait for the Bear Sanctuary's shuttle. Taxis also drive

WHERE TO STAY IN PRISTINA

Oda Hostel
Conveniently located hostel with a homely shoes-off vibe and good recommendations. Not particularly social. **€**

Grand Boutique Hotel
Family home turned hotel with a walnut-tree-shaded garden, farm-fresh breakfasts and free bottle of wine. **€€**

City Inn
This modern, swish hotel is a quiet refuge from street noise and includes a breakfast buffet. **€€€**

here from Pristina and you can pay extra if you want them to wait. However you come, fill out the day with a visit to the nearby 14th-century Gračanica Monastery.

See Serbian Orthodox Frescoes

Medieval monastery close to Pristina

While more than 90% of Kosovo is made up of Albanians, Serbians remain in ten enclaves (or exclaves depending who you ask) around the country, especially in the north. One of the largest is **Gračanica** southeast of Pristina, which is home to a Serbian Orthodox monastery built in 1321 by King Stefan Milutin. The Unesco World Heritage-recognised five-dome church is filled with gorgeous frescoes, including on the domes themselves, with Jesus depicted in the centre and apostles Matthew, Mark, Luke and John in the rest. Frescoes detail stories from the New and Old Testaments, including the Crucification and Judgement Day, at a time when many believers couldn't read. There's also a fresco depicting King Milutin's Nemanjić bloodline watched over by Jesus and angels. In total, there are 4000 faces in the church, which, as legend has it, were painted by Greek artists in under 20 seconds each. Religious figures have golden halos over their heads, symbolising their angelic status.

The monastery remains active with morning and afternoon services and is taken care of by its resident nuns, who sell books and candles in shops on the grounds. Save the candles for another place as burning inside the church isn't allowed (it took years to clean the soot off frescoes after centuries of candles and lanterns). You'll need to cover up if wearing shorts or short sleeves – brown cloaks are provided.

To get to the monastery, take the regional bus towards Gjilan from Pristina's Plepat bus terminal and get off near Gračanica Park. A trip here is ideally combined with a visit to the Bear Sanctuary (p181), 10km away.

KOSOVO WAR & INDEPENDENCE

Nine years after Tito's death, Serbian nationalist Slobodan Milošević took power in 1989 with a plan to dissolve Kosovo's autonomy within Yugoslavia. While Yugoslavia was falling apart, Kosovar leader Ibrahim Rugova pushed for Kosovar independence by peaceful means, without success. The rebel group Kosovo Liberation Army (KLA) formed in 1996 and led guerrilla attacks on Serbian police.

Milošević retaliated and in January 1999 UN representative William Walker witnessed the Račak massacre where 45 Kosovo Albanians were killed. Quickly labelled a crime against humanity, the massacre led NATO forces to bomb Serbia, and 850,000 Kosovo Albanians fled.

Kosovo declared independence in 2008 and was recognised by about half of UN member countries, though not by Serbia, Russia and governments such as Spain resisting their own independence movements.

WHERE TO DRINK COFFEE IN PRISTINA

Dit' e Nat'
Have a coffee or a cocktail and a light meal with a good book at this bohemian cafe and garden.

Soma Book Station
Cafe cut from a decor magazine serving Mediterranean cuisine with a laptop-friendly library.

Sonder
Jazzy cafe and restaurant with smoothies, bagels, breakfast and healthy eats on a quiet side street.

PRISTINA WALKING TOUR

Start your exploration of Pristina from the ❶ **Ethnological Museum** with its two Ottoman-style houses dating as far back as three centuries. Walk down to the ❷ **Xhamia e Madhe (King's Mosque)** built in 1461 and the ❸ **Kosovo Museum**, which has an impressive collection of artefacts dating back to the Bronze Age on the second floor and weapons and uniforms commemorating Kosovo's independence struggle on the third. Pass the city's oldest mosque ❹ **Xhamia e Çarshisë**, first built in 1390, and look across the street at the white fork-like ❺ **Monument of Brotherhood and Unity** in honour of Yugoslavia (the good days, at least). Follow the pedestrian Blvd Mother Teresa to the ❻ **Skanderbeg Statue**, depicting the Albanian hero who fought off the Ottomans from his fortress in Kruja (p57).

Continue past outdoor cafes, then turn right on Rr Sheshi Edit Durham to see a ❼ **mural of Dua Lipa**. The beloved Kosovo Albanian pop star was born in London but lived in Pristina from the ages of nine to 15. Across the street is Kosovo's ❽ **Newborn Monument**, which celebrates Europe's newest country and currently says NONEWBR (No New Broken Republic) in opposition to a Serbian republic within Kosovo. Across the street is the ❾ **Heroines Memorial** dedicated to victims of rape during the war. Turn left on Rr Garibaldi to see Pristina's most aesthetically controversial building, ❿ **the National University Library of Kosovo**, which combines Ottoman-style domes and Byzantine cubes encased in a metal beehive. See a temporary art exhibit at ⓫ **the National Gallery of Kosovo** and then take an elevator up the clock tower at the airy ⓬ **Cathedral of Saint Mother Teresa** for the best view over Pristina.

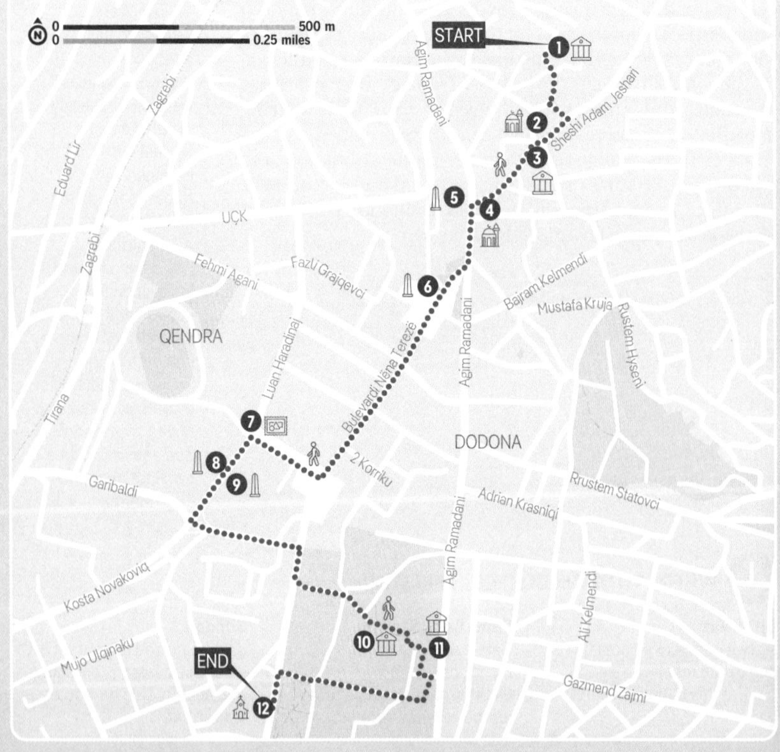

Prizren

HISTORY | ARCHITECTURE | RELIGION

Where else can you take a photo of a fortress, mosque and Orthodox church all in the same frame? Picturesque Prizren, Kosovo's most obvious town to visit, has long been a hub for various cultures, sitting halfway between Constantinople (Istanbul) and Rome. In the 14th century, Prizren was the capital of Serbia and as many as 20,000 Serbians lived here before the 1998–99 war, but the Serb population is near zero these days.

Hop from one religious site to the next, visit Prizren's two museums, shop for fine filigree jewellery and climb up to the fortress before joining locals for a meal along the river or at a cafe near the bustling old-town fountain. You won't need more than a day or two to explore Prizren unless you come for one of its summer festivals, such as the world-renowned DokuFest in August, or to drive up to the nearby Shar Mountain.

GETTING AROUND

Prizren's primary sites are close together in the old town, so you can walk around. The bus station is located northwest of the old town and has frequent connections to Pristina and Peja. If driving, park outside the historic centre or at your accommodation. Car parks will charge €1 per hour, but you can negotiate an overnight rate.

Fortress, Mosque & Archaeology

Wander through history

Sitting high above Prizren's red roofs and earth-tone homes is the **Prizren Fortress**, which has been inhabited by various conquerors for over 2000 years. Most of the wavy-walled castle in its current form dates back to the Ottoman days in the 18th century and has recently been restored. Follow the signs labelled Kalaja from the old town to reach the fortress in about 10 minutes and wander its dark tunnels and along its stone walls. Around the back of the castle is a lovely, tree-lined paved trail down to the river. It takes around 30 minutes to walk down, longer to climb up, and the riverside has a few cafes and restaurants, with the best being **Restaurant Marashi**.

TOP TIP

Join locals and visitors, many of whom are from Muslim countries, for sunset atop the Prizren Fortress. This time of day is less hot in summer and takes on a festive atmosphere. Visiting the fortress at any other time of day is a bit bland.

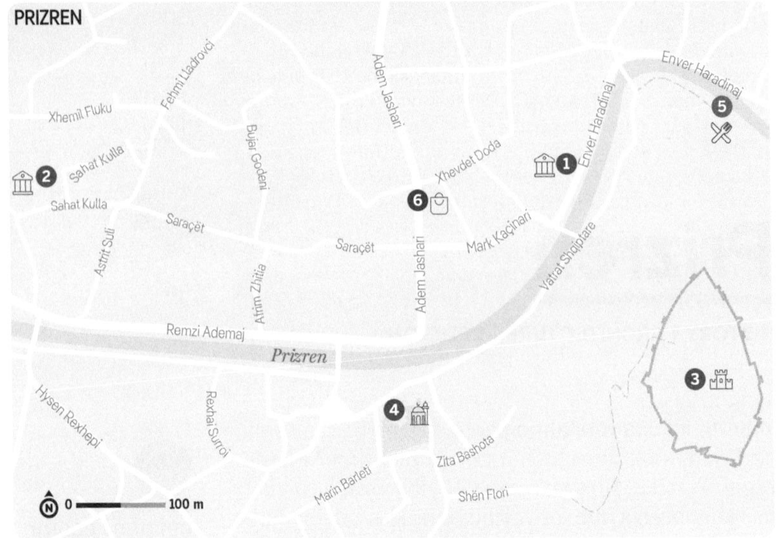

SIGHTS
1 Albanian League of Prizren
2 Archaeology Museum
3 Prizren Fortress
4 Sinan Pasha Mosque

EATING
5 Restaurant Marashi

SHOPPING
6 Rr Adem Jashari

PRIZREN FESTIVALS

In early August, Prizren hosts Kosovo's biggest film festival: **DokuFest**, International Documentary and Short Film Festival. The nine-day event shows more than 240 documentary screenings at unique locations across Prizren, including on a platform over the river as well as the Prizren Fortress. The festival often hosts internationally acclaimed directors and organises mountaintop raves for the late-night crowd.

In July, the new **Prizren Fest** showcases theatrical arts over five days, with theatre performances, poetry readings and more, also held at locations across Prizren.

Prizren's other main site is the **Sinan Pasha Mosque**, which towers over the old town. Dating back to 1615, its impressive dome, minaret and colonaded facade form a fabulous sight from the street, though it's also well worth going inside (outside of prayer times) to see the detailed frescoes and architectural highlights. Remove your shoes; women should wear a head scarf.

Across the river in an alley off of Rr Saraçët is Prizren's impressive **Archaeology Museum**. This well-maintained white and glass museum inside a former *hammam* houses hundreds of artefacts spanning thousands of years, some dating back to the Neolithic period. There are Roman tombstones and a sarcophagus lid in the garden, plus pottery shards, tools and maps with plenty of text explaining Prizren's important place in history. Climb up the clock tower for 360-degree views over the city.

Shop for Intricate Jewellery

A tradition of artisanship

In the 15th and 18th centuries, Prizren was known throughout the Ottoman Empire for filigree – the delicate art of silver threading. Back then, filigree techniques were used to decorate the handles of curved pistols and rifles. Today, the art form continues in jewellery shops found near the fountain in the historic centre and across the bridge on **Rr Adem Jashari**. Shop or gaze longingly through the window at filigree rings, necklaces, bracelets, amulets and other precious items. Thanks to EU and UN Development Project funding, Prizreni youth are being trained in the art form, and the use of these ancient techniques is likely to continue.

Though not necessarily particular to Prizren, Kosovo is also known for its intricately designed traditional clothing. While you won't see many wearing these clothes, you can see examples at the **Albanian League of Prizren**. The museum, which is unfortunately short on explanations, also showcases archival texts, photographs, busts and, best of all, paintings that tell Albanian legends and war stories. On Rr Adem Jashari you'll find modern bright and beaded dresses that, while not traditional per se, show off the persisting desire in Kosovo to dress to impress. On the corner of Rr Bajrakli, head (literally) into the shop selling *plisa* (cone-shaped traditional Albanian wool hats). It's been in business for a century.

BEST RESTAURANTS & BARS IN PRIZREN

Qebaptore Ura Gurit
Choose your own meat at this tiny, beloved *qebabtore* across from the stone bridge. €

Noja
Family-run vegetarian restaurant with falafel wraps, *jufka* (cheese and dill pasta) and breakfast. €

Hani i Vjetër
Eat organic traditional food the Illyrian way – from a pot that's sliced open with a sword. €€

Syrrush
Kosovo's first female-run distillery with flavour-packed gin, *rakija*, vodka and liqueurs.

DestiLL
Join Prizren's bohemian youth at this cool beer garden and attached restaurant serving international snacks.

MARKETA1982/SHUTTERSTOCK ©

Traditional clothes shop, Prizren

WHERE TO STAY IN PRIZREN

Ura Hostel
Clean, modern hostel with air-con, a big hangout area and terrific location in the historic centre. €

My Home Hostel
Backpacker-style hotel and Mo-Zam-Bik cafe (the owners spend winter in Mozambique) just steps from the mosque. €

Hotel Prizreni
A pleasant combination of traditional and modern, with 12 small-but-stylish rooms and a perfect location. €€

Peja

HIKING | ADVENTURE SPORTS | MONASTERIES

GETTING AROUND

Peja has a bus terminal northeast of the centre with connections to Pristina, Prizren, Deçani and trailheads along highway M9 (take a bus towards Boge for the Accursed Mountains). Driving in the city is a nightmare - avoid if possible. Parking lots charge just €1-2 to park for the day.

Peja (Peć in Serbian) took a lot of damage during the Kosovo War and has mostly been reconstructed in the last two decades. The city has a strong sense of community (it's said that locals think more about their neighbours than themselves), a small bazaar lined with busy cafes and bars, and lovely pedestrian walkways that get jammed during post-dinner strolls known as *xhiro*. The main reason to visit Peja is as a base for Kosovo's northwestern peaks, which are some of the most beautiful in the Balkans and home to the transnational Peaks of the Balkans Trail. Meet your guide in Peja and gather supplies for the trek, which can take up to two weeks if hiking into Montenegro and Albania. Peja is also near the Rugova Canyon with thrilling *vie ferrate* (climbing routes) and two Serbian monasteries that have some of the most amazing medieval frescoes in Europe.

TOP TIP

Accommodation options in Peja aren't great, especially the hostels which don't have air-con nor full-time receptionists. For something more comfortable and scenic, stay in the mountains at a guesthouse or an A-frame cabin, many of which have been freshly built to meet the tide of travellers hiking the Peaks of the Balkans.

Hike the Peaks

Epic multi-day trek

During the Kosovo War, the Balkan peaks in the Accursed Mountains and Rugova region west of Peja filled with thousands of refugees fleeing to Montenegro, Albania and abroad, some carrying their parents and children in their arms through the ancient mountain passes. A dozen years later, local tourism organisations and hiking associations joined the German Development Agency to create a transnational trail in the mountains that would keep Kosovars in the country by boosting tourism and creating jobs. The strategy appears to be working, as the resulting 192km Peaks of the Balkans Trail has become one of the most buzzworthy hikes in Europe.

Stretching over the borders of Kosovo, Montenegro and Albania, the Peaks of the Balkans Trail ranges from day hikes to a 12-day circuit, with shorter crossings available. Leave two or three days if you just want to hike in Kosovo. The trail is

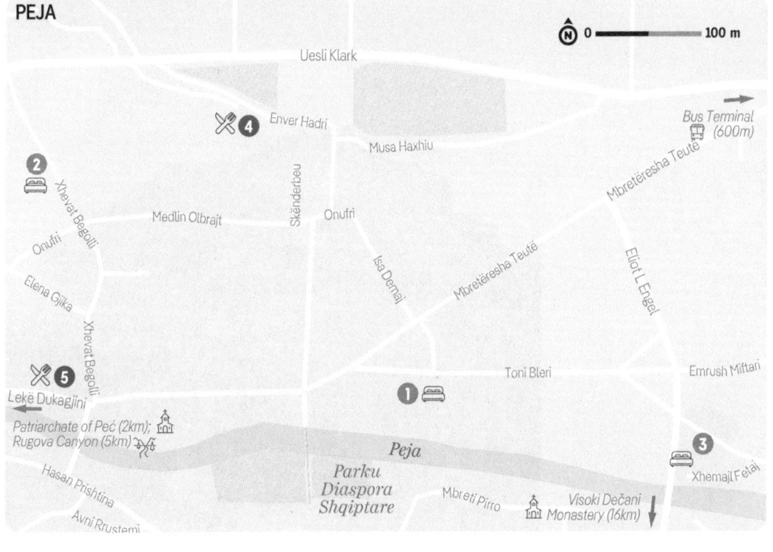

SLEEPING
1 Dukagjini Hotel
2 Hotel Kulla e Zenel Beut
3 Stone Bridge Hotel

EATING
4 Art Design
5 Qebaptore Bujce

well-marked in red and white so you can do it self-guided, but it's wise to contact a local hiking operator like **Balkans Natural Adventure** if only to coordinate border-crossing permits. The organisation, which operates a visitor centre and the helpful peaksofthebalkans.info, can also link you up with a guided group, book guesthouses, provide detailed maps and gives free advice.

The trails cover a surprisingly diverse stretch of terrain, with spectacular vistas, high-altitude lakes and plenty of villages with traditional and modern cabins to spend the night. If you just want a taste, take a bus from the terminal Peja towards Boge and get off near Kuqishtë to climb up **Guri i Kuq** (2522m). The hike is gorgeous, even just to the first mountain lake, and there are plenty of guesthouses and the superb **Guri i Kuq Restaurant**.

Vie Ferrate, Zip Line & Rock Climbing

Adrenaline in Rugova Canyon

Minutes west of Peja, find the Rugova Canyon, a cluster of spectacular peaks towering over the river and bolted with four *via ferrata* routes operated by the Climbing Association of Peja and **Balkans Natural Adventure**. For the unacquainted, *via ferrata* involves clamping carabiners onto ropes secured into the cliff face and shuffling your

ALBANIAN UNIFICATION

If you ask Kosovars or Albanians, many would call a united Albania a dream. After all, Kosovo's division with Albania was penned not by its own hand, but by European powers following the breakup of the Ottoman Empire. In 2021, Albanian Prime Minister Edi Rama said he'd favour Albanian unification if a referendum were held, and the two countries agreed to de facto remove border controls for vehicles and goods, meaning travellers don't need to show their passports when travelling between the two. Still, it's hard to imagine unification becoming official while border disputes with Serbia persist.

WHY I LOVE PEJA

Joel Balsam, Lonely Planet writer

While it's certainly worth visiting Pristina and Prizren, don't you dare skip Peja. This town has a lively, young vibe, but it's the nearby Accursed Mountains that can't be missed. I loved hiking a section of the Peaks of the Balkans Trail and found the paths even prettier (and far less crowded) than Albania's. I also got to try a *via ferrata* (climbing trail with permanent cables and ladders) for the first time and, wow, my heart thumped so hard I think it dropped to the canyon floor.

Peaks of the Balkans Trail

feet along metal pegs or rock steps. The *via ferrata* here is in the Italian style, so it has tight metal ropes as opposed to the loose-hanging ropes in the French style.

Among the routes, try Shpellat, which takes you up 470m on a heart-thumping two- to three-hour journey past seven natural caves and stark sheer-rock faces. You can explore inside some of the caves, and it ends with a short hike downhill. First-timers and the nervous should consider the 500m Mat route, while experienced climbers can take on the three-hour Marimangat, which starts 2km further west than the rest. You may be able to join a group trip at the weekend, but

WHERE TO STAY IN PEJA

Stone Bridge Hotel
Newish hotel with 10 white-and-grey rooms smack in the heart of Peja. **€**

Hotel Kulla e Zenel Beut
An Ottoman-era stone-and-wood building with modern rooms and a fantastic restaurant. **€€**

Dukagjini Hotel
Peja buzzes around this 1951 hotel renovated in 2008, with smart rooms, a pool and hot tub. **€€**

it's only private tours during the week. Equipment rentals are also available for experienced *via ferrata* adventurers, and you can ask about other routes set up in the country, including in Berim and Deçani.

Alternatively, take a flight over the Rugova Canyon along a 650m zip line. It only takes a few minutes, but it's fun and can be done on its own or in a package with a *via ferrata*.

The Rugova Valley is also a popular rock-climbing destination with 100 routes, including one recently put up by Italian climber Federica Mingolla. Rent equipment and book guides from the visitor centre.

Marvellous Medieval Monasteries

The finest in Europe

While most of Kosovo, especially outside the northern region around Mitrovica, doesn't have many Serbians since the war, important Serb religious sites remain. Closest to Peja is **Patriarchate of Peć**, a World Heritage-recognised medieval monastery for sisters of the Serbian Orthodox faith that was historically used to crown kings. The monastery complex dates back as far as the 1230s and includes a captivating cavernous church covered in vivid frescoes. The church is also filled with marble coffins where skeletons remain. You'll need to show your passport or ID card to the KFOR guards at the gate to enter.

South of Peja, don't miss the **Visoki Dečani Monastery**, which was built by Serbian King Stefan Dečanski in the early 14th century. Located on the outskirts of the town of Deçani, the onyx and breccia stone building features 10,000 painted figures including the only medieval fresco of Jesus carrying a sword (meant to chop sins, not enemies in battle). The frescoes here are astonishing and in the best condition of Kosovo's monasteries. Look up at the ceiling, which reaches 28m on the inside, and admire the Byzantine blue paint, which was priced as high as gold during Roman times. Then look over at the tapestry showcasing dozens of religious figures from the Old Testament leading up to Jesus and take a peek behind the pulpit to the main chapel, of which there are three. A staff member or father can show you around. You'll need to leave your passport or ID card with the soldiers at the gate. Before you leave, stop by the shop to grab a bottle of wine and cheese produced by the monastery's 25 resident monks.

OFFBEAT KOSOVO

Virtyt Gacaferri, a former journalist and current tour operator, shares a day trip itinerary from Peja.

Isniq
Take a minibus to the village of Isniq and visit **Kulla e Osdautaj**, a three-storey stone museum that gives insight into Kosovo Albanian rural life, and visit the **Visoki Dečani Monastery**.

Gjakova
Continue 20km to Gjakova to visit cultural centre **Teqja e Madhe** and learn about Kosovo's Dervish tradition.

Rahovec
This small agricultural town has a wine tradition uninterrupted at least since the Romans. It's also home to annual Dervish rituals that include face-piercing and sword swallowing.

Prizren
Finish in Prizren, the most diverse city in Kosovo, with mosques, churches and *tekkes* (shrines), and make sure to try a *boza* (fermented drink).

WHERE TO EAT IN PEJA

Qebaptore Bujce
Juicy meat plates served with spicy dip on the curve of Rr Mbretresha Teute and William Walker. **€**

Art Design
Kosovar restaurant with artistic decor. It's been one of Peja's best restaurants since the war. **€€**

Kulla e Zenel Beut
Classy hotel-restaurant and grapevine-covered patio serving traditional food like *tavë* (casseroles). **€€**

DARKO CVETANOSKI/SHUTTERSTOCK ©

Wizz Air flight

Arriving

Entering Kosovo is generally a breeze, with welcoming and bureaucracy-free immigration and customs. Citizens of many countries don't need a visa to stay less than 90 days. One thing to be aware of, however, is that if you wish to travel from Kosovo to Serbia, you'll need to have entered Kosovo from Serbia first.

By Air

Pristina International Airport is 18km from the centre of Pristina. Due to the ongoing conflict, flights cannot enter through Serbian airspace, so fly through North Macedonia or Albanian territory instead, which sometimes adds extra journey time. Airlines include Wizz, Austrian and Swiss.

By Land

There are land borders with Montenegro, Albania, North Macedonia and Serbia (only inbound to Kosovo). All are by vehicle, save for the direct train connection between Pristina and Skopje in North Macedonia. Be sure to forewarn police if hiking across borders.

Money

Currency: Euro (€)

CASH

Kosovo has been allowed to use the Euro as legal tender since 2002 despite not being a member of the EU or Eurozone. Virtually everywhere prefers cash, with few having the technology to accept cards. You'll receive euros when withdrawing at bank ATMs found across the major cities. Credins Bank ATMs were transaction-fee-free at the time of writing, though they do charge now in Albania, so that may change. Other ATMs will charge €5 or more.

CARDS

Bank and credit cards are just starting to be accepted in Kosovo, and the option to pay with one is still rare at restaurants or accommodation. It's worth asking if the business accepts card, if that's your preference, though they may ask you to pay cash instead so they can avoid the transaction fee.

TIPPING

Tipping isn't expected in Kosovo, though you can round up or give up to 10% if you appreciated the service.

Getting Around

Road conditions in Kosovo are generally good, though watch out for potholes on some poorly maintained stretches. The driving, however, is erratic at best, especially in Peja and Prizren where small roads aren't prepared for modern vehicles. Taking the bus is a great, affordable option, though the going can be slow on Kosovo's single-lane roads.

DRIVING

Driving can be erratic, with cars pulling over unexpectedly to make stops, though roads are generally good.

SARIME/SHUTTERSTOCK ©

Public bus, Pristina

CYCLING

Kosovo's small size and abundance of less-busy country roads make it a fun place to cycle. If bikepacking, wild camping is tolerated, though not technically allowed.

PUBLIC TRANSPORT

Bus 1A connects the airport to Pristina's Main Bus Station every couple of hours and buses between Pristina, Prizren and Peja are frequent. Buses stop at distinct blue signs, but can be flagged down anywhere.

TAXI

Kosovo doesn't have Uber or Lyft, but you'll see plenty of official marked taxis, especially in Pristina. Pay a little extra on a day trip if you want the driver to wait.

CAR HIRE

Pristina has car-hire options from the main companies like Europcar and Avis as well as less expensive local companies.

DRIVING ESSENTIALS

You can't rent a car with Serbian plates and drive to Kosovo (and vice versa)

Purchase vehicle insurance at the border, though it's not necessary for Albanian rentals; traffic stops are common

Driving in cities is intense and it's common to block traffic if you want to merge

ECSTK22/SHUTTERSTOCK ©

Above: Kotor (p200) and the Bay of Kotor (p205). Right: Lake Skadar National Park (p220)

Montenegro

MOUNTAINS, COAST AND ANCIENT TOWNS

With so much natural beauty squeezed into such a small area, Montenegro is a miniature marvel.

It may be one of the Western Balkans' smallest nations but Montenegro is simultaneously one of its tourism heavy-hitters. A large reason for that is the extravagant beauty of its compact coastline. Nowhere is this more pronounced than in the extraordinarily pretty Bay of Kotor, where the enclosing mountains dip their feet directly into crystalline waters.

Every summer tens of thousands descend on Montenegro's tiny Adriatic coastline, cramming the beaches and packing into the picture-perfect walled towns scattered along it. When the crowds get too much, it's easy to escape to the mountains. In less than an hour you can be hiking along wild trails, wine-tasting in remote villages or kayaking through the water lilies on vast Lake Skadar. Push a little further and there's rafting, canyoning and skiing on offer, and even wilder places to explore.

Montenegro's often-painful position on the dividing lines of civilisations has bequeathed it a diverse and fascinating set of historic relics. You'll find Illyrian ruins, Greek cemeteries, Roman mosaics, Byzantine frescoes, Serbian monasteries, Venetian palaces, Ottoman mosques, Austrian forts and lots of zany Yugoslav-era hotels and monuments scattered all over the country.

Combine that with a Mediterranean climate and lots of delicious things to eat and drink, and you'll begin to see why this wee nation has such an outsized reputation.

JURIAN CUYPERS/SHUTTERSTOCK ©

THE MAIN AREAS

KOTOR
Fairytale walled city. **p200**

BUDVA
Beach town with an ancient heart. **p208**

CETINJE
Historic mountain capital. **p215**

DURMITOR NATIONAL PARK
Hiking, rafting and skiing. **p223**

Find Your Way

Less than 300km from tip to toe, Montenegro is as compact as they come. A wall of mountains separates the coast from the interior, but they're well connected by highways.

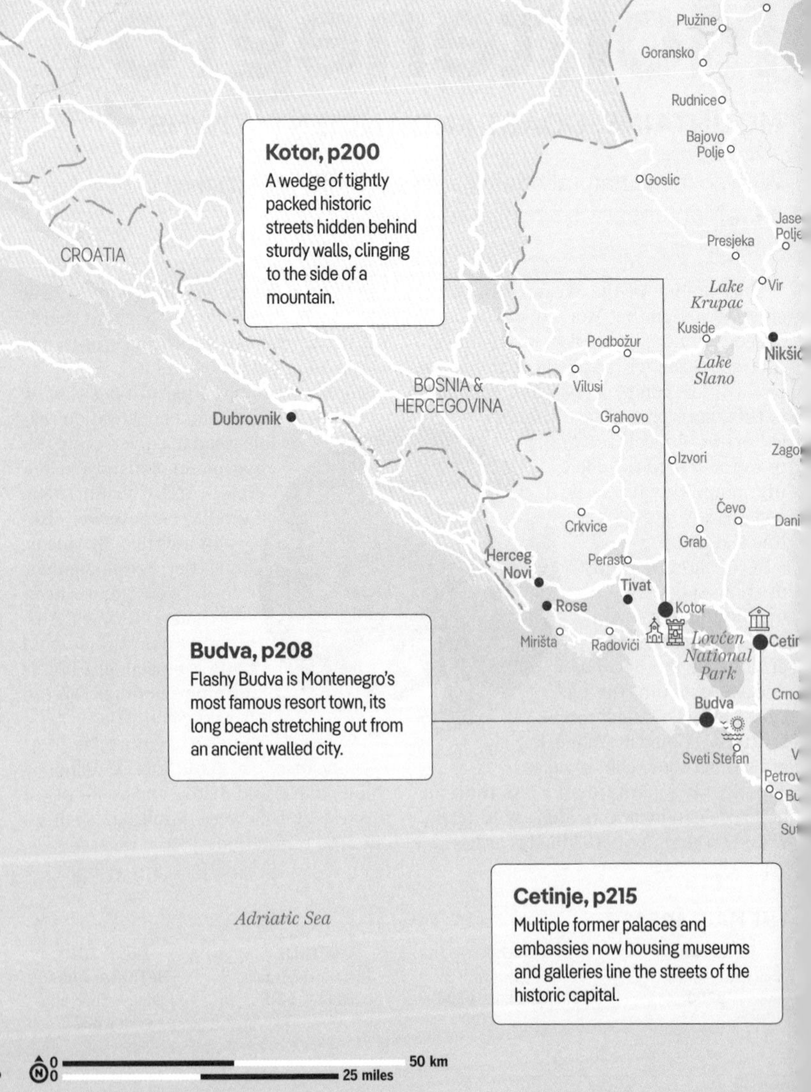
Šćepan Polje
Brstanovica
Trsa
Plužine
Goransko
Rudnice
Bajovo Polje
Goslic
Jasen Polje
Presjeka
Vir
Lake Krupac
Kuside
Nikšić
Podbožur
Lake Slano
Vilusi
CROATIA
BOSNIA & HERCEGOVINA
Dubrovnik
Grahovo
Izvori
Zagor
Čevo
Crkvice
Dani
Grab
Herceg Novi
Perasto
Tivat
Rose
Kotor
Mirišta
Radovići
Lovćen National Park
Cetinje
Budva
Crno
Sveti Stefan
Petrovac
Adriatic Sea
0
50 km
0
25 miles

Kotor, p200
A wedge of tightly packed historic streets hidden behind sturdy walls, clinging to the side of a mountain.

Budva, p208
Flashy Budva is Montenegro's most famous resort town, its long beach stretching out from an ancient walled city.

Cetinje, p215
Multiple former palaces and embassies now housing museums and galleries line the streets of the historic capital.

Durmitor National Park, p223

The crowning glory of the north, offering lofty vistas, highland hikes and unforgettable rafting through a dizzying canyon.

CAR

Having a private vehicle at your disposal will give you the most flexibility and access to some spectacular routes. Driving isn't without its stresses, however, with heavy summertime traffic, parking problems, narrow roads and daredevil local motorists.

TRAIN

Train services are limited to the main line linking Bar to Belgrade via Virpazar, Podgorica and Kolašin, and a spur line from Podgorica to Nikšić. Trains tend to be old and less comfortable than buses.

BUS

Buses are the major mode of public transport. They connect all of the towns and cities, and are generally comfortable and reliable. Each major town has a bus station with timetables prominently displayed and easy to understand.

Plan Your Time

Don't let its size fool you: you could easily spend weeks exploring Montenegro and not be bored, especially if you factor in time for hiking, kayaking and lazing on the beach.

CHRISTINA VARTANOVA/SHUTTERSTOCK ©

Gospa od Škrpjela (p205), Perast

Just One Day

- Make **Kotor** (p200) your priority. Tackle the city walls before it gets too hot and then roam around the Stari Grad. Get lost in the maze of lanes, call into whichever churches you stumble across and stop to pat the cats. Visit the Maritime Museum if you have time.

- In the late afternoon, head to **Perast** (p205) and take a boat to **Gospa od Škrpjela** (p205) island.

- Afterwards, stroll along the waterfront to watch the sunset before sitting down to a seafood feast. Head back to Kotor and finish up with a nightcap at one of the bars.

Seasonal Highlights

July and August mark, the peak of the summertime craziness, but Montenegro's tourism season now extends from around April to October. Skiing and tourist-free walled towns make winter appealing, too.

FEBRUARY

The **Venetian carnival** tradition lingers in Tivat (p206) and Kotor (p200) with masked balls and parades in the lead-up to Lent.

APRIL

Rafting starts up on the **Tara** (p225), with spring thaws revving up the river. The coast emerges from its slumber.

JUNE

Summer is ushered in with long, warm days and the **Boka Navy Day** festivities in Kotor (p200) on 26 June.

FROM LEFT: OLGA ILINICH/SHUTTERSTOCK ©, ANDREW MAYOVSKYY/SHUTTERSTOCK ©, OLGA ILINICH/SHUTTERSTOCK ©

Four Days on the Coast

- Base yourself in **Kotor** (p200) for the first two nights, spending the first day exploring the Stari Grad and climbing the city walls.

- On day two, drive around the Bay of Kotor, stopping first at **Perast** (p205). Have lunch at **Konoba Ćatovića Mlini** (p206) in Morinj and continue on to **Herceg Novi** (p206). Return via the ferry to **Tivat** (p206).

- Relocate to **Budva** (p208) on day three and spend it exploring and lazing on the beach.

- On your final full day, head to Pržno and walk to **Sveti Stefan** (p212), an impressive backdrop for a swim, then head on to **Stari Bar** (p213).

The Full Monte in a Week

- Start in **Herceg Novi** (p206) and spend the first day driving along the bay to **Perast** (p205) and on to **Kotor** (p200).

- On day two take the serpentine road up through **Lovćen National Park** (p219) to **Cetinje** (p215).

- Visit **Ostrog Monastery** (p222) on day three, en route to **Durmitor National Park** (p223).

- On day four stop at **Biogradska Gora National Park** (p227) before spending the night in **Kolašin** (p226).

- Spend day five visiting **Morača Monastery** (p228), **Podgorica** (p221) and **Lake Skadar** (p220).

- Chill out in **Budva** (p208) on day six before continuing along the coast on your last day, stopping at **Sveti Stefan** (p212), **Stari Bar** (p213) and **Ulcinj** (p213).

JULY

Peak summer with high temperatures and large crowds. On the plus side, it's also the peak festival season.

AUGUST

Crowded beaches and traffic snarls, but also warm waters, sunny days and music festivals in Kotor, Bar and Nikšić (pictured).

SEPTEMBER

A wonderful month to visit, with the waters still warm but the crowds thinning substantially. Great hiking weather.

DECEMBER

Snow falls on the mountains and skiing starts in the north. **Virpazar** (p222) holds its traditional wine and food festival.

Kotor

CHURCHES | CITY WALLS | MUSEUMS

GETTING AROUND

It's easy to explore Kotor on foot. The entirety of the Stari Grad is vehicle-free, so be prepared to lug your bags if you're staying there. There's a paid parking lot on the waterfront directly across from the Stari Grad, another just over the Škurda River, and still more in the Škaljari neighbourhood. Kotor's bus station is a five-minute walk from the Gurdić Gate. Water taxis and excursion boats depart from Park Slobode, immediately north of the Stari Grad.

TOP TIP

Museums Kotor consists of three minor museums in Kotor along with the Perast Town Museum and Risan's Roman mosaics. Combined tickets are available for all of them (€12), just the Kotor trio (€5) or just the other two (€8).

Wedged between brooding mountains and a moody corner of the bay, achingly atmospheric Kotor (pronounced '*koh*-tor') is perfectly at one with its setting. Hemmed in by staunch walls snaking improbably up the surrounding slopes, the town is a medieval maze of churches, cafe-strewn squares and Venetian palaces. It's a place where the past coexists with the present; lines of laundry flutter from wrought-iron balconies and hundreds of cats loll in marble laneways. Come nightfall, the illuminated city walls glow as serenely as a halo. Behind the bulwarks, the streets buzz with bars, live music and castle-top clubbing.

Kotor's main downside is its popularity. In the tourist season multiple cruise ships arrive daily, blocking the view of the bay and disgorging thousands of passengers who instantly overwhelm the compact Stari Grad (Old Town). If you're staying here you'll learn to savour the relative peace in the morning before they arrive and after they've departed in the evening.

Explore Kotor's Many Churches

Treasures of art and architecture

The hushed ambience, the smell of beeswax and incense, the emotive paintings and the uplifting architecture – Kotor's beautiful churches have been steering visitors towards the divine for centuries. They're also the custodians of much of the city's artistic and architectural legacy.

Kotor's most impressive church is **St Tryphon's Cathedral**, consecrated in 1166 but reconstructed following several earthquakes. The Catholic cathedral's gently hued interior is a masterpiece of Romanesque architecture. Slender Corinthian columns alternate with pillars of pink stone, thrusting upwards to support a series of roof vaults. Look for the remains of Byzantine-style frescoes in the arches. Behind the altar, the gilded silver bas-relief screen is considered Kotor's most valuable treasure.

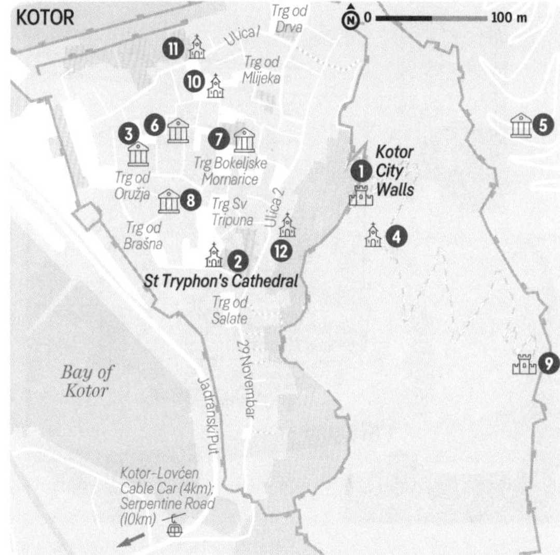

HIGHLIGHTS
1 Kotor City Walls
2 St Tryphon's Cathedral

SIGHTS
3 Cat Museum
4 Church of Our Lady of Health
5 Ladder of Kotor
6 Lapidarium
7 Maritime Museum of Montenegro
8 Solidarity Gallery
9 St John's Castle
10 St Luke's Church
11 St Nicholas' Church
12 St Paul's Church

The cathedral is the only one of Kotor's churches to charge an admission fee (€4, outside of services) but it includes access to the sacral art museum upstairs, filled with paintings, vestments and a grisly wooden crucifix dating from 1288. Behind the grill in the reliquary chapel are relics of assorted saints, including Tryphon himself, a saint venerated by both Catholic and Orthodox Christians.

The city has long had a mixed Catholic and Orthodox population, with a history of co-operation through the ages. Nowhere is this collegial spirit more apparent than in sweet little **St Luke's Church**. It was constructed in 1195 as a Catholic church but, from 1657 until 1812, each denomination took turns to hold liturgies here. It's now Orthodox. Fragments of 12th-century frescoes still survive, along with two wonderful iconostases from the 17th and 18th centuries.

The grand domed **St Nicholas' Church** nearby is the city's largest Orthodox church, built in 1909.

Climb the City Walls

Historic battlements with vertiginous views

Kotor's defining feature is its system of defensive walls and fortifications which arc up the mountain to a height of 260m above sea level. It's a hard, shadeless slog to the top and there's a hefty admission charge (€8) but the views are glorious. When tackling the walls in summer, avoid the heat of the day and bring water.

The main entry point is near the River Gate. From here there are 1350 steps and 1200m of path before you. At a solid pace, it takes around 45 minutes to reach **St John's Castle** at the very top, built in the 15th century on the site of an ancient fortress.

BEST DINING IN KOTOR

Taraca Resto Bar
Tucked-away alongside the Škurda River, with vegetarian/vegan options and Yugoslav memorabilia on the walls. €

Ladovina
Mediterranean fare served in an elegant conservatory under a canopy of trees in the Škaljari neighbourhood. €€

Marenda Grill House
Traditional grills including massive mixed platters for sharing, near the roundabout in Škaljari. €€

Galion
Kotor's best restaurant serves upmarket modern cuisine (especially seafood) in a romantic waterfront setting, gazing directly at the walled town across the luxury yachts in the marina. €€€

KOTOR THROUGH TIME

It's thought that an Ancient Illyrian fortress once stood where St John's Castle is now. However, Kotor first entered the historical record in 168 BCE as the Roman town Acruvium, which survived until the 5th century Ostrogoth invasion.

After the coming of the Slavs, Kotor developed as a city-state. During the Middle Ages, it passed through periods of Byzantine, Bulgarian, Serbian, Hungarian and Bosnian suzerainty before the Venetians eventually got the upper hand in 1420.

The city owes much of its present look to nearly 400 years of Venetian rule, when it was known as Cattaro. In 1813 it briefly joined with Montenegro for the first time, but the Great Powers handed it to Austria, who held it until WWI.

Maritime Museum of Montenegro

On the return journey you can branch off below the 15th-century **Church of Our Lady of Health** onto a path labelled '*barutni magazin*' (power magazine) to come out at the other entrance near Trg od Salate.

Museum-Hop Through Palaces & Churches

Collections historical and whimsical

More than just a rainy-day option, Kotor's museums give access to buildings that would otherwise be off limits while also providing insights into the city's story.

Nowhere is this more true than the **Maritime Museum of Montenegro**, housed in the impressive Grgurina Palace. Built in 1732, its three grand storeys display items relating to Kotor's proud naval history.

Museums Kotor has three outposts in Kotor: the **Solidarity Gallery** on the ground floor of the 17th-century Pima Palace; the **Lapidarium** in St Michael's Church; and **St Paul's Church**. The latter is now devoted to a single incredible object: the stone head of a sculpture of 1st-century Roman emperor Domitian (ironically, a noted persecutor of Christians).

Finally there's the **Cat Museum**, a private collection of thousands of moggie-themed postcards, lithographs, prints, jewellery and antique advertisements.

WHERE TO STAY IN KOTOR

Old Town Hostel
Sympathetic renovations have turned this 13th-century palazzo into one of the best hostels in the country. €€

Apartments Wine House
Cosy stone-walled apartments offering a warm welcome in the heart of the Stari Grad. €€

Hotel Astoria
The decor straddles a line between fantastic and fantastical, but the rooms are luxurious. €€€

KOTOR STARI GRAD WALKING TOUR

Start at the ❶ **Sea Gate**, constructed in 1555 when Kotor was under Venetian rule. Venice's symbol, the winged lion of St Mark, is displayed prominently on the wall. Above the gate, the date of the city's liberation from the fascists during WWII is celebrated with a communist star and a quote from Tito. As you pass through, look for the 15th-century stone relief of the Madonna and Child flanked by St Tryphon and St Bernard.

The gate opens onto the Stari Grad's largest square, Trg od Oružja (Armoury Square). Straight ahead is a ❷ **Clock Tower**, built in 1602, with a pyramid-shaped pillory in front of it; unruly citizens were once shackled here for public shaming.

Walk left across the square and then take the first lane to the right. In short succession you'll pass ❸ **St Claire's Franciscan Church**, ❹ **Kotor Bazaar** (in an old monastery cloister), ❺ **St Nicholas' Church** (p201), ❻ **St Luke's Church** (p201) and ❼ **St Mary's Collegiate Church**. Cut across Trg od Drva (Wood Square) to the ❽ **River Gate**, built in 1540.

Gaze on the clear waters of the Škurda River, which forms a moat on the town's northern flank, then return along the main lane. Duck to the right onto Trg Bokeljske Mornarice (Boka Navy Sq), where you'll find the ❾ **Maritime Museum of Montenegro**, and then continue on to Trg Sv Tripuna (St Tryphon's Square), dominated by imposing ❿ **St Tryphon's Cathedral** (p200).

Take the lane to the side of the cathedral, turn right, and continue all the way to the 13th-century ⓫ **Gurdić Gate** at the southern end of town. The clear waters of the gurgling Gurdić Spring form the southern moat.

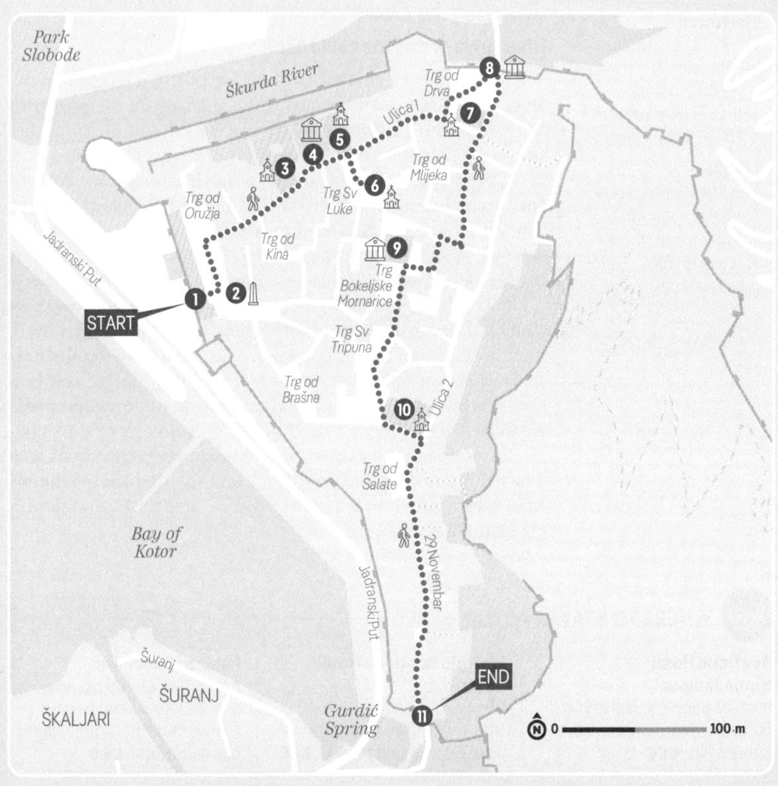

BEST CAFES & BARS IN KOTOR

Platanus
Popular local cafe along the Dobrota waterfront with excellent service and a good breakfast selection.

Pier 65 Gastro Bar
Turkish-style breakfasts on one of the Stari Grad's quieter squares, near the cinema.

Bandiera
There's still a local flavour to this long-running hangout near the Gurdić Gate.

The Nitrox
The drinks are pricy, but Bandiera's neighbour caters well to craft-beer and hard-rock enthusiasts.

Letrika
The Stari Grad's party bar has a vaguely steampunk aesthetic and a side-alley location.

ROKAS TENYS/SHUTTERSTOCK ©

Kotor–Lovćen Cable Car

Journey to Old Montenegro

Hike, drive or ride the cable car

There are no better views over the Bay of Kotor than from the slopes of Lovćen. For centuries the zigzagging caravan trail known as the **Ladder of Cattaro** was the main route between Old Montenegro and the rest of the world. In the 19th century, the Austrian occupiers of Kotor built a 17km road to the top including a serpentine section with 25 hairpin turns. Then, in 2023, the **Kotor–Lovćen Cable Car** was added to the mix. It's capable of transporting 1200 passengers per hour to the top via 48 gondolas, in a journey lasting 11 minutes.

The Ladder hike starts near the old hydroelectric power station on the Škurda River, immediately north of the Stari Grad, and it's as tough as you'd expect. The serpentine road starts near Austrian-built Fort Trojica, a 10-minute drive south of the old town. It's thrilling and unsettling in equal measure, especially if you meet a large vehicle coming from the opposite direction. Take your time and keep your wits about you. The cable car stretches from Dub, on the other side of the Vrmac road tunnel, to a remote edge of Lovćen National Park (1348m above sea level).

WHERE TO STAY IN KOTOR

Boutique Hotel Hippocampus
Elegant design and attentive staff, all within 17th-century stone walls. €€€

Historic Boutique Hotel Cattaro
Perched within the city walls, with spacious rooms and a vista that's tough to beat. €€€

Palazzo Radomiri
A honey-coloured palazzo on the Dobrota waterfront, transformed into a first-rate boutique hotel. €€€

Beyond Kotor

Majestic mountains rise precipitously from slate-grey waters, defining and enclosing a peculiarly shaped double bay with a historic settlement around each bend.

Places

It's hard to avoid superlatives when talking about the Bay of Kotor (Boka Kotorska). Simply put, this is one of the world's great beauty spots. It's not a fjord, despite often being described as one – although that word does help to conjure a sense of the grandeur of the surrounding mountains. Rather it's a ria, the submerged valley of a river that once flowed from Mt Orjen and out to sea.

Driving around the Bay of Kotor, the views are never short of gorgeous. Exploring by boat is even better, with tours departing from the history-filled towns of Kotor, Tivat and Herceg Novi to explore isolated bays, ethereally lit sea caves and once top-secret submarine docks.

GETTING AROUND

The Bay of Kotor is extremely compact with only 40km of wiggly road separating Herceg Novi, in the west of the outer bay, from Kotor, at the eastern extremity of the inner bay. Car is the quickest and most flexible way to get around, but be prepared for traffic jams in the busy summer months. Buses regularly traverse the main coastal highway between Herceg Novi and Kotor. Some services between Herceg Novi and Tivat cross by ferry, while services between Kotor and Tivat pass through the toll-free Vrmac Tunnel.

Perast

A tiny slice of Venice

Once a rich and powerful Venetian maritime hub – churning out ships and sea captains in quantities completely disproportionate to its diminutive size – Perast has had to learn to be content with being merely gorgeous. Despite having only just one main street, this small town (a 20-minute drive from Kotor) boasts 16 churches and 17 formerly grand palazzi, two of which are regularly open to the public. Both date from the 17th century: **St Nicholas' Church** and the Renaissance-baroque Bujović Palace, which now houses the **Perast Town Museum**.

Boats line up on the waterfront to ferry people to **Gospa od Škrpjela** (Our Lady of the Rock Island), one of a pair of picturesque islets that lie just off Perast (€5 return). Capped by a stone church with a sky-blue dome, the island was artificially created around a crag where, on 22 July 1452, an icon

TOP TIP

The vehicle ferry across the Verige Channel speeds up trips between Herceg Novi and Tivat considerably.

BEST DINING & DRINKING AROUND PERAST

Konoba Ćatovića Mlini
One of Montenegro's best restaurants, serving traditional fare in a historic mill building in Morinj. €€€

Restaurant Conte
With its island views, table-top flowers and attentive service, this long-standing Perast seafood restaurant is sublimely romantic. €€€

Verige65
Upmarket restaurant with an international menu and clifftop views perched on the edge of the Verige Strait. €€€

Konoba Školji
This traditional Perast restaurant is all about the thrill of the grill: fresh seafood and falling-off-the-bone meats. €€

Beach Bar Pirates
Seaside bar serving beers, cocktails and coffees to Perast's buffed and beautiful board-shorts-and-bikini brigade.

REPINA VALERIYA/SHUTTERSTOCK ©

of the Madonna and Child was found. Every year on that date locals row over with stones to continue the task in a festival known as **Fašinada**. The magnificent church at its centre was erected in 1630 and has sumptuous Venetian frescoes, hundreds of silver votive tablets and a small museum (€2).

Tivat

Superyachts and salubrious shopping

Tivat is like nowhere else in Montenegro. Only a 15-minute drive from Kotor (when there's no traffic), this workaday town in the outer bay was looking a little shabby in the early 2000s. Then along came **Porto Montenegro**, transforming Tivat's 24-hectare Yugoslav-era navy base and shipyards into a surreal town-within-a-town catering unashamedly to the uber rich.

It's tastefully done, seamlessly connecting the existing town promenade to a new enclave full of sunny walkways, luxury accommodation, restaurants, bars, a beach club, a superyacht marina and shops with names like Bulgari, Balenciaga and Boss. A couple of dry-docked Yugoslav-era submarines offer a token reminder of the past.

Herceg Novi

Battlement views and seaside strolls

With its compact walled town and its long waterfront promenade, Herceg Novi (an hour's drive from Kotor) has a breezy lived-in feel all year round but in summer it balloons in size,

Tivat

its seaside cafes, bars, restaurants and concrete sunbathing platforms buzzing with holidaymakers.

A gate topped by an elegant crenulated **clock tower**, built by the Ottomans in 1667, provides a suitably atmospheric entrance to the Stari Grad. From here a short lane leads to gleaming **Belavista Square**. Its centrepiece is the beautifully proportioned Serbian Orthodox **Church of the Holy Archangel Michael**, completed in 1905.

Two mighty fortresses bookend the Stari Grad: 16th-century **Kanli Kula** (Turkish for 'Bloody Tower') on the landward side and **Forte Mare** (Italian for 'Sea Fort') on the seaward side. From their battlements you can easily see why Herceg Novi was prized, being positioned just within the bay and with views gazing straight out to sea. Each screens interesting short videos within their stone chambers, recreating scenes from the town's tumultuous history (admission €4 each).

Tucked away between the coastal tourism strip and the hilltop Savina Forest, **Savina Monastery** offers a serene escape from the summertime bustle down below.

BEST DINING IN TIVAT & HERCEG NOVI

Buregdžnica AS kod Dutea
Humble deliciousness in pricy Tivat, serving just *burek* (savoury pastries) and pizza slices. **€**

Ponta Veranda
Tucked-away Tivat barbecue restaurant offering outstanding grilled vegetables, seafood and meat. **€€**

One
Porto Montenegro's best restaurant, with a waterfront location and a menu as jet-setting as the clientele. **€€€**

Peter's Pie & Coffee
Vegetarian bakery/cafe on the promenade, selling sandwiches, savoury pastries, cakes, juices and the best flat whites in Montenegro. **€**

Konoba Feral
Atmospheric tavern on the Herceg Novi waterfront serving Dalmatian-style seafood, pasta and traditional Montenegrin grills. **€€**

WHERE TO STAY BEYOND KOTOR

Lazure Hotel & Marina
Restoration of an 18th-century Venetian quarantine station at the eastern end of the Herceg Novi promenade. **€€€**

Regent Porto Montenegro
Located within Tivat's superyacht enclave, the Regent is a luxurious place for a splurge. **€€€**

Hotel Conte
Not so much a hotel as a series of deluxe apartments in neighbouring Perast buildings. **€€€**

Budva

BEACHES | HISTORY | OLD TOWN

GETTING AROUND

Most places in Budva are within 30 minutes' walk of the beaches and Stari Grad. The intercity bus station is in the centre of town, and local buses stop along the highway. If you're not lucky enough to snare a street park, there are paid lots near the Stari Grad and Slovenska Plaža. In any case, once you've parked you're unlikely to want to move the car, as the traffic is formidable.

TOP TIP

In summer, taxi boats from Slovenska Plaža ferry sunseekers to the main beach on uninhabited Sveti Nikola (St Nicholas' Island) for just a few euro. Known locally as 'Hawaii', the island stretches for nearly 2km. Alternatively, hire a kayak and look for a secluded spot on the far side.

Budva is a place where history and beach culture collide. A photogenic walled town with ancient provenance anchors one end of a long sweep of beach that's jam-packed in summer with thousands of holidaymakers. Spreading back from the beach and starting to make its way up the surrounding slopes is a chaotic jumble of hotels and apartment blocks, with flashier and bigger ones being built all the time.

The origins of Budva are literally the stuff of legends, with the Ancient Greeks naming Cadmus and Harmonia as the town's founders in an elaborate story involving gods, dragon's teeth and the couple turning into snakes. In any case, Budva's Stari Grad has been settled for at least 2500 years, the Venetians ruling the roost for nearly 400 of them. Within its sturdy walls it's as if time stopped in the renaissance, and overdevelopment is but a troubling rumour.

Beach Hop in Budva

A consummate Mediterranean beach experience

Ah, the Med in summer: endless rows of sun umbrellas, local pop music blaring and handsome waiters delivering garishly coloured cocktails to sweaty sunbathers. On this front, Budva doesn't disappoint.

Budva's heaving main beach, **Slovenska Plaža**, stretches for 1.6km. In summer, the beachside promenade morphs into a bustling, hustling strip of fast-food outlets, beach bars in the guise of pirate ships and global landmarks, travel agencies hawking tours, market stalls and a fun fair. It's quite a scene. If you don't fancy forking out for a lounger there are places where you can spread out your towel directly on the pebbles.

Things are marginally less chaotic at the two small beaches on either side of the Stari Grad: **Pizana Beach** to the north and **Ričardova Glava** (Richard's Head) to the south. The latter is the prettier of the two, with the town walls as its backdrop. It takes its name from Academy Award–winner Richard

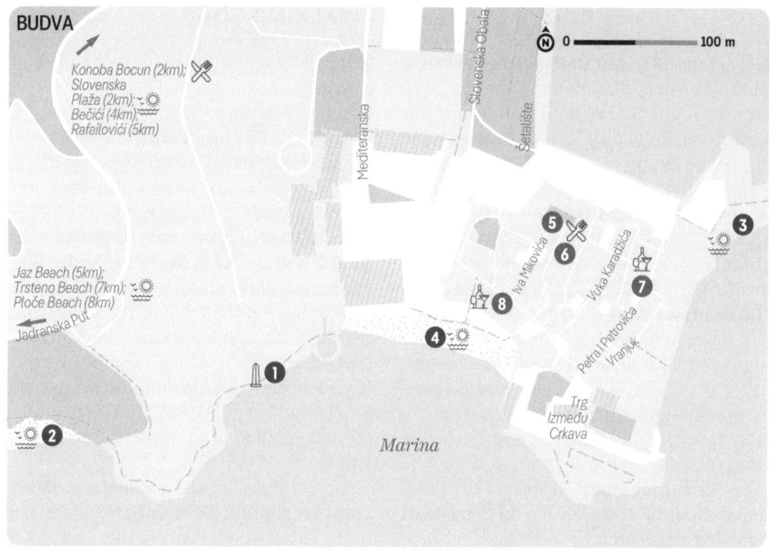

Widmark who was frequently spotted here during the filming of *The Long Ships*.

To reach Budva's best beach, continue along the shoreline from Ričardova Glava. On the way, you'll pass one of Budva's most photographed landmarks, a **statue of a ballerina** posing perpetually en pointe and unclothed. Around the next headland is beautiful double-bayed **Mogren Beach**. You can hardly see any buildings when you're lying on the fine pebbles here – a rare treat for the Budva Riviera. The high cliffs provide plenty of afternoon shade, along with the vicarious entertainment of watching the fearless and foolhardy leap into the water below.

Stroll to Bečići & Rafailovići

Another long beach to explore

If you want a change from Slovenska Plaža or just fancy a stroll or a jog, head to the far end of the beach and continue through the pedestrian tunnel to **Bečići**. If you thought Budva was built up, brace yourself. This nearly 2km-long stretch of sandy beach has been completely swallowed by large resorts, complete with swimming pools, nightclubs and casinos. It caters well to those whose primary holiday objective is to flit between the pool, pokies and sand, cocktail in hand. Even if it's not your scene, it's somehow fascinating.

BEST DINING & DRINKING IN BUDVA

Konoba Bocun
Friendly little locals' tavern tucked away in a residential neighbourhood. **€€**

Rivijera
Great service and delicious Dalmatian-style food in an atmospheric Stari Grad lane. **€€€**

Piano Nobile
Upmarket 'steak and burger bar' in a beautiful Venetian building, spilling onto a little square. **€€€**

Casper
Chill out with local craft beers, cocktails or house-roasted coffee in this Stari Grad garden bar.

Rakia & Wine Bar
Appealing hole-in-the-wall wine bar in the Stari Grad.

BUDVA STARI GRAD WALKING TOUR

Start at the ❶ **Giant Bell** outside the walls, a leftover from 1964 Viking movie *The Long Ships* starring Sidney Poitier and filmed in Yugoslavia. Enter the Stari Grad through the last portal on this side, the ❷ **Pizana Gate**.

Head along the marbled lane, following it past ❸ **Budva Museum** to Trg između crkava (literally, 'the square between the churches'). Immediately to the left is the former Catholic Cathedral, now ❹ **St John the Baptist Church**, with a bell tower and Gothic-style Bishop's residence. Behind the main altar is a colourful mosaic by Croatian artist Ivo Dulčić, while a side chapel houses the Madonna of Budva, a 12th-century icon venerated by Catholic and Orthodox Budvans alike.

An open space nearby displays the ruined foundations of a 5th-century ❺ **Christian basilica** uncovered by a devastating 1979 earthquake. Beyond this is the ❻ **Citadela** (admission €4.50 for sea views and model ships).

Plonked in the centre of the square is fresco-filled ❼ **Holy Trinity**, an Orthodox church constructed in 1804 from stripes of pink and honey-coloured stone. Built into the town walls nearby are two abandoned churches: tiny 12th-century ❽ **St Sava the Sanctified** and ❾ **St Mary in Punta**, Budva's oldest, dating from 840.

Backtrack to the edge of the square and turn left. The lane opposite the ❿ **Tourist Office** leads to a small square containing a 1st-century ⓫ **Roman altar**. Exit the Stari Grad via the ⓬ **Main Gate**, noting the winged lion of St Mark (the symbol of Venice).

Straight ahead are the remains of an ⓭ **ancient necropolis**, found during construction of the Avala Hotel. Many of the artefacts in Budva Museum were discovered here.

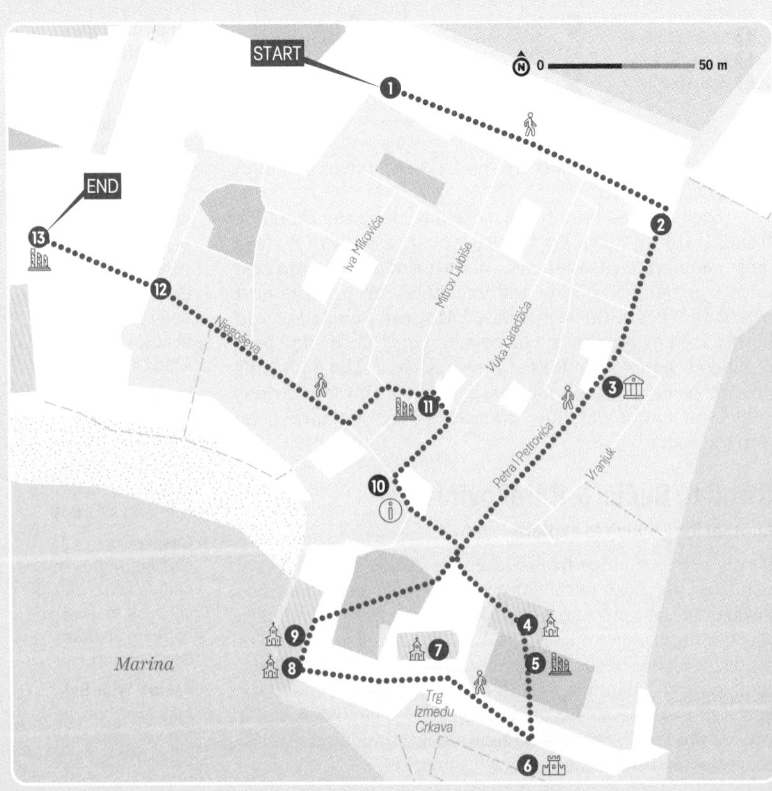

JANA JANINA/SHUTTERSTOCK ©

Pizana Beach (p208)

Rafailovići, at the beach's eastern end, is similarly overdeveloped but retains the vaguest echoes of a village feel. Older-style apartment hotels hug the cliffs and restaurants line the shore. It's a popular spot for families, but at high tide there's hardly any beach.

Drive to Less Built-Up Bays

Change your beach view

If you're after slightly less high-rise with your beach views, try the bays west of Budva. The blue waters and broad sands of **Jaz Beach** (ronounced 'yahz') lie just off the highway, 10 minutes from Budva (traffic allowing). Sun umbrellas and beach bars line the main section but you'll find more peace and quiet down the eastern end. Continue around the headland if you prefer to swim and sunbathe naked.

West from Jaz is **Trsteno Beach**, a sandy cove with shallow waters. Next up is pumping **Ploče Beach**. You'll either love or hate its beach-club vibe, with its swimming pools, sunbathing terraces and wade-in bars.

BUDVA'S SLIPPERY FOUNDERS

The founding of Budva is celebrated in the sort of mythical soap opera that the ancient Greeks loved so much. It involves Cadmus, founder of Thebes and brother of Europa (who the continent is named after).

Cadmus' luck ran out after he killed a sacred dragon, so he and his wife Harmonia hitched up their oxen and set off to make a fresh start. Far away they founded a new city, naming it Bouthoe (later Budva) after the Greek word for oxen.

The miserable luck didn't lift, and Cadmus was heard complaining that if the gods were so fond of serpents then he wished he was one. The gods, never missing an opportunity for a spot of black humour, obliged – promptly turning him into a snake.

PLACES TO STAY IN BUDVA

Freedom Hostel
Beloved sociable hostel with a small courtyard and tidy little rooms spread between three buildings. **€**

Sailor House
Centuries-old Stari Grad house with welcoming hosts, nicely decorated bedrooms and a guest kitchen. **€€**

Villa M Palace
There's a seductive glamour to this modern block of luxurious apartments near the Stari Grad. **€€€**

Beyond Budva

Rugged mountains frame a sublime stretch of coast peppered with walled towns, monasteries and mosques steeped in history.

Places

GETTING AROUND

The Adriatic Highway is a highly scenic route. When there's no traffic you can drive the entire length of the coast in 90 minutes but be prepared for snarls in summer. Buses ply the highway from Budva to Ulcinj, stopping in all towns in between.

Montenegro's entire Adriatic coastline stretches barely 100km as the crow flies, but it still manages to pack a lot in. The highlights are a set of picture-perfect walled towns jutting out over turquoise waters, and another hidden within the folds of the surrounding mountains.

The presence of Venice can be felt throughout, but the southeastern half has the added overlay of three centuries of Ottoman rule, contributing a different flavour entirely.

In recent years, apartment blocks and high-rise hotels have sprouted in profusion, catering to the masses that pack the many beautiful beaches in summer. Visit outside of the peak season to experience the seaside towns and villages at their most charming.

Sveti Stefan

Beautiful beaches and island views

The fortified island village of Sveti Stefan (St Steven), a 10-minute drive south of Budva, is like something from a fairy tale. From the highway above it appears as a photogenic jumble of terracotta roofs set against turquoise waters, anchored to a pink-hued beach by a narrow causeway. Make the most of the view as it can only be admired from afar. The entire island village was nationalised in the 1950s and is now part of the luxurious **Aman Resorts**, meaning it's off-limits to all but paying guests.

A magnificent **walk** cuts through the forested parkland separating Pržno from Sveti Stefan. This route traverses some of Montenegro's most beautiful beaches, although Aman Resorts has been known to charge exorbitant fees for non-guests to access them. If that's the case, throw down your towel on the public **beach** south of the island causeway.

Sveti Stefan

Stari Bar

Ancient streets and tasty treats

Tucked away on the lower slopes of Mt Rumija above the scruffy modern city of Bar (an hour's drive from Budva), Stari Bar (Old Bar) is a lost-in-time, partially ruined, ancient settlement that is one of the most enchanting locales on the entire seaboard. Its current state is mainly a result of Montenegrin shelling when they captured the town in 1878.

The cobbled lane leading up to the gloriously dilapidated walled city (admission €3) is home to some of the best restaurants in the region, humble places specialising in a local cuisine which draws heavily from the region's Turkish past.

Ulcinj

Beaches, mosques and ancient walls

All of Montenegro's walled coastal towns are spellbinding but Ulcinj (an 80-minute drive from Budva) has its own unique magic. For a start, its **Stari Grad** is still largely residential and even a little ramshackle, a legacy of the 1979 earthquake.

TOP TIP

Bar is a transport hub, welcoming ferries from Italy, trains from Serbia and buses from all over the region.

BEST RESTAURANTS BETWEEN BUDVA & BAR

Caffe Caffe
Casual dining halfway up the hill in Sveti Stefan, serving smoothies, breakfasts, sandwiches, pizza, pasta and grills. **€**

Paštrovića Dvori
Hospitable, family-run restaurant in Blizikuće village with incredible views, serving authentic, homemade Paštrovići cuisine. **€€**

Knjaževa Bašta
Excellent regional fare in the lush gardens of King Nikola's Palace in Bar. **€€**

Kaldrma
Atmospheric Stari Bar eatery serving traditional fare, including five-course vegetarian, meat or fish tasting menus. **€€**

Konoba Bedem
Also in Stari Bar, tuck into delicious vegetarian meze platters and massive serves of roast lamb. **€€**

PLACES TO STAY BEYOND BUDVA

Stara Čaršija Hotel & Spa
Atmospheric hotel with luxurious rooms, Stari Bar views, memorable breakfasts and a gorgeous spa centre. **€€**

Hostel Pirate
A friendly, comfortable hostel in Ulcinj which organises barbecues, bike rentals, kayaking and boat trips. **€**

Hotel Palata Venezia
Beautiful Ulcinj palazzo with great views, attentive staff, excellent facilities and spacious rooms. **€€**

BEST RESTAURANTS IN & AROUND ULCINJ

Bella Vista
Friendly place on the main street serving pasta, seafood and local grills. **€€**

Dulcinea
Stari Grad restaurant delivering crispy grilled fish and Mala Plaža views. **€€**

Antigona
Excellent seafood served on a romantic clifftop terrace tucked away in the walled town. **€€€**

Restaurant Lovac
Family-run restaurant near Velika Plaža delivering warm hospitality and delicious food since 1928. **€€**

Miško
The best of the Bojana River restaurants, serving delectable seafood including outstanding fish soup. **€€**

Stari Grad (p213), Ulcinj

That's all part of its charm – with its uneven cobblestones and sketchy street lighting, this Old Town really does feel old. Ulcinj is also the only one of the coastal walled towns with an Albanian (61%) and Muslim (68%) majority. The minarets of multiple mosques punctuate the skyline, a legacy of 300 years of Ottoman rule.

In summertime, the compact curve of **Mala Plaža** (literally 'Small Beach') is the energetic heart of Ulcinj. During the day it's hard to see the sand under all the suntanned flesh. As night descends, the beachside cafes and kebab stalls crank up the music, kids race along the promenade and everyone enjoys the mayhem.

Mala Plaža's counterpoint is **Velika Plaža** ('Big Beach'). It's Montenegro's longest sandy stretch by far, starting a 10-minute drive southeast of Ulcinj and extending for 12km. For most of its length it's backed by low scrub and not much else. The only catch is that the water is shallow – toddlers will love it but adults less so. Where it does excel is as a kitesurfing and windsurfing destination.

The **Bojana River** separates Velika Plaža from the clothing-optional island, **Ada Bojana**. The fish restaurants hanging over the river (on the clothed side) are some of the best in the country.

PIRATES' PLAYGROUND

Even before the arrival of the Venetians in 1405 and the Ottomans in 1571, Ulcinj had a reputation as a pirates' lair. For more on Ulcinj's grim history of **piracy and slavery**, see p373.

Cetinje

CULTURE | MONASTERIES | CAVES

The capital of Montenegro until it was subsumed into the first Yugoslavia in 1918, Cetinje (pronounced '*tse*-tee-nyeh') is the very core of the historic Montenegrin heartland. It sits within an idyllic green basin within the Lovćen Massif, the mountain's craggy karstic peaks visible on every horizon.

With a population of just over 14,000, Cetinje is more like a large town than a city but it overachieves when it comes to museums and galleries. Podgorica may be the nation's administrative capital, but this is its cultural capital.

Zetan ruler-on-the-run Ivan Crnojević founded Cetinje in the late 15th century. However, much of Cetinje's present-day look dates from the reign of King Nikola, when European ambassadors rubbed shoulders with Montenegrin princesses in the city's palaces, embassies and streets. What remains is a refined, low-rise, pedestrian-friendly city filled with parks and elegant early-20th-century buildings. Cetinje has a charm all of its own.

GETTING AROUND

Cetinje is easily traversed on foot and the main street is blissfully car-free. It only takes five minutes to walk from the bus station to the centre of town. There's a large car park beside a tourist information point just below the palaces; coach tours disembark here.

Tackle the Multi-Pronged National Museum

Royal palaces and interesting art

If you prefer to soak up history and culture by osmosis while you're poking around royal palaces and other heritage buildings, the National Museum of Montenegro is for you.

Topping the list is the **Museum of King Nikola** (€8). This maroon-coloured palace on the main square was built in 1871 and, while grand, it still manages to feel like the kind of place that a family could live in.

King Nikola didn't have far to move from his previous palace, neighbouring **Biljarda**, which now houses the **Njegoš Museum** (€5). It was designed and financed by the Russians

TOP TIP

The National Museum offers a combined ticket (€20) which includes admission to its branches in Cetinje as well as the Njegoš Mausoleum (p219) in Lovćen National Park and the Njegoš Birth House in Njeguši. By the time you've visited the mausoleum, palace and one other, you've already justified the hefty price.

HIGHLIGHTS
1 Museum of King Nikola

SIGHTS
2 Biljarda
3 Cetinje Monastery
4 Ethnographic Museum
5 History Museum and Art Museum
6 Miodrag Dado Đurić Gallery
see 2 Njegoš Museum

EATING
7 Kole
8 TavèRna

DRINKING & NIGHTLIFE
9 Scottish Pub Academia

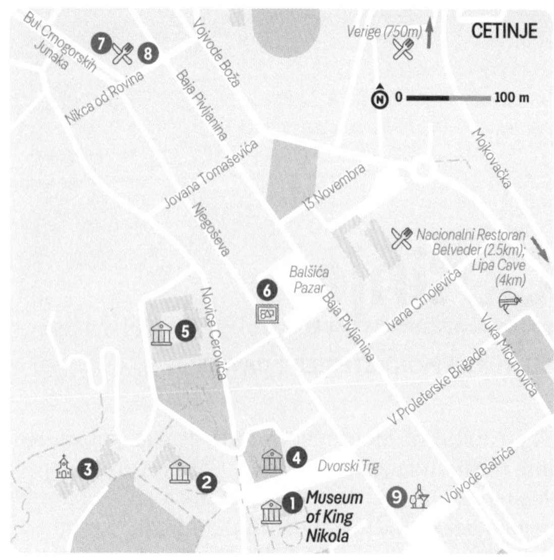

BEST RESTAURANTS & BARS IN CETINJE

Verige
Food is prepared the traditional way, over wood and charcoal, in this hospitable *pečenjara* (roastery). €

Nacionalni Restoran Belveder
Occupying a scenic eyrie near Lipa Cave, this memorable roadside restaurant serves top-notch traditional fare. €€

Kole
Kole serves tasty omelettes and pasta, but it's well worth delving into their meaty local specialities. €€

TavèRna
Pasta and pizza rub shoulders with spit-roasted meats, stuffed cabbage rolls and grilled fish. €€

Scottish Pub Academia
Cosy and companionable, this popular pub offers beer, whisky, hearty food and live music.

in 1838 for Montenegro's favourite son, Vladika (Prince-Bishop) Petar II Petrović Njegoš. Upstairs are Njegoš' personal effects and the nation's first billiard table (hence the building's nickname, which stuck). Included in the Biljarda admission (or €3 separately) is a large-scale **relief map of Montenegro**, built by the Austrians for military use during WWI.

The other big hitter is the **History Museum and Art Museum** (€5 combined). The history wing follows a straightforward timeline from the Stone Age onwards. The attached art gallery provides an excellent introduction to Montenegrin art, with each of the most celebrated names of the highly creative Yugoslav period assigned their own separate space. To check out what's going on in Montenegro's art scene today, call in to the five-storey **Miodrag Dado Đurić Gallery** (admission free) on the main street.

Housed in the former Serbian Embassy, the **Ethnographic Museum** (€4) has a well-presented collection of traditional folk costumes and tools.

Visit Cetinje Monastery

Icons and revered relics

It may not be the most friendly of Montenegro's Serbian Orthodox monasteries, but Cetinje Monastery is historically significant and one of the city's defining sights. Founded in 1484 by Ivan Crnojević, it was repeatedly destroyed during Ottoman attacks and rebuilt each time. This sturdy incarnation dates from 1786, with its only exterior ornamentation being the capitals of columns recycled from the original building.

The church to the right of the courtyard holds the monastery's proudest possessions: a **shard of Christ's Cross** and

CETINJE WALKING TOUR

Start outside the pretty ❶ **Blue Palace** (Plavi dvorac), built in 1895 for Crown Prince Danilo but now the official residence of the Montenegrin president. The elegant raspberry-coloured building next door was the ❷ **British Embassy**; it's now a music academy. Continue along leafy Njegoševa, the car-free main thoroughfare, which is lined with multicoloured early-20th-century buildings: the former ❸ **German Embassy** is apricot-hued, the ❹ **Tourist Office** mint green.

Turn left onto Dvorski trg (Palace Square) where the erstwhile ❺ **Bulgarian Embassy** and ❻ **Serbian Embassy** face off. Next up is the royal palace, now the ❼ **Museum of King Nikola** (p215), with a ❽ **Statue of Ivan Crnojević** in the small park opposite.

Head towards fortress-like ❾ **Biljarda** (p215) and turn left towards the ❿ **Court Church**, built in 1886 on the ruins of the original Cetinje Monastery. Inside are the tombs of Ivan Crnojević, King Nikola and Queen Milena. Follow the Biljarda walls to ⓫ **Cetinje Monastery** then turn right towards imposing Government House, now the ⓬ **History Museum and Art Museum**.

Return to Njegoševa and turn right at the flamboyant art nouveau ⓭ **French Embassy**. On the small square straight ahead is the ⓮ **Fairy of Lovćen**, a monument to 350 American Montenegrins who died when their boat was sunk off Albania while they were returning to fight in WWI.

Behind it is the ⓯ **Vlach Church**. The Vlach people are believed to be the remnants of the Roman population who retreated into less accessible areas when the Slavs arrived. The fence is made from 1544 gun barrels taken from the Ottomans during the 19th-century wars.

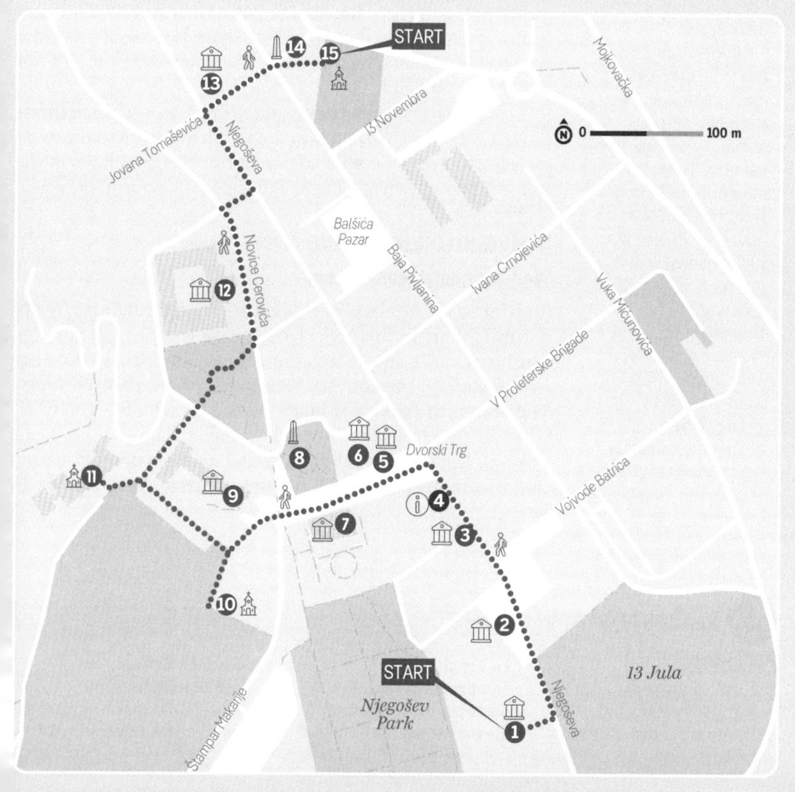

WHY I LOVE CETINJE

Peter Dragicevich, Lonely Planet writer

There's something cosy, comfortable and hugely appealing about Cetinje. It would be hard to imagine that this oversized village was ever a royal capital if it weren't for all the palaces and former embassies. Everywhere you look there are well-kept heritage buildings and leafy parks.

Car-free Njegoševa has to be the nicest main street in all of Montenegro. On summer evenings, the cafes spill onto the streets, friendly dogs laze about, and just about the whole town promenades up and down.

Cetinje is the crucible of Montenegrin history and culture. If you want to begin to get a handle on Montenegrin identity, here's where to start.

DJORDJE NIKOLIC/SHUTTERSTOCK ©

Lipa Cave

the mummified **right hand of St John the Baptist**. The hand is only occasionally displayed for veneration, so if you miss out you can console yourself with the knowledge that it's not a very pleasant sight.

The monastery **treasury** is only open to organised tour groups but, if you are persuasive enough and prepared to wait around, you may be able to tag along. The highlight is the 14th-century crown of King Stefan Uroš III Dečanski of Serbia.

Delve into Lipa Cave

Well-lit underground caverns

Step into a wonderland of stalactites, stalagmites and freaky natural pillars in this large karstic cave complex, 10 minutes southeast of Cetinje. Stretching for 2.5km, this is the only cave system in the country that is open for organised tours. The standard trip (€14) takes an hour, including the tourist train ride from the car park to the entrance. Tours head through large illuminated halls and along concreted paths, so it's suitable for all ages. Be sure to bring warm clothes as temperatures hover around 10°C year-round.

PLACES TO STAY IN CETINJE

Casa Calda
A cluster of attractive and thoughtfully equipped apartments set behind a large lawn. €

La Vecchia Casa
This period house with a gorgeous rear garden captures the essence of old Cetinje. €

Gradska Cetinje
New hotel, partly in a converted mansion next to the palace in the city centre. €€

Beyond Cetinje

The Old Montenegro of Mt Lovćen and Lake Skadar meets modern Montenegro's biggest city in this compact and diverse region.

At the dawn of the 20th century almost all of Montenegro fitted within this small area, making its claim as the nation's heartland beyond dispute. A large chunk of the landscape is protected by two national parks: mountainous Lovćen (the famed 'Monte Negro') and low-lying Lake Skadar, together forming a wildlife corridor that harbours bears, wolves and a multitude of bird species.

It was here that the Montenegrin national fable started to take shape – that of the 'best of the Serbs' stubbornly holding on to their independence while lands all around them fell to the Ottoman Turks. The reality may have been somewhat different (Cetinje was sacked several times) but everyone loves a good origin story.

Places

GETTING AROUND

Having a car will give you easy access to wonderful routes around Lovćen National Park, the fringes of Lake Skadar and sights such as Ostrog Monastery. Podgorica is the major bus hub, with regular services to and from Cetinje and Virpazar.

Lovćen National Park

Mighty mountains and magnificent mausoleum

A 10-minute drive southwest from Cetinje will bring you to the entrance of Lovćen National Park (entry €3), a 62 sq km expanse taking in the highest peaks of Mt Lovćen (1749m) and large tracts of forest crisscrossed with hiking paths and mountain-biking trails.

Lovćen's undisputed highlight is an exhilarating combination of architecture, sculpture, cultural significance and extraordinary views. Opened in 1974, the **Njegoš Mausoleum** (admission €8) sits atop the massif's second-highest peak, Jezerski Vrh (1657m). A long stairway (461 steps in total) leads through a cool tunnel and pops out just before the entrance where two granite giantesses guard the final resting place of Montenegro's greatest hero. Inside, under a golden mosaic canopy, a 28-tonne Petar II Petrović Njegoš rests in the wings of an eagle, carved from a single block of black granite by renowned Croatian sculptor, Ivan Meštrović. The actual tomb lies below and is a simple hushed crypt, entered from the rear.

TOP TIP

It costs €3–5 per day to visit Montenegro's national parks. Save money with an annual pass (€14).

BEST RESTAURANTS AROUND LAKE SKADAR

Stari Most
Freshwater fish experts (especially eel, trout and carp), located on Rijeka Crnojevića's riverside promenade. Perhaps surprisingly, given its sleepy village location, this is one of Montenegro's best restaurants. **€€**

Poslednja Luka
Friendly spot above the Crnojević River near Rijeka Crnojevića offering a short menu of lake fish and other local produce. **€**

Konoba Demidžana
Upmarket restaurant by the water in Virpazar showcasing traditional fish dishes and meaty grills. **€€**

Restoran Jezero
By the park office in Vranjina, serving tasty local fish dishes on a lovely lakeside terrace. **€€**

IRINA PAPOYAN/SHUTTERSTOCK ©

Behind the mausoleum a path leads to a circular platform providing dramatic views over the Bay of Kotor, Cetinje, Lake Skadar and all of Montenegro's mountain ranges.

Lake Skadar National Park

Birds, lilies, monasteries and wineries

It's said that the tears of a fairy created **Lake Skadar** (Skadarsko jezero). Once you cast your eyes over its vast tranquil waters, encircling mountains and floating meadows of water lilies, you too might suspect that there's something magical afoot.

Skadar, the largest lake in the Balkans, is shared between Montenegro (two thirds) and Albania (one third). On the Montenegrin side, an area of 400 sq km is now a national park (entry €5), protecting one of the richest habitats for birdlife in Europe. Aside from all that nature there are fortresses, island monasteries, historic villages and wineries to explore. It's easy to arrange a boat tour or to hire a kayak from stalls in **Virpazar**, **Vranjina** and **Rijeka Crnojevića** (60, 50 and 30 minutes from Cetinje, respectively).

TOURS IN LAKE SKADAR NATIONAL PARK

Undiscovered Montenegro
Specialises in multi-day itineraries which can include guided hikes, kayaking, wine/gastronomy and yoga.

Golden Frog
Highly regarded trips from Virpazar on an attractive wooden boat, plus kayak rentals.

Boat Milica
Boat tours and kayak hire from Virpazar, with informative English-speaking captains.

Lake Skadar National Park

Podgorica

The nation's unassuming capital

Set on a large plain ringed by mountains at the confluence of two rivers (a 40-minute drive from Cetinje), Montenegro's capital is home to just over 150,000 people. Penetrate the ring of brutalist apartment blocks that encircle it and you'll find a pleasant core filled with parks, public art, pedestrian-friendly shopping streets and a lively hospitality precinct.

The rivers divide the central city into distinct sectors with divergent personalities. On the south bank of the Ribnica is **Stara Varoš**, the old Ottoman town, with mosques and a blocky clock tower. The orderly low-rise grid of **Nova Varoš** sprang up on the north bank in the late 19th century and quickly became Podgorica's civic heart. Following WWII, Podgorica became Titograd and the Socialist-style blocks of **Novi Grad** sprouted west of the broad green waters of the Morača River.

Podgorica's most striking sight, the Serbian Orthodox **Cathedral of Christ's Resurrection**, literally can't be missed as it's nearly 42m high. It was finally consecrated in 2013 after 20 years of construction with a design brief that must have read: 'maximum impact, no expense spared'. Inside, 6200 sq metres of gilded frescoes engulf every surface.

On the southern outskirts of Podgorica, **Niagara Falls** are worth a look, provided you get your timing right. They're at their dramatic best after the spring thaws when the green waters of the Cijevna River crash over a small dam while a portion skims along the side and feeds dozens of separate cascades. The unusual eroded limestone surrounding it looks

BEST DINING & DRINKING IN PODGORICA

Masala Art
Unexpectedly, Podgorica's best restaurant is an upmarket Indian eatery hidden between Nova Grad's apartment blocks. **€€**

Steak House
Grab a seat on the covered terrace and tuck into beef tartare, steak or grilled fish. **€€**

Street Bar
Hip little bar within a brutalist Novi Grad block, with a tree-shaded terrace and an eclectic interior.

Culture Club Tarantino
Exemplifying the offbeat flavour of the Bokeška strip, this quirky spot promotes local music and art.

Vanilla Heartbeat Place
Large upmarket bar with a semi-enclosed terrace and a busy roster of DJs and live music.

CRMNICA WINE REGION

The fertile area on the western shore of Lake Skadar is Montenegro's most important wine region. Vranac is the most significant variety grown here, an endemic grape that makes a full-bodied red wine.

Crmnica's wineries are generally small, family-run operations that require advance notice of a visit (the Virpazar tourist office has a brochure listing contacts). However, they may not speak English or even have any signage.

A typical tasting session involves a personalised tour followed by generous pours of wine accompanied by food; expect to pay around €10 and to leave somewhat inebriated. The best wineries are in tucked-away villages but the easiest to access is **Vinarija Mašanović** in the new part of Virpazar near the train station.

TATIANA POPOVA/SHUTTERSTOCK ©

Ostrog Monastery

like it was drawn by Dr Seuss. In summer the river reduces to a trickle; don't bother visiting between July and September unless there's been heavy rain.

Ostrog Monastery

Montenegro's most revered religious site

There's something strangely affecting about Ostrog Monastery, located a 90-minute drive north of Cetinje. The setting is certainly part of it. Founded in 1665 within two large caves in a cliff face – 900m above the verdant Zeta valley and visible for miles around – the gleaming white Upper Monastery gives the impression that it has grown out of the very rock. Even with its Orthodox pilgrims, tourists and souvenir stands, it remains a peaceful place.

Behind **Holy Trinity Church** (1824) in the **Lower Monastery** is a natural spring where you can fill your bottles with deliciously cold water. From here the faithful, many of them barefoot, plod 3km up the steep road to the **Upper Monastery** where the remains of its founder, St Basil of Ostrog (Sv Vasilije Ostroški), are kept in a tiny chapel. Non-pilgrims and the pure of heart may drive up to the main car park and limit their penitence to just the final 200m.

PLACES TO STAY BEYOND CETINJE

Villa Miela
Beautifully restored and stylishly furnished traditional house near Virpazar with tranquil views and a pool. €€

CUE Podgorica
Slick design hotel within the Capital Plaza centre in Podgorica, with a swish lounge bar downstairs. €€€

Hotel Sokoline
Perched near Ostrog, this newish hotel has upmarket rooms, extraordinary views and a rooftop restaurant. €€€

PODGORICA

Durmitor National Park

SCENERY | ADVENTURE SPORTS | HIKING

As if the rest of Montenegro's landscapes weren't dramatic enough, rugged Durmitor takes things to operatic heights. Dozens of its limestone peaks soar over 2000m, while 2523m Bobotov Kuk lays claim to being the highest mountain that's completely within Montenegro (there's a peak in the Prokletije mountains bordering Albania that's 11m higher).

Durmitor National Park incorporates both the ruggedly good-looking mountains and a lush green corridor stretching east along the Tara River enclosing old-growth forests, a medieval monastery and a noteworthy bridge.

The park's main gateway is scrappy little Žabljak which sits at a height of 1456m, making it the highest town in Montenegro (and one of the highest in the Balkans). It was burnt to the ground during WWII and the names of hundreds of locals who were killed are inscribed on a space-age pyramid-shaped *spomenik* (monument) on a hill in the centre of town.

Circle the Black Lake

Easy walk among splendid scenery

For an easy and satisfying introduction to the Durmitor landscape, there's no better short walk than the 3.6km circuit of **Black Lake** (Crno jezero). This is the largest of the 18 glacial lakes within the national park, known locally as *gorske oči* (mountain eyes). The track is well-formed and easy to follow, although there can be slippery ice to negotiate in the shadier sections right up until late April.

GETTING AROUND

From Podgorica, the quickest route is through Nikšić and Šavnik, or you can head west from Mojkovac and follow the Tara River. There's a wonderful back road through the mountains leaving the highway near Plužine, but it's impassable as soon as the snows fall. The bus station is at the southern edge of Žabljak, on the Šavnik road. From Žabljak it's possible to walk or cycle to some trailheads but a car will give you more options.

TOP TIP

Durmitor's higher altitudes are prone to fog, heavy snow, treacherous ice, spring avalanches and summer thunderstorms. The National Park Visitor Centre can advise on track conditions and arrange local guides (€80 per day), which is highly recommended if you're heading out in winter or considering serious mountaineering.

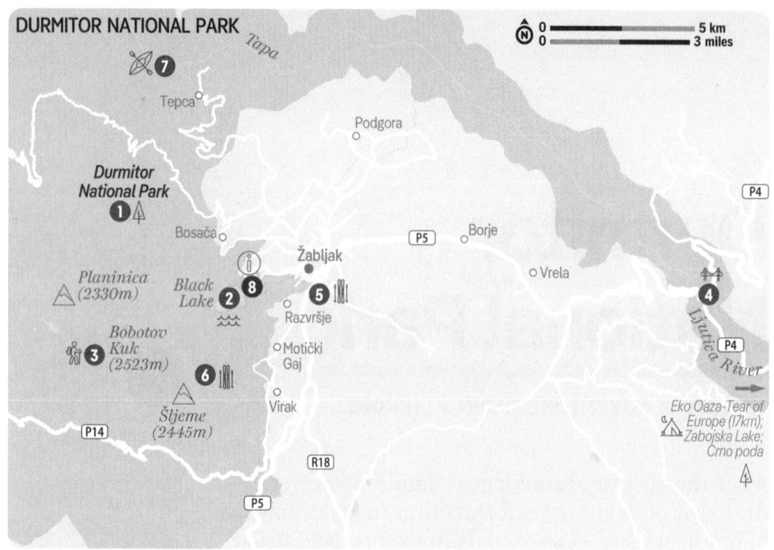

HIGHLIGHTS	ACTIVITIES, COURSES & TOURS	
1 Durmitor National Park	3 Bobotov Kuk	6 Savin Kuk
SIGHTS	4 Đurđevića Tara Bridge	7 Tara Canyon
2 Black Lake	5 Javorovača	**INFORMATION**
		8 Durmitor National Park Visitor Centre

BEST RESTAURANTS IN ŽABLJAK

Soa
This hotel restaurant offers elevated takes on local specialities, such as lamb baked in sour cream and *ajvar* (roasted red capsicum relish). **€€€**

O'ro
The focus is firmly on local specialities at this appealing wood-and-glass restaurant in the town centre. In summer grab a seat on the large terrace and tuck into a *Durmitorska večera* (Durmitor dinner) platter. It also serves lamb, veal and trout dishes. **€€**

Restoran Dvorište
An atmospheric stone cottage heated by antique stoves, serving belly-warming mountain food. **€**

Strap on the Skis

Low frills, high thrills

In winter Durmitor is a glittering fairyland – and with 120 days of snow cover, it offers the most reliable skiing in Montenegro. The prices are great, too, but don't expect glamour.

The main ski resort on **Savin Kuk** (2313m), 5km from Žabljak, has nearly 5km of runs (three blue, one red and one black). There's another little ski centre on the outskirts of Žabljak itself, near the bus station. **Javorovača** has two lifts and a gentle slope that's good for kids and beginners.

Take a Hike

High-altitude karstic scenery

The sculpted crags and grassy plateaux of Durmitor make for magnificent hiking country. There are 25 marked trails in the national park stretching to 150km in total, providing plenty of opportunity to seek some solitude. Ask the staff at the visitor centre about tracks to suit your level of experience and fitness.

Experienced mountain hikers can tackle **Bobotov Kuk** in summer, but they'll need to set out early (it's a 10-hour return hike) and be prepared for a tough scramble at the end.

Call into the Visitor Centre

Taxidermy and track advice

The main **National Park Visitor Centre** on the approach to Black Lake is well worth a look for its displays of local flora and fauna. Along with innumerable mounted beetles and butterflies, there are stuffed lynx, chamois, deer, birds, a wired-looking fox and a snarling wolf.

The friendly staff can help you out with track advice and park passes (€5 per day, or €14 for an annual pass to all parks).

Raft along the Tara River

Traverse the Tara Canyon

A rafting expedition on the green waters of the Tara is the best way to experience the 1300m-high **Tara Canyon**, as it's impossible to see its jaw-dropping depths from the land. While it's not the most white-knuckled ride, there are some rapids to add to the thrills. Trips run between April and October but, if you're after speed, visit in April and May when the last of the melting snow revs up the flow.

Tara Bridge Views & Thrills

Gracious architecture and crazy zip lines

The elegant **Đurđevića Tara Bridge** is an imposing sight, its gently curved 365m length carried on five sweeping arches, the largest of which is 116m wide. Looking down at the green sliver of the Tara River 150m below isn't for the lily-livered, although the only real danger is from passing cars (there's no proper footpath). Yet that experience can't compete with the adrenaline rush offered by the three competing **zip lines** now set up to hurtle you at speeds of up to 100km per hour over the canyon.

Zipline, Đurđevića Tara Bridge

LESS-VISITED NATIONAL PARK HIGHLIGHTS

Pavle Đurišić from Eko-Oaza Suza Evrope shares special places around Dobrilovina. @ eko_oaza

Zabojska Lake
To get to it you need to follow a gravel road up the mountain for 8km. Only people in the know go there, so it's never crowded. The waters are clear and it's surrounded by forest.

Crno poda
The air is different in this old forest, filled with the scent of the black pine trees. There is no designated parking area or trails; just walk in off the highway.

Ljutica River
This impressive torrent of white water shoots out of the rock and only travels for about 130m before it hits the Tara River.

PLACES TO STAY IN DURMITOR NATIONAL PARK

Eko-Oaza Tear of Europe
Exceptional 'eco oasis' near the river in Dobrilovina offering camping, wooden cottages and cabins. €

Apartments Peaks
Self-contained wood-lined apartments in central Žabljak with reasonable prices and friendly owners. €€

Hotel Soa
Rooms at this Žabljak hotel are kitted out with monsoon shower heads, robes and slippers. €€€

Beyond Durmitor National Park

Places

GETTING AROUND

Although distances are short as the eagle flies, the mountainous nature of the terrain slows journeys down. Many of the minor roads traversing the mountains close with the first snow and don't reopen until well into spring. Buses from Podgorica (and some from the coast) head to the main towns, although getting between them by bus can be more problematic. The Bar-Belgrade trainline cuts straight through the centre, stopping in Kolašin.

Two more national parks vie for attention in a landscape that provides a drama-filled backdrop for outdoor activities and medieval monasteries.

The top half of Montenegro is nearly all mountains – punctuated by the occasional mirror-like lake and deep river canyon. Small towns make the most of the rare patches of flat land to be found in elevated plateaux and the broadest of the river valleys. If you think that all sounds painfully picturesque, you'd be right.

For over 400 years this entire region was ruled by the Ottoman Empire. Montenegro swallowed the first slice (Plužine to Andrijevica) in 1878 and the remainder in 1912.

The terrain lends itself to all manner of outdoor pursuits. But arguably the biggest thrill of all is to be found in simply driving around and soaking up the scenery.

Kolašin

Skiing, snowboarding and stirring sculpture

Tucked into a valley at the foot of the Bjelasica massif, a 30-minute drive from the eastern edge of Durmitor National Park, Kolašin is Montenegro's premier mountain resort.

There are two neighbouring ski centres to choose between: **Kolašin 1450** and **Kolašin 1600**, named after the altitude in metres where the lifts start (the highest reaches to 2035m). They're located about 2km apart from each other, 10km east of Kolašin, with shuttle buses transporting skiers from the major hotels in town. While they're owned and operated separately, a ski lift connects them and it's possible to buy a combined pass, giving access to a diverse set of runs over a huge area. The mountain also presents plenty of opportunity for off-piste skiing, Nordic skiing, snowshoe hiking and snowmobile rides.

If you're a fan of Yugoslav-era buildings and sculpture, Kolašin's town centre has some doozies. In 1943 the town hosted the first 'State Anti-Fascist Council for the National Liberation of Montenegro and Boka' (ZAVNO for short). To commemorate this, the angular concrete **ZAVNO Memorial**

Kolašin 1450

Building was built in 1975. Despite being considered one of the era's architectural treasures it's now looking shabby and neglected. In front of it stands the **Monument to the Victims of Fascist Terror**, a bronze Socialist-Realist statue of a young Partisan man and woman marching forward, guns and flag held aloft. In a much better condition than ZAVNO is the **Bianca Resort** directly behind it, a quirky triangular hotel with hexagonal windows built in 1979.

Biogradska Gora National Park

Lakeside strolls and mountain hikes

Lake Biograd (Biogradsko jezero) is achingly lovely, its placid green waters providing a mirror for the surrounding forest and mountains. The 3.3km circuit around it may well be the best short walk in the country: the path is well-formed and flat, there's no chance of getting lost, information boards are scattered about, and there's a memorable restaurant at the end of it.

TOP TIP

During summer, boats from Plužine offer cruises and expeditions to secret swimming spots on Lake Piva.

PROKLETIJE NATIONAL PARK

The Prokletije Mountains are the southernmost and highest part of the Dinaric Alps, forming the border between Montenegro, Albania and Kosovo. In each country's language, the range's name translates to 'Accursed Mountains', a reference to the harsh environment.

Enquire in **Plav** or **Gusinje** about short hikes to suit your abilities. If you're planning a serious mountaineering expedition, it's recommended that you enlist the services of a local guide. The website of the **Peaks of the Balkans hiking trail** (p188; an epic 192km cross-border circuit) lists guides and border procedures, although the paperwork isn't straightforward to arrange without a local helper.

PLACES TO STAY IN KOLAŠIN

Rooms & Apartments Mirović
Attractive complex by the river. One cottage has a stream running underneath its glass floor. €€

Chalet Kolašin
Stone chalet with handsome rooms and a private spa pool in a central residential street. €€€

Bianca Resort & Spa
Iconic Yugoslav architecture refreshed for the 21st century, with spa and indoor swimming pool. €€€

BEST DINING BEYOND DURMITOR NATIONAL PARK

La Parisienne
Bakery on Kolašin's main square serving sweet treats, savoury pastries and pizza slices. **€**

Restoran Vodenica
A converted Kolašin watermill serving old-style mountain food designed to warm your belly on cold nights. **€€**

Konoba Nišavić
Kolašin standard-bearer for Montenegrin mountain cuisine, such as roast lamb and cheesy carb-heavy dishes. **€€**

Restoran Biogradsko Jezero
Striking architecture among the trees near Lake Biograd, serving local berry juice and crispy trout. **€€**

Restaurant Abas
Intergalactic-castle exterior aside, this Plav restaurant serves tasty local cuisine including mouth-watering grills and a handful of vegetarian offers. **€€**

SANTIAGO URQUIJO/GETTY IMAGES ©

The lake is the main hub of Biogradska Gora National Park (admission €4), located a 15-minute drive from the eastern edge of Durmitor National Park (90 minutes from Žabljak). It's one of six glacial lakes within the 5650-hectare reserve. The park encompasses 1600 hectares of virgin rainforest, said to be one of the last three such forests remaining in Europe today. Many of the trees here are over 500 years old, with some soaring to 60m high.

There are many signposted hiking trails within the park, with the most difficult being the 35km trek up **Crna glava** (Black Head), Bjelasica's highest peak. If you're not game to go it alone, mountain guides can be hired through the park office.

Morača Canyon

Spectacular scenery and medieval monastery

Founded in 1252, **Morača Monastery** stands on the banks of the Morača River, an hour's drive from the eastern edge of Durmitor National Park (90 minutes from Žabljak). As you enter the walled compound into a garden courtyard it's like stepping back into the 13th century. The monastery's two churches contain some of Montenegro's most accomplished religious art.

PLACES TO STAY AROUND DURMITOR

Guesthouse Zvonko
Characterful cottage accommodation attached to a surprisingly hip jazz bar-restaurant in Plužine. **€**

Eco Selo Nevidio
An 'eco village' of easy-on-the-eye A-frame stone bungalows in a remote spot near Nevidio Canyon. **€€**

Hotel Dvor
On the edge of Bijelo Polje, this roadside hotel has a pleasantly old-fashioned ambience. **€€**

Morača Monastery

Heading south from here, the drive gets progressively more awe-inspiring as the highway follows the river into the nearly perpendicular **Morača Canyon**, 300m to 400m deep.

Piva Canyon

Nature tamed by Yugoslav engineering

Once the snow has melted, a 40-minute drive from the western edge of Durmitor National Park (double that from Žabljak) will bring you over the mountains to Piva Canyon.

In 1975 the Piva River was blocked by the construction of a hydroelectric dam, flooding part of the canyon and in turn creating turquoise **Lake Piva** (Pivsko jezero), which plummets to depths of more than 180m. The Durmitor road comes out on the highway near the new site of the town of **Plužine**, which had to be moved to higher ground.

Also moved – brick by brick, fresco by fresco, over the course of 12 years – was **Piva Monastery** (*Manastir Piva*), 10km to the south. The conservators did a fantastic job as the interior of this blocky structure (originally constructed between 1573 and 1586) really does feel ancient. An exquisite door inlaid with mother-of-pearl connects the porch to the nave, where a giant rood cross with golden fish at its base crowns the iconostasis.

In the opposite direction, heading north, the highway is a feat of engineering in itself, clinging to the cliffs and passing through 56 small stone tunnels on its way to the Bosnian border. Stop to admire the 220m-high **Mratinje Dam**, then continue through the natural, unflooded section of the canyon where the steep walls reflect in the blue waters below.

PANORAMIC ROADS

You could argue that most of Montenegro's roads qualify for the title, but the National Tourist Organisation has officially designated four panoramic routes and supported them with road signs, brochures, online GPS coordinates and, for two of them (Durmitor and Korita), downloadable on-the-road audio guides.

The 76km **Durmitorski prsten** (Durmitor Ring, route 2) circles through the mountains from Žabljak, visiting villages that are completely cut off by snow for months on end. It's well worth taking the suggested detour to Ćurevac (1625m) for giddy Tara Canyon views.

The other routes are 716km **Kruna Crne Gore** (Crown of Montenegro, route 1), 270km **More i visine** (Sea and Heights, route 3) and 65km **Krug oko Korita** (Circuit around Korita, route 4).

BEAUTIFUL MONTENEGRO/SHUTTERSTOCK ©

Millennium Bridge, Podgorica

Arriving

Montenegro has two international airports, Tivat and Podgorica. Additionally, Dubrovnik Airport (Croatia) is only 17km from the border. Ferries from Italy disembark in Bar. Citizens of 97 visa-exempt countries are entitled to enter Montenegro for up to 90 days in a 180-day period (30 days for most European nationals). Other nationalities need to apply for a short-stay visa.

By Air

Tivat and Podgorica airports are small and facilities are limited, but both have free wi-fi, ATMs (cash machines), taxi stands and rental-car desks. Many visitors also fly into Dubrovnik, hire a car from the airport and drive into Montenegro.

By Land

Montenegro has land borders with Croatia, Bosnia, Serbia, Kosovo and Albania. At the crossing you'll need to present your vehicle registration/ownership documents and a locally valid insurance policy such as a European Green Card. Check that your policy covers Montenegro.

Money

Currency: Euro (€)

CASH

It pays to have coins and small notes on hand for paying for coffees and the like. However, ATMs tend to dispense large notes and it can be hard to break them. Banks will split them but expect to queue (take a ticket and wait).

CREDIT CARDS & DIGITAL PAYMENT

Credit cards are widely accepted, especially for accommodation, petrol and restaurants. However don't rely on them at cafes, bars, kiosks and museums. The facility to pay by tapping your phone or smart watch isn't yet common but this is likely to change.

TIPPING

Tipping isn't expected but is usually appreciated. Even in restaurants, don't feel obliged to leave anything unless you're particularly wanting to reward good service, in which case up to 10% would be considered generous. In cafes, bars and taxis, round up to the nearest euro. Tipping in hotels is unusual.

Getting Around

Having a car at your disposal will give you access to some extraordinary scenic drives, although some (like the famous serpentine road above Kotor) aren't for the fearful. A small car will make it easier to negotiate narrow roads. The local bus network is extensive and reliable. Trains are only useful for getting between Bar, Virpazar, Podgorica and Kolašin.

HIRING A CAR

It's not difficult to hire a car from the airports and larger towns; book ahead for the best prices and to save time. Most hire cars have manual transmission; you'll pay a premium for an automatic.

SASHKO/SHUTTERSTOCK ©

Railway through Montenegrin Mountains

BUSES

Inter-city buses are usually comfortable, air-conditioned and rarely full. Stations display timetables prominently and staff are on hand to help out with prices and times. Up-to-date timetable information and online booking can be found on busticket4.me.

WATER TAXIS

Water taxis are a common sight during summer but they're harder to find outside the high season; look for them at the marinas. They can be hailed from the shore for a short trip along the coast.

ROAD CONDITIONS

While the standard of roads is generally good, many are winding and narrow. Larger vehicles such as campervans will struggle on some of the secondary roads. Traffic is also a major headache along the coast in summer.

PARKING

Many municipalities have replaced meters with app-based payment, which makes things tricky if you don't have a phone with an internet connection. However most towns also have designated parking lots where you can pay in cash at the exit kiosk.

DRIVING ESSENTIALS

Drive on the right.

Blood alcohol limit is 0.03%.

Drive with headlights on (even during the day).

North Macedonia

NATURE AND HISTORY

Natural beauty, a complex past and a warm welcome make North Macedonia an off-the-beaten-track treasure.

North Macedonia may be small but it has a wealth of glorious scenery and cultural heritage. Part-Balkan, part-Mediterranean and rich in Greek, Roman and Ottoman history, it also has a fascinating past and a complicated identity.

Glittering Lake Ohrid and its historic namesake town have etched out a place for North Macedonia on the tourist map, but travel further and you'll find dramatic mountains with blissfully quiet walking trails, lakes and riding opportunities. The national parks of Mavrovo, Galičica and Pelister are cultivating some excellent cultural and culinary tourism initiatives; these gorgeous regions are little explored, so if you want to get off the beaten track in Europe, this is the place.

The potential for outdoor activities is endless, but a lack of tourist infrastructure makes it difficult to do much independently in North Macedonia. Hiking, paragliding, mountain biking and horse riding are all possible with a bit of planning, though.

Dining out in in the country is relatively cheap and the ingredients are usually fresh, seasonal, locally produced and of superb quality. Traditional cooking in rural villages is a highlight.

Capital Skopje's centre has suffered from a building spree of grotesque neoclassical monuments, buildings and fountains in the last decade. Luckily, its Ottoman old town and buzzing modern areas are untouched and remain charming and authentic.

THE MAIN AREAS

SKOPJE
Historic old bazaar and modernist architecture. **p238**

LAKE OHRID
One of Europe's deepest and oldest lakes, surrounded by traditional villages. **p246**

OHRID TOWN
Byzantine churches set on the stunning lake. **p250**

TU XA HA NOI/GETTY IMAGES ©

Above: Church of Sveti Jovan (p250), Ohrid Town. Left: Skopje (p238)

GALIČICA NATIONAL PARK
Peaks to conquer and eerie island to explore. **p251**

MAVROVO NATIONAL PARK
Magnificent monasteries, pretty villages, blissful hikes. **p256**

PELISTER NATIONAL PARK
Peaceful hikes and village tourism. **p258**

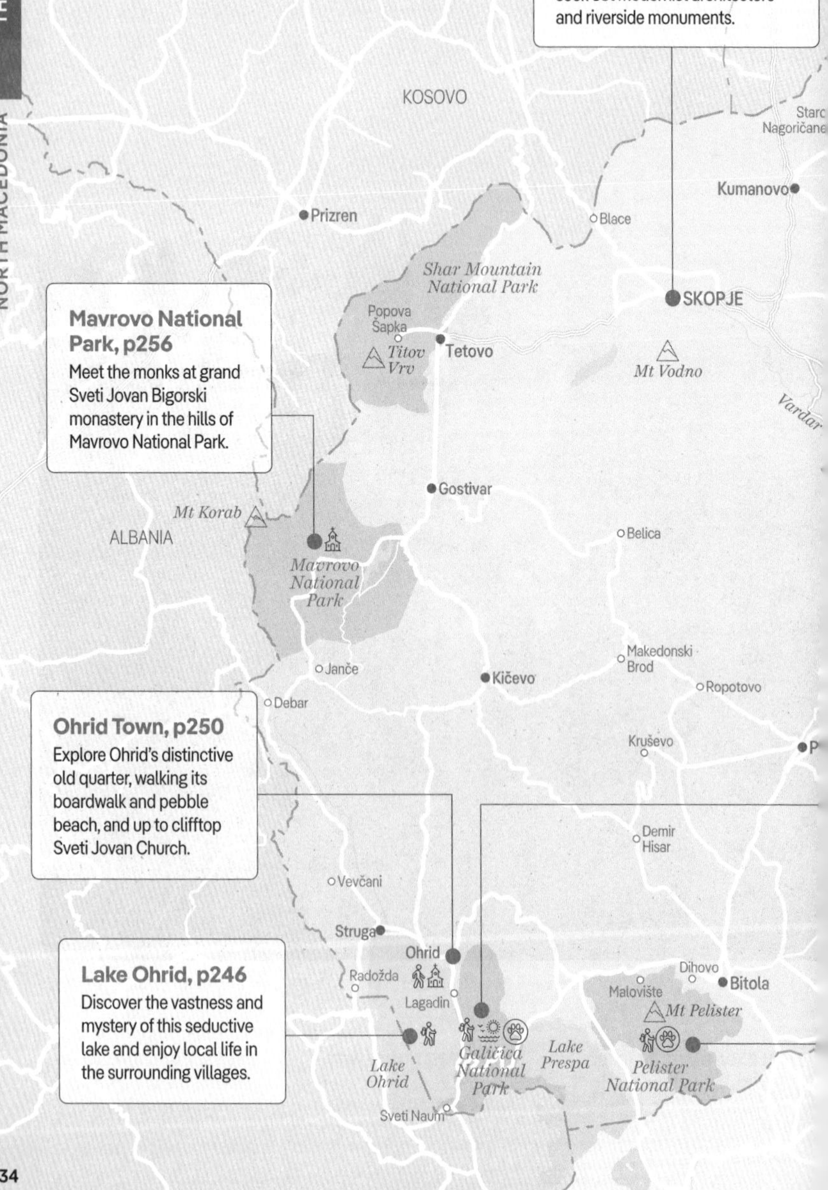
PRISTINA
0 50 km
0 25 miles
Skopje, p238
Dive into the capital's historic Čaršija (old Ottoman bazaar), then seek out modernist architecture and riverside monuments.
KOSOVO
Staro Nagoričane
Kumanovo
Blace
Prizren
Shar Mountain National Park
SKOPJE
Popova Šapka
Titov Vrv
Tetovo
Mt Vodno
Vardar
Mavrovo National Park, p256
Meet the monks at grand Sveti Jovan Bigorski monastery in the hills of Mavrovo National Park.
Gostivar
Mt Korab
ALBANIA
Belica
Mavrovo National Park
Makedonski Brod
Jançe
Kičevo
Ropotovo
Debar
Ohrid Town, p250
Explore Ohrid's distinctive old quarter, walking its boardwalk and pebble beach, and up to clifftop Sveti Jovan Church.
Kruševo
Demir Hisar
Vevčani
Struga
Ohrid
Lake Ohrid, p246
Discover the vastness and mystery of this seductive lake and enjoy local life in the surrounding villages.
Radožda
Lagadin
Dihovo
Bitola
Malovište
Mt Pelister
Lake Ohrid
Galičica National Park
Lake Prespa
Pelister National Park
Sveti Naum

Find Your Way

Take the time to discover compact North Macedonia's cities, towns, traditional villages and, especially, its beautiful national parks, mountains and lakes. Outdoors lovers will find plenty to keep them occupied.

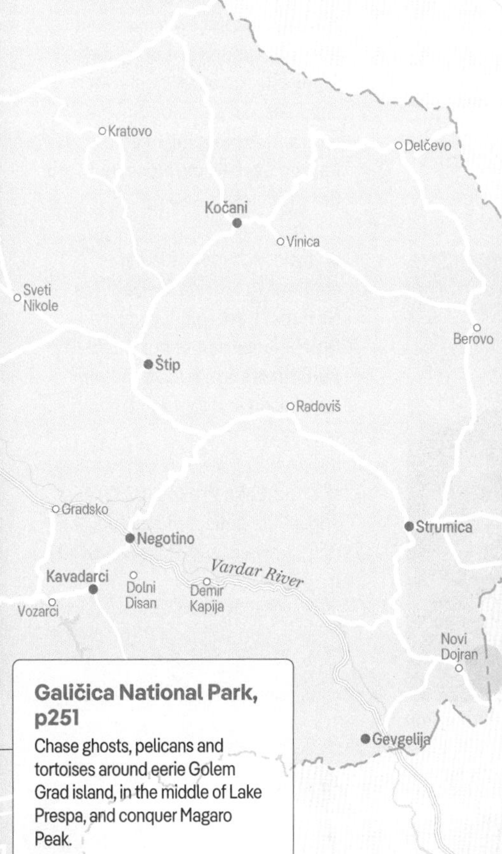

CAR

You don't need a car to get around Skopje and Ohrid Town, but renting one is the best way to discover the rest of North Macedonia, especially if you want to reach villages and outdoor activities spots.

BUS

If you don't have a car, buses can take you between most cities and towns. Skopje serves the majority of domestic destinations. During summer, book ahead for Ohrid. Sunday is often the busiest day for intercity bus travel among locals, so book ahead then too if you can.

TRAIN

Domestic trains are reliable but slow. From Skopje, there is a train to Bitola via Veles and Prilep. Ohrid does not have a train station.

Galičica National Park, **p251**

Chase ghosts, pelicans and tortoises around eerie Golem Grad island, in the middle of Lake Prespa, and conquer Magaro Peak.

Pelister National Park, **p258**

Eat your fill at food-focused village tourism initiatives in this underrated national park, then walk it off the next day.

Plan Your Time

North Macedonia has plenty of possibilities if you like al fresco fun mixed in with historical towns. You'll need a few days to really savour the activities and dig into the history of the country.

ILAN SHACHAM/GETTY IMAGES ©

Cycling around Lake Ohrid (p246)

If You Only Do One Thing

- If you only have time for one thing, head to North Macedonia's most charming and historic town, **Ohrid** (p246), for swimming and drinks by the spectacular lake. Admire its frescoed medieval churches, eat some traditional food and explore the beach-flanked Sveti Naum Monastery and Bay of Bones museum.

- If your schedule allows, continue to the nearby **Galičica National Park** (p251) and hike the Magaro Peak, or head over to **Pelister National Park** (p258) for walking and top-notch home cooking.

- Cross **Lake Prespa** (p253) and admire the pelican-inhabited, ruin-strewn island of **Golem Grad** (p253).

Seasonal Highlights

Summers are hot and great for swimming in Lake Ohrid, while winters are cold. Early summer and autumn are perfect for getting the most out of the outdoors activities on offer.

JANUARY

Join the locals in celebrating **Vevčani carnival** (p248) by Lake Ohrid.

FEBRUARY

Ski in Mavrovo, snuggle up beside fires in chalet-style lodges and experience Ohrid out of season.

JUNE

Go hiking and horse riding in **Pelister National Park** (p358; pictured) and swim in **Lake Ohrid** (p246).

FROM LEFT: MROTCHKA/SHUTTERSTOCK ©, DEJAN GILESKI/SHUTTERSTOCK ©, ANTONIO KARANFILOSKI/SHUTTERSTOCK ©

One Week to Explore

- Spend a couple of days in **Skopje** (p238) and stroll around Čaršija with its historic mosques, churches, museums and Ottoman castle. Visit the nearby **Canyon Matka** (p242) and kayak into it, skirt the cliffside walkway and swim in the cool waters.

- Then head to North Macedonia's top historic destination, **Ohrid** (p246), where you can swim in the picture-perfect lake and stroll waterside villages. Explore the frescoed medieval churches at Sveti Naum Monastery.

- Stay in a guesthouse on the edge of **Pelister National Park** (p258), go on a mountain hike and finish with some homemade traditional food.

- Finish at **Lake Prespa** (p253) to see the pelicans and ruins on **Golem Grad** island (p253).

More Than a Week

- Linger in **Pelister National Park** (p258) and visit the villages of **Brajcino** (p258) and **Dihovo** (p259).

- Make a stop in **Bitola** (p259), loved for its vibrant local life and Ottoman quarter, elegant 19th-century architecture and ancient ruins.

- Next, visit **Mavrovo National Park** (p256) and stay in historic **Janče** (p256) and **Galičnik** (p256) villages for superb Macedonian cuisine, local cheese and horse riding. Visit the impressive **Sveti Jovan Bigorski Monastery** (p255).

- Make a pit stop in the **Tikveš Wine Region** (p261) and spend the night at North Macedonia's top-winery hotel, Popova Kula. End your stay with a visit to the magical and spacey **Ilinden Monument** (p260), near the town of Kruševo.

JULY
Partake in the **Galičnik Wedding Festival** (p256) in Mavrovo National Park.

AUGUST
Enjoy **Ohrid's Summer Festival** (p251) and dive into its deep lake.

SEPTEMBER
Make merry with the locals at the Tikveš Wine Region's **Kavadarci Wine Carnival** (p261).

OCTOBER
Groove at the **jazz festival** in capital Skopje (p238).

Skopje

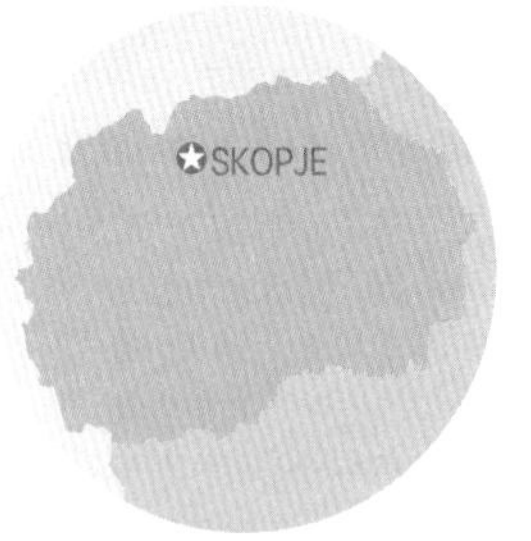

CULTURE | ARCHITECTURE | CUISINE

GETTING AROUND

City buses (including London-style red double-deckers) follow numbered routes; you can buy and validate tickets on board. Driving in Skopje is generally hassle-free; the main worries are finding your way through the city, as signage isn't good and finding somewhere to park in central areas is tricky.

Skopje has an easygoing atmosphere, plenty of charm and some tasty local cuisine. Its Ottoman- and Byzantine-era sights are focused around the city's delightful Čaršija, bordered by the 15th-century Kameni Most (Stone Bridge) and Tvrdina Kale Fortress – Skopje's guardian since the 5th century. Don't miss the excellent eating and drinking scene in Debar Maalo, a lovely tree-lined neighbourhood. The locals are warm and friendly too, so you'll do well to spend a couple of days just getting to know this relaxed capital.

For most of its existence, Skopje has been a modest Balkan city, but in 2014, then-Prime Minister Nikola Gruevski implemented a controversial, nationalistic project called 'Skopje 2014', transforming the city centre into a bizarre set design for an ancient civilisation. Towering warrior statues were erected, along with enormous, gleaming neoclassical buildings, marble-clad museums and hypnotic megafountains.

TOP TIP

One of the best ways to get a panoramic view of Skopje is to take the cable-car ride to Mt Vodno (p243) – it's a ten-minute journey during which you get to see the entire sprawl of the city. Take the 'Millennium Cross' special bus or a taxi from Skopje's bus station to the cable-car station.

Wander Historic Čaršija

Explore Ottoman and Byzantine sights

Čaršija is Skopje's hillside Ottoman old town, evoking the city's past with its winding lanes filled with teahouses, mosques and crafts shops. It also boasts Skopje's best historic structures and a handful of museums, and is the first place any visitor should head.

Just by the entrance, you'll find the **Daut Paša Amam** (1473), once the largest Turkish baths outside of İstanbul. They make a magical setting for the permanent collection of Skopje's National Gallery. There are seven restored rooms housing mainly modern art and sculpture from across the country. Two other National Gallery sites – **Čifte Amam** and **Mala Stanica** – house temporary exhibitions.

A further five-minute walk north will bring you to the partially submerged **Sveti Spas Church**. It sits 2m underground (the Ottomans banned churches from being taller than mosques) and dates from the 14th century. It is the most historically important in Skopje. Its sunken design means it doesn't look like a church, so you might not notice it at first – look

SIGHTS
1 Archaeological Museum of the Republic of North Macedonia
2 Čifte Amam
3 Daut Paša Amam (National Gallery)
4 Holocaust Memorial Centre
5 Mala Stanica (National Gallery)
6 Mother Theresa Memorial House
7 Museum of Contemporary Art
8 Museum of the City of Skopje
9 Mustafa Pasha Mosque
10 Ploštad Makedonija
11 Stone Bridge
12 Sts Cyril and Methodius University of Skopje
13 Sveti Spas Church
14 Tvrdina Kale Fortress

SLEEPING
15 Hotel City Park
16 Hotel Solun
17 Urban Hostel & Apartments

EATING
18 Barik
19 Kebapčilnica Destan
20 Nadžak

DRINKING & NIGHTLIFE
21 Cafe Broz
22 Kotur
23 Old Town Brewery
24 Teeny Тајни
25 The Dude
26 Van Gogh Bar

ENTERTAINMENT
27 Macedonian National Opera and Ballet

SHOPPING
28 Bit Pazar
29 Dželo Filigran

BEST PLACES TO EAT AND DRINK

Nadžak
Lots of Macedonian specialities on the menu, from *skara* (grilled meat) to *tavče gravče* (oven-baked beans); order several dishes and share. €

Barik
An excellent little taverna in Debar Maalo neighbourhood, with some great local dishes – try the veal liver with onion or the baked cheese. €

Kebapčilnica Destan
Skopje's best kebabs, accompanied by seasoned grilled bread, peppers and a little raw onion, are served at this classic Čaršija place. €

Teeny Тајни
Poached eggs and avocado, smoothies and excellent speciality coffees at this Debar Maalo neighbourhood bar.

The Dude
They're really into their coffee at this cafe where antique details are mixed with designer pieces.

Cafe Broz
Great single-bean roasts, together with breakfasts and all kinds of snacks; a great terrace too.

Archaeological Museum of the Republic of North Macedonia

for the pretty bell tower that watches over it, built into the outer courtyard wall. Inside, an elaborate carved iconostasis shines out of the dark.

Standing on a plateau at the very top of Čaršija, **Mustafa Pasha Mosque**, dating back to 1492, is where you can see locals come and go for prayers and for chitchat in the lovely rose garden. It's a seven-minute walk west from the entrance to Čaršija to reach the **Tvrdina Kale Fortress**, a 6th-century CE Byzantine (and later Ottoman) structure that dominates the capital's skyline. Its ramparts offer great views over the city and Vardar River.

Exploring Skopje's Museums

See the city's museums and squares

The **Archaeological Museum of the Republic of North Macedonia**, a huge pile of Italianate-styled marble, was the result of the recent splurge on monuments to boost North Macedonian pride. Inside, there are three floors with Byzantine treasures, a pint-sized replica of an early Christian basilica showing the life phases of mosaic conservation, and a Phoenician royal necropolis.

Just before crossing the **Stone Bridge** that separates the Vardar's south and north banks, you will see the mirrored-glass **Holocaust Memorial Centre for the Jews of Macedonia**,

WHERE TO DRINK IN SKOPJE

Van Gogh Bar
Whisky nights, cocktail nights, live-music nights – something is on here every night of the week.

Kotur
A renovated old house that has art film screenings downstairs and cocktails upstairs.

Old Town Brewery
The siren call of tasty craft beer sings to locals and tourists alike at Skopje's popular microbrewery.

a museum with moving displays that commemorate the all-but-lost Sephardic Jewish culture of the country.

A brief walk across the Stone Bridge brings you to **Ploštad Makedonija** (Macedonia Sq). This gigantic space is the centrepiece of Skopje's audacious nation-building architecture project. The towering, central warrior on a horse, Alexander the Great, is bedecked with fountains that are illuminated at night.

Heading down Makedonija street, southwest of Ploštad Makedonija, takes you to the extraordinary retro-futuristic **Mother Theresa Memorial House**. Its church is the most unique you'll see in North Macedonia. There's a small museum on the first floor displaying memorabilia related to the famed Catholic nun of Calcutta, born in Skopje in 1910.

Continuing all the way to the bottom of Makedonija street, you'll find the **Museum of the City of Skopje**. Occupying the old train station building where the stone fingers of the clock remain frozen in time at 5.17am – the moment a devastating earthquake struck on 27 July 1963, killing 1070 people – it operates as an art gallery for rotating exhibitions. One area is dedicated to the horrific events of the earthquake through video footage and photos.

Skopje's Modernist Architecture

Track modernist architecture masterpieces

After Skopje was hit by a devastating earthquake in 1963, killing 1070 people and destroying around 65% of the city, the Yugoslav government started the reconstruction of the Macedonian capital with help from international governments and the UN. Two years later, Japanese architect Kenzo Tange was enlisted to help after the UN created a master plan for rebuilding. A design team of international and Yugoslav architects was formed and led by Tange. The plan included a 'City Gate', intended to concentrate business and traffic in the centre, and residential buildings outside the 'Gate'. The complex plan aimed to build a sophisticated urban structure (which Tange thought was made easier by the lack of private land ownership in socialist Yugoslavia), celebrating the ability to implement progressive design in this 'revolutionary society'.

The plan itself was not entirely accomplished, but several modernist masterpieces survive in Skopje, including the **train station**, built by Tange, with a vast elevated platform 15m above the ground. Other notable structures are the **Sts Cyril and Methodius University of Skopje** (1974), the country's largest, designed by Marko Mušič; Janko Konstantinov's otherworldly **Main Post Office** and the brilliant **Macedonian National Opera and Ballet**, by Biro 71, completed in 1981.

THE MUSEUM OF CONTEMPORARY ART

This stunning modernist edifice with floor-to-ceiling windows perched atop a hill with wonderful city views, was another building constructed in the aftermath of the 1963 earthquake. Works from around the world were donated to form a collection that includes Picasso, Léger, Hockney, Meret Oppenheim and Bridget Riley. Unfortunately, the highlights are not always on display – you may come here and find its exhibitions extraordinary or mundane, depending on what's on show.

WHERE TO STAY IN SKOPJE

Hotel Solun
Just off the main square, this stylish, beautifully designed place has modern and elegant rooms. **€€€**

Urban Hostel & Apartments
A converted residential house with a sociable front garden, close to the main train station. **€**

Hotel City Park
Fresh rooms, modern and bright, some with balconies; the location is excellent, opposite the City Park. **€€€**

Beyond Skopje

Places

Easy day trips from Skopje range from river canyons and archaeological sites to mountain hikes and a mosque.

The area around Skopje is full of lovely places to visit. Canyon Matka is truly unmissable – the setting, with its Byzantine church ruins and impressive river canyon that is easily explored in a kayak, is wonderful. Mt Vodno, visible from Skopje, has energising hikes and excellent city views. A bit further from the capital is the unforgettable Kokino Observatory, a Bronze Age archaeo-astronomical site at the top of a volcanic hill. On the way down, make sure to stop and gaze at the magnificent frescoes in the 14th-century Church of St George. Finally, Tetovo's Painted Mosque is an hour's drive from Skopje and a veritable beauty, very much worth the trip.

GETTING AROUND

You will be able to reach Matka and Mt Vodno on public transport. To visit the other sites, you'll need your own transport. Skopje's bus station, with ATM, exchange office and English-language information office, adjoins the train station. Bus schedules are only available online in Macedonian (your accommodation's staff should be more than happy to translate for you though). Buy tickets on the day or in advance from the window counters inside the station.

Canyon Matka

Canyon kayaking and Byzantine churches

Early Christians, ascetics and revolutionaries picked a sublime spot when they retreated into the hills of the Canyon Matka from Ottoman advances, building the many churches one can see today: the setting is truly reverential. Matka means 'womb' in Macedonian and the site has a traditional link with the Virgin Mary.

The most easily accessible of Canyon Matka's 14th-century churches is also one of the finest, the petite **Church of Sveti Andreja** (1389), practically attached to the Canyon Matka Hotel and backed by the towering massif of the canyon walls. While you're here, you can discover Matka's underwater caverns – they've been explored to a depth of 212m and the bottom has still not been found, making these caves among the deepest in Europe. **Cave Vrelo** is open to the public – you can enter the inky depths of the bat-inhabited cave by boat (a popular excursion) or hired kayak. Boats depart from Canyon Matka Hotel. The trip takes about an hour.

Canyon Matka

Very close to where the number 60 bus drops you off, framed by mountains and with a serene, peaceful atmosphere, **Sveta Bogorodica Monastery** is a special spot. Still home to nuns, this working monastery has 18th-century wooden-balustraded living quarters. The beautiful 14th-century chapel has frescoes from the 1500s, although a church has stood on this spot since the 6th century. From here, you can go up a trail towards the **Church of Sveti Spas** – it's signpoosted, and takes about an hour to reach. It has a modern bell tower and a crumbling, ancient chapel, which is often locked. Further up on the same trail, another 30 minutes away, **Sveta Nedela Church** is the highest and most spectacularly located, but watch out while climbing up as it's slightly dangerous.

Kokino Observatory

A sublime archaeo-astronomical site

The Bronze Age **Kokino Observatory**, sitting on a volcanic hill at an elevation of 1013m, is a truly marvellous sight.

Observe the two platforms, upper and lower, and the four 'thrones'. This was where the bonding ritual between the sun god and their representative on earth – the ruler, who sat on one of the thrones – was meant to take place. The ritual happened after the harvest, when the sun's energy was starting to fade and plant life was at its seasonal end. The ruler's power was said to be reinforced by absorbing the sunlight, reuniting

TOP TIP

Matka is served by bus number 60 from Skopje; for Vodno take the special 'Millennium Cross' bus. You'll need to rent a car to reach other destinations.

MT VODNO: HIKES & A HOLY SITE

Looming over Skopje to the south, Mt Vodno – easily recognised by its 66m Millennium Cross – is an enduring symbol of the city. A cable car climbs the mountainside from halfway up, where a couple of restaurants cater to day trippers. Take the 'Millennium Cross' special bus or a taxi from Skopje's bus station to the cable car. There's a popular, shaded hiking trail once you reach the top.

Around the western side of Vodno, the village of Gorno Nerezi is home to the Sveti Pantelejmon Monastery, one of North Macedonia's most significant churches, built in 1164. Its Byzantine frescoes depict a pathos and realism predating the Renaissance by two centuries. It's 5km from Skopje city centre and it takes about 20 minutes to get here by taxi (350MKD, using the meter).

CHURCH OF ST GEORGE

Sitting in the inconspicuous village of Staro Nagoričane, some 15km northeast of Kumanovo, this 14th-century church has some magnificent frescoes and outstanding architecture. The paintings, dating back to 1317–18, are the work of masters Michael and Eutychius, notable artists of the time, and are thought of as their most significant creations. Note the depictions of the life of St George and the Passion of Christ.

You'll need a car to reach the village – it's on the road between Skopje and Kokino Observatory, about an hour from the city. The church is usually open during mass.

ALEXNAKO/SHUTTERSTOCK ©

them with the sun god and bringing peace and good crops for the community.

The site's primary purpose was for the daily recording of the rising of the sun and the moon, and measuring the length of the lunar months so that a calendar for a periodic cycle of 19 lunar years could be produced – the cracked volcanic rocks here were soft and could be easily inscribed to mark the position of the sun at the summer and winter solstices, and the spring and autumn equinoxes. The exceptional complexity of the calendar shows that the people of the time had a keen understanding of astronomy.

To get to the observatory you'll need your own transport. It's 70km northeast of Skopje: from Kumanovo, follow the signs for Staro Nagoričane, then for Kokino. The observatory is signposted. There are some English-language information boards. If you're here in midsummer, remember to bring a hat and sunscreen, since there is very little shade.

WHERE TO FIND FOOD, DRINKS & KAYAKS IN MATKA

Restaurant Canyon Matka
Fine dining with a focus on Macedonian and Mediterranean cuisine. **€€**

Canyon Matka Hotel
The lakefront setting by the canyon walls makes this hotel a fine place for a night's rest. **€€**

Canyon Matka Kayaking
Don't miss this lovely excursion, where you can enjoy the scenery and the sunlight.

Kokino Observatory (p243)

Tetovo

Uniquely decorated Painted Mosque

An hour's drive from Skopje (43km to the west) is **Tetovo**, an unremarkable town save for its beautiful **Painted Mosque** (its official name is Pasha's Mosque – Painted Mosque is the popular name), which is like something out of *The Arabian Nights* and quite unique in the Balkans. First built in the 15th century by Abdurrahman Pasha of Tetovo, it was razed to the ground two centuries later in a great fire that wiped out half the town; the design and architecture you see today is a 19th-century reconstruction. The facade is a patchwork of rectangular panels worked in a fresco technique; inside, the decoration becomes rich and floral, with geometric and arabesque ornamentation.

The mosque sits on the southern bank of the Pena River, which bisects Tetovo. Buses run here every hour, if not more frequently, from Skopje.

KUKLICA ROCK FORMATIONS

Natural erosion and its varying effects on the area's volcanic rocks are behind the formation of these bizarre 'rock dolls', which are estimated to be nearly 30 million years old. The tall structures look like human figures, and many stories and myths have unsurprisingly been attached to them.

One of the prevailing legends tells of a man who could not decide which of two women to marry, so he decided to marry both, but at different times of the day. After turning up early, the second bride was so upset at the sight of the man marrying another woman that her curse petrified the whole wedding – and here they are today, still standing mid-ceremony.

WHERE TO SHOP IN SKOPJE

Monozero
A brilliant local carpentry enterprise, Monozero makes everything out of solid, sustainably sourced wood.

Dželo Filigran
Based in Čaršija, master filigree craftspeople and their works are considered fine examples of this art form.

Bit Pazar
A large market where you can buy just about anything.

Lake Ohrid & Around

UNESCO HERITAGE | MONASTERIES | SPRINGS

GETTING AROUND

Frequent buses ply the Ohrid Town–Sveti Naum route (€1) in summer, stopping off at various points along the lake road, including Trpejca and the Bay of Bones.

Taxis are expensive; however, during summer some charge bus-ticket rates when filling up fast (check with the driver).

Boat transfers from Ohrid Town to Sveti Naum (€10 return) run every day in summer.

TOP TIP

Mosquitoes aren't much of a problem around Lake Ohrid – until the height of summer. Arm yourself with repellent if visiting in July or August.

Vast, mysterious Lake Ohrid is a wonderfully seductive sight. Mirrorlike and dazzling on sunny days, it's a beautiful place – especially in and around the ancient town of Ohrid, with its cobbled streets, distinctive architecture, city beach and lakefront bars.

At 300m deep, 34km long and three million years old, Lake Ohrid is among Europe's deepest and oldest. It's shared by North Macedonia (two-thirds) and Albania (one-third): the North Macedonian portion is inscribed on the UNESCO World Heritage list for its cultural heritage and unique nature – it's considered the most biodiverse lake of its size in the world.

To the east of Ohrid lies Galičica National Park with mountain villages and Magaro Peak, which can be climbed. To the south, a long, wooded coast has pebble beaches, churches and camping spots. In summer the big, resort-style hotels and beaches can be crowded but there are better options beyond them.

Lake Ohrid Highlights

Lakeside monasteries, villages and springs

Sveti Naum Monastery, 29km south of Ohrid Town, is an imposing sight on a bluff near the Albanian border. St Naum was a contemporary of St Kliment, and their monastery became an educational centre. The iconostasis inside the church dates to 1711 and the frescoes to the 19th century; it's well worth paying the fee to enter. Sandy beaches hem the monastery in on two sides and are some of the best places to swim around the lake.

Inside the monastery, colourful covered motorboats sit waiting to whisk visitors to see the **Springs of Sveti Naum**. The water here – considered a small lake in itself, with two small

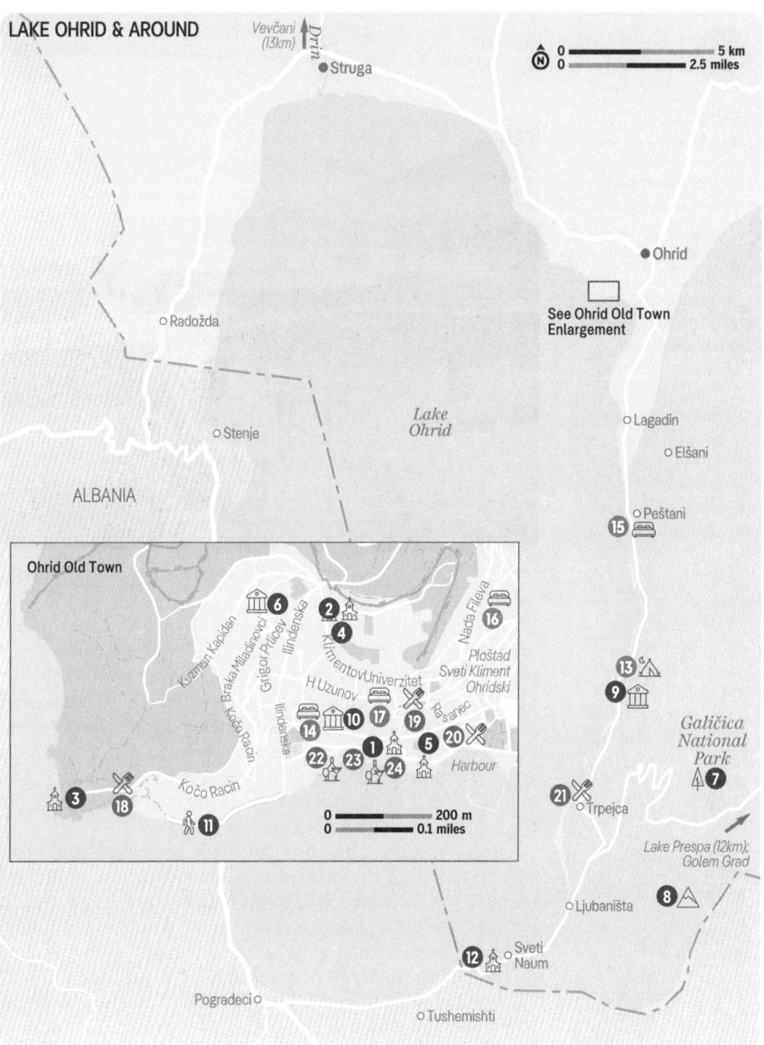

SIGHTS
1 Church of Sveta Bogorodica Bolnička
2 Church of Sveta Bogorodica Perivlepta
3 Church of Sveti Jovan at Kaneo
4 Church of Sveti Kliment
see 12 Church of Sveti Naum
5 Church of Sveti Nikola Bolnički
6 Classical Amphitheatre
7 Galičica National Park
8 Magaro Peak
9 Museum on Water – Bay of Bones
10 National Museum
11 Ohrid Boardwalk
see 12 Springs of Sveti Naum
12 Sveti Naum Monastery

SLEEPING
13 Gradište Camping
see 12 Hotel Sveti Naum
14 Jovanovic Guest House
15 Robinson Sunset House
16 Sunny Lake Hostel
17 Villa Jovan

EATING
18 Letna Bavča Kaneo
see 12 Ostrovo
19 Restaurant Antiko
20 Restoran Čun
21 Ribar

DRINKING & NIGHTLIFE
22 Jazz Inn
23 Liquid
24 NOA Lounge Bar

VEVČANI CARNIVAL

This traditional pagan carnival is thought to have existed for 1400 years, and is celebrated in Vevčani with great pomp. The elaborate costumes are reminiscent of Halloween and locals go to great lengths to design their own gory costumes. There's food, wine, music and general revelry. It takes place annually, mid-January.

DEJAN TRAJKOVIC/SHUTTERSTOCK ©

Museum on Water – Bay of Bones

islands in the middle – is fed by Lake Prespa and is astoundingly clear. At some points it's 3.5m deep but you can still see the bottom. The main reason to take the boat trip is to witness the springs bubbling up from the lake bed. Because of the water clarity they're extremely easy to see, and in some places calcification has caused the rocks to turn white – it's quite a sight. At the end of the small lake is a chapel. The charge for this trip is per boat, so if you wait for more people the price per person will drop.

Naum's original Church of the Holy Archangels (900 CE) was destroyed by the Ottomans in the 15th century and reincarnated as the **Church of Sveti Naum** when it was rebuilt between the 16th and 17th centuries as a multidomed, Byzantine-style structure on a cliff overlooking the lake. Inside, put an ear to the tomb of Sveti Naum to – allegedly – hear his muffled heartbeat. then head to the monastery walls for inspiring lake views.

Surrounding the core of the monastery is a **tranquil garden**, looped by fountains and dotted with roses and peacocks. Exploring the church, going for a paddle and having lunch or

WHERE TO SLEEP AROUND LAKE OHRID

Robinson Sunset House
Lake views, free paddling surfboards and a sprawling garden with lots of relaxing nooks and crannies. **€**

Gradište Camping
The cabins are popular as summer houses – high season evenings are dedicated to noisy barbecues. **€**

Hotel Sveti Naum
In the grounds of the Sveti Naum Monastery, some of this hotel's rooms have lovely lake views. **€**

drinks at one of the handful of restaurants and bars outside the monastery complex will keep you here for half a day; if you go swimming at the beach, count on spending the whole day.

Cupped between a sloping hill and a tranquil bay, northeast along the lake from Sveti Naum, is **Trpejca**, Ohrid's last traditional fishing village, featuring clustered houses with terracotta roofs and a white-pebble beach. At night, the sounds of crickets and frogs are omnipresent. Trpejca has limited services, though in midsummer its small beach gets very crowded. Locals like to swim here, but the frogs and flotsam and jetsam can be a bit off-putting.

In prehistoric times, Lake Ohrid was home to pile dwellers who lived literally on top of the water, on a platform supported by up to 10,000 wooden piles anchored to the lake bed. The remains of this settlement were discovered and gradually excavated by an underwater team between 1997 and 2005, and today the **Museum on Water – Bay of Bones** is an elaborate reconstruction of how archaeologists think the place would have looked between 1200 and 600 BCE. It's 16km south of Ohrid Town; buses will stop here en route to Sveti Naum, or you could combine a taxi stop here with Sveti Naum.

The slightly theatrical name, Bay of Bones, is a nod to the many animal remains and fragmented vessels that have been found here. On shore, there's a small, interesting exhibition of some of the relics, including a fascinating wall-sized photograph of the foundations as they now look under the water. Better still, for divers it's actually possible to visit the underwater excavations in the flesh with Diving Center Amfora. To the north of the site, on the cliff head, there's also a reconstruction of a Roman fort that can be visited as part of your museum ticket.

Northwest across the lake, keeping a sleepy eye on the water from its mountain perch, **Vevčani** dates to the 9th century and is a quiet rural settlement beloved by locals for its traditional restaurants and natural springs. The old, brick streets flaunt distinctive 19th-century rural architecture and the village is dominated by the Church of St Nicholas.

Vevčani Springs writhe and wriggle through leafy forest at the top of the village. The area includes a number of paths and boardwalks, and is popular for picnics and as a place to cool off on hot days, though it's a beautiful, contemplative spot at any time of year. Vevčani lies 28km north of Ohrid Town, at the northerly edge of the lake. You'll need a car to reach it.

DIVING AMID THE BONES

Diving Center Amfora (amfora.com.mk), a Lake Ohrid outfit, can take you diving under the Museum on Water to see the remains of the ancient lake settlement that sits in a watery grave at the Bay of Bones. Bones, teeth, amulets and fragments of pottery can be seen at depths between 5m and 8m, and the instructor is happy to take beginners as well as certified divers. Book at least a day ahead.

WHERE TO EAT AROUND LAKE OHRID

Ribar, Trpejca
Right on Trpejca's waterfront, Ribar serves local fish, *skara* (grilled meats) and coffee. €

Ostrovo, Sveti Naum
Of all the restaurants at Sveti Naum, this one has the prettiest setting by the water and serves good local fish. €€

Kutmičevica, Vevčani
A lively restaurant with immense views from its dining room. Go for the grilled meat and local wine. €€

BEST PLACES TO EAT IN OHRID TOWN

Letna Bavča Kaneo
Of the three waterside, terrace restaurants in Kaneo neighbourhood, this is the best – great atmosphere, fantastic food and professional service. **€€**

Restaurant Antiko
In an old mansion in the middle of the town, famous Antiko is where to try classic Macedonian dishes such as stuffed peppers or *tavče gravče* (beans baked in tomato sauce). **€€**

Restoran Čun
Good food, large lakefront windows and a breezy elevated terrace in a traditional-style Ohrid old town building. **€€**

Exploring Ohrid Town

An enchanting lakeside town

Sublime **Ohrid Town** is North Macedonia's most alluring destination. It sits on the edge of its serene namesake lake and has an atmospheric old quarter that cascades down steep streets, dotted with beautiful churches and topped by the bones of a medieval castle. A holiday atmosphere prevails all summer, when it's a good idea to book accommodation in advance: Ohrid's busiest time is from mid-July to mid-August, during the popular summer festival.

The **Ohrid Boardwalk** takes you to a beautiful outcrop of rocky beaches and a handful of small restaurants and bars. On a hot day the area is thronged with bathers, drinkers and diners: the cool waters are translucent and inviting. Strolling from here up to the **Church of Sveti Jovan** is an Ohrid must. This stunning 13th-century building is set on a cliff above the lake and is possibly North Macedonia's most photographed structure. Peer down into the azure waters and you'll see why medieval monks found spiritual inspiration here. The small church has original frescoes behind the altar.

Saluting the lake from Ohrid's hilltop, **Plaošnik** is home to the multidomed medieval **Church of Sveti Kliment i Pantelejmon**, the foundations of a 5th-century basilica and a garden of intricate early Christian flora-and-fauna mosaics. It's unusual in having glass floor segments revealing the original foundations and framed relics from the medieval church, which date to the 9th century.

Sandwiched between Car Samoil and Kosta Abraš in the heart of the old town, the tiny 14th-century churches of **Sveta Bogorodica Bolnička** and **Sveti Nikola Bolnički** have interiors heaving under elaborate icons. During plagues, visitors to the town faced 40-day quarantines inside their walled confines.

To the north, just inside the Gorna Porta gate, the 13th-century Byzantine **Church of Sveta Bogorodica Perivlepta** has vivid biblical frescoes painted by masters Michael and Eutychius, and superb lake and old town views from its terrace. The **Icon Gallery** next door highlights the founders' artistic achievements.

Ohrid's **National Museum** is housed over three floors of a remarkably well-preserved old town house which dates from 1863 and was once owned by the Robev family of merchants. On the top two floors are Roman archaeological finds, a 5th-century golden mask found locally and woodcarving, while the ground floor is reserved for art exhibitions. Across the road, the Urania Residence, part of the museum, has an ethnographic display.

WHERE TO SWIM AROUND LAKE OHRID

Orevche Beach Bar
Near the Bay of Bones Museum, you can spend a few hours lounging on the beach bar's day beds and swimming.

Trpejca Beach
The white-pebble beach gets crowded midsummer but is good for a dip.

Vevčani Springs
This spot is popular with locals who gather here in the summer to enjoy the coolness of the area's many streams.

Church of Sveti Kliment i Pantelejmon

The town's grandest religious building, 11th-century **Sveta Sofija Cathedral**, is supported by columns and decorated with elaborate, if faded, Byzantine frescoes. Its superb acoustics mean it's often used for concerts. To one side of the cathedral is a peaceful, manicured garden providing a small oasis of green in the heart of the old town.

The impressive **Classical Amphitheatre** to the north was built in the Hellenistic period (around 200 BCE); the Romans later removed 10 rows to accommodate gladiators and used it as a site for Christian executions. In summer, it's brought to life as a venue for **Ohrid's Summer Festival** performances.

Galičica National Park

A wild lake and magical island

The rippling, rock-crested massif of **Galičica National Park** separates Ohrid and Prespa Lakes and is home to **Magaro Peak** (2254m), a handful of mountain villages and 1100 species of plant, 12 of which can be found only here. Climbing Magaro Peak and swimming in Lake Prespa are fantastic activities here; exploring Golem Grad island is a must too.

You can dedicate half a day to hiking Magaro Peak. It's a moderate, 8km loop hike (around 4hrs in total), and from the top you get spectacular views of both Ohrid and Prespa

GALIČICA NATIONAL PARK FLORA & FAUNA

The wealth and diversity of Galičica National Park's flora and fauna is one of the area's main draws. There are so far around 170 registered animal species, including the brown bear, grey wolves and the red fox, which populate the park's dense forests. Golem Grad island is home to a variety of birds: you're likely to spot cormorants and herons, Dalmatian pelicans, as well as buzzards and eagles. Botanists will delight to spot some of the 12 known species of endemic plants, such as the rare *Crocus cvijicii, Centaurea soskae* and the *Malus florentina,* commonly known as the Florentine crabapple.

WHERE TO SLEEP IN OHRID TOWN

Villa Jovan
By far the most charming place to stay in Ohrid, this 1856 mansion offers nine rooms in the heart of the old town. €

Sunny Lake Hostel
Excellent hostel that is a bustling hub for backpackers. There's a snug upstairs terrace with lake views. €

Jovanovic Guest House
Two studios set in the heart of the old town. Each is well-equipped and comes with a shady balcony. €€

OHRID TOWN STROLL

Begin at the eastern end of **1 Car Samoil street**, lined with beautiful traditional architecture. Pop down to see the tiny **2 Sveta Bogorodica Bolnička & Sveti Nikola Bolnički** churches and admire the frescoes stretching across the domed ceilings. Return to Car Samoil and visit the **3 Marta Pejoska Gallery** to see the work of this local artist who practises the traditional technique of silver filigree. As you reach the end of Car Samoil, you emerge into the main town square and **4 Sveta Sofija Cathedral**, best visited if there is a concert on; take in the tranquillity of its small gardens.

From here, follow the small street that heads towards the lake's lapping waters and step onto the **5 Ohrid Boardwalk**. The winding path will take you to the old fishing neighbourhood of **6 Kaneo**, once totally cut off from the rest of Ohrid but now accessible thanks to the walkway. Have a coffee or meal break at **7 Letna Bavča Kaneo** and check out the restaurant's old photographs of the fishing community from the 19th century.

Next, head uphill to one of North Macedonia's most scenic structures, the **8 Church of Sveti Jovan**. Continue climbing, along Kočo Racin and the fig- and pine-tree-lined residential streets, and glance down at the **9 Classical Amphitheatre**, mostly quiet except for Summer Festival performances. Then follow the street past the Gorna Porta gate towards the **10 Church of Sveta Bogorodica Perivlepta**. Gaze up at the ancient frescoes, then take a look in the **11 Icon Gallery** next door to see depictions of Byzantine saints. Before heading back down the hill, enjoy the views of Lake Ohrid and the cascading town – it's a magical sight.

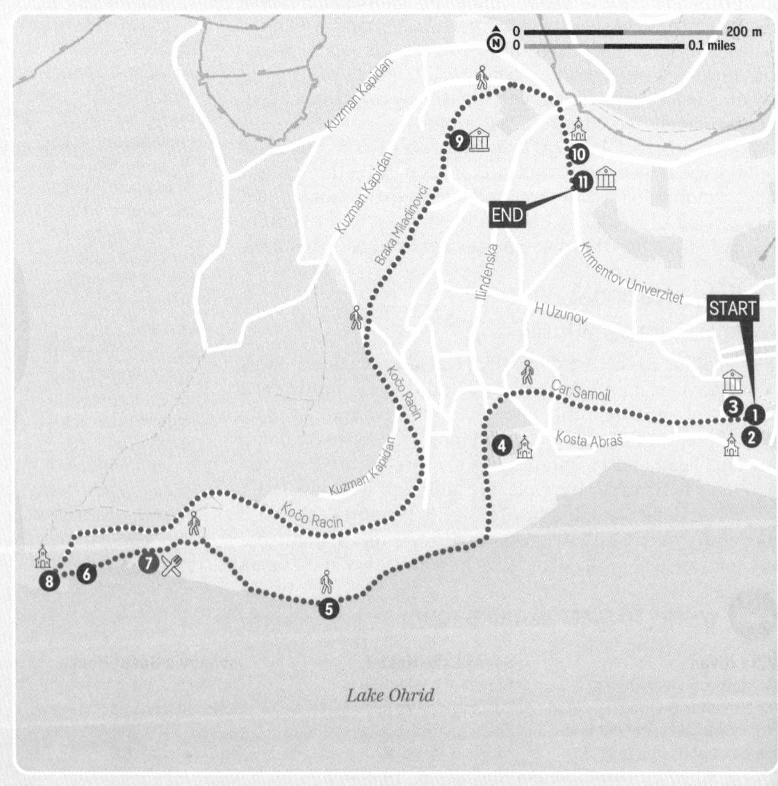

D. PAP/SHUTTERSTOCK ©

Pelicans, Lake Prespa

Lakes. Cool off by swimming at **Lake Prespa**, the highest tectonic lake in the Balkans (853m). The borders of North Macedonia, Albania and Greece converge in the lake's centre. Tourism around this lake is much less developed than on Ohrid and you won't encounter the same trickle of hotels or restaurants, so if you prefer something a bit wilder, this is the place for you. There are several beaches on the lake – **Slivnica Beach** has facilities, while sandy **Dupeni Beach**, near the Greek border on its eastern side, is quieter.

Spend a day visiting the island of **Golem Grad**, Lake Prespa's star attraction. Once the king's summer playground, it's now home to wild tortoises, cormorants and pelicans. A settlement endured here from the 4th century BCE to the 6th century CE, and during medieval times there was a monastery complex. Ongoing excavations have unearthed dozens of ruins, many of which have been marked out for visitors with information boards (in English). The battered **Church of St Peter**, close to the boat docking area, contains remnants of 14th-century frescoes. You'll also find the remaining stumps of a **Roman house**, the overgrown foundations of **early Christian basilicas** dating to the 5th and 6th centuries, and an impressive waterside ruin of a 4th-century **Roman cistern**.

GOLEM GRAD VISITING TIPS

Golem Grad is only 750m long and 450m wide, so very walkable. Note that the shoreline is backed by high rocks and cliffs 20m to 30m high, so it's not much of a swimming spot – particularly as it's also home to a high concentration of (harmless) water snakes. Its nickname is 'snake island'; wear hiking boots as there are also some venomous land snakes to watch out for.

The only way to book a trip to Golem Grad at the time of research was through **Villa Prespa Hotel** (villaprespa.com). Visits take place June to October, and cost around €80.

WHERE TO DRINK IN OHRID TOWN

Jazz Inn
A great little jazz-themed bar with a more bohemian vibe than the other options on Ohrid's lakefront.

Liquid
Ohrid's most stylish waterside bar is a relaxed place by day, serving coffee and drinks; nights have good music.

NOA Lounge Bar
The lake-facing terrace here has lovely views to complement a full cocktail and wine list.

Western North Macedonia

FORESTS | NATURE | MONASTERIES

GETTING AROUND

Without your own wheels, it's difficult to reach the various places of interest in the national park independently, or to do any hiking.

Two buses a day run from Skopje to Mavrovo town, Monday to Saturday. For Sveti Jovan Bigorski Monastery, buses transiting Debar for Ohrid or Struga will be able to drop you off. The monastery is very close to the village of Janče, so you would no doubt be able to make it to the village if you can get as far as the monastery (even if it means walking between the two – it's about 5km).

The gorges, pine forests, karst fields and waterfalls of the west of the country – Mavrovo National Park in particular – offer a breath of fresh air for visitors travelling between Skopje and Ohrid. Beautiful vistas abound, and the national park is home to North Macedonia's highest peak, Mt Korab (2764m). Locally the park is best known for its ski resort (the country's biggest) near Mavrovo town. Summer is a glorious time to visit too.

Mavrovo National Park is home to North Macedonia's most important – and accessible – monastery, Sveti Jovan Bigorski, as well as the pretty villages of Galičnik and Janče, divided by a hikeable mountain ridge. Galičnik's traditional village wedding is a great time to dip into traditional culture and party with the locals.

Driving in the park is extremely scenic, but a word of caution: car GPS doesn't work well here and signposting is poor.

Byzantine Monasteries & Traditional Villages

Atmospheric settlements and majestic monasteries

Spend a day visiting the monastery of Sveti Jovan Bigorski and the atmospheric villages of Galičnik and Janče. The Galičnik traditional village wedding is one of the country's most popular and quirky summer festivals. Mavrovo National Park is also home to some of North Macedonia's most revered cheesemakers.

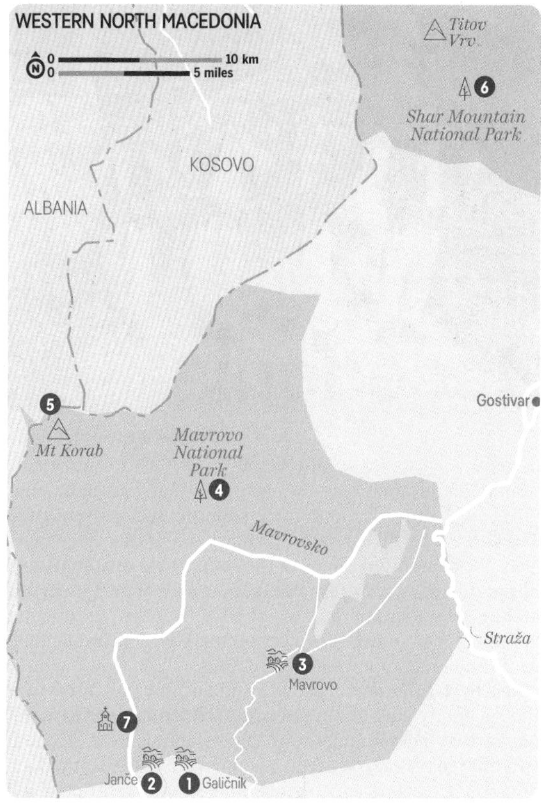

Sveti Jovan Bigorski is a revered 1020 Byzantine monastery located, fittingly, up in the heavens along a track of switchbacks off the Debar road, close to Janče village. Legend attests an icon of Sveti Jovan Bigorski (St John the Baptist) miraculously appeared here, inspiring the monastery's foundation; since then it has been rebuilt often – apparently, the icon has occasionally reappeared too. The complex went into decline during communist rule, but has been painstakingly reconstructed and today is as impressive as ever, with some excellent views over Mavrovo's mountains.

The frescoed church here also houses what is alleged to be St John's forearm, while its awe-inspiring iconostasis was the final of just three carved by local craftsmen Makarije Frčkovski and the brothers Filipovski between 1829 and 1835. This colossal work depicting biblical scenes is enlivened with 700 tiny human and animal figures. Gazing up at the enormous, intricate masterpiece is breathtaking. Upon finishing the job, the carvers allegedly flung their tools into the nearby Radika River, ensuring that the secret of their artistic genius would be washed away forever.

SIGHTS

1. Galičnik
2. Janče
3. Mavrovo
4. Mavrovo National Park
5. Mt Korab
6. Shar Mountain National Park
7. Sveti Jovan Bigorski

TOP TIP

Although Janče and Galičnik are very close to each other as the crow flies (6km), there is no road between the two and to visit both involves a drive of about 1½ hrs looping through Mavrovo National Park. A picturesque walking trail connects the two villages, climbing up and over the mountain that separates the two. Take a GPS with you if you plan to do this walk.

HORSE RIDING

Sherpa Horse Riding (horseriding.com.mk) arranges lovely horse excursions around Mavrovo. You can go on daily rides (2½ to 5½ hrs) through the mountain valleys, starting in Galičnik and stopping by traditional villages. The daily treks include an hour's training for beginners, visits to sheep farms to witness ancient working methods, cheese and yoghurt tastings, a picnic lunch and incredible landscapes throughout. Multiday excursions involve camping and going up to the Medenica Peak (2169m). The views from the top encompass Mavrovo Lake to the north and Korab Mountain to the west. June to October only.

MAVROVO NATIONAL PARK

The largest of North Macedonia's four national parks, Mavrovo National Park spreads over 780 square kilometres. It is rich in lakes – Lake Mavrovo being the largest – forests and vertiginous canyons. There are three Alpine mountains: Shar, Korab and Bistr. Shar Mountain is particularly good for hiking: Shar Outdoors (sharoutdoors.com) organises amazing summer hikes.

Thanks to the large differences in altitude and climatic conditions across the park, the diversity of flora and fauna is impressive – the endemic tree species such as the Macedonian pine and the Greek maple can be seen here. The park's forests are also home to an abundance of wildlife, the most important of which is the European lynx, a near-extinct species.

NURPHOTO/CORBIS VIA GETTY IMAGES ©

Galičnik Wedding Festival

South of the monastery, the blip on the map that is the small village of **Janče** is a picturesque spot that scales the hillside. The views from up here are awesome, even if the village itself feels like a forgotten corner of the country. Its cluster of stone houses includes some fascinating examples of decaying rural architecture with *bondruk* wooden frames (from the German 'bundwerk', a timber construction method), packed earthen walls and creaking wooden porches.

Nearby, **Galičnik** is a placid rural outpost that bursts into life each July with the **Galičnik Wedding Festival**, when one or two lucky couples have their nuptials here. It's a big two-day party that you can join, along with 3000 happy Macedonians. Everyone eats, drinks and enjoys traditional folk dancing and music.

The event draws on customs that are hundreds of years old, but the festival became especially popular during the 1950s when people who had gone abroad to work or had moved into the cities came back to the village to get married in the traditional style. The local council chooses the couples each year out of many applicants.

Some of the highlights include the public shaving of the groom, the bride arriving at the groom's house on horseback, and everyone parading through the village dressed in traditional wear. Some of the women's dresses, heavy with decorations, are more than 300 years old, so do admire the intricate, antique embroidery. Music is constant for the two days of the party, as is plenty of eating, drinking and dancing; if you're in the country at this time, don't miss it.

WHERE TO EAT & SLEEP IN WESTERN NORTH MACEDONIA

Hotel Tutto, Janče
One of North Macedonia's most enterprising community projects is this eco-hotel with a great restaurant. €€

Baba i Dede, Galičnik
Charming guesthouse with a restaurant serving traditional homemade food. €

Sveti Jovan Bigorski Monastery
For a unique experience, bed down in this famous monastery. €

SKOPJE

Central & Southern North Macedonia

NATIONAL PARKS | HISTORIC CITIES | WAR HISTORY

This large swathe of North Macedonia has some of its most beautiful spots. Pelister is the country's oldest national park, covering 171 sq km of North Macedonia's third-highest mountain range, the quartz-filled Baba Massif. Eight peaks top 2000m, crowned by Mt Pelister. Two glacial lakes, known as 'Pelister's Eyes', sit at the top. Summiting both Mt Pelister and the lakes is one of the park's biggest hiking attractions.

The villages of Brajčino and Dihovo sit at the base of the mountain, offering some excellent traditional homemade cooking in rustic settings – a visit to the local beekeeper in Dihovo is a highlight too.

Nearby, and buttressing Pelister National Park, elevated Bitola has a sophistication inherited from its Ottoman days when it was known as the 'City of Consuls'. It's a lovely place to spend a night, meandering around the old Čaršija (bazaar district) and people-watching on the main street. Finally, visiting spacey feats of Yugoslav architecture is an unusual attraction in this area.

GETTING AROUND

There's one main road into Pelister National Park, which enters from the eastern side coming from Bitola and skirts very close to the village of Dihovo. If you visit the park in your own car, there's an entry fee.

Public transport does not service the park. If you're staying in one of the surrounding villages, your host will be able to organise transfers.

Skopje to Bitola buses run every hour, and there are four daily buses to and from Ohrid. The bus station is 1km south of the centre.

SIGHTS
1 Bitola
2 Brajčino
3 Dihovo
4 Heraclea Lyncestis
5 Kruševo
6 Mt Pelister
7 Pelister National Park
8 Prilep
9 Treskavec Monastery

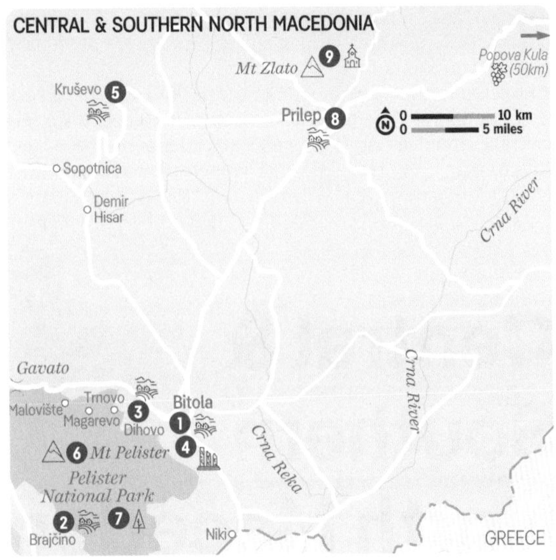

TOP TIP
Pelister National Park has excellent village guesthouses nearby and is just 30 minutes away by car from historic Bitola. With its fresh alpine air and good day hikes, the park is an underrated Macedonian stopover.

Hiking the Pelister National Park

A spectacular and underrated park

North Macedonia's oldest national park, **Pelister** has some excellent activities on offer, with number one being climbing Mt Pelister (2601m) and admiring its two glacial lakes (dip in its icy waters if you dare). It's also a haven for flora and fauna: Pelister's 88 tree species include the rare five-leafed molika pine, while its wildlife ranges from endemic Pelagonia trout, deer and wolves to chamois, wild boars, bears and eagles.

In WWI, the foothills were used by the Macedonian Front, and it was here and Bitola that bore the brunt of the country's involvement in the war – now commemorated in a moving **historical trail** (p260) within the park.

Pelister's signature hike is the full-day ascent to the national park's highest peak, namesake **Mt Pelister** and nearby lakes, **Big Lake** and **Small Lake**, which puncture the mountaintop like a pair of deep blue eyes (hence their nickname, 'Pelister's Eyes'). There are numerous starting points for the hike but none are reliably marked so it's advisable to take a guide – arrange one for about €50 through Villa Dihovo, in Dihovo, or Villa Raskrsnica in Brajčino; most speak English.

Cradled by the foothills on the southwestern edge of the national park, little **Brajčino**'s lungs are fit to bursting with fresh mountain air, making it a thoroughly idyllic place for outdoor fun. Rushing water resounds around the village, cherry trees blossom in spring and migrating swallows stop by; traditional rural architecture adds further charm. There are five churches and a monastery hidden in the leafy environs circling this well-kept place, and a two- to three-hour, well-marked trail takes in all of them.

Brajčino is on the other side of the park to the single road that climbs into the heart of Pelister NP. Hence, it's a longer hike from here up to Pelister's glacial mountaintop lakes (there's a marked trail from the village: plan for around 12 hours for this walk). The village lies within easy reach of Lake Prespa (p253), however, and makes a good base if you wish to explore both the lake and the mountains.

Propping up the eastern flank of Mt Pelister, just 5km from Bitola, the 830m-high mountainside hamlet of **Dihovo** is a pretty spot, surrounded by pine forests and mountain streams. The village's proximity to the main access road into Pelister National Park makes it a popular base for walkers, and locals have shown impressive initiative in developing their traditional community into a pioneering village tourism destination.

Dihovo's pretty coil of stone houses includes three guesthouses, a beekeeper, the icon-rich **Church of Sveti Dimitrije** (1830) and access to mountain paths, plus a waterfall to cool off in on hot summer days. The latter isn't signposted and can be tricky to find: follow signs for the now-defunct open-air swimming pool, take the forest track to the pool that veers off the paved road to the left, head past the pool down the field track to its left, and keep walking for about 10 minutes to reach the waterfall.

BEE GARDEN BN

A fantastic opportunity to learn about beekeeping and taste local honey, pollen and royal jelly, Bee Garden BN (pcelarnikbn.mk, in Macedonian) is located in Dihovo village and run by Blagoj and Naco Jovčevski (hence the 'BN' in the name).

The friendly apiarists will give you protective beekeeping clothing and demonstrate the workings of the hives and honey making. You can buy some of the delicious products – honey, propolis, pollen, royal jelly and beeswax, perfect for souvenirs. The beekeepers' family also prepare excellent traditional homemade food. Book a visit to the bee garden and reserve a traditional lunch by phoning in advance on 00389 75 269 535.

Historic Bitola

Hang out with the locals

Crumbling and colourful 18th- and 19th-century townhouses, coupled with an authentic, workaday Čaršija (old Ottoman bazaar), make Bitola worth a day trip or overnight stay. Join the locals in sipping a coffee and people-watching along pedestrianised Širok Sokak, the main promenade and heart of the city, and explore wonderful Čaršija. Don't miss visiting the ancient ruins of Heraclea Lyncestis, one of the country's best archaeological sights, too.

Bitola's **Čaršija** boasted about 3000 artisans' shops clustered together during Ottoman times. Today, only about 70 different trades are conducted in this old neighbourhood, but it's still an interesting place to wander – particularly as it's got a much more lived-in feel to it than Čaršija in Skopje (p238). Here, you'll see locals zipping about buying provisions, clothes and so on; one of the most lively sections of the bazaar is the

WHERE TO SLEEP IN PELISTER NATIONAL PARK

Villa Dihovo
Villa Dihovo comprises three pretty, traditionally decorated rooms in a historic house. €€

Villa Patrice
Attached to Villa Dihovo, this is a gorgeous little 1970s chalet, with spacious rooms and a large garden. €

Villa Ilinden
Beautiful, old stone house with creaking wooden floors and a secluded patio. €

WWI TRAIL

This gentle trail starting at the national park's headquarters meanders uphill through Pelister's cool alpine forests, and is accompanied by engaging information boards (in English) exploring this area's experiences during WWI. The route is easy enough to follow without a map or GPS – it's 2.5km and generally takes about one hour to complete.

During WWI, the Macedonian Front was stationed in and around Bitola and tasked with fighting off Bulgarian and German forces. Villages in the shadow of Pelister were dragged into the turmoil and suffered two years of consistent bombardments, with an estimated 20,000 bombs dropped on Bitola alone.

food market in the eastern corner, selling all kinds of medicinal herbs, cheeses and local products.

Bitola's **Širok Sokak** is the city's best-known and busiest street – its multicoloured facades and European honorary consulates attest to the city's Ottoman-era sophistication. Enjoying the cafes here, as everyday life promenades past, is an essential Bitola experience.

Located 1km south of town, **Heraclea Lyncestis** is among North Macedonia's best archaeological sites, though the neglected state of the museum here might make you think otherwise. See the Roman baths, portico and amphitheatre, and the striking early Christian basilica and episcopal palace ruins, with beautiful, well-preserved floor mosaics – they're unique in depicting endemic trees and animals. There's a small shady cafe in the grounds and the setting is bucolic.

Otherworldly Monuments

Relics of most brilliant architects

The **Burial Mound of the Unbeaten** is a magnificent monument to the town of Prilep's Partisan soldiers who died in WWII. It is the 1961 work of one of the former Yugoslavia's most brilliant architects, Bogdan Bogdanović, who specialised in mixing up the historical with the antic and celestial. The eight marble monoliths, each between 3m and 5m tall, depict what is thought to be a traditional circle dance, with feminine bodies and double faces representing a continuity between beginnings and ends. Simultaneously modern and ancient, this is a treat to behold.

The town's high number of Partisans and their activism during WWII gave Prilep the status of 'Town of National Heroes' in Yugoslavia, hence Bogdanović's prestigious commission. The marble carving of the monument's figures was done by Prilep's stonemasons, and there was a great emphasis on local workers and stone. The mound is set in Prilep's Revolution Park, just out of town on the Bitola road. Prilep is 44km northeast of Bitola.

The **Ilinden Uprising Monument**, built in 1974 to commemorate the Ilinden Uprising of 1903 (when the Macedonians rose up against the Ottoman Empire) is a marvel of Yugoslav architecture and a fantastic example of abstract historic symbolism. Designed by Prilep architects Iskra and Jordan Grabul, and commonly known as Makedonium, this otherworldly globular structure is meant to represent a 15th-century warrior mace. Inside is a series of stained-glass windows and abstract sculptures, each marking a turning point in North

WHERE TO EAT IN PELISTER NATIONAL PARK

Villa Dihovo
Macedonian specialities are prepared here beautifully; food prices are decided by the guests. €

Bee Garden BN
Homemade traditional food is served up here by the beekeper's family; book in advance. €

Hotel Molika
Nothing to write home about but this hotel has a cafe if you're looking for food while in the park. €

Floor mosaic, Heraclea Lyncestis

Macedonia's history. The monument's guardian will be happy to guide you through more of the symbolism if it's quiet. It's close to Kruševo, itself a pleasant little mountainside town, well off the tourist trail.

Tasting Tikveš Wines

Tour a Macedonian vineyard

Five hundred years of Ottoman rule buried North Macedonia's ancient winemaking culture, and the practice was confined to monasteries for centuries. In the last 50 years though, the Tikveš region has developed as the country's most lauded (and developed) wine region. If you want to visit a vineyard, opt for **Popova Kula** in Demir Kapija (128km east of Bitola), the region's only winery, hotel and restaurant. The owner took inspiration from his experiences of California's wine industry, and what he's achieved here is in a different league to everything else in Tikveš. Tours of the property are held four times a day for guests and nonguests. Book by calling 00389 76 432630. In September the area celebrates its viticultural heritage with the **Kavadarci Wine Carnival**.

TRESKAVEC MONASTERY

The 13th-century Treskavec Monastery rises from Mt Zlato (1422m), a bare massif replete with imposing twisted rock formations. It's hard to say which is more impressive – the bare granite boulder mountainside or the half-ruined monastery. Vivid frescoes, including a rare depiction of Christ as a boy, adorn the 14th-century Church of Sveta Bogorodica, inside the monastery, built over a 6th-century basilica.

Treskavec is 10km north of Prilep and there's no public transport, so driving or hiking are the only options. A pristine asphalt road whisks you up to the monastery along a steep and winding route. Start from Prilep's cemetery and turn uphill at the sign; it takes about 10 minutes to drive up from there.

WHERE TO SLEEP, EAT & DRINK IN BITOLA

Hotel Teatar
One of the loveliest hotels around, the sensitive design keeps true to the image of a traditional Ottoman house. €

Vino Bar Bure
Overlooking Širok Sokak, this restaurant specialises in Macedonian and Turkish cuisine. €

Porta Jazz
Live jazz and blues play at this popular place that's packed every night in summer.

MATTHEW BENN/SHUTTERSTOCK ©

Bus station, Ohrid Town (p250)

Arriving

Skopje and Ohrid are well connected to other Balkan tourist hubs as well as some international destinations further afield. Air connections have increased thanks to the growing number of budget airlines flying here. Buses are generally more frequent and cover a broader range of destinations than trains (they're also just as fast).

By Air

Skopje is the only airport in North Macedonia to fly in to from the rest of Europe. Budget airlines have improved its modest number of connections, and it's now linked pretty well to major European cities.

By Land

Buses serve North Macedonia well and international routes generally arrive at and depart from Skopje or Ohrid. Pristina, Tirana, Sofia, Belgrade and Thessaloniki are the most common connections. From Skopje it's also possible to get to Ljubljana, İstanbul and Zagreb.

Money

Currency: Denar (MKD)

CASH

Most tourist businesses, including lower to midrange hotels, accept cash only.

DIGITAL PAYMENTS

Restaurants and hotels in Skopje and Ohrid will usually accept digital, contactless payments, but don't count on it outside of these two towns.

CREDIT CARDS

Credit cards can often be used in larger cities (especially in hotels and restaurants), but you can't really rely on them outside Skopje.

Getting Around

Buses will take you between Skopje and most other towns across North Macedonia; train routes are slower and less extensive.

HIRING A CAR

Hiring a car is the best way to see North Macedonia. Skopje's rental agencies include international big names and local companies. Ohrid has many options; other cities have fewer. Note that it's virtually impossible to rent a car with automatic transmission.

ANDOCS/SHUTTERSTOCK ©

Porta Macedonia, Skopje (p238)

BUS

Skopje serves most domestic destinations. Larger buses are new and air-conditioned. During summer, book ahead for Ohrid. Sunday is often the busiest day for intercity bus travel among locals, so book ahead if you can.

TAXI

Taxis are relatively cheap, except for some journeys around Ohrid. Make sure the driver switches on their meter. Intercity taxis are expensive if travelling alone, but can sometimes work out preferably for international travel, for example on the Skopje to Pristina (Kosovo) route.

TRAIN

Domestic trains are reliable but slow. From Skopje, one train line runs to Negotino and another to Bitola via Veles and Prilep. A smaller line runs Skopje–Kičevo. Ohrid does not have a train station.

DRIVING ESSENTIALS

Drive on the right side.

Speed limits are 120km/h on motorways, 80km/h for open road and 50–60km/h in towns.

Seatbelt and headlight use is compulsory (yes – headlights even during the day).

XBRCHX/GETTY IMAGES ©

Above: City Hall (p282), Subotica. Right: Novi Pazar (p293)

Serbia

DIVERSITY OFF THE BEATEN PATH

History aplenty, festive spirit and a medley of landscapes and cultures all define this little-visited country in the heart of the Balkans.

A sense of history permeates Serbia. The nation's fate has been shaped by its position on Europe's crossroads ever since the Slavs' arrival to the Balkans. Some would say sheer *inat* – a trait of proud defiance – steered it through epic tribulations and triumphs alike, from the centuries of Turkish and Habsburg dominance to victories in two world wars and the boom and bust of Yugoslavia.

No wonder, then, that Byzantine, Ottoman, Austro-Hungarian and socialist modernist architectural styles compete across Serbia in a visual timeline of its turbulent past. The 20th century left swathes of communist-era concrete atop a multicultural urban mosaic: between the art nouveau of Subotica and minaret-studded Novi Pazar, medieval Orthodox monasteries and Belgrade's brutalist showpieces, the contrasts couldn't be more pronounced.

The diversity is equally apparent in Serbia's great outdoors. Vojvodina's sunflower-covered lowlands rise through the forested hills of Šumadija towards the edges of the Dinaric and Carpathian mountain ranges, while enormous river gorges, ancient karst caves and peculiar rock formations punctuate the country's remote corners. These distinctive landscapes, abounding in wildlife and endemic flora, invite a gamut of active pursuits.

Still, it's the social dynamism – be it age-old village traditions or cutting-edge Belgrade cool – that stays with you. Trumpet-blasting festivals and *rakija*-making prowess are vital manifestations of Serbian élan, as much as the country's sporting successes and acclaimed arts inherited from Yugoslav days.

THE MAIN AREAS

BELGRADE
Spirited metropolis in constant transition. p270

NOVI SAD
Multicultural hub on the Danube. p276

KRAGUJEVAC
Proud history and industrial heritage. p285

NIŠ
Staggering past in rugged surroundings. p295

Novi Sad, p276

The capital of northern Vojvodina province has a relaxed vibe, Austro-Hungarian architecture and a perfect setting by the Danube and Fruška Gora hills.

Belgrade, p270

A study of contrasts, balancing urban bustle with green pockets of tranquility, socialist blocks with fin-de-siècle grandeur, and alternative clubs with high culture.

CAR

The most convenient way to get around, especially for rural and more remote areas (though note that minor roads can be in poor condition). Various car hire companies have offices at Belgrade airport.

BUS

There are extensive services between major towns, resorts and national parks. In more rural areas connections can be sporadic and you may have to connect via larger transport hubs; check ahead for return times.

TRAIN

Apart from the excellent high-speed train between Belgrade and Novi Sad, services are slower and fewer than buses. The Belgrade–Bar railway has day and night departures to Montenegro's coast, traversing southwestern Serbia.

Find Your Way

Serbia's main places of interest to travellers are fairly spread out in all four directions from the capital, but extensive public transport and good freeways make exploring the country pretty straightforward.

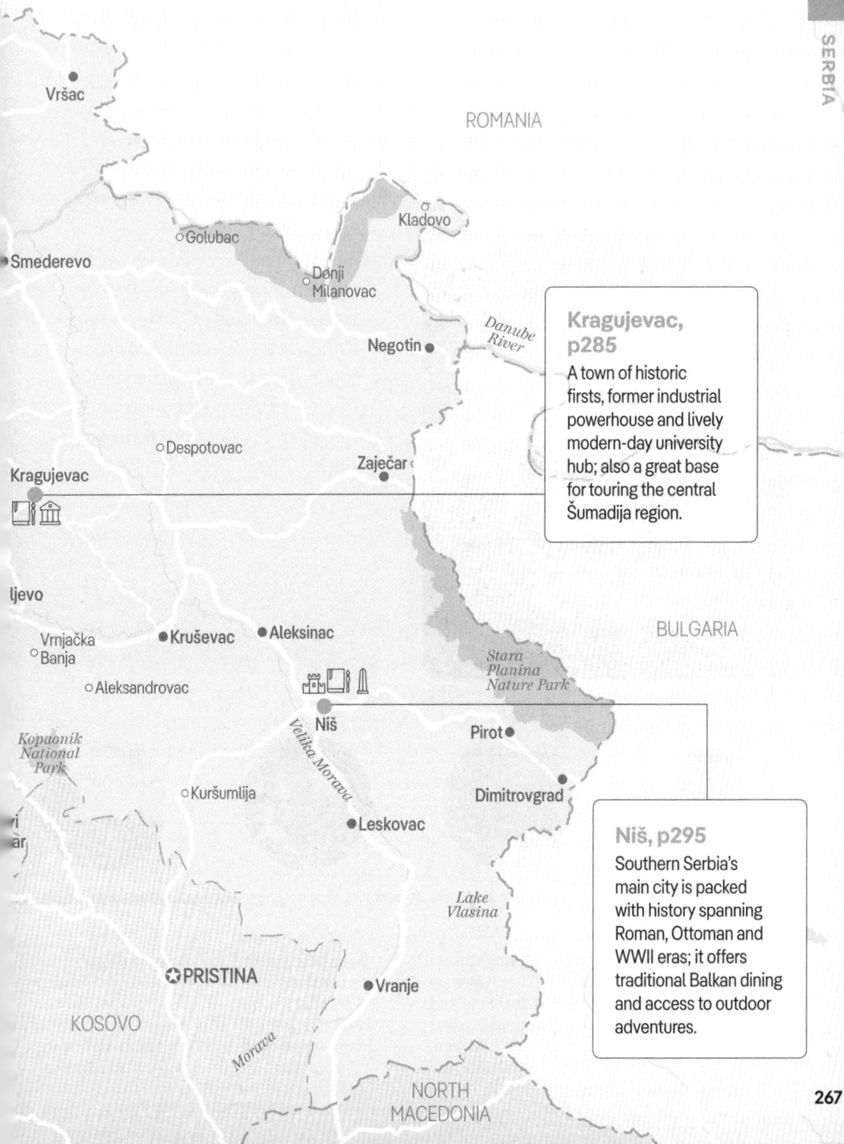

Kragujevac, p285
A town of historic firsts, former industrial powerhouse and lively modern-day university hub; also a great base for touring the central Šumadija region.

Niš, p295
Southern Serbia's main city is packed with history spanning Roman, Ottoman and WWII eras; it offers traditional Balkan dining and access to outdoor adventures.

Plan Your Time

There's more than Belgrade's big-city buzz to keep travellers engaged. With a national park in each region, plus historic towns, monasteries, spas and wineries countrywide, you can pick the experiences that suit your interests.

ALEXEY OBLOV/SHUTTERSTOCK ©

Kopaonik National Park (p294)

A Long Weekend

- It's tempting to spend all three days in **Belgrade** (p270), enjoying the capital's historical, epicurean and outdoor highlights. Learn about its past at **Kalemegdan Fortress** (p270) and the **Museum of Yugoslavia** (p273), sample **New Balkan cuisine** (p274) and go bar-hopping in the **Dorćol** (p275) quarter. In summer, cool off on **Ada Ciganlija** (p273) or take in the views over Belgrade from **Mt Avala** (p273).

- Alternatively, catch the fast train to **Novi Sad** (p276) for a day in this pretty Vojvodinian town, touring its galleries, cycling by the Danube or visiting the wineries of next-door **Fruška Gora National Park** (p279).

Seasonal Highlights

Serbia has a packed calendar year-round, with music festivals in summer and a lineup of Belgrade cultural events during winter. May and September are best for getting active in national parks.

JANUARY

Orthodox Christmas is observed on 7 January. **Küstendorf Film and Music Festival** (p292), run by Emir Kusturica, warms up Drvengrad village.

APRIL

Belgrade Dance Festival gathers global dance troupes. Fruška Gora hosts a **mountaineering marathon**.

JUNE

Danube Day (29 June) is celebrated around Đerdap Gorge. In Tara National Park (p290), it's **bear-watching** season until October.

FROM LEFT: CHERRIES/SHUTTERSTOCK ©, MARKO RUPENA/SHUTTERSTOCK ©, ALIAKSEI KRUHLENIA/SHUTTERSTOCK ©

A Week to Travel Around

- After the long-weekend itinerary, take a day trip north to **Subotica** (p282), the town of Hungarian Secession marvels, and **Gornje Podunavlje** (p284) for cycling, canoeing and birdwatching.

- South of Belgrade, several days filled with outdoor adventures, tradition and hedonism await. Two national parks, **Tara** (p290) in the west and **Đerdap** (p297) in the east, both offer excellent hikes, bike rides and boat trips on the Drina and Danube rivers respectively.

- In central Serbia, historic **Kragujevac** (p285) or **Vrnjačka Banja** (p292) spa resort make good bases for visiting the medieval **monasteries** (p287) and **Župa** (p293) wine region.

More Than a Week

- You can simply extend the week-long trip by exploring Serbia's more remote destinations. In the far southwest, the town of **Novi Pazar** (p293) is a slice of the country's Ottoman heritage, while nearby **Kopaonik National Park** (p294) provides a variety of all-season outdoor activities.

- Over in the east, ancient **Niš** (p295) is worth a visit for its heavyweight historical sights and traditional cuisine, and is a jumping-off point for treks to the secluded waterfalls of **Stara Planina** (p301) or an outing to the spa town of **Sokobanja** (p299) and the **Negotin** (p300) region's old wine villages.

JULY

As the **Exit Festival** (p276) shakes up Novi Sad's Petrovaradin Fortress, the **Drina Regatta** (p291) commemorates western Serbia's rafting tradition.

AUGUST

Nišville Jazz Festival (p295) attracts international acts to Niš Fortress. Manasija Monastery hosts the **Just Out** knights' tournament (p288).

SEPTEMBER

The renowned **Bitef** (Belgrade International Theatre Festival) showcases the latest theatre tendencies, while Niš stages **Burek Days** (p295).

OCTOBER

Prokupac Day (14 October) celebrates the indigenous grape, and **slava** (family patron saint's day in Orthodox tradition) season begins.

Belgrade

HISTORY | GASTRONOMY | NIGHTLIFE

GETTING AROUND

From the airport, take bus 72 to central Zeleni Venac stop, A1 minibus to Slavija Sq or bus 600 to the train station. If catching a taxi, head to the information desk in arrivals hall to get a receipt (the fare is fixed according to zones).

Belgrade's public transport includes buses, minibuses, trolleybuses and trams; tram 2 is a circular route around Stari Grad. Buy paper tickets at city kiosks or (if paying by card) on board, or pay the fare using the Beograd Plus app or by SMS. Night transport (midnight to 4am) is free.

Local rideshare apps include CarGo and Yandex. Naxis Taxi accepts payments by credit card.

Belgrade is full of contradictions. Seemingly its only constant is the urban bustle, with a controversial waterfront development the latest addition to an ever-evolving skyline – but the sunsets on Kalemegdan's ramparts remain as serene as they would have been when the Celts first settled on the promontory above the Sava and Danube rivers. Its Ottoman conquerors, battling over the city with Austria-Hungary, called it Dar-ul-Jihad (House of Wars); yet it arose from the ashes countless times over two millennia and came to be a cradle of progress during its Yugoslav heyday. Its Serbian name, Beograd, translates as 'White City', although its fin-de-siècle mansions and communist-era monoliths sport many shades of grey.

Belgrade is both a microcosm of Serbia (just stroll any of its green markets) and a world apart. Its history is bewildering, its nightlife enviable, and its spirit – from theatre stages to basketball courts, from street art to cocktail bars – is the reason to keep coming back.

A Crash Course in Belgrade's History

Tracing the White City's past

Although destroyed and rebuilt countless times in its 2300-year existence, Belgrade has significant relics of this tumultuous past.

The White City's ground zero is **Kalemegdan Fortress**, first settled by the Celts and expanded by the Romans who named it Singidunum. Get an audio guide at the souvenir shop and look for the Big Gunpowder Magazine (housing Roman sarcophagi and tombstones), lonesome Nebojša Tower (a Turkish-era dungeon), spooky Roman Well (actually built by the Austrians) and ivy-swathed Ružica Church (a former garrison chapel). Nearby, symbols of Belgrade's 20th-century suffering include the **river monitor Sava**, which fired the first

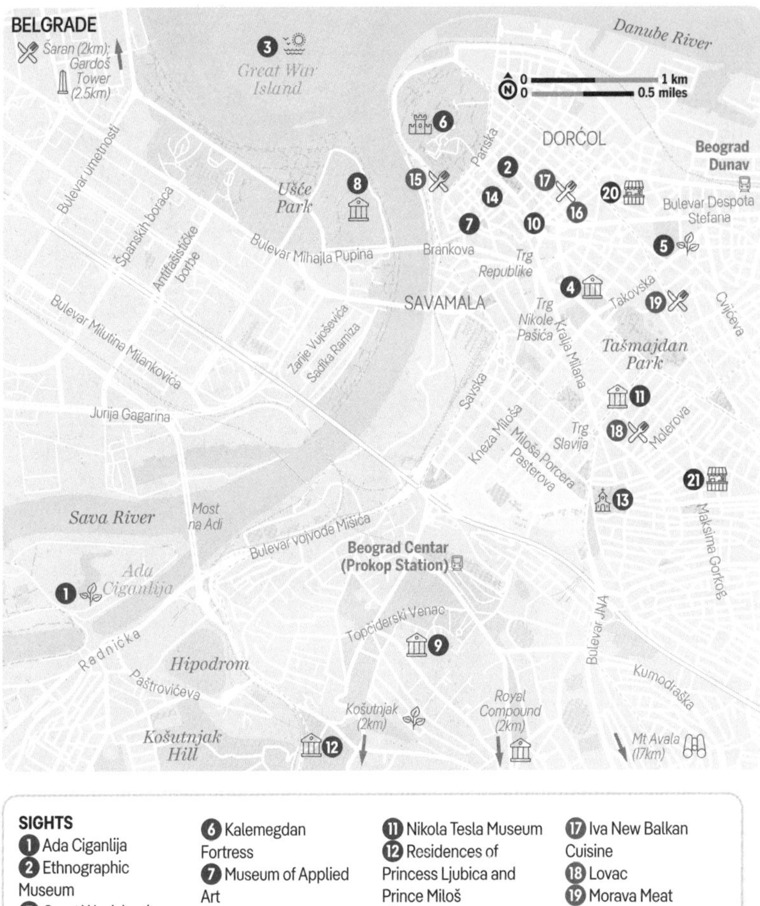

SIGHTS
1 Ada Ciganlija
2 Ethnographic Museum
3 Great War Island
4 Historical Museum of Serbia
5 Jevremovac Botanical Gardens
6 Kalemegdan Fortress
7 Museum of Applied Art
8 Museum of Contemporary Art
9 Museum of Yugoslavia
10 National Museum
11 Nikola Tesla Museum
12 Residences of Princess Ljubica and Prince Miloš
13 Sveti Sava Temple
14 Zepter Museum

EATING
15 Ambar
16 Dva Jelena
17 Iva New Balkan Cuisine
18 Lovac
19 Morava Meat Concept Store

SHOPPING
20 Bajloni
21 Kalenić

Austrian artillery strikes of WWI, and the **ruins of the National Library of Serbia**, burnt down in the 1941 Nazi bombing along with its priceless medieval collection.

One of the world's largest Orthodox basilicas, the **Sveti Sava Temple** in Vračar holds special historical significance – on this spot the Turks burnt the relics of St Sava, the Serbian Orthodox Church founder. Ponder the scale of the project, completed after almost a century; inside, the glittering mosaics are astonishing. Over in Zemun, **Gardoš Tower** was erected in 1896 to mark the millennium of Hungarian statehood

TOP TIP

Stari Grad (Old Town) is loosely defined by pedestrian Knez Mihajlova, central Republic Sq and the thoroughfare of Terazije. Other key neighbourhoods include Dorćol, Vračar and Zemun.

MEMORY OF THE WORLD IN BELGRADE

Inscribed on Unesco's Memory of the World register of documentary heritage are two treasures found in Belgrade's museums.

Miroslavljevo Jevanđelje (Miroslav's Gospel) is a liturgical book dating from around 1180, illuminated with 296 gilded miniatures. This extraordinary manuscript is Serbia's oldest known example of Cyrillic writing. Guarded in the National Museum, it's on display for only a short period each year.

Meanwhile, the archive of Nikola Tesla – containing thousands of books, documents, letters, notes, photographs and blueprints – is kept in the excellent **Nikola Tesla Museum**. On display are some of the great scientist's inventions and tools, as well as his personal items and the golden orb with Tesla's ashes.

VIRIENN/SHUTTERSTOCK ©

Japanese garden, Jevremovac Botanical Garden

and has wonderful Danube views. Mosey around this baroque neighbourhood – Austria-Hungary's border town for nearly two centuries – to appreciate its quaint atmosphere.

Awaiting a new home in Belgrade's former railway station (once it's renovated), the **Historical Museum of Serbia** tells the story of the country's rival royal dynasties. For more insight into their life and times, tour the 19th-century Ottoman-style **residences of Princess Ljubica and Prince Miloš** in Stari Grad and Topčider, followed by the 20th-century neoclassical **Royal Compound** in Dedinje. The latter, a lavish home to Karađorđević family (p288) descendants, can be visited through the Tourist Organisation of Belgrade.

WHERE TO STAY IN BELGRADE

Mama Shelter
Philippe Starck's designer hotel has fun rooms and fab sunset views from its huge rooftop restaurant. **€€€**

Savamala Bed & Breakfast
Cool B&B located in a 1908 building in Savamala, with 11 rooms furnished in mid-century modern style. **€€**

El Diablo Hostel
Lovely townhouse hostel right next to Skadarlija, with dorms plus two private rooms, and friendly staff. **€**

Serbia's capital has a particular Yugo-nostalgic appeal, and Yugotour offers a mini road trip through the era in the iconic Zastava (p286) car, taking in the socialist modernist architecture of Novi Beograd (New Belgrade) along the way. The **Museum of Yugoslavia** is ex-Yu history HQ and home to the mausoleum of Marshal Tito, the former socialist federation's lifelong president; free guided tours take place on Saturdays.

Green Belgrade

Find oases in the Big Smoke

While Kalemegdan Park is Belgrade's central outdoor sprawl, with unmissable views over the Sava and Danube's confluence, there are plenty of nature havens in this city on 20 hills.

On the edge of Stari Grad, **Jevremovac Botanical Garden** is a serene spot for a stroll or a picnic, featuring a Victorian-style greenhouse and a tranquil Japanese garden; come for open-air concerts and wine-tasting events in summer. South of the centre, the former royal hunting grounds of **Košutnjak** comprise 330 forested hectares criss-crossed with walking trails; the Ski Track provides fantastic city views. An easy escape from the urban buzz (16km from central Belgrade), **Mt Avala** is a favourite with cyclists. Take in the panoramic vista over Belgrade, the plains of Vojvodina and Šumadija's hills from the observation platform of the tallest tower in the Balkans (204.5m).

Come summertime, Belgraders flock to the pebbly lakeside beach on **Ada Ciganlija**, a verdant island – now attached to the riverbank – on the Sava. For more solitude, the bird sanctuary of **Great War Island** at the rivers' confluence has a small sandy beach (connected to Zemun by a pontoon bridge in summer).

A great way to enjoy the city is on a cycling tour with **iBike-Belgrade**, heading everywhere from Ada Ciganlija to Zemun. **No Fat No Stress** kayaking tours take you out on the Danube to secluded Beljarica wetlands, aka 'Belgrade's Amazonia'.

The Culture Map of Belgrade

Tour the capital's art museums

Belgrade's fantastic lineup of festivals may leave the cultural calendar blocked, but its museums keep art lovers on their toes year-round.

The stately home of the **National Museum** has archaeological treasures – with a special focus on the prehistoric culture of Vinča, Lepenski Vir (p298) and the Roman era – and

BELGRADE FOR SPORTS FANS

As the capital of a sports-obsessed nation, Belgrade hosts many exciting sporting events and options for getting active.

Marakana Stadium is home to the legendary Red Star football club – their 1991 European Champions Cup is exhibited at the attached museum, while the season's highlight is the Eternal Derby with bitter rival (and city neighbour) Partizan. **Hala Pionir** is Belgrade's temple of basketball, where fans of the game can catch some world-class action when EuroLeague matches are on.

Tašmajdan Sports Centre has indoor and outdoor swimming pools plus open-air ice skating in winter; it also stages international water polo competitions. And at **Novak Tennis Centre**, the home of Serbia Open, public clay courts by the Danube welcome Đoković wannabes.

WHERE TO GO CLUBBING IN BELGRADE

Barutana
Summer club located in a former gunpowder magazine on Kalemegdan Fortress, hosting open-air parties.

Klub 20/44
Cult *splav* (river barge) on the Sava open year-round; it draws an alternative crowd and top electronica DJs.

Drugstore
Stalwart of Belgrade's underground scene – party to techno and indie sounds in a former slaughterhouse.

galleries filled with Serbian masterpieces; observe the development of the nation's artistic expression from Romanticist Đura Jakšić to surrealist Milena Pavlović-Barili. The modernist building of the **Museum of Contemporary Art**, surrounded by a sculpture garden, stages exhibitions from its treasure trove of 20th-century art such as video performances by Belgrade native Marina Abramović and graphic production by Yugoslav avant-garde Zenitism movement.

Two repositories of Serbia's cultural heritage, the **Ethnographic Museum** and the **Museum of Applied Art**, are worth a visit for their permanent collections – displaying everything from traditional tools and folk clothing to jewellery and furniture – but more so for eclectic temporary exhibitions; you may chance upon a deep dive into women's dowry, Slavic carnivals, historical caricature or young Balkan designers. The **Zepter Museum** collection is a well-curated retrospective of Serbian modern-art tendencies ranging from socialist realism by Yugoslav Partisan Đorđe Andrejević Kun to pop art by Belgrade underground icon Srđan Đile Marković.

Explore independent art galleries and the city's subculture with **Belgrade Art Tours**, or find its thriving street art with **Belgrade Alternative Guide**.

THE URBAN SCENE

Dragana Koštica, editor of *Still in Belgrade* online magazine (@stillinbelgrade), reveals her favourite hangouts:

Clubbing
A club/bar in a former brewery in Dorćol with a striking interior design, **Dim** showcases diverse local and international electronic musicians, from techno to experimental live acts.

Exhibitions
Located in downtown Belgrade, **Hestia** is one of the city's finest art galleries. It collaborates with artists from the Global South and their exhibitions also nurture the local art scene.

Design
In Cetinjska bar district, **Kula** adds an artistic flair to the surroundings with a shop selling original pieces such as digital graphics, trendy T-shirts and stylish bags by local designers.

From Kafana to New Balkan Cuisine

Dining extravaganza, Serbian-style

There's no better place to appreciate Serbian cuisine's inextricable link with the land than a neighbourhood *pijaca* (green market); two of Belgrade's best are **Kalenić** in Vračar and **Bajloni** in Dorćol. Go foraging for homemade *kajmak* (salty clotted cream), *čvarci* (pork cracklings), *turšija* (pickled vegetables) or the ubiquitous raspberries.

Another local institution is the *kafana* (tavern), introduced by the Ottomans. On the touristy cobblestoned strip of Skadarlija they come complete with violin serenades. Pick **Dva Jelena**, established in 1832, for its old-school elegance and order national classics like *Karađorđeva šnicla* (*kajmak*-stuffed escalope). For a bohemian Yugo-era *kafana,* head to **Lovac** in Vračar, renowned for game dishes such as wild boar with truffles.

Zemun has the city's best fish restaurants, lining the Danube quay – sample the daily catch turned into delicacies like the 'Smederevo-style' pike at **Šaran**. Meanwhile, **Morava Meat Concept Store** in Palilula Market serves premium steaks, burgers and *ćevapi* (grilled kebabs) at the bar.

WHERE TO SHOP IN BELGRADE

Belgrade Design District
A dilapidated passage off Terazije hides miscellaneous small boutiques showcasing emerging local designers.

Parfimerija Sava
Endearing old-world perfumery (established in 1954) selling unique hand-mixed scents in vintage bottles.

Yugovinil
One of Europe's best record stores, with some 20,000 albums; great window into Yugoslav-era new wave.

JOHN WREFORD/SHUTTERSTOCK ©

Restaurant, Skadarlija

Beton Hala, a former Savamala port warehouse, is a hub of in-vogue contemporary dining; **Ambar** is popular for its small-plate takes on Balkan staples and a long craft *rakija* (fruit brandy) list. Leading Belgrade's culinary revolution is Dorćol's **Iva New Balkan Cuisine** – now a Michelin Bib Gourmand – whose head chef Vanja Puškar reinvents local gastronomy in a fusion of flavours and organic ingredients.

Get introduced to Serbian cuisine and customs with **Food and Culture Tour Belgrade** or the passionate foodies from **Taste Serbia**.

BAR-HOPPING IN DORĆOL QUARTER

The **Cetinjska 15** complex, occupying the ramshackle grounds of a former brewery in Dorćol, draws Belgraders with many ultra-cool bars sharing the address. Other neighbourhood picks:

Leila
Part bar, part record shop, often hosting live sessions.

Blaznavac
Bar, cafe and quirky art gallery that also stages live music.

Lenja Buba
Belgrade Urban Distillery's cocktail bar serves top concoctions.

Druid Bar
Speakeasy-style bar with old-time ambience and inventive cocktails.

Krafter
Sip excellent local craft beer at this industrial-chic venue.

Podrum Wine Art
Enjoy a glass of Serbian *vino* on the wonderful rooftop terrace.

Novi Sad

CULTURE | FESTIVALS | CYCLING

GETTING AROUND

The best way to get around Novi Sad is by bike. The city has more than 100km of cycling paths; NS Bike bicycle-sharing system has a downloadable app and 16 rental stations across town (you need to get a user card first by registering with your ID at the tourist information centre located on Trg Slobode).

Red Taxi (Crveni) is a recommended local company.

While much younger than Belgrade, Novi Sad is no ordinary second city. Known as the 'Serbian Athens', during the 18th and 19th centuries the capital of Vojvodina province was a stronghold of national culture in the Habsburg-ruled north – earning the status of free royal town from Empress Maria Theresa – and remained a beacon for the Serbs south of the Danube and Sava rivers while they languished under Ottoman rule. To this day, the city's multicultural heritage is evident in its four official languages.

Novi Sad's trademark is Petrovaradin Fortress, dubbed 'Gibraltar on the Danube' – a feat of 18th-century Marquis de Vauban engineering that morphs into a huge music stage each July for the mega-popular Exit Festival. But there's much more to this laid-back yet happening place, from candy-coloured Habsburg-era architecture and venerable museums and galleries to one of Europe's best Danube beaches and a thriving bicycle culture.

Vojvodina's Capital of Culture

Get a culture hit in Novi Sad

It's no accident that in 2022 Novi Sad became the first non-EU city to carry the prestigious title of European Capital of Culture. To appreciate the significance of this creative hub, tour its esteemed museums and galleries.

Within Petrovaradin's ramparts, the **City Museum of Novi Sad** outlines civic life through history; pieces of Biedermeier, Rococo and Altdeutsch applied art attest to the development of the city's bourgeois class under Habsburg influence. A standout among many artists' ateliers nearby is **Atelje 61**, which specialises in tapestries.

Trace the province's past from the earliest days at the **Museum of Vojvodina** to understand its multiethnic character, and stroll through an early-20th-century urban landscape for a glimpse into the trades of the epoch. Next door, fast-forward to the future at the **Museum of Contemporary Art**

☑ TOP TIP

For a unique perspective on Petrovaradin Fortress, visiting the City Museum of Novi Sad located within its ramparts allows you to tour the citadel's underground *katakombe* with a guide (the tour includes a fraction of the 16km and four levels of tunnels).

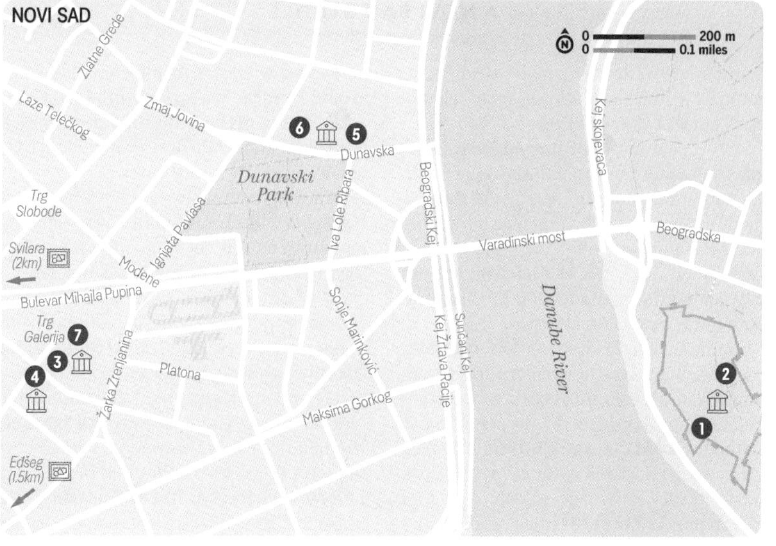

SIGHTS
1 Atelje 61
2 City Museum of Novi Sad
3 Gallery of Matica Srpska
4 Gift Collection of Rajko Mamuzić
5 Museum of Contemporary Art Vojvodina
6 Museum of Vojvodina
7 Pavle Beljanski Memorial Collection

Vojvodina, which stages exhibitions of digital and conceptual art and design, and much more.

The **Gallery of Matica Srpska** displays centuries of masterpieces, from Byzantine icons to modernist paintings by the likes of Vojvodina's own Sava Šumanović (take a curator-led themed tour on weekends). It's bookended by two more galleries, **Pavle Beljanski Memorial Collection** and **Gift Collection of Rajko Mamuzić**; as a perfect complement, they showcase 20th-century Yugoslav art.

Recently joining these established institutions are 'culture stations' **Eđšeg** and **Svilara** – along with a new creative district in the former industrial zone near Štrand beach – which host exhibitions, performances, concerts and other events worth checking out. **Street Art Novi Sad** has an online map and organises cycling and walking tours of the city's alternative side.

MUSIC FESTIVALS

Novi Sad's Exit may be world-famous, but Kragujevac and Niš give it a run for its money with popular summer music festivals in historic locations – **Arsenal Fest** (p286) and **Nišville Jazz Festival** (p296), respectively.

BEST PLACES TO STAY & EAT IN NOVI SAD

Leopold I
Luxury hotel set atop Petrovaradin Fortress, with baroque-style and modern rooms and Danube views. €€€

Hotel & Cafe Veliki
Unbeatable central location, huge modern rooms and a hip restaurant representing Vojvodinian cuisine. €€

Varad Inn
Great budget option in an 18th-century building with a garden cafe in Petrovaradin's Lower Town. €

Project 72
Modern bistro with inventive small plates based on organic produce and a strong list of Serbian wines. €€

A NOVI SAD STROLL

Laid-back Novi Sad is made for strolling. Its compact historic core allows you to take the city's pulse at your leisure.

Start at peaceful ❶ **Dunavski Park**, which has shaded lanes and a pond. Across the boulevard, the white-marble, modernist ❷ **Banovina** building is the seat of the Vojvodina Government and Assembly. Back through the park, you'll reach the ❸ **Fish Market**, the city's oldest. It's now a regular green market with some good cafes attached.

Continue along pedestrian ❹ **Dunavska**, lined with Austro-Hungarian townhouses, popping into passages to check out boutiques and souvenir shops. Nearby, the baroque-style Orthodox ❺ **St George Church** (1734) features the iconostasis painted by Paja Jovanović, master of Serbian realism.

Turn into ❻ **Zmaj Jovina**, another pedestrian street with pastel-coloured facades; it's perfect for window-shopping or chilling out at outdoor cafes. You can't miss the neo-Gothic ❼ **Church of the Name of Mary** (1895), a Roman Catholic cathedral with stained-glass windows and a soaring tower.

To the right of the central square, ❽ **Serbian National Theatre** is another white-marble modernist edifice; the company was the first theatre among the Serbs. Cross the road to enter ❾ **Jevrejska**, a slice of old Novi Sad with some traditional craft stores. Its highlight is the huge Secession-style ❿ **Synagogue** (1909), which served the city's once-large Jewish community; it's now used as a concert hall.

At the street's end is ⓫ **Futoška Market**, Novi Sad's largest. Browse its stalls heaving with groceries, clothes and bric-a-brac. End the walk in sprawling ⓬ **Futoški Park**, home to a gorgeous Secession-style hospital building.

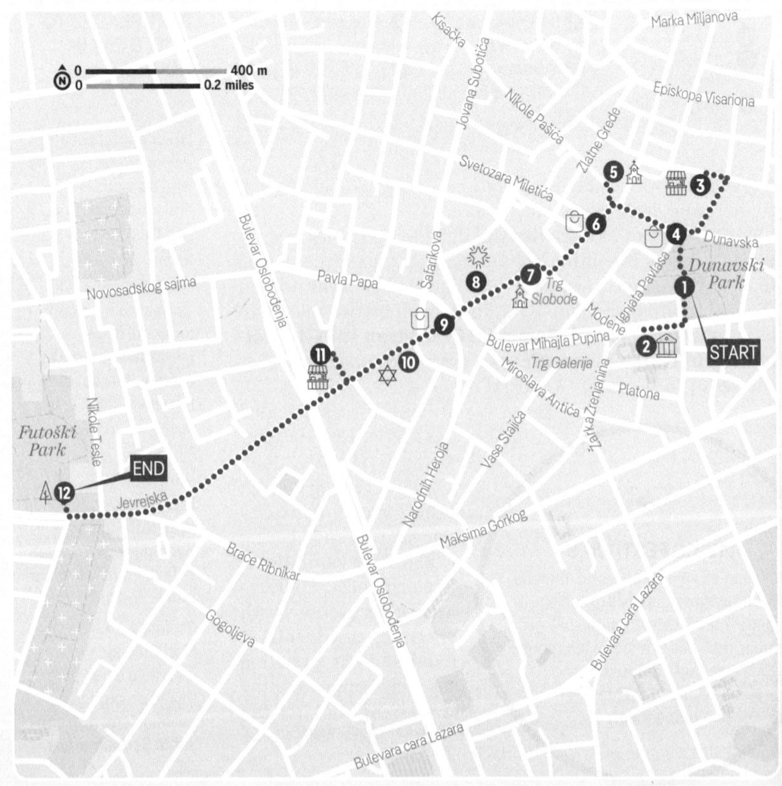

Beyond Novi Sad

With gourmet farmstead dining, thriving wine routes, riverside cycling and forest hikes, the plains of Vojvodina are surprisingly dynamic.

Zooming through sunflower fields on the Belgrade–Novi Sad train, you might assume that the flatlands of Vojvodina are a dull place. You'd be mistaken. Its green havens include birdlife-rich Pannonian marshes and the sand dunes of 'the European Sahara'. Just outside Novi Sad, Fruška Gora National Park is threaded with kilometres of hiking trails, while the EuroVelo 6 cycling path meanders along the Danube.

Vojvodina is also Mitteleuropa in microcosm, counting six official languages. Its northern Habsburg-era town, Subotica, is famed for Secession-style architecture; to the south, Fruška Gora hills shelter a bevy of medieval Orthodox monasteries. Sustaining it all is the time-honoured gastronomy of *salaši* (farmsteads), along with some of Serbia's best small wineries.

Fruška Gora

Taste Vojvodinian wines

First grapes were planted on Fruška Gora in the 3rd century by the Romans; today its villages (a half-hour drive from Novi Sad) are famous for countless small, family-owned wineries.

Get introduced to the region's viniculture at the **Museum of Beekeeping and Wine Cellar Živanović** in Sremski

GETTING AROUND

The gateway to Fruška Gora is Sremski Karlovci; take a taxi or local buses 61 or 62 from Novi Sad (25 minutes). For getting around the national park, it's best to have your own wheels.

Subotica is an easy 1¼-hour drive from Novi Sad along the E75 motorway; buses go hourly but take longer. The high-speed railway line from Belgrade to Novi Sad is currently being expanded to Subotica and on to Budapest across the border.

From Subotica, it's an hour's drive west to Bački Monoštor in Gornje Podunavlje. From Novi Sad, either drive directly or catch a bus to the town of Sombor and then a taxi (it's a 20-minute ride) to the village.

WHERE TO STAY AROUND FRUŠKA GORA

Lala Vineyard Glamping Resort
Set in a vineyard with a pool just outside Sremski Karlovci; breakfast included. €€€

Vila Prezident
Boutique hotel in Sremski Karlovci with elegant rooms and apartments, a restaurant and wine cellar. €€

Vrdnička Kula
Village-style complex in Vrdnik with wooden bungalows and modern rooms, located on the edge of the forest. €€€

FRUŠKA GORA'S WINES

Mirjana Maksimović, president of the Women and Wine association (@zene_i_vino), recommends Fruška Gora's native grapes:

Fruška Gora is home to small family wineries and unique varieties. Among them are several that you can't try anywhere else.

Neoplanta
White muscat wine with exceptional freshness and floral aroma.

Morava
White wine with crisp freshness and unique character.

Seduša
Gently coloured red wine, with elegant texture and refined taste.

Probus
Strongly coloured red wine, with velvety tannins and powerful body.

Bermet
Enhanced-flavour dessert wine, containing many local herbs.

Karlovci. Apart from displaying the 300-year-long family winemaking history, it offers degustations of seven different wines and three types of honey. The aromatic dessert wine, *bermet,* is obligatory. Meanwhile, the young **Deurić Winery** near Vrdnik organises four-hour wine classes; its standouts include local *morava* and *probus* varieties.

Kovačević Winery in Irig – one of Fruška Gora's oldest, and known for an intense chardonnay – provides a complete gastronomic experience. Degustations take place at its Wine House, where gourmet Vojvodinian cuisine is knowledgeably paired with the wines. Alternatively, head to the park's western end for fine dining at the Gastro Chalet of equally long-standing **Erdevik Winery**, which earned a reputation for its shiraz grape.

In Rakovac village, **Imperator** is pioneering biodynamic winemaking and producing Serbia's first organically certified wines; try its juicy *grašac,* or Welschriesling. Also look for **Chichateau** from Šišatovac (its cabernet franc rosé is perfect in summer), **Verkat** from Čerević (uniquely in the region, it cultivates Istria's malvasia grape), and **Bikicki** from Banoštor (popular for its orange wine *traminac,* or Gewürztraminer).

The annual **Fruška Gora Walk and Wine** provides tastings along the park's forest trails (check dates at vojvodina.travel). End with a splurge in Vrdnik – its luxury spa, **Fruške Terme**, has a thermal-water infinity pool with panoramic views of sylvan hills.

WINE REGIONS

Serbia's winemaking tradition dates back to Roman times. Fruška Gora is Vojvodina's principal wine route; other key regions include **Župa** (p293) in the south of Šumadija, and the wine villages of **Negotin** (p300) in eastern Serbia.

WHERE TO EAT AROUND FRUŠKA GORA

Pasent
Shabby-chic interior and a gorgeous garden in Sremski Karlovci; order fish straight from the Danube. **€€€**

Kod Četiri Lava
This Sremski Karlovci stalwart dishes out traditional Vojvodinian cuisine and has a strictly local wine list. **€€**

Fruškogorski Jelen
Popular restaurant in Vrdnik with a folksy ambience serving Serbian grill staples as well as game specialities. **€€**

A FRUŠKA GORA DRIVE

The gentle hills and linden forests of Fruška Gora are cherished by hikers and cyclists. Home to picturesque villages, small wineries and 16 medieval monasteries, they also make for a great drive.

Set out from ❶ **Sremski Karlovci**, whose historical sights belie its sleepy feel. Clustered around the main square are St Nicholas Orthodox Cathedral (1762) and the oldest Serbian grammar school (1791); the nearby Museum of Beekeeping and Wine Cellar Živanović (p279) offers wine and honey degustations. Sremski Karlovci is the gateway to Fruška Gora; it's only a short drive to ❷ **Stražilovo**, which marks the start of a hiking trail through forested hills. A pleasant 1km walk leads uphill to the grave of Branko Radičević, the famous poet of Serbian Romanticism.

Backtrack via Sremski Karlovci southward to the 16th-century ❸ **Velika Remeta Monastery**. It has the remains of vivid frescoes and the highest bell tower in Fruška Gora (40m). Then head west to ❹ **Iriški Venac**, a picnic area in the heart of the park at an altitude of 502m. Here, the Yugoslav-era Freedom Monument commemorates the Partisans' struggle during WWII – a soaring obelisk topped with a statue of a woman, her raised hands symbolising the people's uprising.

A short drive away, break the journey (if you have a designated driver) at ❺ **Kovačević Winery** to relax over some wine tasting and gourmet dining. It's one of Fruška Gora's most famous wineries. Just down the road is the 15th-century ❻ **Novo Hopovo Monastery**, with the iconostasis by Serbia's leading baroque painter Teodor Kračun.

End the drive in ❼ **Vrdnik**, a village with thermal hot springs and a luxury spa on Fruška Gora's southern slopes.

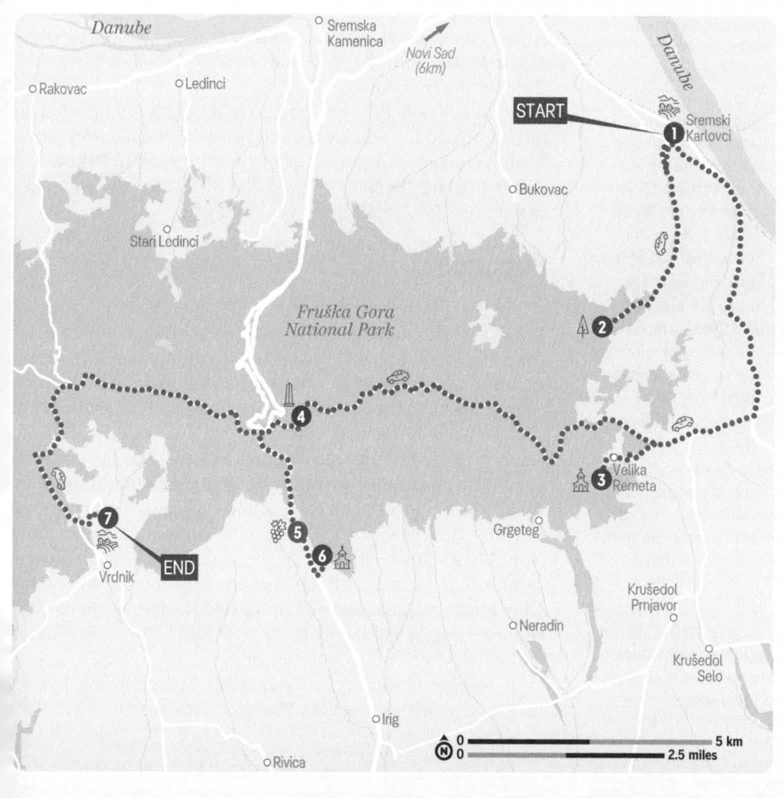

TOP TIP
The Danube and Tisa rivers, plus many canals and wetlands, make Vojvodina ideal for kayaking; contact Dunavski Rafting in Novi Sad.

VOJVODINA'S HISTORIC BREWERIES

Part of Vojvodina's Austro-Hungarian heritage, first breweries were established across the province in the 18th century with the settlement of Germans in the Pannonian lowlands. The 19th century was the golden age for the brewery in **Pančevo**, which was owned by the Weifert family and grew into the largest one in the Balkans; as well as those in **Čelarevo** and **Zrenjanin**, both properties of the most famous Vojvodinian landowner Lazar Dunđerski. While the Weifert building in Pančevo is currently abandoned, some of Vojvodina's industrial heritage can be seen at the beer museums in Čelarevo (its brewery is now part of Carlsberg Group) and Zrenjanin (the town also hosts Beer Days in August).

Vojvodina

A gastronomic road trip

For most Serbs, any mention of Vojvodina immediately brings to mind two gastronomic institutions – *salaši* (traditional homesteads) and *čarde* (riverside taverns), both of Hungarian origin. These strongholds of wholesome rural-style dining dot the flatlands where 'slow food' and 'farm to table' were the way of life long before they became global buzzwords.

The most famous is **Salaš 137** in Čenej village, 10km north of Novi Sad. Work your way through the locally focused menu, from *salašarski čekić* (prunes stuffed with cheese, rolled in bacon and grilled) to *šnenokle* (whipped egg whites floating atop vanilla custard), then sleep it off in one of its Altdeutsch-style rooms with gorgeous clay furnaces.

On Fruška Gora's southern slopes, in Neradin village, the rustic house at **Perkov Salaš** is a veritable ethnographic museum, preserving two centuries of family heritage. Book ahead for lunch (perkovsalas@yahoo.com) to enjoy belt-busting, home-cooked courgette moussaka and poppy-seed strudel, or just stop by for a sip of *višnjevača* or *orahovača* (cherry or walnut *rakija*).

Majkin Salaš, at Palić Lake outside Subotica, is a sprawling estate with orchards, farm animals, a fish pond and a horse stable. Regional delicacies not to miss here include *morčija supa* (guinea-fowl soup) and *gomboce* (plum-stuffed potato-dough dumplings). You may even be serenaded by lute-style *tamburica* music.

The best *čarde* are, obviously, right on the Danube; their menus invariably revolve around freshwater fish specialities. Within Gornje Podunavlje (p284), head to **Čarda Pikec** near Bezdan village for spicy *riblja čorba* (fish soup, usually carp), slow-cooked in a cauldron over open fire.

Subotica

Secession-style architectural marvels

Leafy, elegant Subotica in Vojvodina's north, a 1¼-hour drive from Novi Sad, was once a thriving town of the Austro-Hungarian Empire where renowned architects of the time created fine works in the Secession style – a variant of art nouveau – at the turn of the 20th century.

Subotica's oldest and most impressive art nouveau edifice is the 1902 **synagogue** designed by Marcell Komor and Deszö Jakab. It's a riot of pastel colours and stylised ornaments such as tulips and peacock feathers, with stained-glass windows from Miksa Róth's studio and roof tiles made of Zsolnay ceramics. The same architects were responsible for Subotica's **City Hall**; admire the elaborate decoration in its council chambers on a guided tour (at noon Tuesday to Saturday), and climb the 76m-high tower for great city views.

An example of Vienna Secession style – recognisable by geometric elements – is the **City Museum**, designed by Budapest's

Synagogue, Subotica

Vago brothers. Don't miss the gallery displaying the Hungarian fine arts in Vojvodina; the portrait of Empress Maria Theresa by realist Mór Than was commissioned for the centenary of Subotica as a free royal town. The iconic Raichle Palace, once architect Ferenc Raichle's design studio and now home of the **Modern Art Gallery**, shows Transylvanian folk art influences in its floral patterns. Stop by for rotating exhibitions or just to admire the Dalí-esque building itself.

Only 7km from town, **Palić Lake** has yet more art nouveau gems including the Grand Terrace, the Women's Lido and the water tower. Visit in July, when its acclaimed week-long **European Film Festival** celebrates the continent's cinematography.

SLOVAK NAÏVE ART

The Slovak-majority village of Kovačica in Vojvodina's east, while home to only 6000 people, is famous for its naïve art. Since 1939, its self-taught painters have created over 50,000 works in a colourful, rural-themed style. **Kovačica Naïve Art Gallery**, established in the village in 1955, now owns around 800 works by more than 40 painters – staging rotating exhibitions – and also has paintings for sale. Some of the village's homes have their own collections.

Over time, the artists' colony has embraced painters from other villages in Vojvodina as well as the province's other ethnic groups. Their art is a delightful window into the customs, folklore and daily life in the Pannonian Plain.

WHERE TO STAY, EAT & DRINK IN SUBOTICA

Artist Hotel
Stay in a restored Secession-style building with modern design touches and a 130-year-old wine cellar. €€€

Boss Caffe
Stylish restaurant with a diverse mix of international cuisine; it shares the garden with the Modern Art Gallery. €€

Grunf
In genteel Subotica, find alternative-scene vibes at this sociable cafe/pub that hosts live music and art events.

THE EUROPEAN SAHARA

Dubbed the 'European Sahara', the 330-sq-km nature reserve of **Deliblato Sands** (Deliblatska Peščara) in Vojvodina's southeast is the continent's largest sandy area. Formed in the Ice Age and sculpted into dunes by the strong easterly *košava* winds in the more recent era, it's home to a vast range of plants - a mix of steppe, forest and marsh vegetation - as well as wildlife including wolves.

The reserve is a designated Important Bird Area (IBA), with many rare species nesting here, such as little cormorant, little egret, yellow heron and ibis. The undulating, Hobbiton-like hillocks of Zagajička Brda are located near the village of Grebenac; their colours are most attractive in May and October.

LEON KISS/SHUTTERSTOCK ©

Kingfisher, Gornje Podunavlje

Gornje Podunavlje

Escape to the Amazon of Europe

Part of the five-country floodplain billed as 'the Amazon of Europe' and a Unesco Biosphere Reserve, the 196-sq-km **Gornje Podunavlje** occupies Vojvodina's northwestern corner (two hours' drive from Novi Sad). With alluvial forests and wetlands, river islets, saline marshes, Danube meanders and canals, the nature reserve shelters Serbia's largest population of red deer, plus otters, badgers, black storks and white-tailed eagles. In early autumn, the deer's mating call bellows through the woods.

Two idyllic villages are gateways to Gornje Podunavlje and a showcase of its cultural heritage. In **Bački Monoštor**, the reed-roofed Mali Bodrog 'ethno house' preserves the rural ambience from over a century ago; visit the Periškić beekeeping household for a sip of *medovača* (honey brandy), and watch horseshoe or fishing-net makers at work. **Bezdan** has an authentic 1871 silk damask workshop where custom-made pieces are still handwoven on traditional wooden looms.

The reserve's **Karapandža Eco-centre** provides signposted walking trails with bird observatories - try the 5km circular route by the Danube or the 3.5km forest path to Šarkanj pond. Alternatively, rent canoes to explore in blissful solitude along the pristine Bajski canal, strewn with reeds and white and yellow water lilies.

Gornje Podunavlje's flat terrain is perfect for two-wheeled adventure. Its cross-border cycling paths include the 80km **Pannonian Peace Route** between Sombor in Vojvodina and Osijek in Croatia; **EuroVelo 6**, rambling onwards to Đerdap National Park (p296); and the **Amazon of Europe Bike Trail** that follows the Mura, Drava and Danube rivers from Austria to Hungary. Bački Monoštor's tourist centre (backimonostor.rs) rents out bikes.

Kragujevac

HISTORY | GASTRONOMY | AUTOMOBILES

Both geographic and administrative centre of Šumadija region, Kragujevac holds a special place in Serbia's eventful history. Chosen by Prince Miloš Obrenović as the fledgling state's capital upon its liberation from the Turks in 1818, the city was home to a series of firsts. Independent Serbia's first courthouse, grammar school, theatre and printing house were all founded here during the 1830s; however, the glory days didn't last long, because in 1841 the capital moved to Belgrade.

Kragujevac was also the birthplace of Serbia's industrial revolution and the site of one of the country's greatest WWII tragedies – a proud past that's preserved both in local museums and memories – while the Yugoslav era catapulted it into the car lovers' alternative hall of fame. Today, this university hub brims with youthful energy and rocks out at the summer's Arsenal Fest; nonetheless, the surrounding green hills of Šumadija offer rural escapes aplenty.

GETTING AROUND

The historic core of Kragujevac is easy to get around on foot. To reach the sprawling grounds of Šumarice Memorial Park, located about 2.5km from the city centre, it's best to catch a taxi.

Serbia's City of Firsts

Ponder the past in Šumadija's capital

A trio of museum complexes makes Kragujevac a worthwhile destination for anyone with an interest in history.

While most of the city's 19th-century architecture was destroyed in WWII, you can go back in time to old Kragujevac at **Milošev Venac** (Miloš Crescent), whose unassuming edifices are relics of some of the nation's proudest moments. The **National Museum of Šumadija** is centred around a humble Ottoman-style mansion from the old court complex housing an exhibition on Serbia's rebirth. Ponder the simplicity and significance of the **Old Court Church** and **Old Assembly**

TOP TIP

Kragujevac has countless small wineries and *rakija* (fruit brandy) distilleries in its vicinity. For a taste of regional produce, visit the Wine and Rakija Hub in the city centre. It offers degustations of some of Šumadija's best brandies and wines; there's also a shop.

SIGHTS
1 Knežev Arsenal
2 Milošev Venac
3 National Museum of Šumadija
4 Old Assembly Building
5 Old Court Church
6 Old Foundry Museum

KG CAR ICONS: FIĆA, ZASTAVA & YUGO

In the post-WWII period, Kragujevac became an industrial powerhouse; its new Crvena Zastava automobile factory was where the iconic Fića (a version of Fiat 600) was produced, followed by Yugoslavia's trademark Zastava 101 (also known as Stojadin) and Yugo (famously starring in *Die Hard with a Vengeance*). Fića was responsible for the country's motorisation – once driven by everyone from police to ambulance and used for driving tests, the miniature model was also the first family car for many Yugoslavs. Between 1955 and 1985 the Kragujevac factory rolled out nearly a million vehicles. Today, June's **Fića Fest** car show attracts old-timer fans from across Serbia and the Balkans to Šumadija's capital.

Building, where the principality's first constitution (1835) and full independence (1878) were proclaimed.

In 1853, Serbia's first industrial plant – a cannon foundry – was established in Kragujevac and grew into a major armaments factory; the first light bulb in the country was switched on here in 1884. Today, the disused industrial complex of **Knežev Arsenal** (Prince's Arsenal) includes the original factory building, converted into the steampunk-feel **Old Foundry Museum**; visit to see why a TV series about the construction of the *Titanic* was filmed here. Come July, its outdoor zone becomes the stage for **Arsenal Fest**, featuring international alternative rock bands.

Kragujevac suffered heavily in WWII: on 21 October 1941, the Nazis executed around 3000 civilians in a single day, in reprisal for the Partisans' attacks. The massacre was carried out in the area that's now **Šumarice Memorial Park**. A 7km circular road leads through the peaceful 352-hectare park, past 10 Yugoslav-era memorials and 30 mass graves; learn the tragic story at the site's sombre museum.

THE SPIRIT OF SERBIA

Read our ***rakija* essay** (p376) to learn more about Serbia's national spirit and the renaissance this traditional fruit brandy has been enjoying in recent years.

Beyond Kragujevac

Places

The southwest is Serbia at its most captivating, from its revered medieval monasteries to the outdoor playground of the Dinaric Alps.

To truly experience Serbia, venture southwest. Cradled in the green valleys of Šumadija, or 'forest land', the most sacred of Orthodox monasteries echo with memories of the nation's past glories. And in the highlands of Raška (aka Sandžak), Serbia's medieval heartland, Muslim-majority Novi Pazar is the epitome of the country's Ottoman heritage.

Mother Nature has been generous in these parts, still inhabited by endangered brown bears and griffon vultures. Out west, Tara National Park makes a scenic stage for an array of outdoor activities; down south, the slopes of Kopaonik mountain range are a favourite winter playground. Elsewhere, the serpentine Ovčar-Kablar Gorge and Uvac Canyon provide some of the best vistas in the region.

GETTING AROUND

The towns of Kragujevac, Užice, Vrnjačka Banja and Novi Pazar, as well as Kopaonik and Tara national parks, are well connected by bus with Belgrade. Užice is also a stop on the Belgrade–Bar train, which has night and day services.

For travel between these destinations and to more remote areas – including the Ovčar-Kablar Gorge, medieval monasteries and Župa region's wineries – it's best to have a car. The gateway to Tara is the town of Bajina Bašta, which has good bus connections with Užice. The nearest town to Kopaonik is Raška, with an infrequent bus connection to Novi Pazar.

Studenica to Manasija

Step into medieval Serbia

More than architectural beauties adorned with ancient frescoes, Serbian monasteries are guardians of the nation's identity and Orthodox faith and a precious bond with the medieval empire that was crushed by the Ottoman conquest. The highest achievements of two architectural styles – the Raška School of the 12th and early 13th centuries and the Morava School of the late 14th and early 15th centuries – are hidden in verdant valleys of southwestern and central Serbia.

The Raška School, named after the medieval state's heartland, is distinguished by Romanesque influences. Its tour de force is Unesco-listed **Studenica**, established in 1196 by Stefan Nemanja (founder of the royal Nemanjić dynasty). Within the Church of Our Lady's marble walls lies Stefan Nemanja's tomb; the smaller King's Church has the renowned *Life of Virgin Mary* fresco cycle. To follow in pilgrims' footsteps, tackle the 2.5km hike to the **hermitage of St Sava** (Nemanja's son

TOP TIP

For more than day-tripping around Šumadija, consider an authentic village stay; Serbian Rural Tourism (selo.rs) has plenty of bookable options.

ANGELAOBLAK/SHUTTERSTOCK ©

Monastery, Studenica (p287)

THE ROYAL HEARTLAND

It was from the small town of **Topola** in the heart of Šumadija that 'Black George', or Karađorđe – founder of the Karađorđević dynasty that ended up ruling Yugoslavia – led the First Serbian Uprising against the Turks in 1804.

Due to its historical significance, Topola holds a special place in the hearts of Serbs; the royalists, in particular, come to pay their respects at **Oplenac**. Here, tranquil parkland shelters the white-marble Church of St George, adorned with fantastic mosaics made from 40 million pieces of coloured glass; its crypt is the Karađorđević family mausoleum. Nearby are King Peter's House (with the royal family's portrait gallery), King's Winery, plus Karađorđe's old barracks, fort and church.

and first Serbian Orthodox Church archbishop), where cave-like monks' cells are built into cliffs.

Studenica is two hours' drive south of Kragujevac. Other revered Raška School monasteries in the region include **Žiča**, **Mileševa** and **Sopoćani**.

The pinnacle of the Morava School, named after the Morava River valley and combining elements of Romanesque and Serbian-Byzantine styles, is **Manasija**. Established in 1418 by Prince Stefan Lazarević (son of Prince Lazar, who perished in the fatal battle of Kosovo) and fortified by massive walls with 11 towers, the monastery was a refuge for scholars keeping the national culture alive. Its frescoes, including the *Holy Warriors*, are considered predecessors to Serbia's Renaissance art. For a taste of medieval times, visit in August when the **Just Out** knights' tournament takes place here.

Manasija is a 1¼-hour drive east of Kragujevac. Further south, **Ravanica** and **Ljubostinja** are also notable Morava School monasteries.

WHERE TO STAY IN KRAGUJEVAC

Industrial 1853
The design of this boutique hotel in Prince's Arsenal is inspired by Kragujevac's industrial heritage. €€€

Hotel Zelengora
Refurbished historic hotel (dating from 1884) with cozy rooms, conveniently located in the pedestrian zone. €€

Woodland Resort
Tucked away behind Šumarice park, with exposed-brick and wooden-beam features, a huge garden and pools. €€€

Ovčar-Kablar Gorge

Roam Šumadija's rugged outdoors

In Serbia's central Šumadija region, the so-called 'clenched' meanders of the West Morava River have carved a gloriously green 15km gorge between the **Ovčar** (985m) and **Kablar** (889m) mountains. Ten small, active monasteries built as hideouts for Orthodox monks between the 15th and 18th centuries lend the area its image of a 'holy mountain', while the thermal spa of **Ovčar Banja** – with sulfuric water of 38°C springing from the limestone – attracts wellness tourists and serves as the gateway to the gorge. This 49-sq-km protected area is popular with hikers and cyclists; being a 1¼-hour drive west from Kragujevac, it's an easy day trip.

Ten marked hiking trails (2.5km to 9.5km) lead through oak and beech forest, past the secluded monasteries and to the mountain peaks – the lookout at the top of Kablar, in particular, offers an iconic panorama of the West Morava's meanders. For exploring the area on two wheels, choose between seven signposted mountain-biking routes (3km to 29km) including the converted tracks and tunnels of the narrow-gauge railway that once ran through the gorge; Ovčar Banja rents out bikes. To relax, take a catamaran ride on tranquil **Međuvršje Lake**.

Užice

Revisit the heroic past

A jumping-off point for adventures around western Serbia, Užice (two hours' drive from Kragujevac) is also well worth a visit for its inspiring past.

Užice's most imposing feature is the 14th-century **Old Town Fortress**, perched high on a cliffside above the curving Đetinja River. Repeatedly razed throughout history, it has weathered Austro-Turkish wars and Serbian uprisings and – recently reconstructed – offers dizzying views over the verdant gorge and the town's socialist-era skyscrapers. Beneath the fortress, the small and picturesque **hydroelectric powerplant** on the Đetinja dates from 1900 and was famously among the first in Europe (shortly after the one at Niagara Falls) built according to Tesla's principles of alternating current. Its original interior is now the Museum of Technology.

But the town's greatest claim to fame hails from WWII. The short-lived Užice Republic – the first liberated territory in Nazi-occupied Europe – was proclaimed here by Yugoslavia's resistance movement. It covered about 19,000 sq km and lasted 67 days, until the Partisans' heroic defeat at

THE TRUMPETS OF GUČA

The sleepy village of Guča, south of Ovčar-Kablar Gorge, turns party central each August for a four-day gathering of *trubači* (trumpeters) from across Serbia. Going strong since 1961, the hugely popular **Guča Festival** attracts tens of thousands of brass music fans; the village even hosts a Trumpet Museum. While the event has become more commercialised in recent years, it remains a coveted competition for (largely Roma) performers who dream of becoming the next Trumpet Master – like now-legendary Boban Marković.

Rakija-fuelled revellers join in the fast-paced *kola* (circle dances) as brass orchestras roam the village streets. The sound of *trube* is both soulful and frenzied; famously, past visitor Miles Davis was left impressed.

WHERE TO EAT IN KRAGUJEVAC

Gastro Komitet 27
Slick contemporary venue with a short but creative fusion menu of Italian, French and Balkan influences. **€€€**

Restoran Toro
Modern restaurant with city views; expect European cuisine and reinterpreted Serbian dishes. **€€**

Kafana Balkan
Historic tavern (established in 1890) in the pedestrian zone serving typical *kafana* fare paired with regional wines. **€**

Kadinjača in November 1941. Learn more at the **Užice National Museum**, incorporating the national bank's vaults turned Partisans' armaments factory. Serbia's most grandiose Yugoslav-era memorial, **Kadinjača** commemorates the Workers' Battalion that perished on this green hill fighting the Germans; it's 14km from Užice. Resembling a futuristic Stonehenge, the 15-hectare complex comprises a series of white granite monoliths culminating in two soaring pillars that form a symbolic 'bullet hole' sculpture.

Užice's **Republik Tours** can take you cycling to Kadinjača and along the former narrow-gauge railway line (Serbia's first Greenway), ziplining and rock climbing in the Đetinja Gorge – where local daredevils jump off the old railway bridge by the fortress in summer – or touring other memorials in the region.

OLD CRAFTS OF ZLAKUŠA & SIROGOJNO

Sirogojno village, on the slopes of Zlatibor mountain, has a wonderful **open-air museum** featuring wooden houses furnished with artefacts that bring to life 19th-century Serbia. But Sirogojno is also renowned for its knitters. Woolen clothing items hand-knitted by women from the region now make the Sirogojno Style brand, recognisable by its fusion of a centuries-old tradition with contemporary fashion. The **Knitters' Museum** in Sirogojno offers workshops.

Further north near Užice, Zlakuša village is celebrated for its traditional pottery, still made from earth and stone on a hand wheel like hundreds of years ago. Today, Zlakuša hosts the **International Colony of Fine Art Ceramics**. Its picturesque **Terzića Avlija** 'ethno-park' showcases a typical early-20th-century rural household.

Tara National Park

Go wild in the Dinaric Alps

Some of Serbia's most impressive scenery is found within the 250-sq-km **Tara National Park** (2¾ hours' drive west from Kragujevac). With densely forested slopes and the dramatic Drina River canyon, this westernmost outpost of the Dinaric Alps is a true outdoor playground. Traipsing its spruce, fir and beech forests is Serbia's largest population of endangered brown bears; bear-watching with a park ranger is possible between May and October. A wide range of adventures is organised by Užice-based **Republik Tours**, and if you prefer to go solo, the visitor centres at Perućac and Mitrovac have maps and rent out kayaks and bikes.

Cutting through steep limestone cliffs, the emerald Drina creates a stunning background for water-based activities. **Tara Tours** offers rafting for beginners and full-day boat trips to historic Višegrad (p96) in Bosnia. Contact **Green Bear** for stand-up paddleboarding from Vrelo waterfall to the iconic 'little house on the Drina' (three hours). The placid **Perućac** (dotted with houseboats) and **Zaovine** lakes are popular kayaking spots.

Hikers are in for a treat along Tara's 30 marked trails; see the park website for maps. For easy treks, nine official lookouts provide stupendous views – **Banjska Stena** (1065m), 6km from Mitrovac, overlooks Perućac Lake, while **Crnjeskovo** (980m), 3km from Kaluđerske Bare, rises above Rača Gorge. Also criss-crossing the park are major mountain-biking routes. **Visoka Tara** is a 26km loop along forest and gravel paths, starting and ending at Šljivovica village. **Carska Tara** is a 42km trail from Kaluđerske Bare to Perućac, on a combination of macadam and asphalt.

WHERE TO STAY, EAT & DRINK IN UŽICE

Užički Konak
Family-run, modern townhouse accommodation with doubles and dorms; breakfast optional. €

Moja Reka
Try local delicacies like *Užički kajmak* (salty clotted cream), and the turkey specialities, on a riverside terrace. €€

Vremeplov
This cozy cafe and bar with a retro salon-style interior and a small flower-filled terrace also hosts live music.

NENAD NEDOMACKI/SHUTTERSTOCK ©

'Little house on the Drina', Tara National Park

Railway, regatta and silver screen

The outskirts of Tara National Park offer more than sweat-breaking action, with modern-day attractions a window into the area's traditional heritage.

The **Šargan Eight** steam train, linking Mokra Gora and Šargan Vitasi stations, was once part of a narrow-gauge railway line that connected Belgrade, Sarajevo and Dubrovnik in the former Yugoslavia. Today, the vintage tourist train chugs through serpentine mountain scenery of western Serbia for 2½ hours, passing five bridges and 22 tunnels, and stopping at several viewpoints as it completes a perfect figure-of-eight loop over a 300m incline.

Each July, the rowdy **Drina Regatta**, featuring anything that floats, commemorates the centuries-old tradition of rafting the Drina River. The intrepid rafters – who once braved the rapids to transport timber – disappeared in the 1960s with the damming of the Drina. **Tara Tours** can organise hosted visits to the annual regatta; side events include music concerts, foodie events and a handicrafts fair in Bajina Bašta.

Held in January in Drvengrad (meaning 'Timbertown'), **Küstendorf Film and Music Festival** is hosted by two-time

SERBIAN DINARIC ALPS ADVENTURES

Pavle Pavlović (@serbiatouristguide), licensed tourist and mountain guide from Kraljevo, outlines top outdoor adventures in western Serbia:

Hiking and snowshoeing

Golija, Stolovi, Čemerno, Kopaonik, Zlatar, Zlatibor, Kablar and Tara are the most attractive mountains for moderate hiking year-round – full of wildlife and viewpoints over canyons and valleys.

MTB and cycling

From May until October, explore western Serbia on two wheels. Long-distance trails link cultural heritage with remote villages that keep ancestral traditions and prepare authentic local food.

Water sports

Kayaking, rafting and SUP are favourite summer activities on Ibar, Lim, Drina and West Morava rivers. Canyoning and swimming are also great ways to refresh.

WHERE TO STAY AROUND TARA

Mećavnik Resort
Chalet-style accommodation in Drvengrad village, featuring smart wooden lodges with folk design touches. €€€

Hotel Turist
Comfortable, elegant rooms decked out in neutral colours, plus an upmarket restaurant; located in Bajina Bašta. €€

Hotel Tara
A great option at Kaluđerske Bare on Tara; built of stone and wood, with spacious rooms and a restaurant. €€

BALKAN TOMBSTONES

Inscribed on the Unesco World Heritage list in 2016, mystical *stećci* are medieval tombstones in the shape of slabs or chests that can be found scattered across Bosnia, parts of Croatia and Montenegro, as well as western Serbia.

Within Tara National Park, two 15th-century necropolises – known as **Mramorje** – are located in the villages of Perućac (which has 88 tombstones, all without inscriptions) and Rastište (with 33 and 35 tombstones in two separate locations; their reliefs include motifs of a circle, a crescent or a cross, and there's even a relief of a bow and arrow and two swords). Another necropolis, known as **Grčko Groblje**, is preserved in the village of Hrta in southwestern Serbia.

MLADEN TOMIC/SHUTTERSTOCK ©

Vineyard, Aleksandrovac, Župa

Palme d'Or winner Emir Kusturica. The village itself, built in 2002 for Kusturica's film *Life Is a Miracle,* blends Serbian rural life with global culture – its streets are lined with authentic, restored cottages from the region and named after legends of world cinema like Jim Jarmusch or Abbas Kiarostami. The festival has a strong *film d'auteur* focus; nightly live concerts create a party atmosphere.

Vrnjačka Banja

Hit the ancient hot springs

Vrnjačka Banja, an hour's drive south of Kragujevac, is renowned for its therapeutic waters – its seven mineral springs include the one with a temperature of the average human body (36.5°C). The springs have attracted health-seekers from the ancient Romans to the Yugoslav elite; at its peak, the town received more visitors than Dubrovnik. These days, a vast range of wellness treatments are available.

Landscaped parkland and fin-de-siècle villas hint at the resort's illustrious past. Take in the faded grandeur of **Belimarković Mansion**, now hosting art events, and inspect the small but fascinating **Museum of Spa Treatment**. During Vrnjačka Banja's 19th-century heyday, balls were frequently organised;

WHERE TO EAT AROUND TARA

Viskonti
Drvengrad's stylish restaurant serves a range of pizzas and pastas in addition to Serbian and Balkan classics. **€€€**

Studenac
Terrace views of the famous 'Little House on the Drina' in Bajina Bašta; go for *pljeskavica* (spicy hamburger). **€€**

Tarsko Jezero
Mountain views accompany a range of dishes, from fresh trout to game stew; located at Zaovine Lake on Tara. **€€**

today, this festive spirit embodies Serbia's biggest **Carnival** each July, complete with a parade of international troupes.

Župa

Ancestral wine region

Wine-growing in Župa (meaning 'parish') thrived in medieval Serbia – according to a charter from 1196, Stefan Nemanja gifted the parish vineyards and cellars to Studenica Monastery (p287). Some of the rustic 19th-century winegrowers' lodges *(poljane)* are still preserved across the region.

The heart of Župa is Aleksandrovac, an hour's drive south of Vrnjačka Banja. Its **Museum of Winemaking and Viticulture** provides insights into the centuries of winemaking in these parts. Throughout September's **Župska Berba** (Parish Harvest) festival, free *vino* is poured from a unique 'wine fountain' in the town centre.

Župa's indigenous *prokupac* (red) and *tamjanika* (white) varietals have been at the forefront of Serbia's wine revival of recent decades. **Ivanović Winery** in Aleksandrovac, established in 1919, is the region's most famous; book ahead for degustations.

Novi Pazar

Ottoman heritage in Sandžak region

The cultural centre of Sandžak (Raška) region, Muslim-majority Novi Pazar – established by Isa-beg Ishaković in 1461, soon after the Turkish conquest – is distinguished by slender minarets piercing the hillsides and a jumbled Stara Čaršija (Old Bazaar) area reminiscent of those in Balkan capitals Sarajevo and Skopje. It's a 2¾-hour drive south of Kragujevac.

Get a glimpse of the region's diverse history at the **Museum Ras Novi Pazar**. This 19th-century Ottoman-style mansion is an ethnographic inventory of weapons, jewellery, folk clothing and period furniture. Illustrating the crucible of cultures are writings in Arabic, Hebrew and Old Church Slavonic, and Roman and Islamic tombstones.

Among the town's many mosques, the most significant – and one of the oldest Islamic buildings left in Serbia – is the 16th-century, two-arched **Altun-Alem Mosque**, named after a precious stone. Nearby ruins of the Ottoman-era **fortress**, enveloped in greenery, make for a pleasant stroll. **Amir-aga's Khan**, a 17th-century inn, once welcomed travelling merchants (along with their mules and horses) and now houses some traditional stores, while partially restored **Isa-beg's Hammam** (which had men's and women's baths) features an open-roofed cafe – a perfect spot to linger over chill-out music.

MADE IN SERBIA: OPANCI

Once traditional peasants' footwear and today part of folk dancers' costumes, *opanak* (a moccasin-like leather shoe upturned at the toes; plural *opanci*) is a Serbian national symbol. The humble shoe even got the Serbian army through its epic Balkan odyssey during WWI.

Ever since the Middle Ages, *opančarstvo* was a major local craft, and in the 19th and early 20th centuries *opanci* were often awarded at international fairs. Various styles of this traditional footwear (both men's and women's) are found across Serbia, particularly in the Šumadija region.

While the craft has dwindled in the modern era, a great place to find high-quality products is **Opanak Strugarević** in Vrnjačka Banja, a family operation for nearly a century.

WHERE TO STAY, EAT & DRINK IN VRNJAČKA BANJA

Vila Savka
Tastefully furnished rooms with large balconies in a restored 1906 villa at the edge of the central park. €€

Tri Golubice
National cuisine and a good range of regional wines; set in a heritage building with a lovely garden. €€

Caffe Scena Teatar
A relaxed spot for a drink on a hill beside the open-air amphitheatre; it also hosts live music events.

NATURE'S MARVELS IN SOUTHERN SERBIA

Serbia's deep south shelters some of the country's top natural wonders. Southeast of Kopaonik, an eerie cluster of 202 stone towers looms over red-hued, acidic mineral streams. Reaching up to 15m in height and topped with peculiar volcanic caps, these intriguing rock formations are symbolically named **Devil's Town** (Đavolja Varoš).

To the northwest of Novi Pazar, the Uvac River's spectacular meanders are the highlight of the Uvac Nature Reserve. This startlingly green river zigzags through steep limestone rock of up to 350m in height – a feat of nature best admired from a lookout high above. **Uvac Canyon** is the habitat of the endangered griffon vulture and comprises a 6km-long cave system.

Turkish culinary influences are everywhere: try *ćevapi* (grilled kebabs) or *mantije* (tiny meat pastries), and choose between sugar-soaked *baklava, tulumbe, kadaif* or *urmašice*. Bars are thin on the ground in this predominantly Muslim town; head to a *kafečajnica* (literally 'coffee-teahouse') for viscous Turkish coffee cooked over embers.

Kopaonik National Park

Snow slopes and Ibar rapids

Serbia's largest mountain range, 'the Sunny Mountain' was known for silver mining in the Middle Ages and today features a 118-sq-km national park; it's three hours' drive south from Kragujevac. Covered in thick spruce, beech, fir and oak forest, and with the 2017m-high summit of **Pančić's Peak**, Kopaonik's slopes are perfect grounds for hiking, mountain biking and various other outdoor activities (see infokop.net). One don't-miss lookout is at the **Nebeske Stolice** (1913m) ridge. Aptly named 'Heaven's Chairs', it has the remains of a 5th-century basilica and, on a clear day, views of Montenegrin, Albanian and Macedonian mountains in the distance.

With 200 sunny days annually and snow cover from November to May, Kopaonik is Serbia's premier winter-sports destination. The resort – at an altitude of 1700m – has 67km of pistes (including alpine, Nordic and night skiing) and 24 lifts; organise passes at skijalistasrbije.rs. A fantastic way to enjoy the slopes in winter, even if you're not a skier, is snowshoeing. **Snowshoeing Serbia** has licensed mountain guides who will take you away from the ski-centre crowds on secluded trails to Kopaonik's best viewpoints (two to seven hours) while ensuring safety and sharing local stories; it even organises a night ascent to Pančić's Peak. Go between December and April, when there's sufficient snow cover.

Winding its way around Kopaonik's western slopes, the **Ibar River** provides arguably the best whitewater rafting in Serbia. From April to October, **Kopaonik Tours and Excursions** runs three-hour rafting adventures with experienced skippers; they start at Ušće (the confluence of Studenica and Ibar rivers) and pass under bridges and through some exhilarating Class III rapids. The tours are also suitable for rafting novices. Every July, the Ibar Gorge – aka 'the Valley of Lilacs' – hosts a merry regatta down the river from medieval **Maglič** fortress to Kraljevo.

WHERE TO STAY, EAT AND DRINK IN NOVI PAZAR

Hotel Vrbak
Now fully renovated, iconic Yugo-era hotel with Oriental architectural touches smack in the town centre. €€

Sve pod Sač
Small family-owned cafe dishing out traditional *mantije*, plus pies with meat, cheese, spinach and potatoes. €

The Pub
One of the few places in Novi Pazar that serves alcohol; chill out with a beer over a rock soundtrack.

Niš

HISTORY | GASTRONOMY | FESTIVALS

The birthplace of Constantine the Great – the first Roman emperor to convert to Christianity – and one of the main stops on the Romans' Via Militaris, ancient Naissus (now Niš) is southern Serbia's history-packed urban heart. The staggering five centuries of Ottoman rule left many cultural influences, from cuisine to music to language. As a popular folk song quips, Nišlije (Niš locals) are the masters of *merak* – a Turkish word that refers to the appreciation of life's simple pleasures. Indeed, there's a laid-back hedonism to this rough-around-the-edges place that lights up each summer with the acclaimed Nišville Jazz Festival and honours its other legendary native son, late Roma singer Šaban Bajramović.

But Serbia's third-largest city is not all about history, Balkan blues and bohemian *kafane* (taverns) in cobblestoned alleys. On its outskirts, a chiselled terrain of gorges and mountains draws adrenaline junkies with everything from caving to paragliding.

GETTING AROUND

Niš is easy to get around on foot, but you'll need to catch a taxi to Bubanj Hill, which is located 3km from the city. Niš Constantine the Great Airport is 4km from the centre; buses 34A and 34B go from and to the airport, respectively (stopping at the bus station).

Journey Through Time in Niš

From Naissus to Nišville

A clutch of extraordinary historical sights in Niš helps to get a grasp on the country's storied past.

At the **Mediana** archaeological site, remains of Constantine the Great's 4th-century palace feature 1000 sq metres of splendid floor mosaics. Stroll around appreciating how, back in the day, the waters from nearby Niška Banja mineral springs were transported all the way to Mediana. The excavated artefacts – including marble busts and sculptures of satyrs and goddesses – can be admired on site and at the city's **Archaeological Hall**.

TOP TIP

According to records, the first *burek* (filo-pastry with meat or cheese) in the Balkans was made in Niš in 1498 by a baker from İstanbul, Mehmet Oğlu. These days, Niš celebrates its culinary heritage each September with Burek Days – otherwise try it at any *pekara* (bakery) in town.

SIGHTS
1 Archaeological Hall
2 Niš Fortress
3 Red Cross
4 Bali-beg Mosque

BEST PLACES TO STAY & EAT IN NIŠ

ArtLoft Hotel
Centrally located, modern boutique hotel; paintings by local artists in every room are a nice touch. €€

Hotel Sole
Another central option, with modern design, spacious rooms, great breakfasts and helpful staff. €€

Stambolijski
Upscale restaurant in a Turkish-era house, where chef Saša Mišić demonstrates the creative New Balkan cuisine. €€€

Dagi Plus
This ethno-style restaurant on the town's outskirts has excellent service and is renowned for mutton specialities. €€

Kafana Meze
Traditional *kafana* spread over two levels, worth visiting for the choice of cold and warm meze (appetisers) alone. €

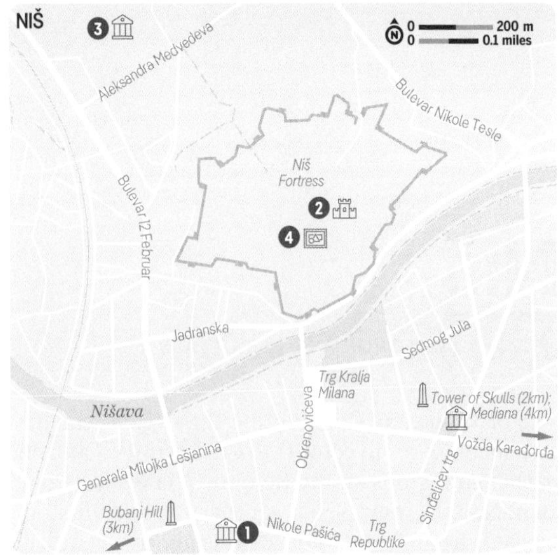

Search for traces of Ottoman rule within the rambling grounds of **Niš Fortress**, home to a 15th-century Turkish *hammam* (now jazz museum) and the 16th-century **Bali-beg Mosque** (now art gallery). These days the fortress hosts the hip **Nišville International Jazz Festival**, one of Serbia's best music events, every August. Another, gruesome reminder of the Ottomans in Niš is the **Tower of Skulls** (Ćele Kula). After the Turks' triumph at the 1809 Battle of Čegar, they embedded the dead Serbs' skulls in this tower – unwittingly creating a defiant testament to local resistance. The tower now stands within a chapel.

Niš didn't escape the horrors of WWII, either. At **Red Cross**, a notorious concentration camp held 30,000 Serbs, Roma and Jews in German-occupied Serbia; visit its harrowing museum to learn about the first-ever major breakout attempt from a Nazi camp. Outside town, **Bubanj Hill** was the site of mass executions of the camp's prisoners. Here, a Yugoslav-era memorial in the form of three gigantic fists rising skyward symbolises the national struggle during WWII.

YUGOSLAV MEMORIALS

During the Yugoslav era, socialist modernist memorials commemoratir major WWII battles and tragedies we erected all over the country. Read ou **essay** (p382) to learn more about these impressive, alien-like monuments.

Beyond Niš

Serbia's rugged southeast has near-mystical appeal, with the Danube's brooding fortresses, ancestral wine villages and hidden mountain waterfalls.

Places

The least developed of Serbia's regions, the southeast is also the most intriguing. This is where the Danube cuts its way through the Carpathians in the far east, substituting the country's lack of coastline with the mighty river's widest and deepest stretches in Đerdap National Park. And it's where the lofty Stara Planina, rising further to the south, accounts for a third of Serbia's waterfalls and its highest peak. This rugged frontier is a fantastic cycling and hiking destination.

Rich legacies of times past abound, too – from the dawn of European humanity in the Iron Gates Gorge and medieval fortresses along the Danube, to Negotin region's historical wine villages and Stara Planina's rural life that has remained unchanged for centuries.

Đerdap National Park

Adventure along the Danube

Serbia's largest national park, the 637-sq-km Đerdap (three hours' drive north of Niš) is where the Carpathian and Balkan mountain ranges meet; it's increasingly a contender for outdoor adventures with Tara in the west. Niš-based **Nature Travel Office** runs multi-activity tours around the park.

The limestone cliffs of the Iron Gates Gorge soar for 100km along the Danube, which reaches its narrowest and deepest points here – a fantastic setting for activities on the water. **Wild Serbia** organises full-day Đerdap kayaking tours with transport from Belgrade; alternatively, see the Iron Gates highlights by speedboat from Tekija (one hour) with **Đerdap Boat Tours** or take a two-hour trip through the gorge with **Golubac from a Boat**.

With signposted paths and lookouts, the park provides rewarding hikes; register with the visitor centre in Donji

GETTING AROUND

Hiring a car is recommended for travel around this region, and necessary for rural destinations like Negotin's wine villages. Sokobanja has good bus connections with Niš.

The scenic Đerdap Hwy (M 25-1) winds its way along the Danube through the national park. Sporadic Belgrade-bound buses connect Kladovo, Donji Milanovac and Golubac.

The gateway to Stara Planina is Pirot, which has hourly buses to/from Niš. There are three routes into the mountain: north to Jabučko Plateau, east to Zavoj Lake, and south to Dojkinci village.

PROTECTING EASTERN SERBIA'S WILDERNESS

Serbia's protected areas include four national parks, along with dozens of nature parks and reserves. Since 2022, Stara Planina (p301) and **Kučaj-Beljanica** are also in the process of being designated as national parks. While Stara Planina has previously been a nature park, only parts of Kučaj-Beljanica have enjoyed protected status.

Covering about 450 sq km in eastern Serbia, it's the largest uninhabited area in the country and comprises the primeval beech forests of Vinatovača and Busovata, Lazar's Canyon (p300) and the 80-million-year-old Resava Cave.

Environmentalists have raised concerns about proposed mining projects in the area; meanwhile, plans for mini hydroelectric powerplants on Stara Planina have been scrapped thanks to ecological activism.

Milanovac before setting off. There are nine marked trails, of which two 7km paths lead from Đerdap Hwy to the peaks of Mt Miroč – **Veliki Štrbac** (768m), overlooking the narrowest part of the Iron Gates, and **Mali Štrbac** (626m), with views of the gigantic Decebalus rock sculpture across the Danube. In Đerdap's hinterland, near Negotin (p300), embark on a forest hike from Vratna Monastery to three massive stone arches – known as **Vratna Gates** (Vratnjanske Kapije) – moulded in the Vratna River canyon. The trails (1km to 5km) are signposted.

The international **EuroVelo 6** cycling path hugs the Danube for 110km through the park. Golubac from a Boat rents out bikes, and **ACE Adventure** offers two-day cycling tours along the river between Silver Lake and Đerdap.

See millennia of Danube history

Bygone civilisations have left their mark throughout what is today Đerdap National Park.

Overlooking the Danube in the heart of the gorge, the **Lepenski Vir** archaeological site was home to mysterious fishing communities in the Mesolithic and Neolithic eras. Displayed within a striking modern building are skeletons and artefacts dating back to 7000 BCE, including the famous stone sculptures of fish-like idols with human faces. Watch the fascinating short film about the site's excavation, and inspect a 3D simulation of the prehistoric settlement.

Signs of ancient Romans' presence during the Dacian Wars are scattered around Đerdap. The **Tabula Traiana** – a relief of Emperor Traianus with a Latin inscription, visible from the Danube 10km upstream of Tekija and a regular stop on boat tours – was carved into the rock in 103 CE to mark the completion of the Roman military road. The remains of **Traian's Bridge** (105 CE), once the longest arch bridge in the world, are found 5km downstream from Kladovo.

The fabled 14th-century **Golubac Fortress**, dominating a rocky promontory at the entrance to the national park, was fought over by the Hungarians, Ottomans and Serbs throughout history. Since its remarkable 2019 restoration, visitors can clamber the nine towers, browse the history-themed exhibitions and enjoy panoramic views of the Danube (which is at its widest point here).

For a full grasp of the area's invaluable cultural heritage, stop by the **Đerdap Archaeological Museum** in Kladovo; its huge collection, spanning prehistoric to medieval times, features tools, jewellery, statues, military equipment and much more.

WHERE TO STAY ALONG THE DANUBE

Hotel Aquastar Danube
Modern hotel next to Kladovo's beach, with spacious rooms, swimming pools, two restaurants and bars. **€€€**

Vila Dunavski Raj
Family-owned B&B in the woods near Golubac, serving organic breakfasts; the rooms have large balconies. **€€**

Vila Delux
B&B located in Negotin in Đerdap's hinterland, with smart rooms, swimming pool and e-bikes for guest use. **€€**

Sokobanja

Sokobanja

Relax in an Ottoman hammam

Sokobanja, an hour's drive north of Niš, is hot on the heels of Vrnjačka Banja in Serbia's spa-tourism stakes. More rural than its Šumadija counterpart, Sokobanja is distinguished by the working Ottoman-era **hammam** (which has men's and women's pools), built on the foundations of a Roman bath; six curative mineral springs have a temperature range of 28°C to 45°C.

A big part of Sokobanja's appeal is its location – framed by mountains, it's a great base for hikes so you don't just get to laze around in a pool. The overgrown ruins of **Sokograd**, a 6th-century hillside fortress, are a 2km trek from the resort. Mystical, pyramid-shaped **Rtanj** (1560m), famous for its endemic herbal tea, is a popular stargazing location; guided trips are advertised around town.

TOP TIP

In summer, the lower Danube towns celebrate the river's bounty with food festivals and cooking competitions; expect lots of fish specialities.

SERBIA & THE ROMANS

It may come as a surprise that as many as 16 Roman emperors were born on the territory of present-day Serbia – but not really if you consider that the Danubian limes served for a long period as the empire's eastern frontier. There are several major Roman-era archaeological sites in these parts, including Mediana (p295) in Niš. Unesco-listed **Felix Romuliana**, the 4th-century palace of Emperor Galerius, lies in ruins 107km north of Niš. **Viminacium** (96km southeast of Belgrade) was the capital of the Moesia province and a military camp for the Dacian Wars. And the remains of **Sirmium**, one of the Roman Empire's four capitals during the tetrarchy, are found in Vojvodina's town of Sremska Mitrovica.

WHERE TO EAT ALONG THE DANUBE

Zlatna Ribica
Riverside *kafana* in Golubac with panoramic views, serving grilled fish dishes and classic Serbian fare. €€

Jezero
Tavern in Kladovo offering regional delicacies such as Homolje cheese along with local wines. €€

La Moara
Contemporary restaurant in Negotin with a changing menu of creative dishes based on seasonal ingredients. €€€

REMOTE HIKES IN EASTERN SERBIA

Rade Stojković (@rademisirac), adventure tour guide from Majdanpek, shares his favourite hidden highlights of eastern Serbia:

Lazar's Canyon
Serbia's deepest and longest (9km) dry canyon offers the country's most extreme hiking. It's essential to go with a guide.

Pustinjac & Pek River
The river canyon has rainforest-like vegetation (for swimmers only). Nearby, decades of ore processing in the former Majdanpek copper mine have resulted in desert-like sandy slopes.

Beli Izvorac, Valja Prerast & Rajko's Cave
Trek to an impressive cascade waterfall, Serbia's highest natural stone arch (over 45m), and a legend-shrouded cave rich in ornaments of snow-white calcite.

DMZ001/SHUTTERSTOCK ©

Wine cellar, Rogljevo

Negotin Region

Traditional wine villages

Winemaking in the Negotin region, two hours' drive north of Sokobanja, reaches back to the 3rd century. Its **Rajac** and **Rogljevo** villages feature bucolic 19th-century wine cellars *(pimnice)*, made of stone and partially buried in the ground. Don't miss the atmospheric Rajac cemetery, with enigmatic pillar-shaped tombstones carved from the same granite as the cellars and decorated with symbolic reliefs.

Raj Winery in Rajac offers tours and degustations including food and wine pairing (one to five hours). Among its wines is the rare black *tamjanika* – the region's ancient red-grape sort with a typically musky aroma. Just outside Negotin town, **Matalj Winery** cultivates the nearly forgotten indigenous *bagrina* (white) and *začinak* (red) varietals in addition to international sorts; there's also a modern restaurant.

WHERE TO STAY, EAT & DRINK IN SOKOBANJA

Nataly Spa
Boutique spa hotel with modern apartments, restaurant, swimming pool and panoramic rooftop terrace. €€€

Pećina Marko Polo
Forest oasis under a rocky arch by the river; order grilled meats, lamb roast or fresh trout. €

Garden Bar
Cheerful lounge in the pedestrian zone; serves snacks and desserts in addition to coffees, juices and cocktails.

Stara Planina

Trek to hidden waterfalls

Part of the Balkan mountain range, **Stara Planina** (Old Mountain) is prime hiking territory featuring Serbia's highest peak, **Midžor** (2169m), timeless villages and secluded waterfalls. It's 1¼ hours' drive southeast of Niš.

Experienced Niš-based operator **Nature Travel Office** runs guided hikes to all corners of the mountain. The marked trails in Stara Planina's north include a 2km route from Babin Zub mountain lodge to tooth-shaped **Babin Zub** (1758m) peak, and an 8.6km route from the lodge to Midžor, with a chance of encountering wild horses along the way. The southern slopes are dotted with scenic natural wonders. Perhaps the most photographed waterfall, **Tupavica** is a 4km trek along a forest path from Dojkinci village; its 15m-high cascades are most impressive in spring and late autumn. Another picturesque spot, a 15-minute walk from Slavinja village, is the **Slavinjsko Grlo** canyon where rung-like layers carved by erosion in the riverbed form a series of whirlpools. For a panoramic vista, the easy 7km trail from Rsovci village leads to the **Kozji Kamen** (1181m) viewpoint overlooking the turquoise meanders of elongated Zavoj Lake. Harder to reach (the 4.5km route from Rsovci includes a steep descent into the gorge) and barely explored is the **Vladikine Ploče** cave in the Visočica River canyon.

Tucked away east of Zavoj Lake, the 'stone village' of **Gostuša** (population under 100) is one of the oldest and most remote hamlets in Pirot region. Its crumbling houses, strewn about on a hillside, are covered from base to roof with plates made of authentic Stara Planina stone. Some households offer homestays.

RIVER CANYONS

While the Iron Gates Gorge is part of Serbia's first Unesco Global Geopark, two other river canyons also offer impressive scenery, boat trips and water-based adventures – **Drina** (p291) in Tara National Park and **Uvac** (p294) near Novi Pazar in the southwest.

MADE IN SERBIA: PIROT RUG

A long-time trade town and gateway to Stara Planina, **Pirot** has been famous for its rugs made from the wool of Stara Planina sheep since the 16th century. Handwoven on a loom, *Pirotski ćilim* is distinguished by striking colours (red is traditionally dominant), geometrical ornaments (stylised birds, flowers and other themes), and the fact that its front and back are identical.

First exhibited internationally at the 1886 Vienna World's Fair, Pirot rug is considered a national treasure: it has adorned monasteries and courts, appeared in period movies and made part of many a bride's dowry over the centuries.

Today, a small community of Pirot women and **Damsko Srce** cooperative keep this beautiful old craft alive.

NATALIYA NAZAROVA/SHUTTERSTOCK ©

Danube River cruise

Arriving

Serbia's central position in the Balkans means it's well connected with all of Europe by good freeways, although the fact it's outside the Schengen Area also means drivers can expect delays at border crossings during busy holiday periods. Belgrade airport receives most international flights. Danube River cruises are the only water route into the country.

By Air

Belgrade's Nikola Tesla Airport (currently being expanded) is the country's main entry point. The national carrier is Air Serbia (co-owned by Etihad Airways). Niš Constantine the Great Airport is small and serviced by Wizz Air, Ryanair, Turkish Airways and Air Serbia.

By Land

Buses connect Serbia with Western Europe and Turkey, while trains link Belgrade with Montenegro. EuroVelo 6, 11 and 13 cycling routes traverse the country. Serbia doesn't acknowledge Kosovo border crossings as international ones, so arriving from Kosovo may not be possible unless you first entered Kosovo from Serbia.

Money

Currency:
Serbian dinar (RSD)

CASH

Both ATMs *(bankomat)* and exchange offices *(menjačnica)* are easy to find in Serbian towns and cities, but cash is still indispensable in villages and remote areas. It's also advisable to have some cash at hand for shopping at markets, newsstands and for taxi rides or public transport in the cities, as well as for sights' admission fees (which are usually very small).

CREDIT CARDS

Major debit and credit cards, particularly Visa and Mastercard, are accepted by hotels, restaurants, shops, petrol stations and other established businesses or when booking tours. Not many taxis accept card payments, however, so specify when booking if you need to pay by card.

TIPPING

Tips in restaurants or for tour guides are not obligatory, but 10% is a good idea for satisfactory service and always appreciated; it's also customary to round up the taxi fare.

Getting Around

With extensive bus services countrywide and good main roads, Serbia is easy to get around. For flexibility and convenience of reaching more remote and rural destinations, it's best to hire a car. Taxis in Serbian towns are affordable, so they may be a better idea than working out the public transport system.

TRAIN

Since the 2018 closure of Belgrade's historic railway station, trains depart from Beograd Centar (aka Prokop) station. The high-speed Soko train to Novi Sad runs frequently and takes 36 minutes. The scenic Belgrade–Bar train passes through Užice in western Serbia.

IVAN PANCIC/SHUTTERSTOCK ©

Novi Sad Train Station

BUS

There are good long-distance bus connections. Major cities have public bus systems. In Belgrade, pay the fare (valid for buses, minibuses, trolleybuses and trams) by SMS, app or credit card or buy tickets at kiosks. In Novi Sad and Niš, buy single-ride tickets from the driver.

TAXI & RIDESHARE

Taxis can be flagged down or ordered; make sure the meter is turned on. Not many taxis accept credit card payments. Belgrade's rideshare app is CarGo; there's also Yandex but no Uber. For long-distance carpooling, use the BlaBlaCar app.

BICYCLE

Cycling is a great way to explore parts of Serbia, particularly the Danube Cycle Path, Vojvodina flatlands and Fruška Gora, Tara and Đerdap national parks. The best town for cyclists is Novi Sad, with over 100km of bike paths and NS Bike bicycle-sharing system.

CAR

Belgrade airport has major car rental offices. Street parking in all bigger towns is regulated by zones/hours; tickets can often be paid only via SMS (in Serbian). The speed limit is 50km/h in towns, 80km/h outside towns, 100km/h on motorways and 130km/h on freeways.

DRIVING ESSENTIALS

Drive on the right.

The BAC limit is 0.2mg/mL.

You must drive with short headlights on, even in the daytime.

Slovenia

A GEM, HIDING IN PLAIN SIGHT

Slovenia is a destination for all seasons, with year-round offerings in sports, culture, food and wine.

It's a strange quirk that we humans have, always looking for the next hidden gem to visit. It may hearken back to our days as explorers, or colonisers, or simply to a time before every centimetre of the earth was catalogued and geotagged. We should stop doing that. Let's start with Slovenia.

Of course, Slovenia is sandwiched between heavy hitters, so you're forgiven if you may not have noticed it at first. But it's got beaches that rival Croatia's to the south, outdoor scenery that northern neighbour Austria covets, and food that even Italians to the west have been known to applaud.

The best part? There are no must-see, bucket-list day trips that you've got to rush through just to feel like you've 'seen it all'. Wander the charming cobblestones of Ljubljana, the pristine peaks of the Julian Alps, and the sloping hills of the Pannonian East. Take your time and don't worry about whether the road you're on is less travelled. Indeed, tiny but mighty Slovenia does it all and does it well. From food to wine to mountains, you'll be spoilt for choice on how best to spoil yourself. As soon as you arrive, you realise that it's all been here, waiting patiently for you to catch up.

FOTO MATEVZ LAVRIC/SHUTTERSTOCK ©

THE MAIN AREAS

LJUBLJANA
Capital fit for foodies and architecture lovers. **p310**

LAKE BLED
Iconic castle and island on the lake. **p317**

THE ALPS
A world of adventure, history and food. **p322**

POSTOJNA
Centre of Slovenia's karst underground. **p328**

MARCO BOTTIGELLI/GETTY IMAGES ©

Above: Bled Island, Lake Bled (p319). Left: Mt Triglav (p322)

PIRAN
A slice of Venice across the Adriatic. **p332**

VIPAVA VALLEY
A paradise for wine and nature lovers. **p337**

NOVO MESTO
Historic spas, castles and bear-watching. **p339**

MARIBOR
Thriving food and wine scene. **p342**

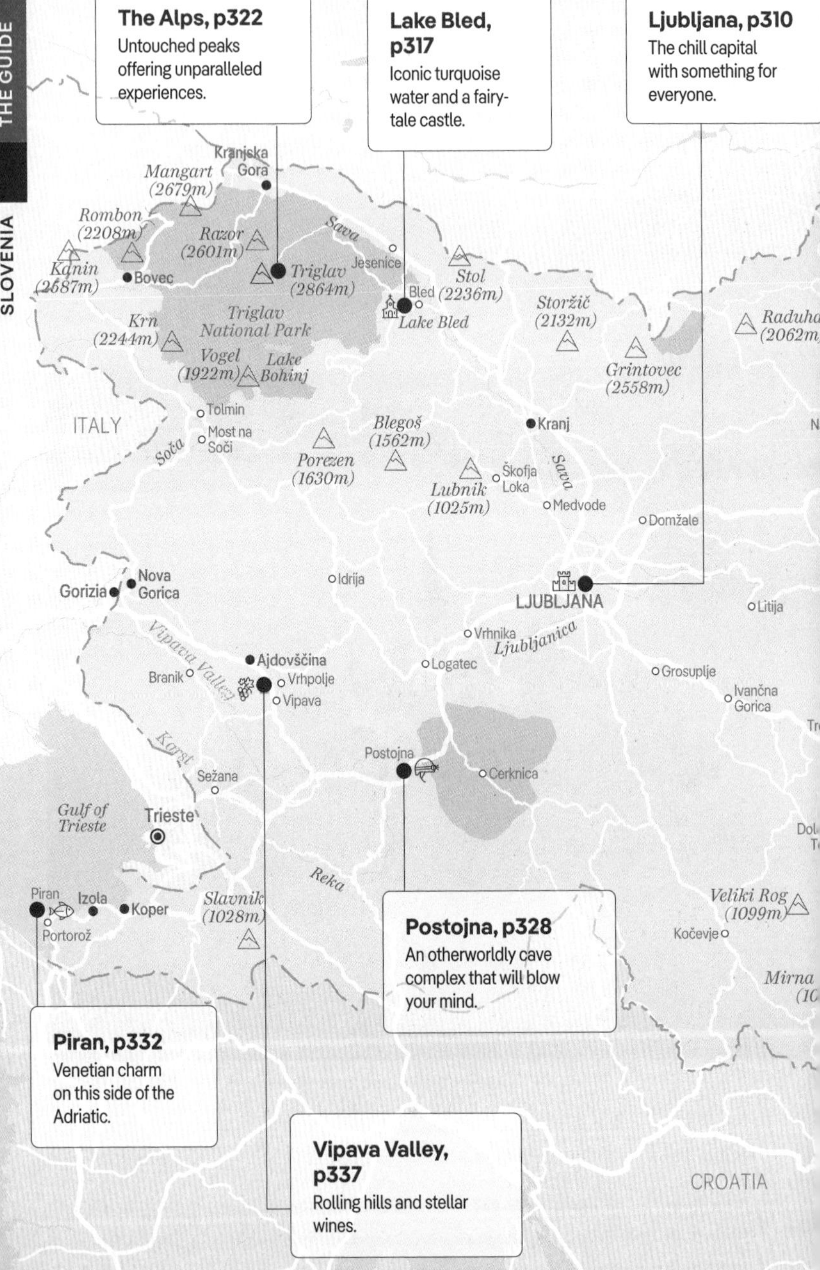
The Alps, p322
Untouched peaks offering unparalleled experiences.
Lake Bled, p317
Iconic turquoise water and a fairy-tale castle.
Ljubljana, p310
The chill capital with something for everyone.
Kranjska Gora
Mangart (2679m)
Rombon (2208m)
Razor (2601m)
Sava
Kanin (2587m)
Bovec
Triglav (2864m)
Jesenice
Stol (2236m)
Bled
Lake Bled
Storžič (2132m)
Raduha (2062m)
Krn (2244m)
Triglav National Park
Vogel (1922m)
Lake Bohinj
Grintovec (2558m)
Tolmin
ITALY
Most na Soči
Soča
Blegoš (1562m)
Kranj
Porezen (1630m)
Lubnik (1025m)
Škofja Loka
Sava
Medvode
Domžale
Gorizia
Nova Gorica
Idrija
LJUBLJANA
Litija
Vipava Valley
Vrhnika
Ljubljanica
Ajdovščina
Logatec
Branik
Vrhpolje
Vipava
Grosuplje
Ivančna Gorica
Karst
Postojna
Cerknica
Sežana
Gulf of Trieste
Trieste
Reka
Piran
Izola
Koper
Portorož
Slavnik (1028m)
Veliki Rog (1099m)
Kočevje
Postojna, p328
An otherworldly cave complex that will blow your mind.
Piran, p332
Venetian charm on this side of the Adriatic.
Vipava Valley, p337
Rolling hills and stellar wines.
CROATIA

Find Your Way

You have to work harder to avoid Slovenia than to pass through it from almost anywhere in Central Europe or the Balkans. Roads run north to south connecting Zagreb and Vienna; trains link Budapest with Trieste via Maribor and Celje. You can even walk from the Alps to the Adriatic, if you're so inclined.

Maribor, p342
The tenacious second city with a little bit of grit and a lot of good food.

…ovo Mesto, …339
…arm-filled city …a bend in the …a River.

AUSTRIA
HUNGARY
CROATIA
Mura
Drava
Sotla
Krka
Dravograd
…roškem
Slovenj Gradec
Velika Kopa (1543m)
Maribor
Žigartov (1347m)
Rogla (1517m)
Murska Sobota
Mursko Središće
Velenje
Slovenska Bistrica
Ptuj
Slovenske Konjice
…peter
Žalec
Celje
Rogaška Slatina
Šentjur
Silavec
Rogatec
Laško
Podčetrtek
Kozjansko Regional Park
Sevnica
Bistrica ob Sotli
Brestanica
…kronog
Krško
Brežice
…Mesto
Trdinov Vrh (1178m)

TRAIN

Rail service between Ljubljana and other capitals (like Zagreb, Vienna and even Trieste) remains slow due to the lack of infrastructure investment after the end of the Cold War. But the rides are scenic!

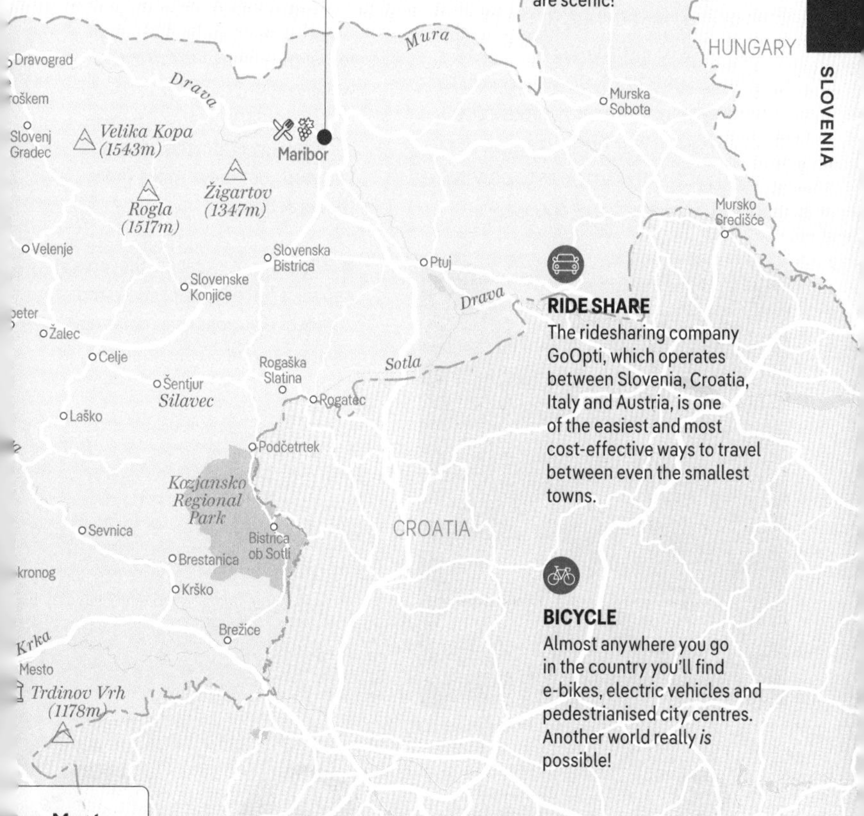

RIDE SHARE

The ridesharing company GoOpti, which operates between Slovenia, Croatia, Italy and Austria, is one of the easiest and most cost-effective ways to travel between even the smallest towns.

BICYCLE

Almost anywhere you go in the country you'll find e-bikes, electric vehicles and pedestrianised city centres. Another world really *is* possible!

0 50 km
0 25 miles

Plan Your Time

One of the best things to do in Slovenia is to simply go slow and let things take time, so when you're planning your itinerary make sure to leave plenty of time to relax and enjoy those impromptu stops you're bound to make along the way.

BLAZG/SHUTTERSTOCK ©

Jezersko (p326)

Just Passing Through

- Refuel in Ljubljana at the **Odprta Kuhna** (Open Kitchen; p312), the outdoor feast in the Central Market, and don't forget to sample some of the award-winning restaurants that abound in the capital. While you're there, sample wines from the venerable vineyards of Vipava to the great whites of Styria.

- Whatever the season, Slovenia's capital is full of charm, style, and plenty of distractions to make it a must on any trip in the region.

Seasonal Highlights

Winter means skiing, and spring is for biking. Summer is the kick-off to alpine ascents. Wine lovers await the end of harvest in autumn. Of course, thermal spas are always open.

JANUARY

Cold, snowy weather keeps things busy in the Alps. If you're hitting the ski slopes you won't be alone.

FEBRUARY

The **Kurentovanje** in Ptuj is the carnival celebration of a lifetime, and not to be missed. Bring on the spring!

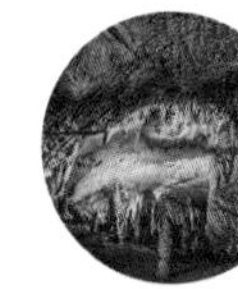

MAY

Caving rules in the **Postojna Cave Park** (p328) with the spring blooms, and biking trails open to full capacity.

FROM LEFT: SAHA_STOZHKO/SHUTTERSTOCK ©, SONSART/SHUTTERSTOCK ©, WENILIOU/SHUTTERSTOCK ©

Three Days of Adventure

- Go cave diving through the secret passageways and hidden corners of **Postojna** (p328), then explore the secrets of **Predjama Castle** (p331).

- Then head to **Bovec** (p324), one of Slovenia's top spots for extreme sports. All that prepares you for climbing Slovenia's highest peak, **Mt Triglav** (p322).

- Once your adrenaline levels off, enjoy the quiet beauty of the **Logar Valley** (p327) and neighbouring Jezersko. Reinvigorate your body with Kniepp Therapy, and a witch-guided schnapps tasting in mystical **Jezersko** (p326).

More than a Week

- You'll need two days to appreciate the bucolic centre of **Ljubljana** (p310), and to navigate an impressive list of places to eat and drink.

- You might see busloads of tourists disembarking at **Lake Bled** (p317) but who cares? Stroll around the turquoise lake and finish by flying high over the **Sava River** (p320).

- From there, head to the **Soča Valley** (p325) and then **Postojna** (p328) to be amazed at the caves and finish up in the salt water of **Piran** (p332).

JUNE

Rivers swell after the spring thaw, making it ideal for rafting. This is also the time to think about summiting **Mt Triglav** (p322)!

JULY & AUGUST

Occasional heatwaves bring crowds to the seaside and lakes. In July and August, **Bohinj** and **Bled** (p317) warm up for swimming.

SEPTEMBER

Wine harvests, mushroom foraging, and just enough sun left to enjoy the evening make this a prime time for pleasure seekers.

NOVEMBER

St Martin's Day (p343) is huge in eastern Maribor, and if you're a wine lover you won't want to miss it.

NJA STROJAN/SHUTTERSTOCK ©, MIKOLAJ NIEMCZEWSKI/SHUTTERSTOCK ©, JRP STUDIO/SHUTTERSTOCK ©, MALJALEN/SHUTTERSTOCK ©

GETTING AROUND

Ljubljana was made for walking. The Ljubljanica River is never far away and serves as a handy reference point. The city is small enough that walking is also practical for reaching outlying areas. A one-hour walk in any direction brings you to the city limits. It's heaven for cyclists, and there are bike lanes and special traffic lights everywhere. Buses are also handy for longer distances and operate from 5am to 10.30pm. A flat fare of €1.30 (good for 90 minutes of unlimited travel) is paid with a stored-value magnetic Urbana card, which you can purchase and top up at newsstands and tourist offices.

TOP TIP

The easiest way to access the castle is a 70m-long funicular that leaves from the Old Town not far from the market on Vodnikov trg. Three paths lead here: Študentovska ulica, which runs south from Ciril-Metodov trg; steep Reber ulica from Stari trg; and Ulica na Grad from Gornji trg.

Ljubljana

FORTRESS | FOOD MARKET | MUSEUMS

Ljubljana has always had the relaxed ambience of a big small town rather than a sprawling metropolis, due in large part to architect and urban planner Jože Plečnik, a native of the city. Almost single-handedly, starting in the early 1920s, he transformed Ljubljana with beautiful bridges and buildings as well as dozens of conscious design elements, such as pillars, pyramids and lamp-posts, which created the impression of a city as a work of art.

Ljubljana is not just about form though. The leafy banks of the emerald-green Ljubljanica River are designed for pedestrians and cyclists, and much of the centre is car-free. Ljubljana's environmental and sustainability policies have seen it named Europe's 'Green Capital', without succumbing to the temptation to scrub historic buildings. The result is the relaxed, graceful, and livable capital that inevitably makes visitors wonder why every city can't be like this.

Visit Medieval Ljubljana Castle

Peek inside the oldest rooms

The castle's 19th-century **watchtower** is located on the south-western side of the courtyard. The climb to the top, via a double wrought-iron staircase and a walk along the ramparts, is worth the effort for views down to the Old Town. Within the watchtower, there is a short video tour of Ljubljana and its history. Situated below, down a small flight of stairs, the remarkable **Chapel of St George** (Kapela Sv Jurija) is one of the oldest surviving remnants of the castle, dating from 1489. It's covered in frescoes and the coats of arms of the Dukes of Carniola.

HIGHLIGHTS
1 Ljubljana Castle

SIGHTS
2 Austrian Embassy
3 Dragon Bridge
4 German Embassy
see 6 Museum of Natural History
5 National Gallery of Slovenia
6 National Museum of Slovenia
7 Triple Bridge
8 US Embassy

SLEEPING
9 City Hotel Ljubljana
10 Cubo
11 Hostel Tresor

EATING
12 Abi Falafel
13 Odprta Kuhna

DRINKING & NIGHTLIFE
14 Cafe Čokl
15 Klub Daktari
16 Slovenska Hiša
17 Supernatural

ENTERTAINMENT
18 National Opera and Ballet

SHOPPING
19 Central Market

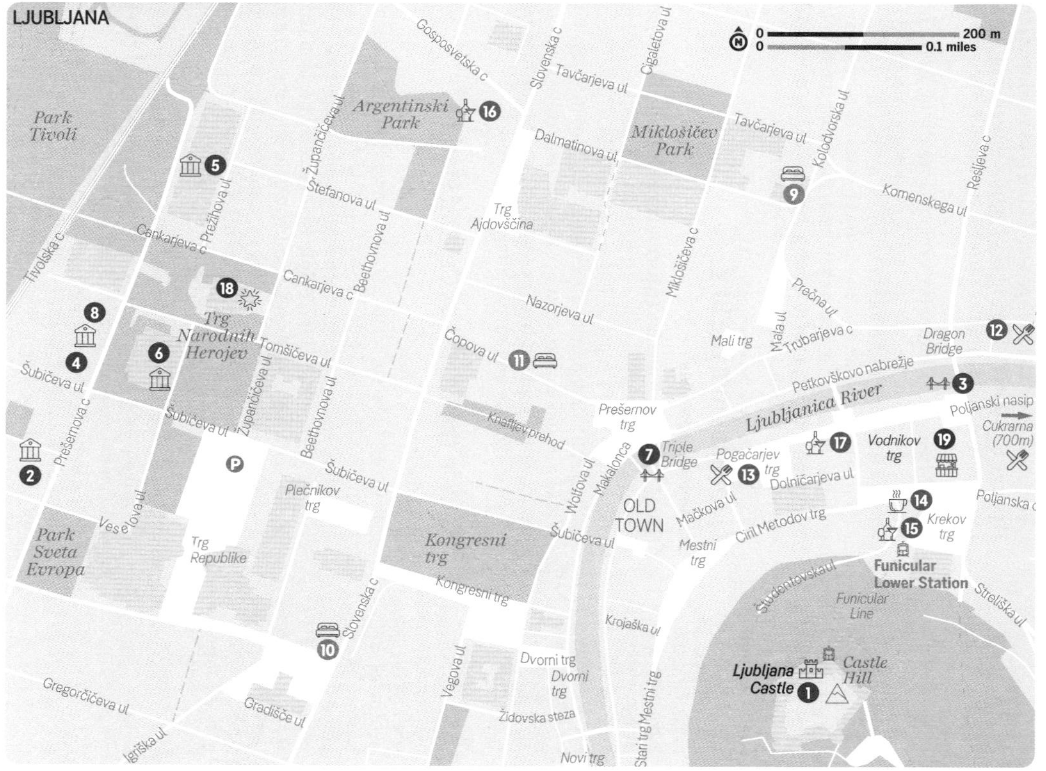

TIME TRAVEL

The castle's medieval layout, with staircases running here and there, can be confusing at first glance. The **Ljubljana Castle Information Centre** (ljubljanskigrad.si) hands out maps and multilingual audioguides and can advise on tours and events.

A better bet might be to travel back in time through one of the castle's guided Time Machine tours. These are 60-minute tours led by costumed guides who walk you through six of the city's most noteworthy periods, starting with Ljubljana's Roman origins as the settlement of Emona. Book through the information centre.

The interesting and well-presented interactive **Slovenian History Exhibition** looks at the country through the ages, running from Roman times through the Middle Ages, up to the two world wars.

The **Museum of Puppetry** explores everything from the making of marionettes to the staging of the shows themselves. It's very interactive and lots of fun.

It's free to ramble around the castle grounds, but you'll have to pay to enter the historic chambers, including the watchtower and the Chapel of St George, and to see the Slovenian History Exhibition and Museum of Puppetry.

Ljubljana from the Sky

Hot-air balloon rides

The **Ljubljana Tourist Information Centre** (TIC; visit ljubljana.com) organises hot-air balloon rides with stunning views of the city, Ljubljana Marsh and the Julian Alps. Check with the TIC for departure times and pickup locations for the ride out to the launch centre. You'll get one to 1½ hours in the air. Other balloon trips can take you near Lake Bled for views of the lake and surrounding mountains.

Take in the Tastes of Central Market

A foodie feast

The Central Market hosts the city's biggest and best open-market food fair on Fridays from mid-March to October. The sprawling market occupies prime riverfront real estate. The market extends east of the **Triple Bridge** along the Ljubljanica River, following Adamič-Lundrovo nabrežje, and runs to about Dragon's Bridge. The area's dominant feature is the dramatic neo-Renaissance **Plečnik Colonnade**, another architectural masterpiece by the city's homegrown urban planner, Jože Plečnik. Besides serving as a setting for people-watching, the massive market – occupying the squares of Vodnikov trg and Pogačarjev trg – is a great place to stock up on fresh produce, fish, and deli items. Outdoor stalls specialise in fruits and vegetables grown by local farmers, while shops and stalls within the colonnade sell meats, cheeses, breads, and other delicacies.

In the same period, the **Odprta Kuhna** (Open Kitchen) features local and international specialties cooked on-site from the country's top restaurants. Go outside traditional meal times or prepare for long lines.

WHERE TO DRINK NEAR CENTRAL MARKET

Cafe Čokl
This fair-trade place at the foot of the lower funicular station roasts its java in-house; see the chalkboard for daily specials.

Klub Daktari
This place at the foot of the funicular to Ljubljana Castle is so chill there's practically frost on the windows.

Supernatural
Located in Central Market; features coffee, beer, wines and a short menu of mostly burgers and light bites.

RAMBLE THROUGH OLD TOWN HISTORY

This stroll through the Old Town calls out architectural and historical highlights that tell fascinating stories, but which one could easily walk by without a second glance.

The tour begins at the Town Hall building on Mestni trg. The bright-white ❶ **Robba Fountain** from 1751 in front of the Town Hall features three titans with gushing urns that represent the three rivers of the historic Slovenian province of Carniola: the Sava, Krka and Ljubljanica. This fountain is a copy; the original, eaten away by urban pollution, is housed in the National Gallery.

Proceed south into Stari trg to find the lovely rococo ❷ **Schweiger House** between Nos 11 and 15. Look for a large Atlas supporting an upper balcony. The figure has his finger raised to his lips, asking passers-by to be quiet (the house name means 'Silent One' in German). The address is 11a (instead of 13), perhaps because bordellos were traditionally located at house No 13 of a street.

Stari trg is the heart of the Old Town. From behind the medieval houses on the eastern side, paths once led to Castle Hill, which was a source of water. The old-looking ❸ **Škuc Gallery** at Stari trg 21 is actually a cutting-edge contemporary art gallery with a studenty vibe.

The ❹ **Hercules Fountain** at the middle of Levstikov trg, the southern extension of Stari trg, is a favourite city meeting place. The original 17th-century statue is now housed in the Town Hall.

Turn left into Gornji trg to spot the ❺ **five medieval houses** at Nos 7 to 15. The narrow side passages here were once used by residents to deposit rubbish so that it could be washed down into the river.

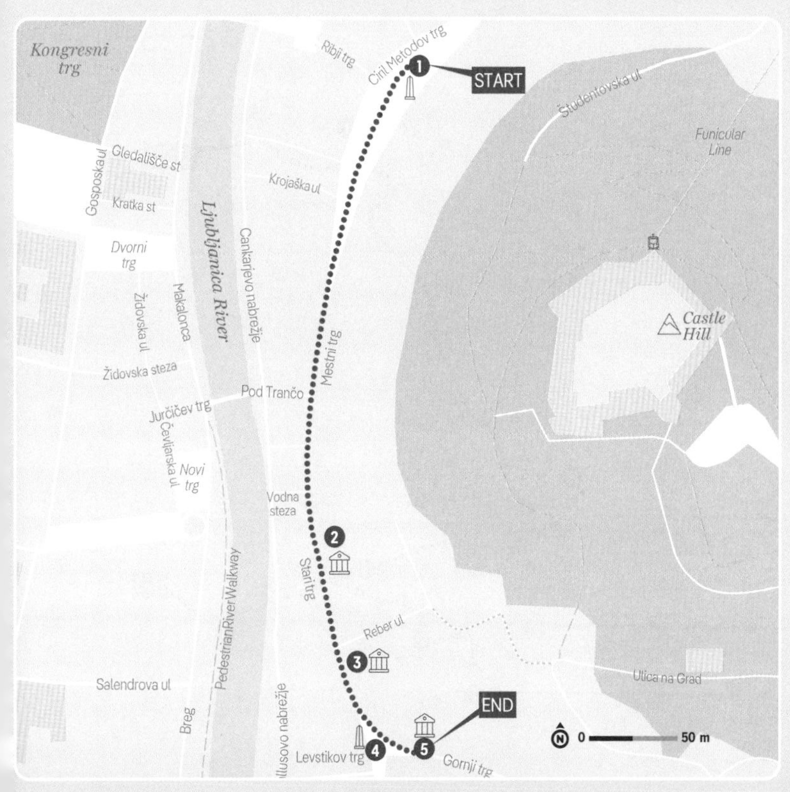

A STROLL THROUGH TIVOLI PARK

This walk begins at the park's main entrance on Celovška cesta and ends toward the south of the park, near the Museum Area. It mostly avoids the park's higher elevations and is suitable for both walking or biking. On foot, it will take around an hour at a leisurely pace.

From the parking lot at the entrance, look to the right to spot ❶ **Hot Horse**, a popular kiosk that sells burgers and sandwiches featuring horsemeat (yes, really). This area has lots of activities for kids, including a playground and mini-golf course. The large building behind Hot Horse, the ❷ **Hala Tivoli**, is a sports and entertainment complex, with a pool and indoor skating rink. Next door, the 18th-century ❸ **Cekin Mansion** is home to the highly recommended Museum of Contemporary History of Slovenia.

From here, follow one of the winding, landscaped paths southward to the ❹ **Bistro Švicarija**, a pretty timbered building that locals adore for a drink or light bite. It's a short hike over to another grand building, the 17th-century ❺ **Tivoli Mansion**, which houses the International Centre of Graphic Arts. The graceful, Jože Plečnik–designed ❻ **Jakopič Promenade** begins here and leads southeast toward the Museum Area.

If you're still in the mood to stretch your legs, the area south of the Jakopič Promenade has more landscaped pathways. Choose any walkway heading south to find ❼ **Čolnarna**, another beloved spot for a drink or meal, and a large children's playground. Retrace your steps back to the promenade and walk through a highway underpass to enter the Museum Area. The ❽ **Museum of Modern Art** will be on your right.

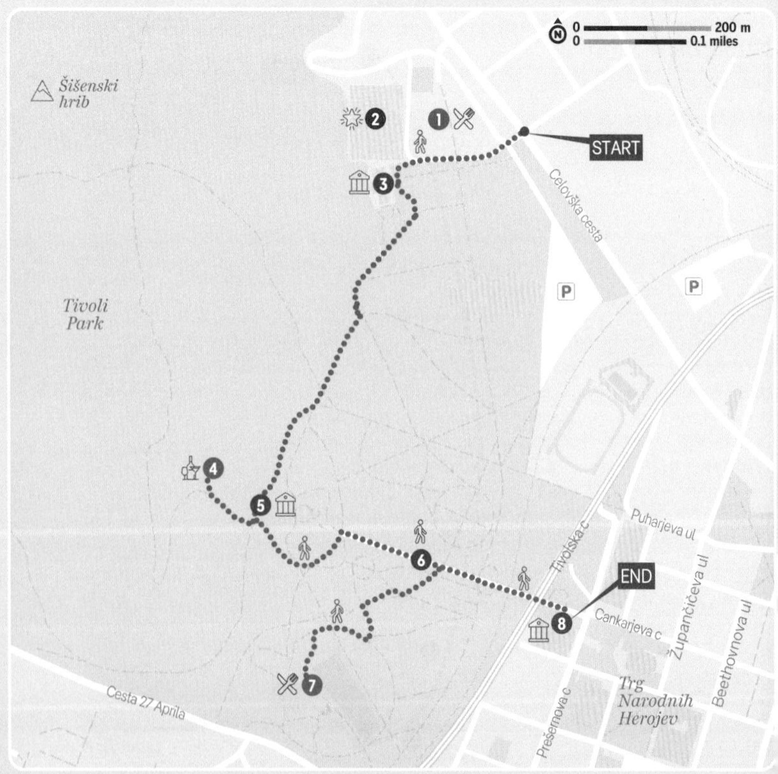

Jakopič Promenade

Museum Round-Up

The city's cultural hub

Ljubljana's Museum Area, though not a true neighbourhood in its own right, is far enough northwest of the centre to feel like a distinct part of the city. The area's claims to fame are four of the city's (and country's) most important museums, all of which are worth visiting.

The **National Museum of Slovenia** shares an address with the **Museum of Natural History** and houses the most important archaeological finds in the country. The Iron Age and Celtic holdings are given pride of place and include a highly embossed Vače Situla, a Celtic pail from the 6th century BCE that was unearthed in a town east of Ljubljana. The holdings go much further back than the Iron Age, and include incredible Stone Age discoveries. You'll see examples of Roman-era jewellery found in 6th-century Slavic graves; there's a glass-enclosed **Roman lapidarium** outside the building to the north.

When you're not looking at the exhibits, check out the ceiling fresco in the foyer of the main building, which features an allegorical image of the ancient Slovenian province of Carniola

LOCAL FAVES AROUND OLD TOWN

Ljubljana native **Matija Bulatović** spent most of his life below Ljubljana Castle, where he opened the ever-popular Daktari (p312) bar. When he's not spending time in his own place, he likes to visit these spots around the Old Town.

Abi Falafel
Not far away on Trubarjeva cesta and run by a young family that's dedicated to their craft. I think they make the best Middle Eastern food in Slovenia.

Slovenska Hiša
Another great place to go for drinks or a light meal, as they source their ingredients exclusively in Slovenia.

Cukrarna
New cultural venue east from the Central Market, not far from the Old Town. It's a very nice place to have a drink or catch a modern-art exhibition.

WHERE TO STAY IN CENTRE

City Hotel Ljubljana
Good-value, central high-rise with clean rooms, a good breakfast buffet and a welcoming reception. €€

Hostel Tresor
A 28-room hostel housed in a former bank, with rooms named after currencies and aphorisms on the walls. €

Cubo
Stylish, upscale Cubo's overall design is minimalist, with an emphasis on neutral tones of grey, beige and charcoal. €€€

LAVISH VILLAS

The villas in this part of the city – including several prominent embassies – are some of the prettiest in all of Ljubljana. Many date from the late 19th and early 20th centuries and form part of the Italian architect and urban planner Max Fabiani's (1865–1962) ambitious scheme to rebuild Ljubljana after the 1895 earthquake, which damaged around 90% of the city's buildings.

Though Italian by ethnicity, Fabiani was born in western Slovenia and attended high school in Ljubljana. Among his creations are the **Austrian Embassy** (Prešernova cesta 23), the **German Embassy** (Prešernova cesta 27) and the impressive **US Embassy** (Prešernova cesta 31). This latter work once served as the family villa for the Austrian portraitist Heinrich Wettach (1858–1929).

MATEJ_Z/SHUTTERSTOCK ©

National Gallery of Slovenia

surrounded by important Slovenes from the past, and the statues of the Muses and Fates relaxing on the stairway banisters. And while you're in the area, see who's performing at the **National Opera and Ballet** companies.

National Gallery of Slovenia

Portraits and landscapes

The National Gallery, Slovenia's foremost assembly of fine art, is housed over two floors in an old building (1896) and a modern wing. It exhibits copies of medieval frescoes, wonderful Gothic statuary and Slovenian landscapes from the 17th to 19th centuries (check out works by Romantic painters Pavel Künl and Marko Pernhart). Also look for the impressionists Jurij Šubic *(Before the Hunt)* and Rihard Jakopič *(Birches in Autumn),* the pointillist Ivan Grohar *(Larch)* and Slovenia's most celebrated female painter, Ivana Kobilca *(Summer).* The bronzes by Franc Berneker and Alojz Gangl are exceptional. In the entrance vestibule stands the original Robba Fountain, which was moved here from the front of the Town Hall (see p313) in 2008.

Lake Bled

SPECTACULAR SCENERY | ISLAND CHURCH | GORGES

There are good reasons to dislike Lake Bled. It is unfairly photogenic: the sort of place that seems painted onto reality by a combination of Studio Ghibli magic and technicolour artistry. It is so consistently crowded that the very suggestion of tranquility vanishes the minute tour buses begin their onslaught. Lake Bled is, quite bluntly, a tease. And yet.

The truth is, Lake Bled is the rarest pearl and has drawn people for millennia, as Bronze Age artefacts attest. They came as nomads, as pilgrims, as royalty, as VIPs in search of a cure. But they were all tourists, just like us. The secret of Bled is an open one: its beauty has never been hidden, never been owned. To truly enjoy it, forget about the crowds and the cameras and all the people passing through. Bled has always belonged to anyone and everyone. Find your corner, and the rest is magic.

GETTING AROUND

Bled is an easy drive to and from the capital, Ljubljana, and close to the Plečnik airport. There are buses that regularly stop in the town and two train stations. Lesce-Bled is a larger station with more frequent connections, but it's further from the lake. Bled Jezero is within walking distance of the lake but has fewer connections to the larger cities.

A Day on Lake Bled

Castles, cream cake and magic

Though many choose to make it a day trip, consider staying in Lake Bled for a couple of nights. You can start out before anyone arrives and enjoy a swim or long lunch while the rest of the world clamours for a look. Finish your day with skies that will transport you far beyond the crowds.

Begin with a sunrise walk around the lake, which is just about 5km and almost entirely flat. Bled in the early morning is peaceful and hushed. You might spot the local fishermen who tend to skip out as the buses start rolling in, and you might be greeted with a hushed *dober dan* from them. Take the opportunity to snap a photo in front of the **Blejsko srce** (Heart of Bled).

☑ TOP TIP

Timing is everything when you're in Bled, especially between May and October when tour buses descend upon the lake from nearby cruise terminals, large groups make their obligatory stopovers, and campervans begin to clog the narrow streets. Start early, enjoy more.

HIGHLIGHTS
1 Bled Island

SIGHTS
2 Bled Castle
3 Blejsko srce (Heart of Bled)
4 Church of the Assumption of Mary

ACTIVITIES, COURSES & TOURS
5 Zipline Dolinka

EATING
see 2 Bled Castle Restaurant
6 Caffe Peglez'n
7 Park Hotel
8 Slaščičarna Zima
9 Vila Prešeren

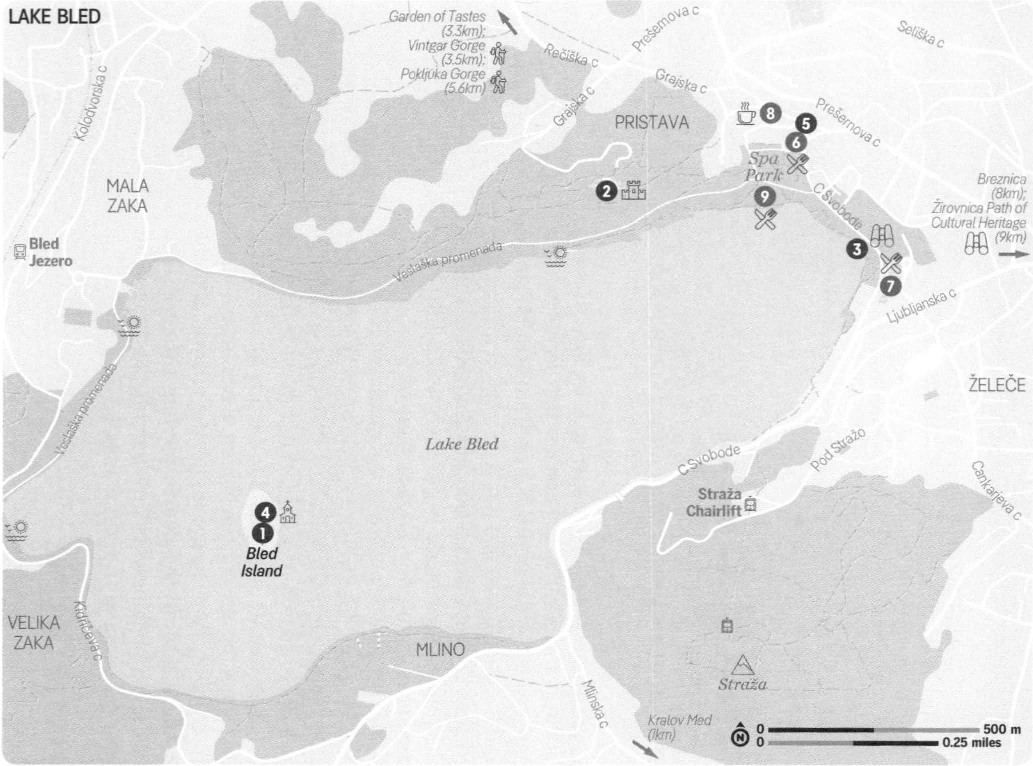

LAKE BLED

Steps to Church of the Assumption of Mary,

There are three footpaths signposted 'Grad' towards **Bled Castle**: all are a climb but in the earlier hours much more enjoyable. The history of this particular hold is slightly offbeat. It was founded in 1011 after German King Henry II conferred the estate to the Bishops of Brixen, who would act as custodians for the castle over the next eight centuries but never actually live there. Instead, it has hosted royalty and dignitaries from all over the world, many of whom left their own small imprint here. Do what they've been doing for millennia: stand back and enjoy the view.

The *kremšnita*, or Bled cream cake, was concocted in 1953 at the **Park Hotel** by a Serbian chef, although its roots likely stretch back to the Austro-Hungarian Empire. The castle cafe serves *kremšnita,* as do many restaurants around the lake. Tuck in before your descent or head to the Park Hotel for the original version.

Then visit the magical, tiny **Bled Island** in the middle of the lake. Board one of the *pletna*, a wooden boat that resembles a Venetian gondola, and head over to climb the 99 stairs into the **Church of the Assumption of Mary**. Local lore states that a groom must carry his bride up all the stairs to ensure a successful marriage. The stairs lead to the bell inside the church, where spouses and anyone else can make a wish and ring their hearts out.

If you still have the energy, go for another walk around the lake at sunset. The sky will look different, but the view will be the same: something utterly magical that even the most hardened traveller would have a hard time denying. Legend has it that Lake Bled was formed when the Slavic goddess Živa filled the valley with water to protect the fairies that lived there. So as the sun dips down over the mountains and those last rays dance on the surface, don't be surprised if you see the twinkling in the water as it laps the shore.

THE SLOVENIAN GONDOLA

Riding a piloted gondola (known as a *pletna*) out to Bled Island is the archetypal tourist experience; in all, the trip to the island and back takes about 1¼ hours. These wooden boats have a long history on the lake. In 1740, Maria Theresa of Austria granted 22 families permission to ferry pilgrims to the church on Bled Island, a tradition that stands to this day. *Pletna* boats are protected and can't be sold, meaning the only place in the world to see them is Lake Bled.

A Tale of Two Gorges

Escape into Bled's hinterland

If the fairies that flit over Bled ever take holidays, it's highly likely that they don't go far. For those without fairy wings, Bled's two gorges are still well within biking, driving or even walking distance from the lakeside.

Open from April to November, the **Vintgar Gorge** is 250m deep and 1.6km long, and accessible via a one-way trail so perfectly wedded to the surroundings that you'd never think it is artificial. The undertaking was a treacherous one: the two men who discovered the gorge in 1891 set about making it accessible to visitors, and two years later it opened to the

WHERE TO EAT IN BLED

Bled Castle Restaurant
Treat yourself at least once to incomparable views (and great food) over the lake. €€€

Hiša Linhart
Chef Uroš Štefelin creates new classics just a short drive from Bled. €€€

Old Cellar Bled
A 500-year-old cellar serving stick-to-your-ribs goodness right in the town centre. €€

BEST PLACES TO EAT KREMŠNITA

The rules of *kremšnita:* when gently shaken, the cream should wobble; when you stab a fork into the crust, it has to make a pop.

Park Hotel
The originator of the recipe is still the best, according to almost anyone. **€€**

Bled Castle Restaurant
That much cream and those panoramic views may just take your breath away. **€€**

Slaščičarna Zima
Grab a stellar slice, a great coffee and a perfect seat outside. **€**

Caffe Peglez'n
The shabby-chic decor makes this tucked-away confectionary feel like your secret. **€**

Vila Prešeren
The genteel surroundings make the decadent cream cake that much more rewarding. **€€**

Beekeeper, Kralov Med

public. It's remained open, and wondrous, ever since. Tickets can be purchased online at vintgar.si. Entry is staggered to protect the gorge and pets are also welcome by purchasing a special ticket.

The wilder **Pokljuka Gorge** is a short drive away from Vintgar and remains one of the least developed attractions near Bled. The tourist path, built in 1930, allows visitors to traverse otherwise impassable rocks to arrive at the upper parts of the gorge. Words don't do justice to the clarity of the water, nor to the awe-inspiring cliffsides of Pokljuka, the rock cave with a sunken ceiling. Take in the sight of a 22m waterfall in silence, to let it speak for itself. In total, Pokljuka is 4km long and though it's signposted and well maintained, there's far less supervision than at Vintgar. If you're a climber or used to more challenging hikes, this is great news. If it's your first run around a gorge, you may want to take a few practice runs at Vintgar first. Either way, bring a helmet.

Soar High with Zipline Dolinka

See Bled from above

Just next to the hamlet of Zasip, Zipline Dolinka offers visitors the chance to soar high above the pristine Sava River,

WHERE TO STAY IN BLED

Ambient Resort Bled
Elegant, airy villas that feel like a retreat in the heart of Bled. **€€€**

Bled Rose Hotel
Swanky modern rooms with lakeside views and spa services. **€€€**

Hotel Triglav Bled
Historic yet modern, and home to the fabulous Restaurant 1906. **€€**

just 3km from Lake Bled. There are over 4km of lines, meticulously placed in the protected forest around the Dolinka Valley. Born out of a community effort to stop a proposed dam that would have permanently altered the landscape, it conserves the area's natural beauty. From the centre of Bled, small groups are shuttled to the starting point and given safety lessons before setting off. The 2½-hour trip involves a hike through the forest to reach the different lines, but it's worth the effort and the scenery is surreal.

Meet the Bees of Bled

Explore a proud beekeeping tradition

The Bled area is a particularly good place to explore the Slovenian art of beekeeping through charming towns, unique experiences and plenty of schnapps. (If you're allergic to bees, this won't be the experience for you.)

On the hills over Lake Bled, **Kralov Med** offers bee therapy sessions, which you can book in advance with owner Daniela. Specially made bunk beds look at the hives, and screens (safely) allow for air from them to enter the bunk, which you breathe in. By engaging all of your senses, the bee therapy calms you down without ever risking a sting. Just beyond the lake in Zgornje Gorje, the bees Mateja Res keeps in her **Garden of Tastes** (Vrt Okusov) may just be fairies themselves. With a variety of experiences available like garden tours, cooking classes and beekeeping lectures, Mateja allows guests to run free and pick anything that strikes their fancy, barefoot or not.

A short drive from Bled, the **Žirovnica Path of Cultural Heritage** is a 10km trail through towns, villages and country lanes that is also the birthplace of Anton Janša, the father of modern apiculture whose contributions are so well known that his birthday of 20 May was declared World Bee Day by the UN. Janša's apiary sits in the tiny village of **Breznica**, alongside the painted beehives that have become a national symbol of a Slovenian art form. The town of **Radovljica** is almost entirely dedicated to bees. Visit the **Museum of Apiculture** to learn about the Carniolian grey bee, a native breed known for a calm disposition, productive output and resilient constitution. Families with children will have fun following a cartoon bee through the town, which makes for a cool walking tour. Stop by the **Pharmacy and Alchemy Museum** and enjoy a honey schnapps in Linart Square.

RIKLI'S BELIEVE IT OR NOT

The **Rikli Trail** in Gorje is named after Arnold Rikli, the infamous Swiss physician who once brought wealthy foreigners to the shores of Lake Bled for 'cures' that were little more than starvation and hypothermia. Indeed, the most successful outcome of his healing methods tended to be the thinning down of visitors' wallets after taking part in his retreats.

However, his legend remains, softened by time, much like the gentle path that you can follow through the countryside surrounding the gorge. It's not clear why the path is named after him, but like Rikli himself, one should never let the truth tarnish a good story.

WHERE TO CAMP AROUND BLED

Camping Sobec
Pitches, bungalows and camping with views that can't be beaten. €

Garden Village Bled
Glamping, treehouses and more at this eco-focused resort in the heart of Bled. €€€

River Camping Bled
This family-run campsite offers glamping and pitches for all budgets. €€

The Alps

ADVENTURE SPORTS | FINE DINING | HISTORY

> **TOP TIP**
> If you're planning to climb Mt Triglav, the best months are typically June, July and September – but avoid the weekends if possible. Always check the mountaineering centres for weather updates, and never go climbing without observing all necessary safety precautions.

There are actually three distinct sections to Slovenia's impressive mountains: the Julian Alps, which run from the Italian border; the Kamnik-Savinja Alps to the east of Bled; and the Karavanke, which straddle the frontier with Austria. While the Julian Alps have become a world-renowned centre for skiing, adrenaline sports and the wondrous Soča Valley, there is a lot to see, do and drink in the rest of the range.

Whatever time of year you're visiting, there will be some form of extreme sport on display in Bovec or Kranjska Gora, just as there will be a million reasons to stop and stay for a while in Velika Planina or Jezersko. So take your time, lace up those hiking boots, and don't forget to practise your schnapps intake. It's a marathon out there.

The Rooftop of Slovenia's Alps

Climbing Mt Triglav

Every Slovene is said to have the duty to summit **Mt Triglav** at least once in their lives, and many have answered the call. At 2864m, Triglav is a challenging intermediate climb, but as long as you're physically fit and aren't afraid of heights, you can plan to climb it.

While the majority is straightforward, the final path to the summit is a *via ferrata* – a climbing route secured with steel cables and fixed pegs to help you ascend. In addition, the weather can change rapidly and differ dramatically as you climb. In short, if you don't have high alpine hiking and *via ferrata* experience, don't even consider climbing Triglav

WHERE TO STAY AROUND KRANJSKA GORA

Vitranc
Hosts Nejc and Laura couldn't be nicer, and the hotel in Podkoren is charming. **€€**

Boutique Hotel Milka
Chic rooms and a sleek kitchen make this Kranjska Gora hotel worthwhile. **€€€**

Hostel Lukna
The place for hikers looking for the basics and a community of climbers at the foot of the mountain in Mojstrana. **€**

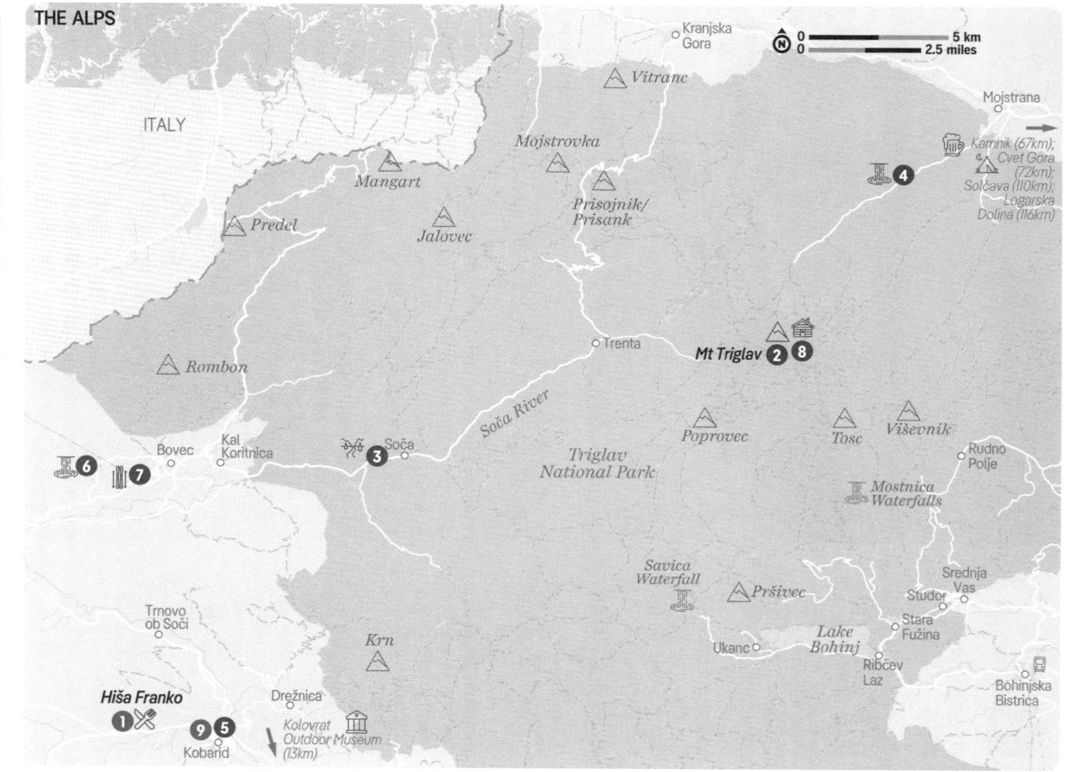
THE ALPS
HIGHLIGHTS
1 Hiša Franko
2 Mt Triglav
SIGHTS
3 Great Soča Gorge
4 Peričnik Falls
5 Planika Dairy
6 Virje Waterfall
ACTIVITIES, COURSES & TOURS
7 Kanin Ski Centre
SLEEPING
8 Triglavski Dom
EATING
9 Hiša Polonka
0 5 km
0 2.5 miles
ITALY
Kranjska Gora
Vitranc
Mojstrana
Kamnik (67km); Cvet Gora (72km); Solčava (110km); Logarska Dolina (116km)
Mojstrovka
Mangart
Prisojnik/ Prisank
Predel
Jalovec
Trenta
Mt Triglav
Rombon
Soča River
Poprovec
Tosc
Viševnik
Bovec
Kal Koritnica
Soča
Triglav National Park
Rudno Polje
Mostnica Waterfalls
Savica Waterfall
Pršivec
Srednja Vas
Studor
Stara Fužina
Trnovo ob Soči
Krn
Lake Bohinj
Ukanc
Ribčev Laz
Bohinjska Bistrica
Hiša Franko
Drežnica
Kobarid
Kolovrat Outdoor Museum (13km)

SUSTAINABLE SOČA

Tourism is a vital part of the local economy, and the towns and villages of the Soča Valley have made sustainable practices a cornerstone of this sector.

Public transport is widely available during the season, with hop-on/hop-off buses running from Tolmin, Kobarid and Bovec. They have also achieved the Green Destination Gold label, which recognises areas that develop tourism infrastructure in accordance with sustainability standards.

Through their website and at tourist information offices in all of the towns in the valley, travellers can also shop for local products and connect with guides that offer small tours designed to respect the natural environment.

MIKADUN/SHUTTERSTOCK ©

Krma Valley

without a certified guide accompanying you. Guides can be hired through operators in Bled or Bohinj, the tourist information centres or the Alpine Association of Slovenia. Make sure you've got proper equipment and up-to-date information on weather and terrain before ascending.

Around **Kranjska Gora**, there are various routes for climbing Triglav, and unless you're an extremely fit mountaineer, you'll need two days, and another day to recover. The first route is via the **Krma Valley**, departing from **Mojstrana**. The trip takes 12 to 14 hours over those two days; you'll overnight in a traditional lodge like **Triglavski Dom**, a weather station on the mountain. More experienced climbers opt for the passage via the **Vrata Valley**, stretching from Mojstrana to the foot of the impressive Triglav North Face. This ascent is done on a *via ferrata*, and there are three to choose from. Whichever way you go, you'll be rewarded with one of the most beautiful climbs in the world. Along the way, be sure to pass by the mythical **Peričnik Falls** just outside Mojstrana, at the entrance to Triglav National Park.

Extreme Sports in Bovec

Canyons, rafting and adrenaline

At the foot of Mt Triglav and surrounded by the imposing peaks of the Julian Alps, Bovec is the northernmost town

WHERE TO HIKE AROUND SOČA

Great Soča Gorge
A flat, beautiful hike just a 10-minute drive from Bovec and the source of stunning views.

Virje Waterfall
Hidden among the trees of Triglav National Park, this swimming spot is coveted (and rightly so).

Kanin Ski Centre
Trails for every level and a cable car for anyone who just wants to enjoy the view.

in the Soča Valley and an extreme-sports twin to Kranjska Gora. If there's a cliff to hurl yourself from or a ravine to jump into, someone in Bovec has done it and can help you do it too.

Whitewater rafting and kayaking are the most popular activities in the area from March to October, when you'll see teams of people paddling, slaloming and splashing along the river. Although you must be a swimmer in order to participate, there are plenty of families with children who go along for the ride. Canyoning is rapidly gaining ground in Bovec; you can make your way down a mountain stream in a gorge with techniques like abseiling, climbing, sliding and jumping. Many companies in Bovec offer excursions for beginners and experts, including **Nature's Ways** and **Kayak Soča**.

Bovec also offers zip lining over the Julian Alps, with more than 3km of lines at the **Adrenaline Park Bovec**. The park rents e-bikes, scooters and kayaks in addition to offering accommodation to anyone who survives the daily roster of activities.

Though it may not be extreme, fly-fishing is one of the most popular pastimes on the Soča River, and Bovec is a great place to try it. Make sure to go with a guide, however, because access to the river to fish is strictly controlled. **Soča Trout** offers guided trips.

Of course, skiing is still king along these mountains, and nowhere is more popular than the **Kanin Ski Centre**. The biggest ski area in Slovenia actually shares custody with Italy, and the starting point for the gondola is in Bovec. Hit the slopes and watch the sea below, whether you're a beginner or an expert.

Fine Dining in the Soča Valley

The Hiša Franko experience

Perhaps you've come to Slovenia precisely to eat at **Hiša Franko**, the three-Michelin-starred restaurant just outside Kobarid. Maybe you've seen chef Ana Roš on billboards or television shows, and now your curiosity is piqued. Whatever the reason, the bite-sized courses will make you giggle at times, make you think at others, and leave you amazed at the end of it.

Hiša Franko isn't for everyone, but then again not all of us will summit Mt Triglav or sail over the Sava River. Some of us will remember the wind in our hair and others the taste of the perfect bite on our tongue. But every one of us remembers that time we did something incredible, and a select few of us will have Ana Roš to thank for it.

Tasting menus start at €255 per person, not including wine pairing. Guests of the restaurant can also reserve rooms (subject to availability).

KOBARID'S CHEESE MUSEUM

Every museum should have a cheese shop, or perhaps every cheese shop should have a museum. In Kobarid, you have both. The **Planika Dairy** celebrates the time-honoured tradition of cheesemaking in the Soča Valley through an interactive exhibit of its origins as well as a look at how cheese was made in the past. Have a walk through the inviting museum and then head across the parking lot to the Kobarid market for a fantastic selection of locally made products from around the Soča Valley. If you're staying in the area, this will be your go-to supermarket; once you head home, you might miss this most of all.

WHERE TO GET A COFFEE IN KAMNIK

Stow Coffee
Ljubljana's hippest coffee is brewed right here, so come to the source.

Kavarna Veronika
Neither the views, the people nor the coffee are stingy.

Korobač
The neighbourhood vibe is as strong as the coffee – which is to say, strong.

WITCHES BREWS IN MYSTICAL JEZERSKO

The tiny municipality of Jezersko is tucked into the remote Kokra Valley. Nestled in the town is **Cvet Gora**, a mountain retreat with various types of accommodation in peaceful surroundings. It's run by Tanja Rebolj, known locally as 'the blonde witch of Jezersko'. She has a deep understanding of over 1000 flowers and herbs in the area, and uses them to create tinctures, soaps and liquors that seem to find their way to exactly the right people, at exactly the right time.

Come to Cvet Gora for a schnapps tasting and healthy samples of Jezerska Pehta, a one-of-a-kind brew made from 102 different herbs that Tanja picks herself. You'll be glad there are glamping pods!

Reconstructed trenches, Kolovrat Outdoor Museum

History Lessons at Kolovrat Outdoor Museum

Walk through WWI trenches

The Kolovrat Outdoor Museum highlights the profound impact WWI had on the Soča Valley by restoring command posts, machine-gun positions, caves and trenches for visitors to explore. From the observation points you'll see the mountain spines that were transformed into battle positions in Italy and Slovenia, and far below, the sparkling contours of the Soča River.

The Walk of Peace website offers precise instructions, guided tours and more information about the museum. For lovers of history and nature, this is a fascinating way to experience, and honour, one of the most difficult periods in Slovenia's history.

Tour Kamnik's Breweries

Drink your way around Kamnik

In a town where beer flows as freely as water, it only makes sense to make a day out of drinking as much of it as you can. However, this is Slovenia: indulgence is always accompanied by some level of strenuous activity that will balance out, or better still, cancel any potential damage.

WHERE TO EAT IN JEZERSKO & LOGARSKA

Vila Planinka
The elegance of the dishes perfectly echoes the almost otherworldly scenery of the surroundings. €€€

Gostilna Kočna
Across the street and a world apart from Vila Planinka, yet totally worth it for hearty meals and garden tables. €

Hiša Ojstrica
Friendly tavern-like atmosphere with copious plates of local products and specialities. €€

While many other parts of Slovenia depend heavily on wine production, the Kamnik-Savinja region relies instead on the water that is an ideal chemical composition for beermaking. Ksenija and Bogdan created **Beer Way** to combine their shared love for hospitality, outdoor activities, a bit of history and, of course, beer. The result is an occasionally raucous, always entertaining, and eminently hydrating tour of Kamnik's history. It's also a perfect day trip from Ljubljana, or a great way to end a day of hiking at nearby Velika Planina.

There are a number of tours to choose from based on how much time (and love) you have to devote to the art of the brew. Beer nerds will find nirvana with the full-day tour of three breweries and tastings with four brewers, along with an invigorating walk on the outskirts of Kamnik, past the river that brings this perfectly balanced water into your glass. Along the way you'll also have food tastings or snacks and plenty of stories about the area. But save room in your belly and your heart for **Maister Brewery** just outside the town centre, where Beer Way tours often conclude. Owner Janez (or Johnny) is too passionate about his craft to resist. He'll show you every detail of his process. Of course, he's always ready to toast to your visit.

Take the Solčava Panoramic Road

Slay dragons in wild nature

It hardly matters if you choose to walk, drive or cycle this 37km trail; you'll be stopping so often to look around you that it might seem like you're hardly moving at all. The Solčava Panoramic Road passes through the Logar, Robanov Kot and Matlov Kot valleys, and along the way offers 15 different hiking trails with more than 20 different scenic points to stop at. There are waterfalls, natural springs and gorges, all of which carry (like most things in Slovenia) traces of legend. This one involves a young shepherd and a dragon, and whether you believe it or not hardly matters. Spend enough time on the road, and you'll start feeling like you're in your own personal fairy tale. The untamed scenery is unlike anything else.

The Solčava Panoramic Road is one of the Slovenia Green itineraries, which are awarded that distinction for their commitment to sustainable tourism and promotion of the local cultural heritage. Not only is the natural environment protected, but the area is full of so-called 'tourist farms' that serve traditional meals using local ingredients, and many offer immersive experiences to visitors. For a complete itinerary, the tourism board of **Solčava** (logarska-solcavsko.si) has a brochure that you can download.

LOGAR VALLEY FAVOURITES

Nina Plesnik (plesnik.si; @hotelplesnik) lives in Logarska Dolina and shares what makes it special.

What do I love most about living in Logarska? Every day here means connecting with nature, embracing sustainable living and introducing people to a different idea of wellness, one that fits their lifestyles. People who come here reconnect, either with their own centre or with the world around them. The valley is a special place for so many reasons: just being here combats burnout, and offers people the chance to really reflect. I'm proud to be able to share this energy with the world, and I know that anyone who makes the trip here is more than rewarded.

WHERE TO HIKE IN JEZERSKO & LOGARSKA

Rinka Waterfall, Logarska
An easy bike ride from the entrance to the valley, find stunning views and a sausage-vending machine.

Mountain Hut Češka Koča, Jezersko
This perch is a rewarding walk to take in the breadth of the Karavanke mountain range.

Podolševa, Solčava
One of the highest-elevation settlements in Slovenia, the Church of the Holy Spirit is a departure point for hikes.

Postojna

CAVES | SPY HOTEL | ADVENTURE

TOP TIP

Most Slovenian caves have a constant temperature of 8°C to 10°C with 95% humidity, no matter the season, so if you plan to do any caving, bring a warm jacket and decent shoes. Note that rainy summer days bring the biggest crowds.

Before the massive underground world of Postojna was fully explored in 1818, the town wasn't known for much other than being a convenient transit point between the sea and Ljubljana. All that changed when the jaw-dropping, 24km-long Postojna Cave opened to the public and became one of Slovenia's top destinations. Nowadays, caving is one of the main reasons to hang out in the Karst, a limestone plateau with sinkholes and funnels stretching from the Gulf of Trieste to Vipava Valley that's home to thousands of underground caverns. Discovering new caves has become a popular pastime for adventurous Slovenes.

Aside from underground treasures, the Karst's deep green hills are rich in fruits, ruby-red *teran* wine, *pršut* (dry-cured ham), old stone churches and, of course, the celebrated Lipizzaner horses. Today, Postojna serves as a convenient gateway to many Karst adventures, from canoeing on the disappearing lake of Cerknica to tracking brown bears in Notranjska Regional Park.

The Subterranean Wonderland of Postojna

Cave with underground train

Discover the tremendous **Postojna Cave**, one of the world's largest, featuring unparalleled stalagmite and stalactite formations. A must-visit when in Slovenia, this ancient two-million-year-old cave has welcomed more than 40 million visitors since Austrian Emperor Franz Joseph I paid a visit in 1818.

WHERE TO STAY AROUND POSTOJNA

Hotel Jama
Literally atop Postojna Cave, this huge socialist-era hotel was renovated into luxury lodging with great views. **€€€**

Lipizzaner Lodge
Pleasant rural guesthouse run by a Welsh-Finnish couple with brilliant local expertise. **€€**

Youth Hostel Proteus Postojna
Fun, chilled-out space offering three-bed rooms, shared bathrooms and bike rental. **€**

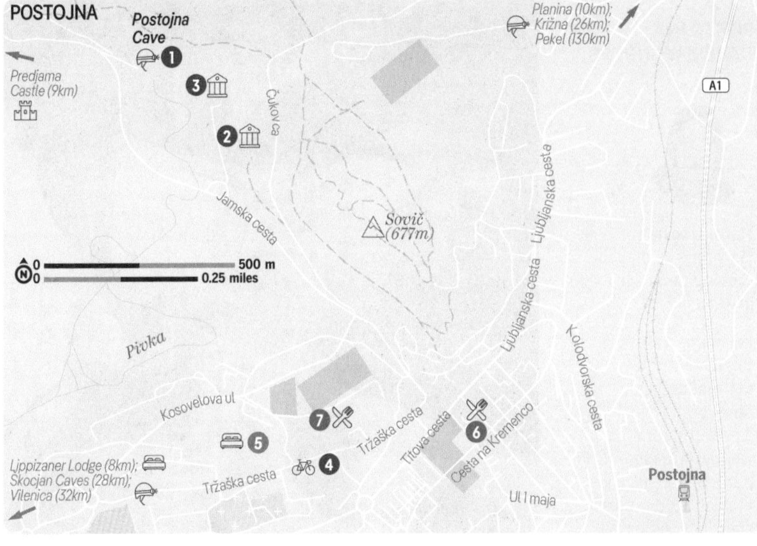

Yes, it gets busy. Surprisingly, the bustling tourist activity does not diminish the wonder; the immense crowds seem to just vanish amid the sheer vastness of this remarkable cave complex. Once inside, you will embark on a 1½-hour tour that unveils 5km of the expansive cave, with more than 3km of the journey covered by a cool electric underground train. Entering the **Great Mountain** cavern feels like stepping into the secret den of a James Bond villain. From there, guides escort you through dry galleries adorned with delicate stalactites, needle-shaped formations and even translucent 'curtains'.

Prepare for the constant chill inside, and if you forget a coat, felt capes are available for hire at the entrance. With wheelchair-accessible options, Postojna stands apart from Škocjan and other caves in Slovenia. Don't miss the attractive package deals, which include a visit to **Vivarium Proteus** (an observatory of cave-dwelling animal species), the new **Expo** (the world's largest exhibition and interactive presentation of subterranean karst formations illustrating the history of the cave) and the dramatic Predjama Castle (p331).

THE BABY DRAGON

Postojna Cave shelters the elusive *Proteus anguinus*, or olm, an enigmatic salamander with skin resembling pink human flesh. The creature can live in pitch-black darkness for over a century and can survive for a decade without food. Named 'Proteus' by a Viennese doctor in 1786, this 'human fish' (*človeška ribica* in Slovenian) reaches 30cm in length and has a swimming tail, stubby legs and atrophied eyes. It thrives on keen olfactory senses and detects weak electric fields in water to navigate, hunt and communicate. The olm can be seen inside Postojna Cave, or near the entrance to Vivarium Proteus.

POSTOJNA CAVE'S WONDERS

Mateja Možina Margon is a Postojna Cave guide who lives in Pivka.

For me, as a local, this cave is proof that wonderland does exist. This amazing natural wonder is unique; it's peaceful, scenic and eternal. So, it's not a coincidence that my former boyfriend, now husband, and I chose it as our mysterious wedding destination, considering we are both cave guides in love with pristine nature and wildlife. Just imagine what a privilege this was for us – getting married in the most beautiful natural cathedral! Rich with cave formations and serving as the home of our baby dragons – the biggest cave animals in the world – Postojna Cave should definitely be considered the eighth wonder of the world!

HAPPY MOMENTS/SHUTTERSTOCK ©

Predjama Castle

A Hard-Hat Postojna Cave Expedition

In the footsteps of early explorers

If you are in the market for an adrenaline-filled cave tour, try the hard-hat excursion, 'In the Footsteps of Luka Čeč', named after the lamplighter who discovered the full extent of Postojna Cave accidentally while getting the cave ready for the scheduled visit of Austrian Emperor Franz Joseph I back in 1818. Equipped with caving gear and led by experienced guides, you will emulate the journey taken by early explorers and venture into parts of the cave not accessible to regular tours – **Pivka Cave** and **Black Cave**, the last underground stations of the Pivka River. At €300 per person, it doesn't exactly come cheap, but this is a unique expedition meant to explore the hardly accessible depths of the cave while solving actual caving tasks, such as descending on a rope or climbing over the river, all while embracing the immense darkness, silence and the rich biodiversity of the karst underground.

WHERE TO EAT AROUND POSTOJNA

Bistro Štorja
This cosy restaurant focuses on local, seasonal dishes including tasting menus paired with wine. **€€**

Gostilna & Pizzeria Čuk
Popular restaurant serving a nice selection of regional dishes; the pizza from a wood-fired oven is the real draw. **€€**

Predjamka Cafe
The service can be spotty at the terrace overlooking Predjama Castle, but the view (and calamari) is worth it. **€€**

Spy on the Former Regime

The Hotel Jama secret rooms

Delve into the secret rooms of **Hotel Jama**, which once concealed some very unusual activities that took place here. It turns out that after it was built in 1971, the hotel lived a well-hidden double life – providing accommodation for the millions of Postojna visitors on one hand, and spying on them on the other. It was only when Hotel Jama was being renovated in 2016 that an unassuming back door was discovered and behind it, an entire hidden communication centre of the Yugoslav secret police was revealed. The hotel cleverly preserved these rooms, along with the eavesdropping recordings and technology, and now offers a fascinating tour during which you become an active participant in a world where truth and lies intermingle. Tickets cost €15 (€8 if purchased as a combo with Postojna Cave).

Fortress Perched in a Cave

Explore the Predjama Castle

Predjama Castle is located only 9km from Postojna, and whether you arrive by car, bicycle or hike up to it (opt for the latter for extra suspense), your jaw will likely drop as you first take a glimpse at this medieval fortification masterpiece. Perched halfway up a 123m cliff, with part of it inside a cave, the fortress looks simply unconquerable. Kids of all ages will enjoy the castle's eerie features – holes in the ceiling to pour boiling oil, a dark dungeon or a treasure chest discovered in the cellar in 1991. For those not afraid of bats, the cave beneath the castle is part of the 14km Predjama cave system and a home to a colony of these nocturnal winged creatures.

A combo discounted ticket for both Predjama Castle and Postojna Cave is on offer, too, as is a convenient free shuttle bus between the two. But the **Predjama Tour** alone is fun, with an audioguide in 15 languages detailing the captivating story of Erazem Lueger, a 15th-century robber baron who, like Robin Hood, robbed the rich to give to the poor. Amid the Hungarian-Austrian wars, Erazem took refuge in Predjama Castle, aided by a secret passage behind the rock wall to continue his daring deeds. In 1484, the Austrians besieged the castle, but it stood impregnable. Erazem taunted them, even showering them with fresh cherries to prove his ease. Yet, the Austrians had the last laugh, striking him with a cannonball while he sat on the toilet – a fateful end for a fascinating character.

BEST CAVES IN THE SLOVENIAN KARST

While Postojna is a spectacular and well known cave complex, it's not the only one. Other interesting caves in the Karst region include:

Križna
Navigate one of the underground lakes of the 'Cross Cave' in a rubber dingy.

Vilenica
The cave's unique, colourful halls even host the Vilenica International Literary Festival in September.

Pekel
It's called 'Hell Cave' in Slovenian because of the steam rising out of it in the winter months.

Planina
With its Slovenian name translating as 'Mountain', this is the largest water cave in the country.

Škocjan
The Unesco World Heritage site is a thrilling experience all of its own.

WHERE TO RENT A BIKE AROUND POSTOJNA

Čeho Bike
Bicycle shop in the centre of Postojna offering road and mountain bikes, children's and youth bikes.

Youth Hostel Proteus Postojna
Bike rental and service (including bicycle storage) as well as cycling guides.

Lipizzaner Lodge
Call ahead to rent one of their eight electric and nine regular bikes.

Piran

SEA | SALT | CYCLING AND HIKING

GETTING AROUND

Piran is small and walkable. From the southwest corner of Tartinijev trg, frequent free minibuses shuttle between Piran's bus station and the Fornače car park, where drivers must leave their cars before entering the Old Town. If venturing to the surrounding coastal areas, biking is a fast and efficient way to get around. Luma Sport, opposite the bus station, rents out bicycles and e-bikes and even offers bike delivery to hotels by prior arrangement.

TOP TIP

Since Piran is mostly a pedestrian zone, driving can be a nuisance. You'll need to leave your car in the town's parking garage, just beyond the Old Town limits. Frequent shuttle buses operate between the parking area and the town centre from 5am to 1am, depending on the season.

Nestled at the tip of a slender peninsula that was once an island, the picture-perfect Piran (Pirano in Italian) shines as the crown jewel of Slovenia's 47km coastal stretch. Wandering the twisty alleyways of Piran's impeccably preserved Old Town with its Venetian Gothic architecture can feel like a cool fix for Venice's frenzy – barely any mob crowds, mosquitoes or rip-off vibes here. An added bonus: a few crystal-clear Adriatic beaches are just a stroll away.

If you are wondering why this pretty little village was so attractive to the Venetians, the answer is: salt. For centuries, the town's wealth and notoriety was tied to the famed Sečovlje Salt Pans, and *piranska sol* is still considered some of the world's finest.

Sure, Piran might no longer be the Adriatic's best-kept secret, but it's hard not to instantly fall in love with its romantic charm, mouthwatering seafood joints and breathtaking sunsets.

The Secret Behind Piran's Sea Bass

Fish-farm boat trip

To get an idea how the celebrated Piran sea bass achieved its culinary fame, head to the **Fonda Fish Farm** (fonda.si) in Piran Bay and hang out with the good people responsible for providing local restaurants with the freshest fish. Slovenian food aficionados, however modest, are proud to point out that even fastidious Italians like to travel from Italy to Piran to taste the most delicious sea bass on the Adriatic coast.

The secret behind the famed local *brancin* apparently lies in Piran's crystal-clear, nutrient-rich waters that provide the sea bass with a diverse diet, resulting in delicate and flavourful meat. According to the Fonda family, farmed fish have an advantage over their wild counterparts – their living conditions and food are highly supervised and free of harmful supplements.

To tour the 'fish garden' pools in the protected area of the Sečovlje Salina Nature Park (p335), you must arrange with the Fonda Fish Farm at least a couple of days ahead. Once meeting your guide, you'll hop aboard their boat or opt for a

PIRAN

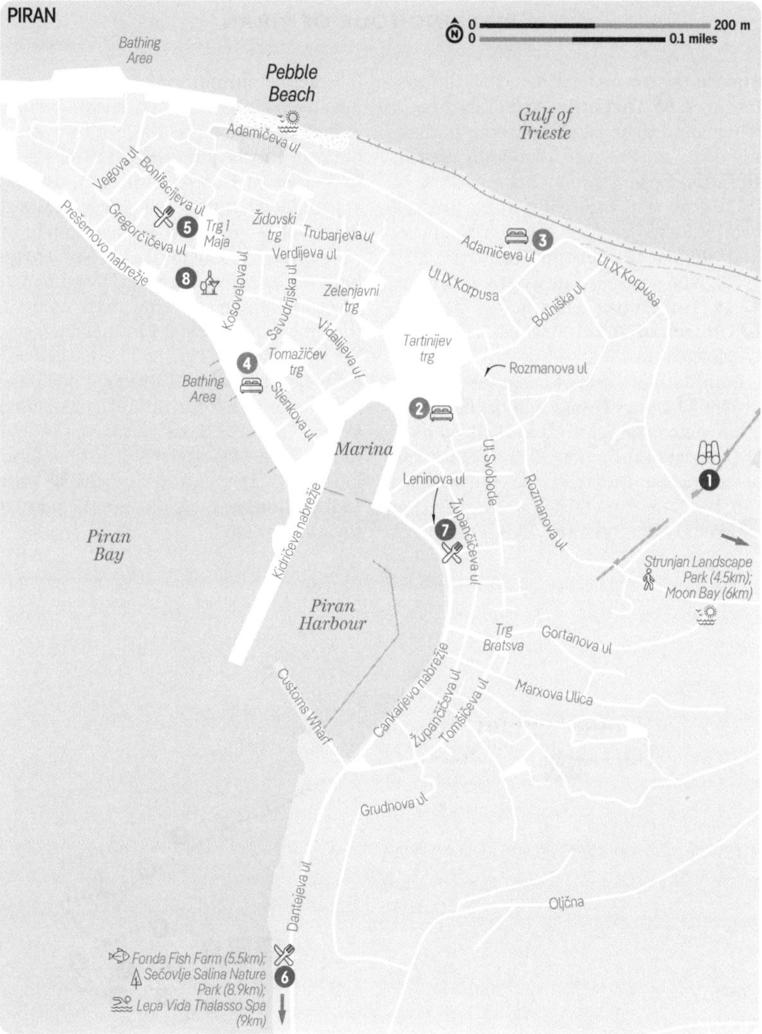

0 200 m
0 0.1 miles

Bathing Area
Pebble Beach
Gulf of Trieste
Adamičeva ul
Vegova ul
Bonifacijeva ul
Prešernovo nabrežje
Gregorčičeva ul
Trg 1 Maja
Židovski trg
Trubarjeva ul
Verdijeva ul
Kosovelova ul
Savudrijska ul
Zelenjavni trg
Vidalijeva ul
Tomažičev trg
Tartinijev trg
Ul IX Korpusa
Bolniška ul
Rozmanova ul
Bathing Area
Stjenkova ul
Marina
Leninova ul
Ul Svobode
Župančičeva ul
Piran Bay
Kidričeva nabrežje
Piran Harbour
Strunjan Landscape Park (4.5km); Moon Bay (6km)
Trg Bratsva
Gortanova ul
Marxova Ulica
Customs Wharf
Cankarjevo nabrežje
Tomšičeva ul
Grudnova ul
Dantejeva ul
Oljčna
Fonda Fish Farm (5.5km); Sečovlje Salina Nature Park (8.9km); Lepa Vida Thalasso Spa (9km)

SIGHTS
1 Piran Town Walls

SLEEPING
2 Art Hotel Tartini
3 Max Piran
4 Piran Hotel Rooftop

EATING
5 Fritolin Pri Cantini
6 Pri Mari
7 Restaurant Neptun

DRINKING & NIGHTLIFE
8 Cafinho

SALT THERAPY

While Istria possesses its fair share of Thalasso Spa centres, which use seawater, check out the mineral baths and legendary spas around **Novo Mesto** (p339).

A WALKING TOUR OF PIRAN

Start at the town's beating heart, the pastel-toned ❶ **Tartinijev trg** (Tartini Sq), which used to be a small harbour for fishing boats until it was filled with sand in 1894 and turned into an open market. In its centre, the statue of a finely dressed gentleman represents native son, composer and violinist ❷ **Giuseppe Tartini** (1692–1770), who was born in what's called the ❸ **Tartini House** today, across from the ❹ **Church of St Peter** which has a richly adorned interior.

Dominating the square's western edge are the ❺ **Court House** and the porticoed 19th-century ❻ **Municipal Hall**, home to the tourist information centre. Before venturing deeper into town, be sure to check out the 'time machine' at the exciting ❼ **Mediadom Pyrhani**. This multimedia interactive museum takes you on an innovative journey through Piran's history.

The striking pinkish mid-15th-century palazzo to the northwest is the famed ❽ **Venetian House**, built by a wealthy Venice merchant to serenade a local girl. Behind it, a cobbled street leads up to Piran's hilltop ❾ **Cathedral of St George**, built in the early 17th century and named after the town's patron saint, who is thought to have saved Piran when it was hit by a violent storm. The cathedral's free-standing ❿ **bell tower** – obviously modelled on the *campanile* of San Marco in Venice – rewards those courageous enough to climb the 147 stairs with some fabulous views. Descend toward the ⓫ **Punta lighthouse** and get lost in the maze of twisty alleyways.

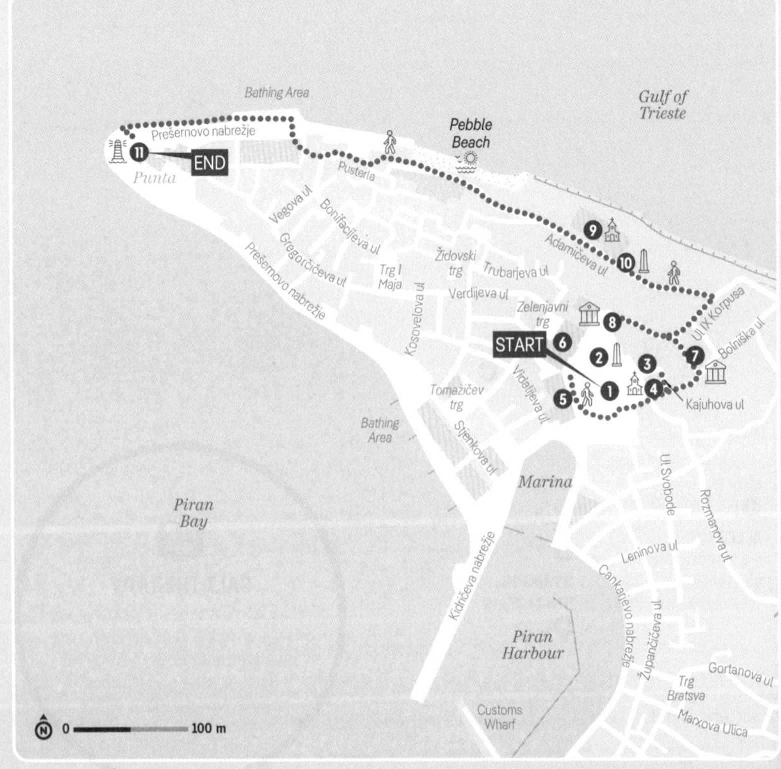

sportier approach with a kayak or a stand-up paddleboard and sail away to learn all about the intricacies of sustainable fish farming. At the end, you get to try both raw and smoked sea bass, paired with the exquisite flavours of Piran's famous *fleur de sel* (sea salt) and Istrian olive oil, perfectly complemented by local wine.

A Saltwater Soak in Sečovlje

Visit a seawater spa

The expansive **Sečovlje Salina Nature Park**, Piran's money-making hub for centuries, is where salt is still extracted by hand using 700-year-old methods. A haven for 290 bird species, crisscrossed by dykes and channels, the entire park is only accessible by foot or bike and can get scorching hot in the summer. The breezy northern end of the salt pans is home to the gorgeous open-air **Lepa Vida Thalasso Spa**, which shuttles visitors from the entrance in a golf cart, and is a marvellous spot to spend a relaxing afternoon soaking in saltwater pools, getting a mud wrap and bird-watching. Bookings are essential.

Slovenian Coast on Two Wheels

Cycle the Parenzana Trail

Starting from Piran, sample at least a portion of the scenic **Porečanka (Parenzana) Trail**, a 130km walking and cycling path that runs along the former narrow-gauge railway, built in the Austro-Hungarian Empire to connect Trieste in Italy with Poreč in Croatia. About 30km of the trail runs through the mesmerising landscapes of Slovenian Istria and its vineyard-clad hills, olive groves and quaint coastal villages, each turn unveiling stunning panoramas, with the azure Adriatic Sea glistening on the horizon.

Conveniently, Piran is located roughly in the middle, and renting a bike in Piran will allow you to choose whether to pedal northeast towards Italy or south towards Croatia. The northbound route will take you through the lively coastal ports of Izola and Koper with a recommended stop along the way at Strunjan Landscape Park (p336) for a dip in the sea. The southbound trail continues through the glitzy resort town of Portorož to the Sečovlje salt pans, with a possible finish line at the lovely open-air Lepa Vida Thalasso Spa.

Both options are about 20km each way and make for an easy day trip, especially if you arrange for a one-way bike rental and use public transport to get back. Multiple day trips, including bike transport and accommodation along the way, can be arranged though parenzana.info.

BEST SUNSET SPOTS IN PIRAN

Piran Town Walls
Soak in the amazing views from the preserved medieval walls high up above town.

Seaside Promenade
Pick any bar along the coastal boardwalk. Cafinho has a lively vibe and a good selection of cocktails and craft beers.

Strunjan Nature Walk
About an hour's walk along the coast from Piran, the trail takes you up on 80m-high cliffs with amazing views.

Piran Hotel Rooftop
The renovated rooftop bar of Piran's iconic hotel is the classiest place in town for a sundowner.

Sunset Cruise
Boat operators offer sunset tours including wine and snacks. Vintage Boat Tours feature a 1947 traditional Istrian wooden sailboat.

WHERE TO STAY IN PIRAN

Piran Hotel
The town's flagship hotel has a commanding seafront position, great service and a century of history. **€€€**

Art Hotel Tartini
Facing Tartinijev trg, this is one of Piran's most stylish options. The rooftop terrace is a winner. **€€€**

Max Piran
This 18th-century townhouse in the heart of town offers good deals on its six colourful double rooms. **€€**

TRADITIONAL DISHES OF SLOVENIAN ISTRIA

Piran sea bass in salt
Baked in the oven in a tray filled with Sečovlje salt.

Mussels or clams alla busara
Cooked with olive oil, white wine, breadcrumbs and garlic.

Calamari
Grilled, fried or stuffed – a staple of any Istrian menu.

Anchovies in šavor
White anchovies served with olive oil, local *malvazija* white wine and vinegar; usually served as a starter.

Fuži with truffles
Local pasta dish made with truffles, Parmesan cheese and cream.

Bobiči
Bean stew made with smoked pork, potatoes and sweet corn.

DESIGNERROOM/SHUTTERSTOCK ©

Moon Bay

Strunjan Park Hike with Dazzling Views

Coastline cliffs and dragonflies

The **Strunjan Landscape Park** provides a great excuse to stretch your legs and breathe some of that healing Adriatic air. Head out some 4km east from Piran along the rocky coastline toward the protected natural reserve.

Right after the **Fiesa meres** – a unique shelter to fish, marsh birds and about 20 rare dragonfly species – the path turns a bit inland before returning to the coast at the Strunjan salt pans. From there, the trail ascends to the edge of one of the tallest cliffs on the Adriatic coast, revealing the stunning views. Stop at the **Church of the Vision of St Mary**, one of the most important pilgrimage points in Slovenia. Continuing further (with the coastline on your left), keep an eye out below the cliff for **Moon Bay**, Slovenia's most photogenic (and hardest to reach) beach. If you fancy a dip in its pristine waters, keep in mind it's a steep hike down and then up again – but it's well worth it. From here, turn inland to return towards Portorož or retrace your steps.

This trail is part of the **Circular Strunjan Footpath** and is pretty well marked, so just follow the post signs. Should you have a longer hike in you, finish the entire 12km (three-hour) loop in Portorož and return to Piran by bus.

WHERE TO EAT IN PIRAN

Pri Mari
This usually packed *gostilna* by the sea, away from the city centre, serves fabulous fresh fish. **€€**

Restaurant Neptun
Try the delicious *dondoli* clams (sea truffles) and other top-notch seafood and pasta at this old-school joint. **€€**

Fritolin Pri Cantini
Order fresh fried calamari and other no-fuss dishes from this self-service window under a cosy grape-wine canopy. **€**

Vipava Valley

FOOD | WINE | ARCHITECTURE

One of the top destinations for foodies this side of Italy, charming Vipava has somehow managed to go mostly unnoticed for decades until a couple of great restaurants opened up. Then another, and another. These days, this charming, wine-rich town is home to so many fine eateries, you might as well postpone your dieting resolution until you leave. Consider yourself warned – they take their food and wine seriously here. It often feels harder to find a humble tavern serving a simple bowl of *jota* (traditional sour turnip or sauerkraut stew with potatoes, beans and meat) than stumble on an exquisite culinary experience of five-course menus paired with appropriate wines. Case in point: the Lanthieri Mansion in the heart of Vipava is home to a 'Wine University'. Yes, the School for Viticulture and Enology is one of the few places in Europe where you can actually get a degree in wine. Cheers to that.

GETTING AROUND

The town of Vipava is easily walkable. About a dozen daily buses connect Ljubljana and Vipava; it's a nearly two-hour journey. For touring the valley, it is feasible to rely solely on two-wheeled transport by renting a bike or e-bike from one of the tourist centres or lodgings in town. However, a car will allow you to be more flexible.

Stroll the Venice of Slovenia

Terracotta roofs and 25 bridges

Starting at Vipava's main piazza, check out the dominating baroque **Lanthieri Mansion**, built by the counts of Lanthieri. Today, the palazzo houses a Wine Museum and the School for Viticulture and Enology, aka the 'Wine University'. Strolling around the sleepy town and over the bridges, you will walk past the defensive **Baumkircher Tower**, a part of the Tabor Castle fortification against Turkish and other invasions. Follow a pleasant footpath uphill to the ruins of the old **Vipava Castle**, which was the residence of the knights of Vipava until the mid-14th century. The highlight of the town is the **Church of St Stephen**, with its classicist white-marble altar and beautiful frescoes from the 18th and 19th centuries. Continue to the **Vipava Cemetery** and you will find perhaps the most surprising attraction – two 4000-year-old Egyptian

TOP TIP

Vipava Valley is a cycling and hiking paradise. The apps Slovenia Outdoor and Outdooractive provide a user-friendly way of discovering the numerous hiking and cycling routes in the area. The tourism board's website (vipavavalleyoutdoor.si) is another good source of trails in both Vipava Valley and Goriška Brda.

BEST PLACES TO EAT IN VIPAVA

Gostilna Pri Lojzetu
Chef Tomaž Kavčič dishes out slow-cuisine miracles at this Michelin-star institution. **€€€**

Gostilna Podfarovž
Excellent five-course degustation menus as well as à la carte dishes in a charming location beside one of the seven springs of the Vipava River. **€€**

Gostilna Theodosius
This family-run restaurant in Vrhpolje is well worth the short drive (or long walk) from Vipava. **€€€**

Krhne
Delicious farm-to-table meals, including wine pairings. **€€**

Faladur
Creative seasonal menus along with a great selection of wines. **€€€**

sarcophagi discovered in the tombs at the foot of the Pyramid of Khafren in Giza were somehow 'brought' here by the diplomat and Egyptologist Anton Lavrin, originally from Vipava. Lavrin's family is buried in them. Continuing the tour, make sure to venture all the way to the Renaissance-style **Zemono Manor House**, also commissioned by the noble family of Lanthieri. Today, it houses one of the best fine-dining restaurants in the country, Gostilna Pri Lojzetu.

Keep an eye out for a local *osmica,* a popular pop-up wine and food event in any Slovenian wine-growing region, when local winegrowers and farmers open their cellars or homes to the public for a limited time. Follow the *osmica* schedule at winedineslovenia.com/osmice.

Vipavski Križ to Štanjel

A scenic gourmet tour

From Vipava, head 12km northwest to the hilltop walled village of **Vipavski Križ**. Stroll its charming, narrow alleys until you stumble on **Darovi Vipavske**, a perfectly positioned wine bar on the square, selling local treats like *pršut* and cheese. From there, continue another 10km toward **Branik**, and visit the mighty, cylindrical **Rihemberk Castle**, built in the 13th century, before making your way to the nearby town of **Štanjel**, a medieval architecture pearl made almost entirely from carefully cut stones. You can easily spend half a day touring the town's prehistoric settlements, gardens and art galleries, but make sure to stop for a glass of local wine and some organically produced dry-cured meats from the local Krškopolje (black-belted) pigs and Brkinian cheeses at **Panorama Štanjel**. The incredible views over the valley from its terrace will make it hard not to stay for sunset. Before returning to Vipava, end the day with a marvellous dinner at either Majerija, a great rustic restaurant in Slap, or the beloved **Cejkotova Domačija** in Goče. While walk-ins might get lucky, reservations are recommended.

From Vipavski Križ, a scenic and easy 8km circular trail takes hikers, cyclists or runners through the villages of **Cesta**, **Plače** and **Male Žablje** past pretty vineyards, olive trees, orchards and even an occasional forest. The surface is part tarmac, part gravel, without major inclines or slopes, with Vipavski Križ (176m) as its highest point. The trail is marked with direction boards and provides some great views of the valley.

WHERE TO STAY IN VIPAVA

Guesthouse Koren
Located in the middle of town, and with a wine shop attached, it's as convenient as it gets. **€€**

Majerija
This popular guesthouse, 4km from Vipava, has 10 simple rooms and a great restaurant. **€€**

Theodosius Forest Village
Some of the finest glamping in all of Slovenia, in a pine forest overlooking the Vipava Valley. **€€€**

Novo Mesto

HISTORY | ART | CYCLING

Novo Mesto, with a population of a little over 23,000, is the region's largest and most important city. A direct train link to Ljubljana as well as some very nice hotels and excellent restaurants make this a natural hub for exploring the lower Krka's castles and sights. The town's setting – atop a sharp, scenic bend of the Krka River with its tranquil, turquoise waters – is surprisingly picturesque. The pedestrian-only main square, Glavni trg, is lined with restaurants and cafes. Spend a relaxing afternoon exploring the square and surrounding walkways, the regional museum and a few churches, or better yet, pick up a regional hiking and cycling map from the tourist information centre.

Distances are deceptively short in this part of Slovenia. Major regional attractions like Otočec Castle and even the lovely Šmarješke Toplice spa resort lie within a few hours' walk or bike ride following the Krka along part of the way.

Otočec Castle

GETTING AROUND

Several daily trains run from Ljubljana with onward service to Črnomelj and Metlika. Note that Novo Mesto has two train stations: the main one on Kolodvorska ulica, and little Novo Mesto-Centre on Ljubljanska cesta at the western edge of the Old Town. The centre of town is small and walkable, though parking can be difficult. For destinations outside the centre, book taxis by calling 041 625 108 or 040 550 785. The tourist information centre rents bicycles (from €10 per day).

TOP TIP

The centre of Novo Mesto is closed to motor vehicles. This keeps the commotion of car traffic nicely away from the main square, but it makes it tricky if you're arriving by car. Arrange parking in advance with your hotel and get precise directions for reaching designated parking areas.

SIGHTS
1 Cathedral of St Nicholas
2 Church of St Leonard
3 Dolenjska Museum
4 Jakac House

SLEEPING
5 Center Hotel
6 Hostel Situla

EATING
7 Don Bobi
see 6 Fink & Situla
8 Kralj Matjaž

INFORMATION
9 Tourist Information Centre

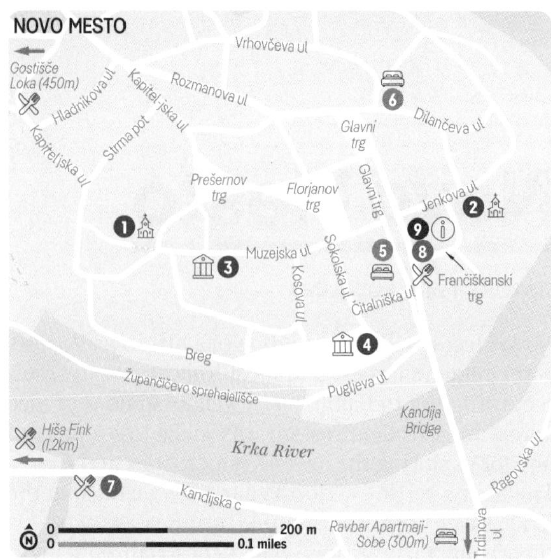

BEST PLACES TO EAT IN NOVO MESTO

Hiša Fink
Refined regional cooking in a scenic locale along the Krka River in the village of Irča, 2km west of the centre. **€€€**

Don Bobi
Delicious Italian food within easy walking distance of Novo Mesto's Old Town. **€€**

Fink & Situla
Inventive takes on local favourites (all gluten-free). Dine under an enormous linden tree in the garden. **€€**

Gostišče Loka
Riverside spot with a huge outdoor terrace covers all the basics: burgers, pasta and risotto. **€€**

Kralj Matjaž
Convenient lunch spot. Decent pizza, cakes, coffee and craft beers on the main square. **€**

Learn Some Local History

Hallstatt princes, Celts and Romans

Novo Mesto was settled during the early Iron Age (around 1000 BCE), and helmets and decorated burial urns unearthed in surrounding areas suggest that Marof Hill, northwest of the Old Town, was once the seat of powerful Hallstatt princes (from the 8th to 4th centuries BCE). The Illyrians and Celts came later, and the Romans maintained a settlement here until the 4th century CE. This fascinating history is on display at the **Dolenjska Museum** in the Old Town. Don't miss the fine bronze *situlae* (pails) from the 3rd or 4th century BCE embossed with battle and hunting scenes, and the Celtic ceramics and jewellery (particularly the bangles of turquoise and blue glass).

The museum also administers the **Jakac House** (at Sokolska ulica 1), which exhibits works by prolific painter and local boy Božidar Jakac (1899–1989). The artist visited dozens of countries in the 1920s and '30s, painting such diverse subjects as Parisian dance halls, Scandinavian port towns, African villages and American skylines. But his best works are of Novo Mesto's markets, people and rumble-tumble wooden riverside houses.

Fabulous Church Art

A Tintoretto in situ

Just beyond the museum, the Gothic **Cathedral of St Nicholas** is Novo Mesto's most important building. It has a 15th-century vaulted presbytery and crypt, plus wall frescoes, a belfry that served as a medieval defence tower, and an altar painting of the patron saint by Venetian master Jacopo Tintoretto (1518–94). Southeast of the main square, the Franciscan **Church of St Leonard** was built by monks fleeing the Turks in Bosnia in 1472. The monastery library has books dating back to the 12th century.

Hike or Bike along the Krka

Sightseeing in slo-mo

Novo Mesto's central location makes it an unbeatable base for exploring the region's most beautiful or important sights at your own pace, on foot or by bike. A logical approach to local sightseeing would be to overnight in Novo Mesto and plan a series of out-and-backs over several days to spots in the surrounding countryside. As a first step, pick up a free copy of Kartografija's *Novo Mesto Cycling and Hiking Trail Map* from the **Tourist Information Centre** (visitnovomesto.si) on the main square. The map outlines 13 cycling trails and five dedicated hiking trails of varying distances and degrees of difficulty (easy, moderate or demanding), with helpful suggestions for meals or wine stops along the way.

The **Thermal Spa trail** is relatively easy and leads to the scenic spa resort of Dolenjske Toplice. The **Bear trail** heads up to the small town of Žužemberk and its 1000-year-old abandoned castle. That trail, helpfully, includes a quick swim in the Krka to cool off. Another recommended ride, the **Šmarjeta trail** is flat for much of its way to the east and takes in both Otočec Castle and the thermal resort at Šmarješke Toplice. As for the dedicated hiking routes, the **Slak trail** includes an important wine-growing area, a hilltop vista, and a stop at a vineyard cottage on the way back for a bite to eat. More adventurous hikers may want to consider the multiday **Trdina trail**, which covers around 160km and takes seven days to finish. There are dozens of variations, many following the pretty Krka River.

As many as 1000 brown bears live in Slovenia and most of them in the Green Karst, specifically in the **Notranjska** and **Kočevsko** forests. Observing them in their natural habitat is usually possible from May to September, when they are not hibernating. Follow an experienced guide deep into the forest, where most bear-spotting outlets have a safe and animal-friendly wooden lookout that is smell-isolated, allowing bears to come into close viewing range. Aside from brown bears, you may often be able to spot foxes, deer, badgers and even wolves.

UNDERRATED NOVO MESTO

Jože Ravbar is a lifelong cyclist and operates the Ravbar Apartmaji-Sobe (ravbar.net) guesthouse in Novo Mesto.

Novo Mesto is beautiful but badly underrated. Many visitors simply stop here for a night on their way to other places. But Novo Mesto offers pretty views over the Krka River, several good restaurants, and is especially suited to active travellers. A new pedestrian bridge over the river is great for taking leisurely walks around town. For people looking for more adventure, several marked cycling and hiking trails lead out into the countryside. Some of the trails follow the Krka and allow you to use Novo Mesto as a base for exploring nearby Otočec Castle and the spas at Dolenjske Toplice and Šmarješke Toplice.

WHERE TO STAY IN NOVO MESTO

Center Hotel
Recently renovated rooms, decent air-con and a lovely setting on Novo Mesto's main square. **€€**

Hostel Situla
One of Slovenia's nicest hostels, built within the walls of an 18th-century townhouse with rooms over five floors. **€**

Ravbar Apartmaji-Sobe
This guesthouse has a bundle of rooms and apartments; all are homely, well-equipped and spotless. **€€**

Maribor

WINE | FESTIVALS | TOWERS

Slovenia's second-largest city was a manufacturing hub in the days of Yugoslavia and doesn't seem to have quite figured out what its next incarnation will be. But there is something bubbling beneath the surface of Maribor, and it's worth taking the time to find it.

The Lent district on the banks of the Drava River is undergoing a transformation, anchored by the oldest grapevine in the world, whose branches still bear fruit every fall. This is a city of rock and roll, of students in cafes that still talk about revolutions, of winemakers who gently coax new flavours out of classic *sipon* and *laški* grapes. This is the city of the Vračko brothers, chefs who have gained international praise yet remain unapologetically faithful to Maribor's iconoclasm. So don't be fooled by its straight face. Maribor is a sly wink from across the room, inviting you in on the joke, ever so grateful to see you there.

GETTING AROUND

As Slovenia's second-largest city and the biggest hub in the east, Maribor is well connected to Ljubljana. Highways connect the two cities in a little over an hour, and trains run throughout the day. Maribor is also the connection point for almost anywhere in eastern Slovenia as well as Austria, Hungary and Croatia. In fact, Zagreb airport is closer than Ljubljana, so it's worth checking the flights (especially for low-cost carriers). The city is ideal for exploring on foot or by bicycle. There are free buses that transport people around the city centre, and information on schedules can be found at the Maribor tourist information centre, where you can also find e-bike rental information and maps of Maribor and surroundings.

A Wine Tour of Maribor

From ancient grape to flying glass

Coming to Maribor and not devoting a day to wine would be like, well, coming to Maribor and not devoting a day to wine. The grape is an essential chapter in the story of Štajerska, or Styrian Slovenia, and although it's been grown since the pre-Roman period, it was only in modern Yugoslavia that Slovenia's wine-growing regions were divided and protected varietals assigned. The east is predominantly white wine, with about 80% of its vineyards devoted to it. You'll find some international grapes around eastern Slovenia, but save your palate for autochthonous varietals such as *sipon* (or *furmint*), Italian Riesling (or Welschriesling), *ranina, traminer* or Blaufränkisch (the most frequent red you'll find).

Old Vine Museum

Start out at the **Old Vine Museum** and pay respects to the 460-year-old Modra kavčina vine, which really does deserve it. The grapevine was planted somewhere in the second half of the 16th century, and the oldest known evidence of it comes in a painting from 1657. It has survived Turkish incursions, Napoleonic invasions, a plague that wiped out nearly all the vines in Europe, two world wars and the breakup of Yugoslavia. Now that's resilience.

Though the vine still produces grapes, the wine is saved for visiting dignitaries and heads of state. Instead, head over to nearby **Vinag 1847**, where a labyrinth cellar dating from 1847 guards an archive of 85,000 bottles. You can't taste all of them but you can certainly try: Vinag offers a variety of guided tours and tastings that range from a walk through the 2km of underground tunnels with two wines, to a larger tasting paired with local foods. If you're so inclined, one of their experts will help you choose an archival bottle to commemorate a special occasion.

TOP TIP

Maribor has free electric transport through the city centre that anyone can use and is equipped to transport people with limited mobility. Call +386 (0)30 700 035 to pre-arrange a pickup, or flag one down in the street. The drivers also make excellent tour guides.

BEST OF MARIBOR FESTIVALS

Festival of Walks
In late March, master storytellers lead walking tours through the city.

Festival Lent
At the end of June, Maribor hosts the largest outdoor party in the country.

Summer Puppet Pier
Every August, Maribor is filled with puppet shows from around the world.

Street Food Festival Tour
This massive tour takes over the streets at the end of summer.

Festival Maribor
Every September, this innovative music festival merges classical and other genres.

St Martin's Day
The Old Vine Festival ends on 11 November, when must turns into wine and Maribor throws a huge party.

BEST BARS AND CAFES IN MARIBOR

HiKoFi Speciality Coffee
HiKoFi feels like exactly the kind of place you want to live above and exactly where you'll go every day you're in town.

Le Vino
The best bar on Maribor's busiest street has a formidable selection of local wines including many of their own.

Rooster Coffee
Home-brewed coffee from local roasters and fabulous brunch menus to be enjoyed on an adorable terrace.

BEST PLACES TO STAY IN MARIBOR

Hotel Maribor
Chic apartments in the historic centre with a focus on sustainability. **€€€**

Fani&Rozi B&B
Family-run B&B with rooms that look out on the Drava and great breakfasts. **€€**

Posestvo Sončni Raj Nesting Resort
Tree houses and other funky dwellings from the folks who brought you the Wine Fountain. **€€€**

Hostel Pekarna
Cheery dorms, rooms and apartments in a complex that used to be a bakery. **€**

Chocolate Village by the River, Luxury Glamping Resort
Your eyes do not deceive you. It's an entire resort dedicated to chocolate, just 5km from Maribor's centre. **€€€**

Plague Tower

Head back overground, where a quick taxi ride will take you to **Fontana Vin** at the Sunny Paradise Estate, 5km outside central Maribor. On a perch overlooking the Styrian hills, you'll be given a specially microchipped wine glass that allows you to access wines from all over the region, which are stored in barrels next to a scenic dining area. If it sounds like something that comes from both the future and the past, it is: the time-honoured tradition of open-air wine tasting and locally produced meats, cheeses, bread and vegetables is mixed with high-tech traceability and sustainable production. But wait, you're thinking: does anything fly here? Well yes, including you if you're so inclined! Food is delivered to guests via flying boxes that arrive on the Wine Fountain platform, and the farm also boasts the longest two-way zip line in Europe. And don't worry, experts are on hand to make sure that both you and your dinner are safely strapped in before either of you take flight.

A WALKING TOUR OF MARIBOR CENTRE

Maribor is a city of stories, and a walk through the centre brings them all to life.

Begin at ❶ **Maribor Synagogue**, one of the oldest still intact in Europe, and today the site of a museum devoted to Slovenian Jewish culture. Continue up Vetrinjska ulica to the ❷ **National Liberation Monument** on Trg Svobode. Built in 1975 by locally born architect Slavko Tihec, the moving piece features the farewells of rebels killed during WWII. It's in front of ❸ **Maribor Castle**, which houses the regional museum and an excellent cafe with seating in the courtyard.

Famous inventor Nikola Tesla took up residence in Maribor in 1878. He spent much of his time at a pub that's since been lost to history, but if you head to Poštna ulica you can imagine the city Tesla might have known. This tiny street is dense with bars and restaurants; sample the local wines at ❹ **Le Vino**. Follow Poštna ulica to Glavni trg, a charming square lined with outdoor cafes. It's also home to the ❺ **Plague Tower**, a white-marble ode erected by 'pious burghers' to commemorate the end of a 1680 plague epidemic.

Stairs lead down to the right of the ❻ **Glavni Most** bridge toward the Lent district on the banks of the Drava. The neighbourhood is undergoing a revamp, with new restaurants, cafes and galleries on both sides of the river, connected by a footbridge.

Take your time strolling along the banks, from the medieval ❼ **Water Tower** on one end, past the ❽ **Old Vine Museum** (p343), Maribor's most famous attraction where you can check out the 400-year-old 'mother' vine, and taste an impressive array of wines from the region, to the perfectly named ❾ **Judgment Tower** on the other.

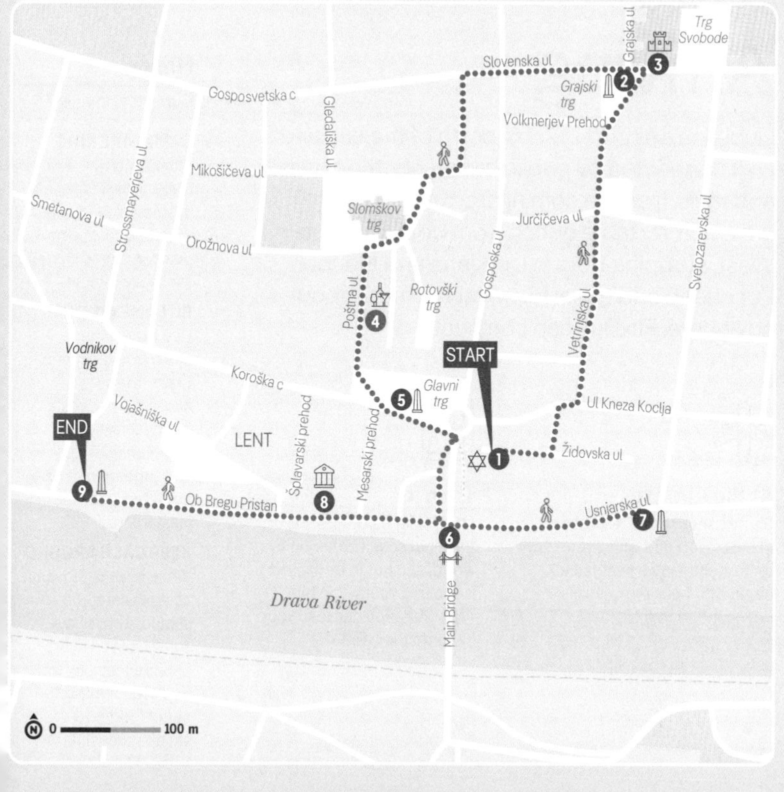

Ljubljana Jože Pučnik Airport

Arriving

Ljubljana's airport is 27km north of the city and well connected by public buses, shuttle buses and taxis. If you're coming from overland, trains are a comfortable option from both East and West, stopping both in Ljubljana and Maribor. For cheap and cheerful travel from just about anywhere, FlixBus can't be beat.

At the Airport

Shuttle services have kiosks at the airport and whisk you to the centre in 30 minutes for about €15. Taxis are quicker but cost €30 to €40.

Train it!

The Bohinj Railway is one of the most scenic rides in the world, and not to be missed if you find yourself in the Alps. Plus, you can load your car onto the train!

Money

Currency: euro €

CARDS ARE KING
Almost anywhere in Slovenia will take card payments, as long as you've got a chip or pincode. Some places even take Bitcoin!

BUT AMEX IS OUT!
Due to the high commission, American Express is not accepted anywhere in Slovenia, even at larger chain shops and supermarkets. Be prepared with Visa or Mastercard.

KEEP CASH AROUND
While most of Slovenia accepts cards, you should always have some cash on hand. This is especially true for outdoor markets, street food, and smaller tourist farms.

Getting Around

Slovenia is a small country and easy to navigate no matter how you choose to travel. If you're driving you can see everything at your own pace, but trains and buses are a viable alternative for anyone looking to travel slow and keep it light.

GET A VIGNETTE

If you're driving on Slovenian motorways and expressways you must have a vignette, or an automatic toll device. You can only buy one through the official website (evinjeta.dars.si) and failure to do so can result in fines of up to €800.

UMOMOS/SHUTTERSTOCK ©

Cycling the Slovenian coast, near Izola

TO THE TRAIN!

Train travel in Slovenia is super convenient – buy tickets online, at the station, or on the train. Unlike many other countries, you do not incur a penalty for buying on board and you don't need to validate your ticket before riding.

GO ELECTRIC

There are nearly 1500 EV charging points in Slovenia, making it really easy to drive an electric or hybrid car. PlugShare has interactive maps on their website to locate charging points, and Google Maps also features the closest station.

SLOVENIA BY BIKE

There are hundreds of kilometres of bike trails in Slovenia that can take you from the mountains to the sea. If you're travelling by car with bikes hitched, there are park&ride points all over the country.

#VANLIFE

Campervan enthusiasts will find over 150 locations to park, whether it's for a brief stop or a few days. Campsites all over the country offer a range of amenities for travellers. Campervans must register for a DarsGo pass for toll booths.

DRIVING ESSENTIALS

Speed limit is 50km/h on residential roads; 90km/h on regional roads; 110km/h on express roads; 130km/h on highways.

From 15 November to 15 March you must have either winter tyres or snow chains in the boot.

Blood alcohol limit for drivers is 0.5 parts per thousand.

1142 001

TOOLKIT

The chapters in this section cover the most important topics you'll need to know about in the Western Balkans. They're full of nuts-and-bolts information and valuable insights to help you understand and navigate the Western Balkans and get the most out of your trip.

Zagreb Train Station (p121), Croatia

Arriving

The Western Balkans is well served by both budget and full-service airlines flying to multiple airports. Each country has its own international airport, with some having several (even tiny Montenegro has two). Buses, trains and ferries also deposit holidaymakers into the region. On top of that, it's possible to enter by car from Italy, Austria, Hungary, Romania, Bulgaria and Greece.

Schengen Area

Slovenia and Croatia are both part of the Schengen Area, which means there are no border checks between the two and their European Union (EU) neighbours (Italy, Austria and Hungary).

Visas

Schengen aside, every country has its own visa regime. You'll need to check the requirements for each place that you're planning to visit. Many nationalities can travel visa-free throughout the Western Balkans.

Airport Facilities

Even the smallest international airports offer free wi-fi and have ATMs (cash machines), cafes and rental-car desks. It's possible to buy local SIMs at some, but not all.

Arriving by Car

At the border you'll usually need to present your vehicle registration/ownership documents and a valid third-party insurance policy such as European Green Card. Check that your policy covers the countries you're visiting.

Public Transport from Airport to City Centre

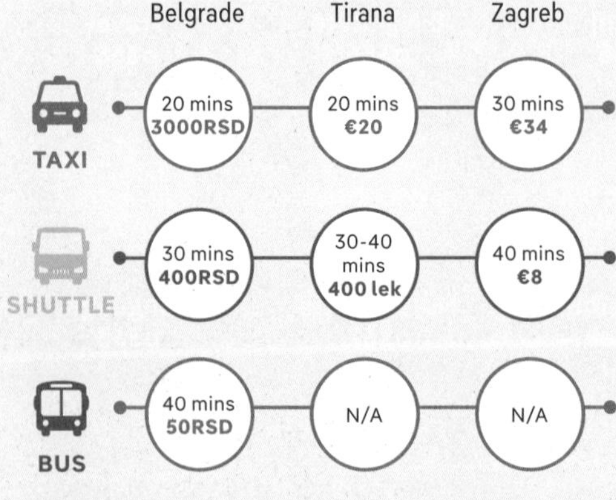

	Belgrade	Tirana	Zagreb
TAXI	20 mins 3000RSD	20 mins €20	30 mins €34
SHUTTLE	30 mins 400RSD	30-40 mins 400 lek	40 mins €8
BUS	40 mins 50RSD	N/A	N/A

KOSOVO–SERBIA BORDER CROSSINGS

While most land borders between Western Balkan nations present no particular problems, the border between Kosovo and Serbia is a special case because Serbia doesn't recognise Kosovo's independence.

There's no problem entering Serbia and crossing to and from Kosovo, as Serbia doesn't acknowledge the Kosovo border as an international one. However, if you enter Kosovo from elsewhere and then attempt to cross into Serbia, this is problematic. As far as Serbia is concerned, you will have entered 'Serbia' illegally, without receiving a valid entry stamp.

It's all a question of the order you travel in, so plan your itinerary accordingly.

Getting Around

Having a vehicle at your disposal will give you access to some truly extraordinary scenic drives, although some aren't for the fainthearted. Buses connect most towns and cities.

TRAVEL COSTS

Car rental
From €45 per day

Petrol
From €1.40 per litre

EV charging
From €0.24 per kWh

Bicycle rental
€8–20 per day

Hiring a Car

It's easy to hire a car from the airports and larger towns; book ahead for the best prices and to save time. Most hire cars have manual transmission; you'll pay a premium for an automatic. A small car will make it easier to negotiate narrow roads.

Road Tolls

Some motorways, tunnels and bridges have tolls. Usually you collect a ticket from a machine on entry and pay at a booth as you leave. In Slovenia, an e-vignette is required (locally rented cars have them). Purchase one online (evinjeta.dars.si) or at a petrol station near the border.

TIP

Ferries play a big role in the transport network in Croatia, including car ferries and high-speed catamarans.

KEEP CALM & CARRY ON

When it comes to driving, the peoples of the Western Balkans aren't immune from the stereotypes of other Mediterranean nations: many drivers speed, tailgate, honk and overtake on blind corners. This is despite the police in some countries being zealous in speed-limit enforcement (sometimes in hope for a bribe). Limits change often and sometimes arbitrarily, but it pays to stick to them even in the face of consternation from behind.

DRIVING ESSENTIALS

Drive on the right

.02

Blood alcohol limit varies per country ranging from 0.02% to 0.05%

Drive with headlights on (even during the day)

Road Conditions

The standard of roads varies but, even in countries where they're well maintained, many are winding and narrow. Larger vehicles such as campervans will struggle on some of the secondary roads. Traffic is also a major headache along the coast in summer.

Buses & Furgons

Bus services in the Western Balkans tend to be extensive, reliable, reasonably comfortable and relatively inexpensive. In Albania, they compete with privately run minibuses known as *furgons*, although these are better suited to unfussy travellers with time to waste as they can be slow, unreliable and uncomfortable.

Trains

In most of the Western Balkans the trains are old and the networks limited. The exception is Slovenia where trains connect many major centres, are more comfortable than buses and can occasionally be cheaper. In Serbia, the high-speed Soko train connects Belgrade to Novi Sad in 36 minutes.

Money

CURRENCY: EURO (€); ALBANIAN LEK (LEK); BOSNIAN CONVERTIBLE MARK (KM); MACEDONIAN DENAR (MKD); SERBIAN DINAR (RSD)

Tipping

Tipping isn't expected but is usually appreciated. In cafes, bars and taxis, round up to the nearest euro. In restaurants, leave up to 10% if you're feeling generous; if you're not completely satisfied with the service, don't leave anything. Same goes for tours. Tipping in hotels is unusual.

Credit Cards

In most countries credit cards are widely accepted for accommodation, petrol and restaurants, but don't rely on them for taxis, cafes, bars and museums. Albania is the exception; it's very much a cash culture and cards are almost never accepted. Kosovo is a little better but cash is preferred.

Digital Payment

The facility to pay by tapping your phone or smartwatch is available in some of the bigger cities but don't rely on it.

Cash

In most countries it pays to have coins and small notes to hand for paying for coffees and the like (essential in Albania).

HOW MUCH FOR A...

museum entry
free–€10

national park entry
€3–40

local bus ticket
€1–2

kayak rental
single/double from €5/10 per hour

HOW TO... Save Money

Students and seniors usually qualify for discounts at museums and other attractions. Look out for special family admission prices: discounts for up to two adults and two children. Some cities offer discount cards bundling together museum entry and public transport, or combo tickets covering multiple sights. If you're not in a rush, take scenic secondary roads to avoid highway tolls.

LOCAL TIP

If you happen to find yourself in a rural area where ATMs are scarce, you can often withdraw cash at the local post office for a fee.

WESTERN BALKANS ON A BUDGET

While prices have shot up, the Western Balkans can still be an affordable destination, especially if you avoid the coast in peak season (July and August). There are some good hostels scattered around and, if there's a group of you, apartment rental can be reasonable. Serves at most restaurants are usually far too big – easy to split between two. Beachside loungers are pricy but it's free to throw down a towel. Monasteries and mosques are always free, and there are plenty of ruined fortresses to hike to.

Accommodation

Private Accommodation

There is a long history of families renting rooms and apartments in these parts. The days of black-clad women holding signs at the bus stations is over, but you'll find a good range of affordable options online. Apartments will always have their own bathroom and at least a kitchenette. Some are downright luxurious, with swimming pools and astonishing views.

Yugoslav-Era Hotels

The explosion of tourism in 1970s and '80s Yugoslavia coincided with the development of a distinctive homegrown style of architecture distinguished by bold, angular shapes. While the whims of fashion have seen many left to languish, some have been restored and are worth seeking out. Thankfully the chain-smoking, surly staff have (mainly) been consigned to memory.

Hostels

Hostels have made a relatively recent appearance on the scene and some great places have sprung up over the last decade – although many didn't survive the pandemic. Some are little different from private rentals split into dorms, but the better custom-built places have well-thought-out communal spaces and some sort of kitchen. Shared bathrooms are the norm.

Mountain Huts & Ethno Villages

Local mountain clubs operate a network of huts offering basic accommodation to hikers; it's essential to arrange them in advance. In some countries (notably Montenegro and Serbia) you will find family-run 'ethno villages', clusters of rustic wooden cabins in remote locations. The facilities can vary widely: from single-room huts sharing toilet facilities to self-contained cottages with kitchens, bathrooms and barbecues.

HOW MUCH FOR A NIGHT IN...

a hostel dorm
from €15

a hotel room
from €60

a one-bedroom apartment
from €40

Camping

Camping conditions can be extremely basic (squat toilets and limited water). However, Slovenia and Croatia have raised the bar. Croatia, in particular, has dozens of large campgrounds offering pleasant bathrooms along with kitchens, pools and restaurants. Both countries have also embraced 'glamping', combining an outdoorsy back-to-nature experience with the kind of amenities normally only offered in five-star hotels.

'THE SEASON' & TOURIST TAXES

A hangover from the Yugoslav days is the idea that tourism should be packed into a tidy 'season', typically summer (when prices peak) but now stretching from around April to October. Outside of these months, it's not unusual for tourism-based businesses to close completely, including some hotels.

In most places accommodation providers are required to collect a tourist tax on behalf of their guests (around €1–2 per person per night, set by the local municipality). It's not always included in the quoted rate.

Family Travel

Throughout the Western Balkans, children are both fussed over and given free rein, making it a stress-free place for a family holiday. The classic combo of sunshine and safe beaches appeals to all ages, and there's plenty of opportunity to escape into nature on hikes, kayaks, bike rides and boat trips.

Getting Around

You'll struggle to get strollers along the cobbled lanes and stairways in the older towns and you'll often find yourself having to trundle them along dangerous roads due to parked cars blocking the footpaths. A baby carrier or sling takes up less luggage space and makes exploring easier. Ask in advance about car seats if you're hiring a car or a taxi.

Eating

You won't often find children's menus, but the ubiquity of child-friendly favourites like pasta, pizza and chips (fries) makes mealtime easy. Bakeries are also a good choice; most kids love *burek* (savoury filo-pastry pie), despite – or because of – the crumbly mess it makes. Fresh fruit is easy to come by. Highchairs are the exception rather than the rule at restaurants.

Accommodation

The better hotels may have cots, cribs and roll-out beds available, but it's best to check in advance. Some of the top-end resorts have dedicated kids' clubs. Self-catering apartments, ethno villages and campgrounds are more affordable options for families.

Concessions

Most sights and activities offer half-price tickets for children under 16. Those under five often pay only a nominal amount or get in for free. Enquire about family tickets, which usually cover two adults and two children.

CHILD-FRIENDLY PICKS

Nikola Tesla Museum (p272)
Guides demonstrate whizz-bang inventions in this interactive Belgrade museum.

Ljubljana Castle (p310)
Ride the funicular to the castle and poke around these Slovenian ruins.

Kravice Waterfalls (p105)
Escape the Hercegovina heat in the emerald waters.

Osum Canyon (p71)
Whitewater rafting near Berat in Albania.

Memo Museum (p132)
Get hands-on with socialist-era computers, typewriters and cassette recorders in Pula, Croatia.

OLD TOWNS & CRUMBLING RUINS

Only the most imagination-deprived grown-ups could fail to be transported into the distant past by the streetscapes of the Western Balkans' old walled towns. The car-less streets and squares offer little princesses and knights the chance to charge around in relative safety.

Older kids will love the opportunity to hike to the ruins of forgotten castles, but be aware that health and safety officers are as rare as dragons in these parts. Don't expect gaping holes to be fenced off or well shafts to be covered.

Health & Safe Travel

INSURANCE

Even where health insurance isn't legally required, it is strongly advised. Consider a policy that covers you for the worst possible scenario, such as an accident requiring an emergency flight home. In Croatia and Slovenia, EU citizens are encouraged to carry their European Health Insurance Card (EHIC), which they can present for free emergency health care.

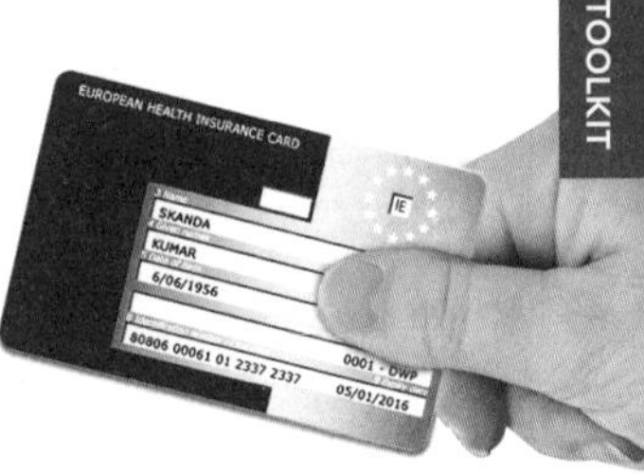

Conflict & Land Mines

You're best to avoid the north of Kosovo near the border with Serbia due to recent skirmishes between ethnic Serbs and NATO peacekeepers (KFOR). There are still minefields in parts of Bosnia and Hercegovina and Kosovo dating from the wars of the 1990s; look out for warning signs (red with skull and crossbones).

Wildlife

Some parts of the Western Balkans are genuinely wild, and bears, wolves and lynx do lurk in remote corners. Relax – you're extremely unlikely to ever actually come across one. You may see snakes, though. There are over a dozen species, but only three of them are venomous: the common adder, karst adder and nose-horned viper (considered Europe's most dangerous).

TAP WATER

Tap water is generally drinkable, unless you're staying in a remote location without a town supply. If you're unsure, ask.

SWIM SAFELY

Green Flag
It's safe to swim.

Yellow Flag
Caution. Moderate surf.

Purple Flag
Marine life spotted (eg jellyfish). Exercise caution.

Red Flag
Danger. Do not enter the water.

Ticks, Jellyfish & Sea Urchins

Ticks can be found in the forests and grasslands, so it pays to use repellents and cover exposed skin. Jellyfish and sea urchins are common in the Adriatic. Not all jellyfish species sting but it's best to avoid swimming if you spot them. Prevent the pain of stepping on spiky urchins by wearing swimming shoes.

SNAKE BITES

To avoid getting bitten, do not walk barefoot or stick your hands into holes. Half of those bitten by venomous snakes are not actually injected with poison (envenomed). If bitten, immobilise the limb with a splint, firmly apply a bandage over the site and seek medical help. Do not apply a tourniquet, or cut or suck the bite.

Food, Drink & Nightlife

When to Eat

Doručak/Zajtrk/Mëngjes (6–9am) Breakfast is usually light; just coffee and bread with jam or cheese.

Marenda/Gablec/Malica (10am–12.30pm) People often take this mid-morning snack to stave off lunch cravings.

Ručak/Kosilo/Drekë (1–3pm) Lunch is traditionally the main family meal. Restaurants serve lunch all afternoon.

Večera/Večerja/Darkë (7–9pm) Dinner is typically lighter, possibly just bread with cured meats, cheese and olives.

Where to Eat

Konoba/gostionica/gostilna/gostišče An informal family-run tavern serving local cuisine.

Restoran/restavracija/restorant A title reserved for more upmarket or nontraditional restaurants.

Pekara/pekarnica Bakery serving bread and pastries, savoury and sweet.

Buregdžinica/byrektorë *Burek* (savoury filo pie; pictured) specialists.

Pečenjara Roast meat specialists, especially spit roasts.

Pizzeria An informal restaurant that also often serves dishes other than pizza.

Slastičarna/poslastičarnica/slaščičarna A pastry shop selling cakes and pastries, and often ice cream and coffee.

MENU DECODER

Bijelo vino/belo vino/verë e kuqe White wine
Čaj/çaj Tea, usually herbal
Crno vino/verë e bardhë Red wine
Domaće Domestic, ie local or homemade
Glavna jela/glavna jed/kursi kryesor Main course
Govedina/mish kau/mish lope Beef
Hladna Cold
Hleb/hljeb/kruh/bukë Bread
Hobotnica/oktapodi Octopus
Jagnjetina/qengji Lamb
Jaje/vezë Egg
Jegulja/ngjala Eel
Jelovnik/jedilni list/menuja Menu
Kafa/kava/kafe Coffee
Krap/karpe Carp
Krompir/patate/kërtolla Potato
Lignje/kallamar Squid
Masline/ullinjtë Olives
Med/mjalt Honey
Meso/mish Meat
Pastrmka/postrv Trout
Piletina/piščanec/mish pule Chicken
Pivo/birrë Beer
Povrće/perime Vegetables
Predjelo/predjed Starter
Pršut/proshutë Prosciutto
Punjene Stuffed
Riba/riblja/peshk Fish
Salate/solate/salatë Salads
Sezonska Seasonal
Sir/djathë Cheese
Sok/lëng Juice
Supa/juha/čorba/supë Soup
Svinjetina/svinjina/mish derri Pork
Teletina/mish viçi Veal
Vegetarijanska/vegjetarian Vegetarian
Voda/ujë Water

HOW TO... Order Seafood

On the coast, seafood restaurants offer a selection of fish soups and stews, seafood risottos, and grilled squid and fish. Inland, freshwater fish such as trout, carp and eel are the norm. At certain times of the year (especially in the interior) dried, marinated or smoked fish may take the place of fresh.

Whole fish is usually priced by the kilogram. At better restaurants you'll be presented with a tray of fish at your table to select from. It's all done with great theatricality, and waiters will usually suggest the fish they consider best. However, local serves are huge, so don't be afraid to ask for something smaller. To avoid paying more than you'd like, ask the approximate weight before deciding. When the grilled fish returns, the performance continues as it and its accompaniments are silver-served to your plate.

HOW MUCH FOR A...

glass of wine
€2–9

beer
€1.50–5

espresso
€1.30–2

soup
€2.50–3.50

burek
€1

main course in a fancy restaurant
€16–25

slice of cake or baklava
€2.50–6

HOW TO... Order & Pay

Serving staff in the Western Balkans may be older and more formally dressed than you're used to, and they're almost always men. While this may suggest that the role is held in greater esteem, it doesn't always equate to better service. In fact there are plenty of things about the local ways of doing things that visitors can find frustrating.

Whether you're in a restaurant or in a bar, keep note of your waiter, as they're the ones responsible for taking all of your orders and settling your bill. There's little point flagging down another member of staff if yours has mysteriously gone AWOL.

When the server delivers your order, they'll drop a bill into a little glass on the table, which they'll then tot up when you're ready to leave. This is a legal requirement, in case a tax inspector drops by. If your waiter is about to finish their shift they may ask you to settle up, but that doesn't mean you're expected to leave. The old bills will disappear and a new waiter will start from scratch.

When you're ready to go, don't be surprised if your waiter is nowhere to be seen or it's impossible to catch their eye. This can be infuriating, especially if you're in a rush. On the other hand, you'll never feel like you're being rushed out.

Take a Seat

In bars, take a seat and wait to be served. While bar staff in tourist areas are used to foreigners coming up to the counter to order, it's not usually the done thing.

GOING OUT

Throughout the Western Balkans, locals love to hang out in cafes. In warm weather, tables spill out onto the streets and groups of friends sit around for hours, chatting and watching the passing parade. You'll never feel hurried to vacate your table. In fact, it's perfectly acceptable to sit on a single drink for as long as you like. If you're heading out with locals, be aware that the person doing the inviting usually does the paying.

Meeting over breakfast or brunch isn't common, although places in touristy areas usually do offer some cooked breakfast options for travellers (omelettes being the most common).

In the golden hour before sunset, locals partake in the ritual the Italians know as *passeggiata* – a long leisurely stroll along the main street or square, stopping along the way to chat with friends and acquaintances. There's no age limit on this simple pleasure. Toddlers potter about merrily while their older siblings kick a ball around and their grandparents reminisce with distant cousins.

In summer, you'll often encounter live music in the squares and on outdoor stages. Keep an eye out for posters advertising performances.

Nightclubs here are quite different from what you'll find in London, New York or Sydney. Rather than the focus being on a packed dancefloor, you'll usually find most people standing in small groups around tiny round tables. Flashy lads order whole bottles of spirits to share with their mates but in some places local women don't tend to drink much, if at all.

Responsible Travel

Climate Change & Travel

It's impossible to ignore the impact we have when travelling, and the importance of making changes where we can. Lonely Planet urges all travellers to engage with their travel carbon footprint. There are many carbon calculators online that allow travellers to estimate the carbon emissions generated by their journey; try resurgence.org/resources/carbon-calculator.html. Many airlines and booking sites offer travellers the option of offsetting the impact of greenhouse gas emissions by contributing to climate-friendly initiatives around the world. We continue to offset the carbon footprint of all Lonely Planet staff travel, while recognising this is a mitigation more than a solution.

Regional Variation

Slovenians and Croatians take sustainability seriously but sadly this is far from the norm in the Western Balkans. Fly tipping is common, and illegal dumps are regularly washed into the rivers during heavy rains.

If you care for bears, it's possible to take a wildlife-watching tour with a park ranger in Serbia's Tara National Park and to visit the Kuterevo refuge for orphaned bears in Croatia.

Outside of the major towns and cities, almost all accommodation and hospitality businesses are owned and operated by local families, meaning your tourist dollars are directly supporting the community.

Recycling

Slovenians take special pride in reducing waste. You can help out by sorting and disposing of your own waste into proper colour-coded bins. In most of the other countries, recycling is difficult to access.

Spread the Love

Many of the seaside towns are filled to the gills every summer. You can avoid contributing to overtourism by visiting other regions which get a fraction of the tourists.

With a little bit of planning, it's possible to get to most places you might want to go by bus. In Croatia it's easy to island-hop by ferry.

Go Loco for Local

Channel money directly to small-scale producers by shopping at roadside stalls and green markets, and visiting village wineries. Traditional treats include prosciutto, honey, cheese and various fruit liqueurs and spirits.

Bike-share schemes in the big cities are cheap and easy on the environment.

Many towns have drinking fountains where you can refill your water bottles.

Avoid Cruise Ships

Cruise ships are contributing hugely to overtourism in places like Dubrovnik and Kotor. If you're committed to a cruise, consider exploring independently when you arrive and thus supporting local businesses directly.

Leg Power

The region is criss-crossed by long-distance hiking and biking trails. Some summit the mountains and hills, other follow the coast and waterways, but all promise unforgettable insights into some of Europe's most beautiful landscapes.

12th

Croatia and Slovenia score highly in world sustainability rankings. In 2023, Croatia was ranked 12th and Slovenia 13th in the UN's Sustainable Development Report. In contrast, Montenegro (the self-declared 'ecological state') had the lowest ranking in Europe (67th).

Care for Trails

If you see plastic bottles or anything else that doesn't belong in the natural surroundings when you're hiking, consider taking it out with you and binning it (preferably in a recycling bin).

Solar Energy Benches

Look out for solar-powered smart benches in towns across Croatia and parts of Montenegro. You can recharge your phone or connect to the internet while taking a break from sightseeing.

RESOURCES

wwfadria.org
Region-wide outpost of the WWF.

slovenia-green.si
Promotes environmentally friendly practices in tourism in Slovenia.

dalmatia-green.com
Find eco-friendly accommodation in Dalmatia.

CLOCKWISE FROM TOP LEFT: NATALIKAVA/SHUTTERSTOCK ©, PIXSELL/ALAMY STOCK PHOTO ©, ZORAN PAJIC/SHUTTERSTOCK ©

LGBTIQ+ Travellers

Aside from relatively tolerant Slovenia, the Western Balkans is deeply homophobic and life for local gays, lesbians and transpeople can be extremely difficult. Though attitudes are changing, most prefer to stay under the radar for fear of harassment or violence. That said, travellers are unlikely to encounter problems as long as they're able to be reasonably discreet.

Pride

Pride celebrations take place in major cities around the region, with **Tirana** kicking things off in May, followed by **Pristina** (June), **Split** (June), **Zagreb** (June), **Ljubljana** (June), **Sarajevo** (June), **Belgrade** (September) and **Podgorica** (October). While violence has marred such events in the past, recent parades have taken place without major incidents. In 2022, Belgrade became the first city in Southeastern Europe to host Europride. Serbian President Aleksandar Vučić initially banned the parade but eventually relented and an estimated 10,000 people took part.

LEGAL SITUATION

Yugoslavia (including most of its former republics) decriminalised homosexuality in 1977, putting it well ahead of most of the world. In Albania, however, consensual same-sex encounters were punishable by up to 10 years in prison right up until 1995. Antidiscrimination laws have subsequently been enacted in all Western Balkan countries. In 2023 Slovenia became the first to permit same-sex marriage.

Bars & Clubs

The best scenes can be found in Belgrade (Mercury, Smiley Bar, Club Musk, Club Pleasure, XL), Zagreb (Hot Pot, Rush) and Ljubljana (Klub Tiffany). Dubrovnik also has one gay bar (Milk). You won't find a single such venue in Albania, Bosnia & Hercegovina, Kosovo, Montenegro or North Macedonia.

MAKING CONNECTIONS

In places where there are no dedicated venues, gay and bisexual men tend to connect via apps or take their chances at a handful of cruisy parks and clothing-optional beaches (caution is advised). Lesbians will find it harder to access the local community.

Serbia's Lesbian PM

In 2017, Ana Brnabić became Serbia's first female prime minister and she is thought to be the first person in the world to head a government while in a same-sex relationship. Ironically, such relationships are not legally recognised in Serbia.

ACCOMMODATION

Throughout the region it is now illegal to discriminate when providing services, including accommodation. You're unlikely to have any problems checking into hotels with your partner, although you might strike the odd surly staff member. Private accommodation is usually fine as well; owners are mindful of online reviews. If you're discreet, they'll probably choose to presume you're straight; sharing beds with friends isn't unheard of here.

Accessible Travel

Provisions for people with disabilities in the region range from reasonable in Slovenia to 'working on it' in Croatia, to very little in most other places. The mobility-impaired will find the many cobbled lanes and steps extremely challenging.

Accessible Beaches

Download the handy Plaja Beach Finder app (plaja.hr) for a list of accessible beaches across Croatia. Some like Borak Beach near Bol have special chair lifts to access the water.

Airport

Most of the airports will provide services for passengers with accessibility issues but require 48 hours notice of requirements. Ljubljana Airport's main Terminal A opened in 2021 and meets modern accessibility standards.

Accommodation

Wheelchair-accessible rooms can be hard to find and tend to be limited to top-end hotels. Newer and bigger hotels in Croatia and Slovenia will normally have at least one specially designed room available.

RESOURCES

Balkan Museums Access Group (accessible.bmuseums.net) Provides an interactive map of museums and heritage sites throughout the Balkans that are accessible to people with disabilities.

Visit Ljubljana (visitljubljana.com) The city's tourist information portal has a special section devoted to visitors with special needs and mobility issues.

Visit Zagreb (visitzagreb.hr) Has a section on accessible attractions in the Croatian capital.

FERRIES

While Croatian passenger ferries operated by TP Line and Kapetan Luka are fully accessible and fitted with ramps, only some Jadrolinija car ferries are equipped with lifts. However, people with reduced mobility have the right to free assistance.

Footpath Obstacles

It's not uncommon for cars to park on footpaths (presuming there is a footpath in the first place), making things exceptionally difficult for wheelchair users.

Public Transport

In Croatian cities such as Zagreb, Split and Dubrovnik there are kneeling buses and low-floor trams. In Slovenia, passengers requiring special assistance are advised to contact operators 48 hours ahead of travel.

PARKING PERMITS

If you have an EU disability parking permit from your country of residence, it's valid in Slovenia and Croatia. As long as it's displayed, you have the same parking rights as local residents.

Over the past decade, Slovenia has taken steps to make the most popular sights accessible to everyone. These include Ljubljana Castle, reached via wheelchair-friendly funicular, and the country's most-visited attraction, Postojna Cave. For a complete overview, see slovenia.info/en/plan-your-trip.

Nuts & Bolts

OPENING HOURS

Opening hours can vary throughout the year and differ between countries and regions. The following are rough estimates:

Banks 8am–5pm Monday to Friday, closing for lunch in some countries and opening Saturday mornings in others.

Bars 10am–midnight or 2am

Cafes 7am–11pm

Restaurants 10am–10pm

Shopping centres 9am–10pm

Supermarkets 7am–9pm

Smoking

Although it may not be immediately apparent, smoking is banned in indoor public spaces in many countries including in restaurants, bars, shops and public transport.

Toilets

Sit-down toilets are the norm, though you'll still occasionally find squat toilets.

Weights & Measures

All countries use the metric system. Decimal places are indicated by commas.

GOOD TO KNOW

Time zone
GMT+1

Country calling codes
355 (Albania), 387 (BiH), 385 (Croatia), 383 (Kosovo), 382 (Montenegro), 389 (North Macedonia), 381 (Serbia), 386 (Slovenia)

Emergency number
112

Electricity

230V/50Hz

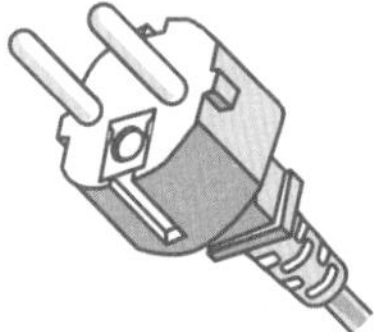

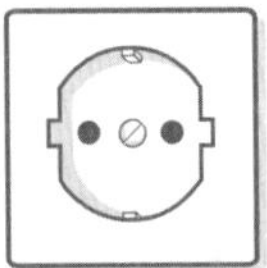

Type F
230V/50Hz

PUBLIC HOLIDAYS

Some countries with mixed populations allow citizens to choose which religious holidays they celebrate. Each country also has its own national and cultural days. The situation in Bosnia and Hercegovina is especially complicated with the Federation celebrating different holidays to the Republika Srpska.

SHARED BY ALL:

New Year's Day 1 January

Labour Day 1 May

IN CATHOLIC AREAS:

Easter March or April

Assumption 15 August

All Saints' Day 1 November

Christmas 25 December

IN ORTHODOX AREAS:

Christmas 7 January

Easter March, April or May

IN MUSLIM AREAS:

Ramadan Bajram/Eid al-Fitr June

Kurban Bajram/Eid al-Adha August or September

Language

Albania, Bosnia & Herzegovina, Croatia, Montenegro, North Macedonia, Serbia and Slovenia each have their own national languages (Albanian, Croatian, Bosnian, Montenegrin, Macedonian, Serbian and Slovenian), although several have mutliple official and regional languages spoken in different areas. In Kosovo, the official languages are Serbian and Albanian.

ALBANIA

In Albanian – also understood in Kosovo and North Macedonia – *ew* is pronounced as 'ee' with rounded lips, *uh* as the 'a' in 'ago', *dh* as the 'th' in 'that', *dz* as the 'ds' in 'adds', and *zh* as the 's' in 'pleasure'. Also, *ll* and *rr* are pronounced stronger than when they are written as single letters.

Basics

Hello. Tungjatjeta. *toon·dya·tye·ta*
Goodbye. Mirupafshim. *mee·roo·paf·sheem*
Yes. Po. *po*
No. Jo. *yo*
Please. Ju lutem. *yoo loo·tem*
Thank you. Faleminderit. *fa·le·meen·de·reet*
What's your name? Si quheni? *see choo·he·nee*
My name is ... Unë quhem ... *oo·nuh choo·hem ...*
Do you speak English? A flisni anglisht? *a flees·nee ang·leesht*
I don't understand. Unë nuk kuptoj. *oo·nuh nook koop·toy*

Emergencies

Help! Ndihmë! *ndeeh·muh*
Go away! Ik! *eek*
I'm ill. Jam i/e sëmurë. (m/f) *yam ee/e suh·moo·ruh*
Call the doctor/police! Thirrni doktorin/policinë! *theerr·nee dok·to·reen/po·lee·tsee·nuh*

Eating & Drinking

What would you recommend? Çfarë më rekomandoni? *chfa·ruh muh re·ko·man·do·nee*
I'll have... Dua... *doo·a*
Cheers! Gëzuar! *guh·zoo·ar*
I'd like the bill/menu, please. Më sillni faturën/menunë, ju lutem. *muh seell·nee fa·too·ruhn/ me·noo·nuh yoo loo·tem*

Shopping & Services

I'm looking for ... Po kërkoj për ... *po kuhr·koy puhr ...*
How much is it? Sa kushton? *sa koosh·ton*
Cheers! Gëzuar! *guh·zoo·ar*
That's too expensive. Është shumë shtrenjtë. *uhsh·tuh shoo·muh shtreny·tuh*

NUMBERS

1 **një** *nyuh*
2 **dy** *dew*
3 **tre** *tre*
4 **katër** *ka·tuhr*
5 **pesë** *pe·suh*
6 **gjashtë** *dyash·tuh*
7 **shtatë** *shta·tuh*
8 **tetë** *te·tuh*
9 **nëntë** *nuhn·tuh*
10 **dhjetë** *dhye·tuh*

BOSNIA & HERCEGOVINA

The official languages are Bosnian, Croatian and Serbian; the guide below is for Bosnian. The official writing system uses both the Roman and Cyrillic alphabets (see p369 for more on the Cyrillic alphabet).

Basics

Hello. Zdravo/Здраво *zdra·vo*

Goodbye. Doviđenja/Довиђења *do-vee-dje-nya*

Yes. Da/Да *da*

No. Ne/Не *ne*

Please. Molim/Молим *mo·lim*

Thank you. Hvala/Хвала *hva·la*

Excuse me. Izvinite/Извините *iz·vee·nee·te*

Sorry. Žao mi je/Жао ми је *zha·o mi ye*

What's your name?
Kako se zovete/zoveš? (pol/inf)
Како се зовете/зовеш?
ka·ko se zo·ve·te/zo·vesh

My name is ...
Zovem se .../ Зовем се ... *zo·vem se*

Do you speak English?
Govorite/Govoriš li engleski? (pol/inf)
Говорите/Говориш ли енглески?
go·vo·ri·te/go·vo·rish li en·gle·ski

I don't understand.
Ne razumijem./Не разумијем.
ne ra·zu·mi·yem

Shopping & Services

I'm looking for...
Tražim ... / Тражим...
tra·zhim

How much is it?
Koliko košta ...? / Колико кошта ...?
ko·li·ko kosh·ta

That's too expensive.
To je preskupo. / То је прескупо.
to ye pre·sku·po

Emergencies

Help! Upomoć!/Упомоћ! *u·po·moch*

Go away! Idite!/Идите! *i·di·te*

Call ...! Zovite ...!/Зовите ...! *zo·vi·te*

a doctor ljekara/љекара *lye·ka·ra*

the police policiju/полицију. *po·li·tsi·yu*

I'm lost.
Izgubljen/Izgubljena sam. (m/f)
Изгубљен/Изгубљена сам. (m/f)
iz·gub·lyen/iz·gub·lyena sam

I'm ill.
Ja sam bolestan/bolesna. (m/f)
Ја сам болестан/болесна. (m/f)
ya sam bo·le·stan/bo·le·sna

Eating & Drinking

What would you recommend?
Šta biste preporučili?
Шта бисте препоручили?
shta bi·ste pre·po·ru·chi·li

Do you have vegetarian food?
Da li imate vegetarijanski obrok?
Да ли имате вегетаријански оброк?
da li i·ma·te ve·ge·ta·ri·yan·ski o·brok

Cheers! Živjeli!/Живјели! *zhi·vye·li*

I'd like the bill/menu please.
Mogu li dobiti račun/jelovnik, molim?
Могу ли добити рачун/јеловник, молим?
mo·gu li do·bi·ti ra·chun/ye·lov·nik mo·lim

NUMBERS

1 **jedan** **један** *ye·dan*

2 **dva/два** *dva*

3 **tri/три** *tri*

4 **četiri** **четири** *che·ti·ri*

5 **pet/пет** *pet*

6 **šest/шест** *shest*

7 **sedam/седам** *se·dam*

8 **osam/осам** *o·sam*

9 **devet/девет** *de·vet*

10 **deset/десет** *de·set*

CROATIA

In Croatian, every letter is pronounced and its sound does not vary from word to word.

Basics

Hello. Dobar dan. *do·bar dan*

Goodbye. Zbogom. *zbo·gom*

Yes. Da. *da*

No. Ne. *ne*

Please. Molim. *mo·lim*

Thank you. Hvala vam/ti (pol/inf). *hva·la vam/ti*

Excuse me. Oprostite. *o·pro·sti·te*

Sorry. Žao mi je. *zha·o mi ye*

What's your name? Kako se zovete/zoveš? (pol/inf) *ka·ko se zo·ve·te/zo·vesh*

My name is ... Zovem se ... *zo·vem se*

Do you speak English? Govorite/Govoriš li engleski? (pol/inf) *go·vo·ri·te/go·vo·rish li en·gle·ski*

I don't understand. Ne razumijem. *ne ra·zu·mi·yem*

Directions

Where's (the station)?
Gdje je (stanica)? *gdye ye (sta·ni·tsa)*

What's the address?
Koja je adresa? *koy·a ye a·dre·sa*

Could you please write it down?
Možete li to napisati?/Možeš li to napisati? (pol/inf) *mo·zhe·te li to na·pi·sa·ti/mo·zhesh li to na·pi·sa·ti*

Can you show me (on the map)?
Možete li mi to pokazati (na karti)? *mo·zhe·te li mi to po·ka·za·ti (na kar·ti)*

10 Phrases to Sound Like a Local

Šta ima? – What's up?

Kužim/Ne kužim – I understand./I don't understand.

To je fora! – That's cool!

To je mrak! – That's awesome!

Idemo na cugu – Let's go for a drink.

To je puno love – That's a lot of money.

Nema šanse! – No way!

Nema veze – Never mind

Idemo na klopu – Let's go for some food.

Nema frke – No problem.

Time

What time is it? Koliko je sati? *ko·li·ko ye sa·ti*

It's (10) o'clock. (Deset) je sati. *(de·set) ye sa·ti*

Half past (10). (Deset) i po. *(de·set) i po*

morning jutro. *yu·tro*

afternoon popodne. *po·pod·ne*

evening večer. *ve·cher*

yesterday jučer. *yu·cher*

today danas. *da·nas*

tomorrow sutra. *su·tra*

Emergencies

Help! Upomoć! *u·po·moch*

Go away! Maknite se! *mak·ni·te se*

Call ...! Zovite ...! *zo·vi·te*

a doctor liječnika *li·yech·ni·ka*

the police policiju. *po·li·tsi·yu*

Eating & Drinking

What would you recommend?
Što biste nam preporučili? *shto bi·ste nam pre·po·ru·chi·li*

Cheers! Živjeli! *zhi·vye·li*

I'd like the bill please.
Mogu li dobiti račun, molim? *mo·gu li do·bi·ti ra·chun mo·lim*

DONATIONS TO ENGLISH

Did you know that the words Dalmatian and cravat come from Croatian?

NUMBERS

1 **jedan** *ye·dan*

2 **dva** *dva*

3 **tri** *tri*

4 **četiri** *che·ti·ri*

5 **pet** *pet*

6 **šest** *shest*

7 **sedam** *se·dam*

8 **osam** *o·sam*

9 **devet** *de·vet*

10 **deset** *de·set*

MONTENEGRO

The official language of Montenegro is Montenegrin, but other languages used in the country include Albanian, Bosnian, Croatian and Serbian.

Basics

Hello. Zdravo. *zdra*·vo
Goodbye. Doviđenja. do·vi·*je*·nya
Yes. Da. da
No. Ne. ne
Please. Molim. *mo*·leem
Thank you. Hvala. *hva*·la
Excuse me. Oprostite. o·*pro*·stee·te
Sorry. Žao mi je. *zha*·o mee ye
What's your name? Kako se zovete /zoveš? (pol/inf) *ka*·*ko se zo*·*ve*·*te/zo*·*vesh*
My name is ... Zovem se ... *zo*·vem se...
Do you speak English? Govorite li (engleski)? *go*·vo·ree·te lee (*en*·gle·skee)
I don't understand. Ne razumijem. ne ra·*zoo*·mee·yem

Directions

Where's...? Gdje je...? gdye ye...
What's the address? Koja je adresa? *ko*·ya ye a·*dre*·sa
Can you show me (on the map)? Možete li da mi pokažete (na mapi)? *mo*·zhe·te lee da mee *po*·ka·zhe·te (na *ma*·pee)

Signs

Ulaz Entrance
Izlaz Exit
Toaleti/WC Toilets
Muški Men
Ženski Women
Otvoreno Open
Zatvoreno Closed
Zabranjeno Prohibited

Time

What time is it? Koliko je sati? ko·*lee*·ko ye *sa*·tee
It's (10) o'clock. (Deset) je sati. (*de*·set) ye *sa*·tee
Half past (10). (Deset) i po. (*de*·set) ee po
morning jutro. *yoo*·tro
afternoon poslijepodne. *po*·slee·ye·*pod*·ne
evening veče. *ve*·che
yesterday juče. *yoo*·che
today danas. *da*·nas
tomorrow sutra. *soo*·tra

Emergencies

Help! Upomoć! *oo*·po·moch
Leave me alone! Ostavite me na miru! *o*·sta·vee·te me na *mee*·roo
I'm ill. Ja sam bolestan/bolesna. (m/f) ya sam *bo*·le·stan/*bo*·le·sna
Call a doctor! Zovite ljekara! *zo*·vee·te lye·*ka*·ra
Call the police! Zovite policiju! *zo*·vee·te po·*lee*·tsee·yoo

Eating & Drinking

What would you recommend? Šta biste preporučili? shta *bee*·ste pre·po·*roo*·chee·lee
That was delicious. To je bilo izvrsno. to ye *bee*·lo *eez*·vr·sno
Please bring the menu/bill. Molim vas donesite jelovnik/račun. *mo*·leem vas do·*ne*·see·te *ye*·lov·neek/*ra*·choon

NUMBERS

1 **jedan** *ye*·dan
2 **dva** *dva*
3 **tri** *tree*
4 **četiri** *che*·tee·ree
5 **pet** *pet*
6 **šest** *shest*
7 **sedam** *se*·dam
8 **osam** *o*·sam
9 **devet** *de*·vet
10 **deset** *de*·set

NORTH MACEDONIA

Macedonian is written using the Cyrillic alphabet. Note that *dz* is pronounced as the 'ds' in 'adds', *zh* as the 's' in 'pleasure', and *r* is rolled.

Basics

Hello. Здраво *zdra·vo*
Goodbye. До гледање *do gle·da·nye*
Yes. Да *da*
No. Не *ne*
Please. Молам *mo·lam*
Thank you. Благодарам *bla·go·da·ram*
Excuse me. Извините *iz·vee·nee·te*
Sorry. Простете *pros·te·te*

What's your name?
Како се викате/викаш?
ka·ko se vi·ka·te/vi·kash

My name is ... Јас се викам ... *yas se vi·kam ...*

Do you speak English?
Зборувате ли англиски? *zbo·ru·va·te li an·glis·ki*

I don't understand.
Јас не разбирам. *yas ne raz·bi·ram*

Emergencies

Help! Помош! *po·mosh*
Go away! Одете си! *o·de·te si*

I'm lost. Се загубив. *se za·gu·biv*

I'm ill. Јас сум болен/болна. (m/f)
yas sum bo·len/bol·na

Eating & Drinking

What would you recommend?
Што препорачувате вие?
shto pre·po·ra·chu·va·te vi·e

Cheers! На здравје! *na zdrav·ye*

I'd like the bill/menu please.
Ве молам сметката/мени.
ve mo·lam smet·ka·ta/me·ni

Waxing Cyrillical

The following list shows the letters of the Macedonian and Serbian/Montenegrin Cyrillic alphabets. The letters are common to all languages unless otherwise specified.

Cyrillic	Sound	Pronunciation
А а	a	short as the 'u' in 'cut' long as in 'father'
Б б	b	as in 'but'
В в	v	as in 'van'
Г г	g	as in 'go'
Д д	d	as the 'd' in 'dog'
Ѓ ѓ	j	as in 'judge' (Macedonian only)
Ђ ђ	j	as in 'judge' (Serbian/Montenegrin only)
Е е	e	short as in 'bet' long as in 'there'
Ж ж	zh	as the 's' in 'measure'
З з	z	as in 'zoo'
Ѕ ѕ	dz	as the 'ds' in 'suds' (Macedonian only)
И и	i	short as in 'bit' long as in 'marine'
Ј ј	y	as in 'young'
К к	k	as in 'kind'
Л л	l	as in 'lamp'
Љ љ	ly	as the 'lli' in 'million'
М м	m	as in 'mat'
Н н	n	as in 'not'
Њ њ	ny	as the 'ny' in 'canyon'
О о	o	short as in 'hot' long as in 'for'
П п	p	as in 'pick'
Р р	r	as in 'rub' (but rolled)
С с	s	as in 'sing'
Т т	t	as in 'ten'
Ќ ќ	ch	as in 'check' (Macedonian only)
Ћ ћ	ch	as in 'check' (Serbian/Montenegrin only)
У у	u	as in 'rule'
Ф ф	f	as in 'fan'
Х х	h	as in 'hot'
Ц ц	ts	as in 'tsar'
Ч ч	ch	as in 'check'
Џ џ	j	as the 'j' in 'judge'
Ш ш	sh	as in 'shop'

SERBIA

The official language is Serbian and the official writing system uses both the Roman and Cyrillic alphabets.

Basics

Hello. Zdravo/Здраво *zdra·vo*

Goodbye. Doviđenja/Довиђења *do-vee-dje-nya*

Yes. Da/Да *da*

No. Ne/Не *ne*

Please. Molim/Молим *mo·lim*

Thank you. Hvala/Хвала *hva·la*

Excuse me. Izvinite/Извините *iz·vee·nee·te*

Sorry. Žao mi je/Жао ми је *zha·o mi ye*

What's your name?
Kako se zovete/zoveš? (pol/inf)
Како се зовете/зовеш?
ka·ko se zo·ve·te/zo·vesh

My name is ...
Zovem se .../Зовем се ... *zo·vem se*

Do you speak English?
Govorite/Govoriš li engleski? (pol/inf)
Говорите/Говориш ли енглески?
go·vo·ri·te/go·vo·rish li en·gle·ski

I don't understand.
Ne razumem./Не разумем.
ne ra·zu·mem

Shopping & Services

I'm looking for...
Tražim .../Тражим...
tra·zhim

How much is it?
Koliko košta ...?/Колико кошта ...?
ko·li·ko kosh·ta

That's too expensive.
To je preskupo./То је прескупо.
to ye pre·sku·po

Emergencies

Help! Upomoć!/Упомоћ! *u·po·moch*

Go away! Idite!/Идите! *i·di·te*

Call ...! Zovite ...!/Зовите ... ! *zo·vi·te*

a doctor lekara/лекара *le·ka·ra*

the police policiju/полицију. *po·li·tsi·yu*

I'm lost.
Izgubljen/Izgubljena sam. (m/f)
Изгубљен/Изгубљена сам. (m/f)
iz·gub·lyen/iz·gub·lyena sam

I'm ill.
Ja sam bolestan/bolesna. (m/f)
Ја сам болестан/болесна. (m/f)
ya sam bo·le·stan/bo·le·sna

Eating & Drinking

What would you recommend?
Šta biste preporučili?
Шта бисте препоручили?
shta bi·ste pre·po·ru·chi·li

Do you have vegetarian food?
Da li imate vegetarijanski obrok?
Да ли имате вегетаријански оброк?
da li i·ma·te ve·ge·ta·ri·yan·ski o·brok

Cheers! Živeli!/Живели! *zhi·ve·li*

I'd like the bill/menu please.
Mogu li dobiti račun/jelovnik, molim?
Могу ли добити рачун/јеловник, молим?
mo·gu li do·bi·ti ra·chun/ye·lov·nik mo·lim

NUMBERS

1 **jedan** **један** *ye·dan*

2 **dva/два** *dva*

3 **tri/три** *tri*

4 **četiri** **четири** *che·ti·ri*

5 **pet/пет** *pet*

6 **šest/шест** *shest*

7 **sedam/седам** *se·dam*

8 **osam/осам** *o·sam*

9 **devet/девет** *de·vet*

10 **deset/десет** *de·set*

SLOVENIA

Slovene belongs to the South Slavic language family, along with Croatian and Serbian (although it is much closer to Croatia's northwestern and coastal dialects). It also shares some features with the more distant West Slavic languages through contact with a dialect of Slovak. Although most Slovene adults speak at least one foreign language, often English, German or Italian, any effort on your part to speak the local tongue will be rewarded.

Basics

Hello. Zdravo.*zdra·vo*
Goodbye. Na svidenje. *na svee·den·ye*
Excuse me. Dovolite. *do·vo·lee·te*
Sorry. Oprostite. *op·ros·tee·te*
Please. Prosim. *pro·seem*
Thank you. Hvala. *hva·la*
You're welcome. Ni za kaj. *nee za kai*
Yes. Da. *da*
No. Ne. *ne*
What's your name? Kako vam/ti je ime? (pol/inf) *ka·ko vam/tee ye ee·me*
My name is ... Ime mi je ... *ee·me mee ye ...*
Do you speak English? Ali govorite angleško? *a·lee go·vo·ree·te ang·lesh·ko*
I don't understand. Ne razumem. *ne ra·zoo·mem*

Directions

Where's the ...? Kje je ...? *kye ye ...*
What's the address? Na katerem naslovu je? *na ka·te·rem nas·lo·voo ye*
Can you show me (on the map)? Mi lahko pokažete (na zemljevidu)? *mee lah·ko po·ka·zhe·te (na zem·lye·vee·doo)*
How do I get to ...? Kako pridem do ...? *ka·ko pree·dem do ...*
Is it near/far? Ali je blizu/daleč? *a·lee ye blee·zoo/da·lech*
(Go) Straight ahead. (Pojdite) Naravnost naprej. *(poy·dee·te) na·rav·nost na·prey*

Time

What time is it? Koliko je ura? *ko·lee·ko ye oo·ra*
It's (one) o'clock. Ura je (ena). *oo·ra ye (e·na)*
half past seven pol osem *pol o·sem* (literally 'half eight')
in the morning zjutraj *zyoot·rai*
in the evening zvečer *zve·cher*
yesterday včeraj *vche·rai*
today danes *da·nes*
tomorrow jutri *yoo·tree*

Emergencies

Help! Na pomoč! *na po·moch*
Go away! Pojdite stran! *poy·dee·te stran*
I'm lost. Izgubil/Izgubila sem se. (m/f) *eez·goo·beew/ eez·goo·bee·la sem se*
Where are the toilets? Kje je stranišče? *kye ye stra·neesh·che*
I'm ill. Bolan/Bolna sem. *(m/f) bo·lan/boh·na sem*
Call ... Pokličite ...! *pok·lee·chee·te*
  a doctor zdravnika *zdrav·nee·ka*
  the police policijo *po·lee·tsee·yo*

Eating & Drinking

What would you recommend? Kaj priporočate? *kai pree·po·ro·cha·te*
Cheers! Na zdravje! *na zdrav·ye*
I'd like the ..., please. Želim ..., prosim. *zhe·leem ... pro·seem*
  bill račun *ra·choon*
  menu jedilni list *ye·deel·nee leest*

NUMBERS

1 **en** *en*
2 **dva** *dva*
3 **trije** *tree·ye*
4 **štirje** *shtee·rye*
5 **pet** *pet*
6 **šest** *shest*
7 **sedem** *se·dem*
8 **osem** *o·sem*
9 **devet** *de·vet*
10 **deset** *de·set*

THE WESTERN BALKANS

STORYBOOK

Our writers delve deep into different aspects of Balkan life

Njegoš Mauseoleum (p219), Lovćen National Park, Montenegro

A HISTORY OF THE WESTERN BALKANS IN 15 PLACES

The Western Balkans story is one of a crossroads of civilisations. Romans, Byzantines, Ottomans, Venetians and Habsburgs all left their marks, before the two incarnations of Yugoslavia achieved some (ill-fated) unity. Today, this captivating region – long defined by diversity and cultural riches as much as division and turmoil – sets its hopes on joining the European Union. By Brana Vladisavljevic

STRADDLING THE CATHOLIC-ORTHODOX fault line ever since Christianity's Great Schism, the Western Balkans is also home to Europe's only Muslim-majority countries. Such religious complexity is the legacy of centuries of foreign dominance that kept the peninsula divided between far-flung centres of power, be it Rome and Constantinople or İstanbul and Vienna. Their intertwining sociocultural influences have likewise enriched the Balkan languages, cuisine, arts and architecture.

But this civilisational crossroads was also – too frequently – a battleground. Countless forces wreaked havoc on the Balkans throughout history (everyone from Alexander the Great to the Red Army makes an appearance), with unfathomable human losses and suffering resurfacing as recently as the devastating 1990s break-up of Yugoslavia.

A noble concept despite its shortcomings, the doomed union of South Slavs once forged its rightful place in the world. Treading a delicate line between East and West, it thrived on the global stage in everything from diplomacy to sport: the Non-Aligned Movement and Sarajevo Olympics are symbols of that rose-tinted era.

The dust hasn't settled in the 21st-century Western Balkans. Will the stalling EU accession process bring stability and once again unite the region? One thing's for certain: Europe is unimaginable without it.

1. Lepenski Vir, Serbia

PREHISTORIC FISHERFOLK

The archaeologists' excitement is palpable as you watch the fascinating short film about the excavation at Lepenski Vir back in the 1960s, screened in a futuristic edifice in the heart of Đerdap National Park. This incredible site on the Danube was home to Mesolithic- and Neolithic-era communities who left beguiling stone sculptures of fish-like idols with human faces. Despite the unearthed skeletons dating as far back as 7000 BCE, little is known about these prehistoric Balkan humans – where did they come from, how did they perish? Yet, reaching across millennia, they speak of the mighty river as the source of life since bygone times.

For more on Lepenski Vir, see p398.

2. Butrint, Albania

ANCIENT TRADERS AND WARRIORS

In the 1st millennium BCE, much of the Western Balkans was dominated by Illyrian tribes, whose language is considered a precursor of Albanian – an isolate unrelated to any other Indo-European language spoken today. Gradually, ancient Greeks established trading colonies along the Ionian and Adriatic coasts. Legendary Illyrian Queen Teuta waged war with the Greeks, precipitating the demise of the Illyrians who vanished, leaving hardly a trace. But echoes of Greek presence remain.

One of their maritime outposts, the Butrint archaeological site lies in a verdant national park wistfully looking out to Corfu. The forest-clad ruins, spanning some 2500 years, are a fascinating insight into the Balkans' distant past.

For more on Butrint, see p59.

3. Split, Croatia

ROMAN GLORY

Rome had conquered the entire region by the 1st century CE, reaching as far as the Danube, building roads and ultimately accelerating the spread of Christianity. The Balkans were to remain united until 395 CE, when the empire was divided into the eastern and western realms. The Adriatic town of Split came into prominence after the Roman emperor Diocletian – a persecutor of early Christians – built a seaside palace there in 305 CE. Its magnificent Cathedral of St Domnius, originally Diocletian's mausoleum, stands as a testament to the Christians' triumph over pagan Rome. The complex remains the beating heart of Split, its alleys and courtyards always thronging with people.

For more on Split, see p148.

Cathedral of St Domnius (p151), Split, Croatia

4. Ohrid, North Macedonia

ORIGINS OF SLAVIC LITERACY

After the Slavs' arrival to the Balkans, today's North Macedonia was in the Byzantine orbit. In the 9th century, Byzantine Orthodox missionaries Cyril and Methodius devised a script called Glagolitic as a tool for spreading Christianity among the Slavs. The Cyrillic alphabet, now in worldwide use, was later developed by their disciples and founders of the Ohrid Literary School, Sts Climent and Naum. Translation of religious works effectively gave birth to Old Church Slavonic, the oldest Slavic literary language that survives in liturgies to this day. The Sveti Naum Monastery on sublime Lake Ohrid – St Naum's final resting place – still has well-preserved Glagolitic epigraphs.

For more on Ohrid, see p246.

5. Višegrad, Bosnia & Hercegovina

ENTER THE OTTOMANS

In the 14th century the Ottoman Turks seized much of the Balkans, stopping short of the Adriatic coast. Centuries of Muslim rule ensued, with many subjugated people gradually converting to Islam. Fine architecture is another lasting reminder of the Ottomans – perhaps none more emblematic of the era than the splendid 11-arched stone bridge on the Drina at Višegrad. It was commissioned by a Bosnian-born Grand Vizier, who was drafted into Ottoman ranks through the infamous 'blood tax' (child levy) system along with many Christian boys from the Balkans. Witness to epic upheavals, the bridge is the symbolic protagonist of the famed novel by Nobel Prize winner Ivo Andrić.

For more on Višegrad, see p96.

6. Ulcinj, Montenegro

THE PIRATES' DEN

Despite the Ottoman 'yoke', the heart of Montenegro held onto its independence under a dynasty of prince-bishops in their mountain stronghold at Cetinje. Meanwhile, the Adriatic town of Ulcinj (passing from Venetian into Ottoman hands) had become the main port of call for pirates from across the Mediterranean. The story goes that the Spanish writer Cervantes languished in Ulcinj for five years waiting to be ransomed. There's a gruesome side to this swaggering episode in the Balkans' history: Ulcinj became the centre of a thriving slave trade. Today, the town is distinguished by its many mosques – among them the Sailor's Mosque, once used as a lighthouse.

For more on Ulcinj, see p213.

7. Dubrovnik, Croatia

REAL-LIFE GAME OF THRONES

Venice's grip on Dalmatia waxed and waned between the 11th and 18th centuries, extending south into Montenegro and leaving behind many architectural gems. Only the tiny Republic of Ragusa (now Dubrovnik) managed to remain an independent city-state, wedged between Ottoman and Venetian domains right up until Napoleon's invasion. Savvy traders and diplomats, the Ragusans played an important role in the region and organised a progressive society – establishing a quarantine system and abolishing the slave trade, for instance – where art and science flourished. While struggling with overtourism (and *Game of Thrones* stardom) today, this majestic walled town on the Adriatic is as irresistible as ever.

For more on Dubrovnik, see p166.

8. Novi Sad, Serbia

THE HABSBURGS' BASTION

In the late 17th century, the Habsburg monarchy governed the Balkans' northern lands from Slovenia to the modern-day Serbian province of Vojvodina. A microcosm of the once-mighty Austro-Hungarian Empire, Vojvodina remains the most multicultural part of the region, counting six official languages. Its story – including the establishment of the 'military frontier' (the Habsburgs' buffer against the Ottomans) – unravels at Novi Sad's 18th-century Petrovaradin Fortress, designed by Marquis de Vauban and nicknamed 'Gibraltar on the Danube'. These days the formidable citadel hosts the rocking Exit Festival; for a different kind of adventure, revellers can descend underground to tour a fraction of its spooky, 16km-long tunnels.

For more on Novi Sad, see p276.

9. Soča Valley, Slovenia

THE END OF EMPIRES

The 'war to end all wars', ignited by Austria-Hungary's 1914 invasion of Serbia, had a staggering human cost and seismic consequences for the region: the downfall of the Ottoman and Habsburg empires and the birth of the Kingdom of Yugoslavia. Some of the bloodiest battles of WWI were fought along the Isonzo Front in the Soča Valley, where the Central Powers defeated the Italians at Kobarid in 1917. Today, a long-distance hiking trail from the Julian Alps to Trieste on the Adriatic connects Slovenia's and Italy's WWI heritage sites – museums, cemeteries, memorials, chapels – honouring the fallen and promoting peace between nations.

For more on Soča Valley, see p325.

10. Sutjeska National Park, Bosnia & Hercegovina

FREEDOM FIGHTERS

Hitler's bombing of Belgrade in 1941 unleashed the horror of WWII. With the royal family in exile and Yugoslavia carved up between the Axis powers, the Partisans – led by communist Josip Broz Tito – put up heroic resistance, ultimately securing the Allies' support and liberating Belgrade in 1944. The decisive battle of the war, fought in Bosnia's Sutjeska canyon, is commemorated with a grandiose socialist modernist memorial (along with a blockbuster 1973 Yugoslav movie starring Richard Burton as Tito). With Bosnia's highest peak, Maglić, and the primeval forest of

Skopje 2014 sculptures, Skopje (p238)

Perućica, Sutjeska makes for fantastic hiking through a terrain loaded with wartime history.

For more on Sutjeska, see p97.

11. Belgrade, Serbia

BROTHERHOOD AND UNITY

The Yugoslav federation held out for half a century largely thanks to its charismatic lifelong president, who kept simmering nationalisms in check and was genuinely mourned by the nation upon his death in 1980. Marshal Tito steered an independent course during the Cold War and introduced a system of workers' self-management within his one-party state – a sports superpower with world-class film and music scenes. Tito's beloved *Blue Train,* which hosted everyone from Queen Elizabeth II to Haile Selassie, is now stationed in Belgrade. His mausoleum in the House of Flowers is attached to the Museum of Yugoslavia, home to ex-Yu memorabilia and thought-provoking exhibitions.

For more on Belgrade, see p270.

12. Tirana, Albania

THE PARANOIA YEARS

For Albania, communism was not a happy time. The isolated regime of Enver Hoxha evolved in the late 1960s from hard-line Stalinism to a style of government modelled on Maoist China's cultural revolution, with every aspect of society firmly under the control of the Sigurimi (secret police). Crumbling concrete bunkers strewn across Albania recall this era of iron-fisted paranoia. In Tirana itself, an enormous concealed bunker once intended for the regime's elite today serves as the informative Bunk'Art history and contemporary art museum, while the intriguingly named House of Leaves whispers scary tales of citizen surveillance and interrogation under Hoxha's dictatorship.

For more on Tirana, see p50.

13. Sarajevo, Bosnia & Hercegovina

A STORY OF SURVIVAL

While the breakup of Yugoslavia was probably unavoidable due to regional inequalities and rising ethnonationalism, the wars that tore it apart are a dark stain on the history of the South Slavs. Bosnia's capital was besieged for nearly four years, but – along with its splendid mosques, synagogues and cathedrals – the city's indomitable spirit has prevailed. The story of the Sarajevo Haggadah is uplifting: this 14th-century illuminated codex, which left Spain with the expulsion of the Sephardic Jews, ended up in a Sarajevo museum to be saved by Muslim curators from both the Nazis (hidden in a mosque) and the 1990s shelling (hidden in a bank vault).

For more on Sarajevo, see p84.

14. Ljubljana, Slovenia

EUROPEAN DAWN

The first of the Western Balkan states to be accepted into the EU (in 2004), adopt the euro and join the Schengen Area was Slovenia. This forward-thinking nation has since made notable strides in everything from sustainability to LGBTIQ+ rights. The capital Ljubljana banished cars from its historic centre, earning the title of Europe's Green Capital in 2016, and in 2022 Slovenia became the first post-communist country to legalise same-sex marriage and adoption. Ljubljana's free-thinking HQ is Metelkova Mesto, a former army barracks turned squatter commune and the place to go for street art, clubbing, workshops, lectures and more.

For more on Ljubljana, see p310.

15. Skopje, North Macedonia

THE LONG ROAD TO EU

The carrot of EU membership has been instrumental in dealing with issues such as corruption and media freedom in the region, but the accession process for the remaining 'Western Balkan Six' has stalled. Along the way, North Macedonia has grappled with a national identity crisis (notoriously forced to change its name under pressure from Greece). Nowhere is this more apparent than in its capital. The former government's hotly debated project with a mind-boggling price tag – aka 'Skopje 2014' – features dozens of buildings and monuments constructed in gaudy neoclassical style, in an attempt to boost national pride with a dubious nod to antiquity.

For more on Skopje, see p238.

Rakija at a bar in Belgrade

BALKANSCAT/SHUTTERSTOCK ©

RAKIJA, REINVENTED

An ever-expanding array of enthusiastically crafted spirits is reimagining the humble age-old tradition into Serbia's *rakija* culture of the future. By Brana Vladisavljevic

SERBIAN ŠLJIVOVICA – the plum-based *rakija*, or fruit brandy, popular across the Western Balkans – was inscribed on Unesco's Intangible Cultural Heritage of Humanity list in 2022. The recognition was well timed: in recent years the country has witnessed a renaissance of its ubiquitous homemade tipple. It's certainly been a long road since 1921, when a *rakija* still was registered as patent number one in the Directorate for the Protection of Industrial Property of the newly founded Kingdom of Serbs, Croats and Slovenes.

That's not to say that the drink hasn't had its moments in the international spotlight. For the 1889 Exposition Universelle in Paris, the young Kingdom of Serbia sent five types of *rakija*, including the one made of plums. And in the 1988 US-produced Yugoslav movie *The Secret of Monastery Rakija*, an American billionaire, impostor monks, petty smugglers and incognito cops all try to get hold of the perfect fruit brandy. Still, most of Serbia's young urbanites would have dismissed *rakija* as a rural drink that can't compete with the likes of whisky or cognac – until recently.

The Spirit of Serbia

Across Serbia, *šljivovica* has accompanied life's defining moments for the last five centuries. It boosted morale and treated wounds in wartime, and was appreciated by Orthodox monks and great scholars alike. Old bottles are cherished like a family heirloom, and the tradition of serving a small glass of *rakija* to visitors has persisted in households to this day. The name itself comes from Turkish, as it was during the Ottoman occupation that the Serbs started brewing fruit to make moonshine. By the 19th century, such was the prevalence of the drink – it was even smuggled across the border – that both Ottoman and Habsburg rulers levied a tax on *rakija* in Serbian lands.

These days, high-quality *rakija* is fermented, then twice distilled in a copper cauldron, followed by the aging process in an oak barrel. Serbs are known to make brandy out of pretty much any fruit (though plums reign supreme), but it can also be made with herbs, walnuts or honey. It's precisely the distinctive fruity aroma that sets *rakija* apart from other spirits.

Game-Changers

In the 20th century, industrialisation brought advances in technology, marketing and export of mass-produced *rakija* from big state-owned companies. However, quantity trumped creativity and,

somewhere along the way, the drink lost its soul. In a hint of change to come, the first privately owned distilleries emerged in the 1980s, diversifying the offer and raising the bar. The one with the oldest tradition is BB Klekovača from western Serbia, founded in 1953. It currently produces 24 *rakija* varieties, including the region's signature *klekovača* (made from plums and juniper berries), which evokes the scents of Tara mountain.

Since the 1990s, sprouting artisanal distilleries have been leaning on ancestral knowledge, using the best of the regional orchards' produce and experimenting with methods to create exciting new flavours. In central Serbia, for instance, the up-and-coming Novićević cellar makes the country's first officially registered *medovača* from double-distilled fermented honey that's aged for up to two years in an ash barrel. 'One litre requires a kilogram and a half of top-quality honey, which is why *medovača* is rightfully called the queen among brandies', says Nevena Novićević, food technology engineer.

Also re-entering the *rakija* scene are monasteries, a hub of national culture that fell into slumber during socialism. Today, Bukovo monastery in Serbia's east cultivates the indigenous black *tamjanika* grape to make *lozovača* (grape brandy); barrel-aged for two years, it has a notably musky aroma.

The Belgrade Scene

While it's small-batch regional producers that shine, one needn't venture outside Belgrade to get immersed in craft *rakija*. At the capital's Rakia Bar and Belgrade Urban Distillery – regular stops on tours offered by local guides – *rakija* rookies can get a crash course through a tasting session with an expert, including tips such as food and drink pairings. Both are the brainchild of Branko Nešić, who is now expanding the franchise internationally.

Strike up a conversation in a Belgrade bar, and you may hear that the first Serbian cocktail was invented by bartender Milan Vujić in the 1920s and served on the *Orient Express*. Called simply Klek & Soda, it was essentially *klekovača* with added soda water – the juniper-berry-infused spirit is a logical stand-in for gin. Today, *lozovača* could make a good base in cocktails due to its more neutral taste, while herbal varieties are appealing given their aromatic qualities. 'I believe that in a few years, *rakija* will be the new mezcal', proclaimed bartender Filip Ivanović at speakeasy-style Beogradski Koktel Klub, while pouring *dunjevača* (quince brandy) to mix up a Victory Julep.

Restaurants have embraced the trend, too. At chic Ambar – a hit with tourists for its reinterpreted Balkan cuisine – the drinks list features 29 types of *rakija* from local cellars, as well as innovative cocktails such as Welcome to Belgrade (made with *jabukovača*, or apple brandy).

Rakija Education

Ultimately, for the newfound appreciation of the traditional drink to really take off, education is key. Back in 2007, Branko Nešić was the driving force behind the Rakija Fest – Balkan Urban Experience. The event took place annually in Belgrade for a decade, creating buzz around the spirit among the big-city audience in a showcase of craft *rakija* and cocktails, accompanied by DJs, workshops, lectures and design competitions. And in 2016, the Museum of Serbian Šljivovica launched just outside the capital as a deep dive into the history, customs and family secrets of producing plum brandy; visitors can even see artefacts that made it into the Guinness World Records. Its distillery, established in 1985, prides itself on award-winning bottles (one apparently ended up on the Mir space station).

Perhaps no one in Serbia, though, is advocating a *rakija* revival more than the duo behind the blog *Rakija, mostly* – sociologists Ilija Malović and Zoran Radoman, whose aim is to develop a local scene of drink connoisseurs. In 2017 they published the book *Rakija* (co-authored with Vladimir Dulović), in which they conclude: 'Serbian rakija is proof of the historical continuity of our people and should be treated as a national treasure.'

A LITERARY ITINERARY

Travel through both time and the Western Balkans landscape via the words of the region's acclaimed authors. By Peter Dragicevich

MANY WONDERFUL WRITERS have emerged from the Western Balkans, including among their ranks Nobel and Man Booker prize winners. Each of these nine books will add insight to your explorations of what can be a difficult-to-understand region.

The Bridge on the Drina

Set in Višegrad (Bosnia), 1570s–1914

Nobel Prize winner Ivo Andrić's 1945 masterpiece has as a main character Višegrad's famous bridge; it's the one constant through the centuries that this intergenerational saga spans. This gripping novel is a window into everyday life in Ottoman Bosnia and vividly illustrates how the millet system worked, where members of each faith (Orthodox Christian, Catholic Christian, Jewish and Muslim) answered in the first instance to their own community leaders.

The Mountain Wreath

Set in Cetinje (Montenegro), 1702

Montenegro's most enduring work of literature is also the oldest and most challenging book on this list. *Gorski vijenac (The Mountain Wreath)* is a verse play romanticising the struggle for freedom from the Ottomans. It was written in 1847 by Montenegro's ruler and acclaimed poet, Vladika (Prince-Bishop) Petar II Petrović Njegoš.

The book is controversial as it glorifies a savage massacre of Muslims. According to the story, Vladika Danilo (founder of the Petrović dynasty) ordered the leaders of the Montenegrin tribes to kill all of their kin – men, women and children – who had converted to Islam. It makes *The Mountain Wreath* a problematic read, given the obvious parallels with the atrocities that took place in Bosnia in the 1990s. It does, however, give some insights into a genocidal mindset.

Death and the Dervish

Set in Sarajevo (Bosnia), 18th century

Struggles under Turkish rule weren't limited to the Christian communities, as this moody 1966 classic by Meša Selimović illustrates. *Derviš i smrt (Death and the Dervish)* tells the story of a fearful Muslim cleric and his dealings with the Ottoman authorities after the arrest of his brother. The story draws on parallels from Selimović's life. His own brother was executed by the Partisans during WWII for alleged theft; both brothers were Partisans themselves and committed communists.

Bosnian Chronicle

Set in Travnik (Bosnia), 1807–14

In the lead-up to WWII, Ivo Andrić had been the Yugoslav ambassador to Berlin. He spent his war years in Belgrade under close surveillance by the German

occupiers. It was during this enforced retreat that he wrote three novels – including *Na Drini ćuprija (The Bridge on the Drina)* – all of which were published in 1945.

Travnička hronika (literally 'Travnik Chronicle') was released in English as *Bosnian Chronicle* and later *The Days of the Consuls*. It's set in Travnik at a time when it was the capital of the Ottoman province of Bosnia. With the Ottoman Empire in decline, the old Muslim men of the market rue the arrival of French and Austrian consuls, representatives of rival empires angling for a stake in the region. It's a fascinating story of political intrigue, no doubt informed by Andrić's own diplomatic career.

The Dawning

Set in Pljevlja (Montenegro), 1870s–1918

In some ways *Svitanje (The Dawning)* is the antithesis of *The Mountain Wreath,* not least because its author, Milka Bajić Poderegin, was a woman and a complete unknown. While it, too, deals with a turbulent period in history, it does so from a domestic lens, focussing on the life of a Serbian family (particularly its daughters, wives and mothers) living in what was then the Sanjak of Novi Pazar. A far rosier vision of Christian-Muslim relations is portrayed, with one of the women befriending the wife of the local pasha.

The unfinished manuscript was completed and published in 1987 by the author's daughter – film actress Nadja Regin (who appeared in Bond flicks *From Russia With Love* and *Goldfinger*) – following her mother's death. It's a great read and a rare glimpse into everyday life for women at the advent of the 20th century.

Chronicle in Stone

Set in Gjirokastra (Albania), 1940s

After Andrić, Ismail Kadare is the other heavyweight of Western Balkans literature, his status cemented when he was awarded the inaugural Man Booker International Prize in 2005 for his entire body of work. Despite living under one of the world's most repressive regimes, Kadare managed to have extraordinary books published, such as this 1971 novel, revelling in the absurdity of the times they describe.

Set during WWII, *Kronikë në gur (Chronicle in Stone)* is simultaneously tragic and very funny. One character changes his name from Gjergj to Giorgio to Yiorgos to Jürgen as the Italians, Greeks and Germans take it in turns to occupy the town, a strategy which fails to protect him from his fate.

The Houses of Belgrade

Set in Belgrade (Serbia), 1960s

This unusual 1970 novel by Borislav Pekić tells the story of terminally ill Arsenije Njegovan, a reclusive property developer and landlord, stepping out of his postwar isolation and confronting his own delusions in a much-changed city. It contains references to the student protests of 1968, the first major protests in Yugoslavia since WWII.

It was first published in Serbian as *Hodočašće Arsenija Njegovana (The Pilgrimage of Arsenije Njegovan),* a recent English-language paperback edition simply titles it *Houses.*

Shards

Set in Tuzla (Bosnia), 1990s

In his remarkable debut Ismet Prcić is a character in his own novel. It describes daily life during the bombardment of Tuzla, a desperate escape through the war zone and, later, living as a refugee in the USA. As uncomfortable as the subject matter is, it's also funny: 'The moment Marshal Tito died I shat myself. These incidents were not connected.'

For a similarly moving/amusing story of an escape from Bosnia and subsequent refugee life, seek out *Bluebird: A Memoir* by Vesna Maric, one of the authors of this guidebook.

Girl at War

Set in Zagreb (Croatia), 1991 and 2001

Jumping between a childhood in Zagreb and an early adulthood in New York, Sara Nović's 2016 novel follows its protagonist as she confronts harrowing wartime memories. The description of a grim journey with her family will stick with you, especially if a road trip through Bosnia is on your itinerary.

Old bridge, Višegrad (p96), as featured in *The Bridge on the Drina* (p379)

Museum of Contemporary Art (p274), Belgrade, Serbia

MIRJANA RISTIC DAMJANOVIC/SHUTTERSTOCK ©

YUGOSLAV MODERNIST ARCHITECTURE & MONUMENTS

Learn the story of Yugoslavia's magnificent Modernist masterpieces. By Vesna Maric

AS A PERSON who grew up in Yugoslavia, I always had a warm feeling in my heart when I remembered the socialist blocks we had lived in and the monuments we visited, their unique designs, beautiful light, the green spaces we played in, the humanist, eccentric and always highly liveable, never exclusive, architecture of our youth.

But when I emigrated to the UK, no one believed me when I said that we had nothing of the kind of the 'drab Soviet tower blocks' that Westerners associated with the so-called Eastern bloc. If I spoke of the spaces and architecture, I was regarded with a headshake that signified my communist brainwashing. Some 20-odd years since the 1990s war, in 2019, the MoMa hosted an exhibition in New York titled Towards a Concrete Utopia – Architecture in Yugoslavia 1948–1980. The museum website states that the exhibition 'introduces the exceptional work of socialist Yugoslavia's leading architects to an international audience for the first time, highlighting a significant yet thus-far understudied body of modernist architecture, whose forward-thinking contributions still resonate today.' I felt vindicated!

The Architecture

Yugoslavia sat between the West and East, politically and geographically – and its socialism was based on 'self-management', an economic model founded by Edvard Kardelj, in which workers were direct owners of their enterprise, whether it was inside the factory or within an architectural endeavour. In order for self-management to work, a massive education project had to take place in the largely agrarian society, where illiteracy was over 80% in the post-WWII period. The rebuilding effort meant that schools, kindergartens and worker universities were of utmost architectural priority. By 1959, 129 universities had been built, with the most impressive design being Radovan Nikšić and Ninoslav Kučan's Novi Zagreb University, with its open spaces and flexible designations, entirely designed to be comfortably inhabited. Other examples are the surreal Museum of Contemporary Art (p274) in Belgrade, designed by Ivan Antić and Ivanka Raspopović, which resembles a space-beehive with its glass grids and angular skylights. Sarajevo's History Museum of Bosnia & Hercegovina is a marble cube impossibly resting atop a transparent, glass structure. It was the pride and joy of the city. Designed in 1963 by Boris Magaš, with Edo Šmidihen and Radovan Horvat, in the International Style, it is now largely dilapidated, poorly funded and forgotten.

But despite much neglect by postwar governments across the former Yugoslavia, most of these structures are still in use and can be visited. In fact, with the

Instagram-inspired resurgence of love for Brutalist architecture, much of Yugoslavia's extraordinary design has become more popular and visible in recent years. Stylistic trends of the moment notwithstanding, it is essential to keep in mind that Yugoslav modernism had important political and historical content. For example, in Yugoslavia, the right to housing was enshrined in the law, and most of the housing and major buildings were the result of architectural competitions. There were vast levels of bespoke design constructed without mass production, for all of the country's population. It was a truly alternative way to organise a state and its housing and working conditions, and it reminds us that design can be a tool of social progress.

The Monuments

Part of the reason why Yugoslavia was able to build its own economic and state model – some have termed it 'market socialism' – was because it had liberated its own territory in WWII, without the need for large-scale Soviet assistance. The country's partisans, under Tito's leadership, did that work for themselves. The WWII partisan struggle was commemorated widely inside Yugoslavia by commissioning those same top-class architects to build monuments honouring landmark moments from the war. These monuments were hugely popular and often visited – not only because of their symbolic celebration of the partisan struggles and victories, but also because of their fantastical, abstract forms that were simultaneously modernist, organic and always set in the most beautiful natural landscapes.

Examples include the Battle of Sutjeska Memorial, in Bosnia and Hercegovina, once among the most visited sites in the country, and the Partisan Memorial Cemetery in Mostar, a memorial park that formed an essential part of the city. Bogdan Bogdanović designed the latter, together with many other monuments – the Jasenovac extermination camp memorial being one of the most emblematic. According to legend, Tito himself picked the design, against the wishes of other Communist Party members. Bogdanović claimed that the only reason Tito had chosen his proposal was because, unlike all the other artists, he had not adopted the Soviet sculptural style of 'headless bodies, wounded figures and stretchers'. Commonly known as the 'Stone Flower', it is simply breathtaking.

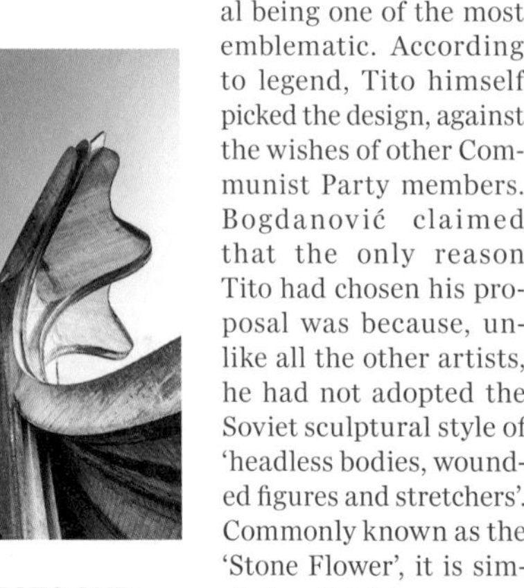

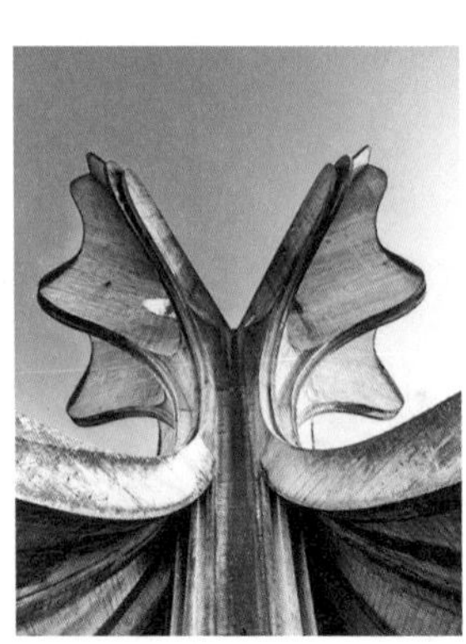

THE ARCHITECTS AND DESIGNERS OFTEN PLAYED WITH SYMBOLS TAKEN FROM NATURE, OR USED SHAPES OF COSMIC BODIES AND INCLUDED WATER AND OTHER ELEMENTS IN THEIR DESIGNS.

Memorial at Jasenovac, Croatia

NENAD NEDOMACKI/SHUTTERSTOCK ©

The architects and designers often played with symbols taken from nature, or used shapes of cosmic bodies and included water and other elements in their designs. As with architecture, where aesthetics and utilitarianism were major factors, local materials and the environment were always essential. The main concern was how the spaces, or the monuments, would be inhabited by human beings. Just as the housing projects provided housing for all (as opposed to the Western notion of 'social housing'), the monuments did not impose or shrink the viewer. The structures inspired awe, but were also always spaces in which to move, have a picnic, and rest.

When you see Yugoslav architecture and monuments today, they feel – considering their context – quite dogma-free. Equally, keeping in mind the subsequent treatment of those structures by post-war nationalist governments (ranging from neglect to outright vandalism and destruction), you can appreciate their enduring symbolic power.

INDEX

A

B

C

Map Pages **000**

Map Pages **000**

T

U

V

W

Z

At Butrint (p59), Albania, save the Greek Theatre until last. Turn right into the forest after the ticket booth for sights such as the Venetian Tower, Triconch Palace and the 6th-century Baptistry (pictured).

Croatia's Istria peninsula, centred on Pula (p130), is known for produce including wild garlic, asparagus and truffles (pictured).

Mapping data sources:
© Lonely Planet
© OpenStreetMap http://openstreetmap.org/copyright

THIS BOOK

Destination Editor Daniel Bolger

Production Editors Katie Connolly, James Appleton

Coordinating Editor Monique Choy

Book Designer Dermot Hegarty

Cartographer Hunor Csutoros

Assisting Editors Kate Mathews, Claire Naylor, Maja Vatrić, Clifton Wilkinson

Cover Researcher Lauren Egan

Thanks Ronan Abayawickrema, Karen Henderson, Alison Killilea, Darren O'Connell, Graham O'Neill

Paper in this book is certified against the Forest Stewardship Council™ standards. FSC™ promotes environmentally responsible, socially beneficial and economically viable management of the world's forests.

Published by Lonely Planet Global Limited
CRN 554153
4th edition – May 2024
ISBN 978 1 78868 392 0

10 9 8 7 6 5 4 3 2 1
Printed in Singapore